# The Non-profit Sector in a Changing Economy

OECD

ORGANISATION FOR ECONOMIC CO-OPERATION AND DEVELOPMENT

# ORGANISATION FOR ECONOMIC CO-OPERATION AND DEVELOPMENT

Pursuant to Article 1 of the Convention signed in Paris on 14th December 1960, and which came into force on 30th September 1961, the Organisation for Economic Co-operation and Development (OECD) shall promote policies designed:

- to achieve the highest sustainable economic growth and employment and a rising standard of living in member countries, while maintaining financial stability, and thus to contribute to the development of the world economy;
- to contribute to sound economic expansion in member as well as non-member countries in the process of economic development; and
- to contribute to the expansion of world trade on a multilateral, non-discriminatory basis in accordance with international obligations.

The original member countries of the OECD are Austria, Belgium, Canada, Denmark, France, Germany, Greece, Iceland, Ireland, Italy, Luxembourg, the Netherlands, Norway, Portugal, Spain, Sweden, Switzerland, Turkey, the United Kingdom and the United States. The following countries became members subsequently through accession at the dates indicated hereafter: Japan (28th April 1964), Finland (28th January 1969), Australia (7th June 1971), New Zealand (29th May 1973), Mexico (18th May 1994), the Czech Republic (21st December 1995), Hungary (7th May 1996), Poland (22nd November 1996), Korea (12th December 1996) and the Slovak Republic (14th December 2000). The Commission of the European Communities takes part in the work of the OECD (Article 13 of the OECD Convention).

*Publié en français sous le titre :*

**Le secteur à but non lucratif dans une économie en mutation**

# Foreword

$O$*ver the past 20 years, the OECD's Co-operative Action Programme on Local Economic and Employment Development (LEED Programme, Directorate for Employment, Labour and Social Affairs) has carried out extensive work in the field of social cohesion and enterprise creation at the local level.*

*The need for* Reconciling Economy and Society *(OECD, 1996) through the creation and spread of "social enterprises" and other non-profit sector organisations* (Fostering Entrepreneurship, *OECD, 1998), as a way of pursuing both economic progress and social cohesion at the local level, is one of the key messages put forward by the LEED Programme.*

*Since 1997, the LEED Programme has conducted an extensive analysis of social enterprises* (Social Enterprises, *OCDE, 1999), which produce not only tangible goods (products and services – often innovative in nature – responding to unsatisfied collective demands) but also intangible goods (social welfare, social capital, social cohesion and social innovation). This research agenda has further expanded into the analysis of the non-profit sector, from which social enterprises originate, and the entrepreneurial "twist" which they have fostered strongly. An international conference on "The Role of the Non-profit Sector in Local Development: New Trends" was organised at the International Monetary Fund in Washington DC in September 2000 as a joint initiative between the European Commission, the German Marshall Fund of the United States and the Corporation for Enterprise Development (USA). This conference – the first to be organised within the framework of the newly-created LEED Forum on Social Innovations (April 2000) – gave new insights into the role and contribution of the non-profit sector to the international, national and local communities.*

*This publication contains some of the papers presented at the Conference. These have subsequently been updated and supplemented by a new set of original contributions, which helped enlarge the initial theoretical framework and geographical coverage.*

*It was prepared by Antonella Noya and Corinne Nativel of the OECD Secretariat.*

*This publication would have been impossible to complete without contributions by many different people inside and outside the OECD's LEED Programme. In particular, we would like to thank Helen Shields, Jennah Huxley, Deidre Claassen, Sheelagh Delf and Valerie Labourdette for their editorial and technical skills, as well as Jean-Pierre Pellegrin, Marie Corman, Sergio Arzeni, Head of the LEED Programme and LEED Programme administrators and consultants for their substantive suggestions.*

*Finally, special thanks go to Professor Carlo Borzaga, whose extensive input has greatly aided the Secretariat's work on the topics covered in this book over the past years.*

*This publication is published on the responsibility of the Secretary-General of the OECD.*

# Table of contents

## List of Boxes

## List of Tables

## List of Figures

ISBN 92-64-19953-5
The Non-profit Sector in a Changing Economy
© OECD 2003

# Synthesis

## The non-profit sector in the 21st century: a stakeholder for economy and society

The non-profit sector, often associated with concepts such as the "social economy", "third sector" and "third system" (see glossary for these terms), is a growing social and economic force all over the world and a key element in employment and social policies in most OECD countries. All of the above terms refer broadly to the same idea: a sector between state and market, fulfilling both economic and social missions, which pursues a general interest, and whose final objective is not the redistribution of profit. Each of these terms underlines only one aspect of the sector. So, while the term "non-profit sector", born in the USA, refers mainly to the absence of the redistribution of profits, the term "social economy" (the French translation of which is "économie sociale") underlines the socio-economic dimension of the sector, and the term "third sector" highlights its position between the state and the market.

This book uses the term "non-profit sector" as it is the most commonly used, and the better understood, in international debates among OECD member countries. However, in its interpretation of the non-profit sector, the book does not merely restrict itself to the "original" definition coined by the Johns Hopkins University (see glossary) but also refers to the social economy and third sector. In fact, the wide spectrum of entities belonging to all these sectors is examined throughout this publication.

We believe that concentrating solely on the non-profit aspect would limit one's understanding of the sector and overlook some of its essential elements. For example, its ability to produce different services of general interest which are not characterised by information asymmetries* (Hansmann, 1986), its ability to produce intangible goods such as social well-being, social capital, social cohesion and finally its ability to produce "relational assets" (GUI, 2001). This term refers to assets that derive from

---

\* Hansmann suggests that non-profit organisations are better at supplying goods to consumers in cases of "contract failure". Contract failure occurs, according to Hansmann, when it is difficult to monitor the quality of the good or service being produced because of information asymmetries caused by a purchaser/provider split, or because the good has collective type benefits. Consumers therefore prefer non-profit-distributing organisations where there is less incentive for producers to act opportunistically to exploit their informational advantage.

interaction amongst the non-profit sector organisations and their "clients" and stakeholders. Relational assets can be defined as local public assets, which are the result of relations in which the identity, the attitude and the motivations of the people involved – the stakeholders – are considered essential elements in the creation and in the value of the assets. "Relational assets" include the relation itself, which represents the economic asset (Bruni, 2002). A clear example of "relational assets" can be found in the field of "proximity services" ("*services de proximité*" in French) and in the healthcare sector. Here, the trust between the supplier (an association delivering home assistance, for instance) and the beneficiary (an aged person receiving the assistance) is a central element of the economic relation. Trust is a relational asset, produced in the relationship and consumed in it. Non-profit sector organisations are characterised by stronger relational assets than those of for-profit enterprises and public institutions (Borzaga, 1997), although the concept of relational assets has also been applied to the private sector (see, for example, Storper, 1997; Nelson and Winter, 1992). Ignoring these elements would mean ignoring the main outcomes of many non-profit organisations whose contribution to local economic prosperity lies indeed in creating positive dynamics which impact on the social fabric and nurture social capital.

The non-profit sector has existed for many years in several OECD member countries and has emerged world-wide during recent decades, mainly as a response to the crisis of welfare systems and to the perceived need to reshape them, notably in the European context and as a new strategy against social and economic exclusion. These are, however, neither the sole nor the principal reasons for the emergence and the modernisation of the non-profit sector. Arguably, the "global associational revolution" (Salamon and Anheier, 1999) has been driven by the non-profit sector's original vision of society and the economy, which give it a legitimacy and function in its own right, over and above the residual role usually attributed to it (OECD, 1999).

The non-profit sector is a far more significant economic force around the world than is commonly thought. Nearly 39.5 million people in FTE (full time employment) jobs are employed in the non-profit sector (excluding traditional co-operatives) in the 35 countries studied by the Johns Hopkins Comparative Non-profit Sector Project. The non-profit sector employs 3.6 per cent of the working-age population, representing 7.3 per cent of non-agricultural employment and 46 per cent of public sector employment. Taken as a separate economy, it would be the sixth largest economy in the world, ranking ahead of United States, Japan, China, Germany and France (Salamon, 2002). In the countries for which comparative data was available, the non-profit sector has also recently shown signs of rapid growth. Between

1990 and 1995, non-profit employment increased by 23 per cent compared to six per cent for the economy as a whole.

Within the European Union, the economic and social significance of the non-profit sector (called the social economy or third sector) is increasingly recognised. Their importance is also growing in the face of new emerging needs. It was recently estimated that approximately nine million EU workers in full-time employment (FTE) are employed by the non-profit sector. This represents 7.9 per cent of salaried civil employment in the European Union (CIRIEC, 2000). Seventy one per cent of the jobs in the sector are provided by associations, 27.5 per cent by co-operatives and 3.1 per cent by mutual organisations.

The sector is active and developing in many areas of the economy, ranging from health and care, culture, environment, social services, education and employment through various entities, which take on a different legal status according to the national legal and cultural framework. These may be associations, traditional co-operatives, social co-operatives, charities, foundations or other types of organisations. While there are many different legal statuses for the different kinds of entities that belong to the non-profit sector, there is no general theory which can explain the limits and competitive advantages of the sector as a whole. Such a theory would probably allow policymakers, and even practitioners belonging to the non-profit sector, a better understanding of the sector and of its mission.

In spite of the national differences, which influence and shape the sector at national level, some common trends can be found in the development of the non-profit sector in the countries examined in this book (EU countries, USA, Mexico, Canada [Québec] and Australia). For example, it is clear that in the countries in which the non-profit sector is well established it is becoming more entrepreneurial, less dependent on public funding and therefore experimenting innovative ways of raising funds. It is also more willing to participate in the design of new evaluation tools, able to measure the outputs of its activities as well as the outcomes (creation of social capital, rehabilitation of individual and collective citizenship, employability of disadvantaged categories of workers, social well-being, revitalisation of local economies, modernisation of local management models) and, therefore, the "social value added".

The overview presented in the book provides evidence of a growing and evolving sector, adapting its management and commercial methods to try to cope in the best possible way with the constraints and the opportunities arising from the major economic and social trends (global markets and the reduction of public resources, for example). In doing so, the sector is facing one major challenge: not to lose its "organisational identity", that is "... *that which is central, distinctive and enduring*" (Albert and Whetten, 1985). While non-profit entities can encompass various organisational identities, such as social enterprises in the USA (Young, 2001), the overall mission for all of them is to contribute to sustainable growth, shared prosperity, social and economic justice, putting human values at the core of their action.

Non-profit sector organisations mainly operate at the local level: they are strongly rooted in territories, which they contribute to shaping, and rely on local formal and informal networks of people, knowledge and resources. The "third system" is able to contribute to local development by:

● defining new goods and services related to the specific needs of the local territory,

● generating integration and creating jobs,

● improving the atmosphere and the attractiveness of the territory,

● consolidating partnership and empowering local actors,

● emphasising "the long run" and therefore by consolidating sustainable projects (ECOTEC, 2001).

The evaluation report on the EU pilot action on Third System and Employment (*www.europa.eu.int/comm/employment_social/empl&esf/3syst/index_en.htm*) concludes that even when the primary purpose of third system initiatives is to serve the needs of individuals, the benefits also extend to local communities. Non-profit sector organisations can help reduce local disparities in terms of service provision, access to goods, services and job opportunities, thereby building cohesion within cities and regions that currently exhibit high degrees of spatial inequalities. However, a gap clearly exists between the role that the non-profit sector plays at local level (which is, in fact, one of the clear trends underlined by the contributors to this publication) and the recognition it receives from policymakers at national and local level, who often do not have a clear understanding of the role that the sector can play. As a result of this lack of knowledge and understanding, support policies tend to have a narrow focus and overlook the broader picture of the whole economy. An increased knowledge of the characteristics and trends of this sector would improve the perceptions and the public policies that surround it: giving the non-profit sector an appropriate legal framework, establishing dedicated public policies and including it in more general public policies such as industrial or employment policies will contribute to the sound establishment of the sector in the economy.

The creation of non-profit satellite accounts, recommended by the Handbook on Non-profit Institution in the System of National Accounts (developed by the Johns Hopkins Center for Civil Society Studies and the

United Nations Statistical Division) will certainly help to better define the sector from a quantitative point of view and to identify the entities belonging to it. Non-profit satellite accounts will put the emphasis on traditional macro-economic data such as number of organisations, number of employees and volunteers, wages, other expenditures, incomes, government support, contribution to GDP, etc.

However, to achieve a better understanding of the non-profit sector from a qualitative point of view, it is vital to identify and evaluate the impact of production and social utility on the sector. This helps "rationalise" the debate over competition between the non-profit sector and for-profit enterprises, as well as between public agencies and non-profit organisations. In addition it helps situate the non-profit sector within a plural economy. With this in mind, both immediate outputs and outcomes must be evaluated. These factors represent the actual, quantifiable contribution of the non-profit sector. However, many for-profit enterprises also achieve these outcomes through adopting a socially responsible attitude. New evaluation methods are therefore required. Although some progress has already been made in evaluating the non-profit sector and developing more comprehensive measurement tools, such as a "social report" (*"bilan social et sociétal"*), many challenges lie ahead.

In conclusion, one of the main messages of this book is that we are in a multi-dimensional market, in which different entities can co-exist and in which the non-profit sector has grown in importance, even if its place in the market is still unclear and somewhat limited. Increasing the visibility and the understanding of the sector could help in creating a better framework for it to contribute in a more appropriate way to a shared growth and prosperity from which more people can benefit. This book is intended to contribute to this objective.

## Shaping, financing and evaluating the non-profit sector: a summary of the key themes of this book

All the chapters contained in this book contend that the non-profit sector is now a recognised and legitimised component of the advanced economies of the OECD. However, in comparison to market or public policy analysis, non-profit studies is a relatively "young" but rapidly evolving field of research. For this reason, the first important aim of this volume is the attempt to identify a number of distinctive trends that could be seen as "new" or "innovative" in different geographical zones of the OECD.

The first four chapters contained in **Part One** give an overview of the latest trends. All take the view that historical dynamics must be taken into account when seeking to understand the role of the non-profit sector and the challenges it currently faces. The authors emphasise that the non-profit sector has played a critical role in community life over the past two centuries, even though it is only recently that it has attracted significant interest. It is suggested that this relatively recent attention goes hand in hand with the broader analysis of welfare restructuring. The complex and changing relationship between the non-profit sector and the Welfare State is thus a central and recurrent theme.

In their contribution on countries belonging to the European Union, Carlo Borzaga and Alceste Santuari (*Chapter* 1) argue that the growing body of literature on the non-profit sector that has emerged since the early 1990s mirrors its remarkable rise following the recent crisis of social welfare systems. Its relative significance over the past decades and centuries has repeatedly been influenced by the overall economic climate and by government policy. For example, while the non-profit sector had gradually established itself over several centuries without State intervention at the end of the 18th century European governments began having a suspicious attitude towards non profit-. With the emergence of universal welfare states, the non-profit sector experienced somewhat of a setback and became more strongly subjected to state regulation. But a "new" revitalised sector emerged in the 1970s whose main concern was the fight against unemployment and social exclusion. Since then, European governments have become increasingly aware of its potential contribution to the social agenda and have sought to establish more systematic funding policies. Dennis Young (*Chapter* 2) attests of a similar trend for the United States in that its existence and legitimacy as a third sector distinct from business or government only emerged in the 1970s when it became a transmission belt for the delivery of federal programmes. Government funding initially fuelled its growth but was cut back by the Reagan administration in the 1980s. Since then, the US non-profit sector has become less dependent on government or traditional sources of charity for its funding. The 1970s was also an important decade for the Mexican non-profit sector, but represented a "birth" rather than a "rebirth" period. Marco Mena's chapter on Mexico (*Chapter* 4) shows that the first generation of civil society organisations can be traced back to this period, although these acted mainly as incipient. But the true rise of the sector occurred in the 1980s as a corollary of the various economic crises and the decline in the political legitimacy of the authoritarian state. The growth of the sector was, as in other countries, also encouraged by public policy programmes, as in the case of a major anti-poverty programme, known as PRONASOL. In Australia, the non-profit sector has also experienced a significant rise in the last two decades. In her detailed overview, Julia Novak shows that today almost 7 per cent of the Australian workforce are employed in the non-profit sector and that its GDP contribution of three per cent surpasses other service sectors such as hospitality and catering.

A further concern among the first four chapters is to stress that the changing patterns of the non-profit sector are not merely a reflection of the passage of time. There is a vibrant *spatial diversity* resulting from distinctive cultural and political factors. Borzaga and Santuari argue, for example, that the extent and modes of co-operation between the non-profit sector and welfare states have varied across Europe as various models have surfaced, from the advocacy role in Scandinavian countries to a residual role, particularly in Southern Europe. Moreover, specific territorial needs also explain why activities developed by the non-profit sector may differ between countries. Novak's overview of multi-purpose family centres in Remote Queensland (*Chapter 3*) is a good example of the non-profit sector's role in rural areas. Additionally, political regimes are major determinants in the shape taken by the non-profit sector. If the Mexican non-profit sector only gained prominence and recognition in the last decade of the 20th century it was mainly because the development of civil society had hitherto been hindered by various factors. These included the creation and consolidation of the nation-state in the post-colonial period and a subsequent history of strong government control. It was only from the mid-1980s that some of the barriers started to be addressed. Nonetheless, Mena argues that the sector still faces many challenges, in particular its conflicting relationship to the State. The political change from an authoritarian to a democratic regime following the July 2000 election spurred hopes that the distrust traditionally expressed by the public sector would decline. While partnership building between the two sectors has been a painstaking process, there is currently a wider recognition of the desirability of achieving good governance.

With the recent emergence and restructuring of the non-profit sector, a common trend is its increasing autonomy and presence within local economies. Novak argues that since their social mission prevents non-profit organisations from distributing any surplus income to their members, they have been encouraged to focus their action on local needs and to adopt a voluntary approach, switching more openly toward the satisfaction of the general interest. Borzaga and Santuari find that in many western European countries, non-profit organisations have come to play a significant role in the direct supply of social services, particularly at the local level. The decentralisation and privatisation of social services provision further reinforced this trend. Since then, the non-profit sector has consolidated its role in local communities and displayed a number of unique characteristics. It has changed in terms of its goals, management and legal structure. In particular, it has established a strong role in the field of labour market re-integration, in the production of social and community services, and in the development of local economies. While in Europe and in the United States, the sector's contribution to employment programmes is seen as a traditional feature, in Australia this is, as argued by Novak, a key shift. In particular, it has come to play a major role with the Job Network introduced by the Department of Employment and Workplace Relations.

The change in internal culture and the occurrence of an entrepreneurial "twist" is undoubtedly a key trend in all the countries described, although more so in Anglo-American countries and in the European Union, than in Latin America. Novak argues that the adoption of an entrepreneurial spirit by the Australian non-profit sector stems from the fact that it is currently undergoing a profound transformation and is increasingly called upon to respond to new social and economic demands. Issues surrounding legal status remain particularly significant in the Australian context as policymakers seek to ensure that the legal status of non-profit organisations accurately reflects changing social and economic conditions. This spurred the Commonwealth Government to commission a major report released in June 2001 to clarify definitions and status of non-profits. In the United States, Young remarks that there has been a trend towards "market integration" in the sense that non-profit organisations have grown used to earning their own revenues in the market place. However, this is not proving unproblematic as it is felt that non-profit organisations may lose their identity and become ordinary commercial ventures. Organisations that conceive of themselves as social enterprises face important structural decisions. They can operate as for-profit businesses that make explicit contributions to the social good, or they can become not-for-profit organisations with social missions that generate income and social benefits through commercial means. Within these forms, they can design their governance arrangements and specify their financial goals and constraints in a variety of ways. Nonetheless, these alternative forms may not fully accommodate a social enterprise organisation's self-conception, *i.e.*, its organisational identity (Young, 2001). Young documents on how the mix of revenues has changed over the years: of the three main sources of revenue for non-profit organisations – gifts and grants, governmental funding, and earned income – the latter has become the chief source of non-profit revenue overall. He argues that the growth of commercial enterprise in the non-profit sector is rarely completely unconnected to mission and hence difficult to separate from so-called related income. Non-profits usually perceive commercial ventures as a direct means to achieve their mission objectives. Hence, the concept of "social purpose enterprise" was introduced to refer to revenue-generating businesses that are owned and operated by non-profit organisations with the express purpose of employing at-risk clients in the business ventures. Various experiences with commercial enterprises by non-profits have put the former into a new light. No longer conceived as primarily a revenue generation strategy, these commercial ventures suggest that market engagement may often be the most effective way to address a non-profit organisation's mission. Moreover, the process of integration in the market place gave rise to hefty debates over unfair competition of non-profits with small businesses. These have, however, declined in recent years as non-profits and corporate businesses established ever-closer links. In fact, traditional non-profit markets, such as education, community development and health care, are increasingly occupied by large corporations. The benefits of collaboration between business corporations and non-profits are mutual. For commercial businesses, benefits include the enhancement of their public images, access to special expertise or future talent, increased demand for their products and increased motivation amongst staff due to opportunities for volunteering. In turn, their non-profit partners gain access to substantial financial, personnel and other corporate resources, obtain wider forums in which to broadcast their messages and appeals, and in some cases influence consumers in ways that indirectly support the non-profit's mission. Nonetheless, collaboration is not without risks to participating non-profits. They may be perceived as neglecting or harming their mission if identifying themselves with questionable products or corporations. At the same time donor sovereignty has put more demands on non-profits in terms of accountability and transparency. As a result non-profit organisations have been challenged to improve management practices. Thus a new market culture is taking root in the non-profit sector.

Of course, the development and sustainability of the non-profit sector is dependent upon the availability of adequate resources and funding. The second aim of the volume is to identify and compare instruments and tools used to finance this sector, focusing on the opportunities and obstacles faced along the way.

**Part Two** brings together three chapters on Canada, Europe and the United States. The notions of *risk, trust* and *uncertainty* are recurrent throughout these three chapters and serve to explain some of the reasons that may have held back, or on the contrary, incited financial investors to consider investing in this sector. These chapters also illustrate the many attempts to develop alternative instruments that would fill the institutional void left by the retrenchment of public or bank funding. The overall message is that many of these new instruments are more fragile and uncertain than well-established financing methods and that further state involvement, notably through programme and mixed funding, should continue to play a role.

Caroline Williams (*Chapter 5*) critically examines how the non-profit sector is financed in the United States. Because the size and the activities of non-profit organisations vary enormously, the sources and levels of funding are also varied. Attracting private capital represents a major difficulty, particularly for small organisations. Echoing Young's earlier overview of the key trends in the US, Williams notes that commercial funding is increasingly sought, especially because governments have cut back their funding on non-profit sector activities. In recent years, the "new wealth" associated with the "rationally exuberant market" of the new economy has aroused many expectations. In particular, it was thought that venture philanthropy would become a major source of commercial funding. The idea that lies behind venture philanthropy is that enlightened investors will accept a lower financial return if the receiving organisation demonstrates that it can generate important social benefits. Since April 2000, the US has been going through some turbulence, including the failure of the dot.com industry, the terrorist attacks of 11th September 2001, as well as various scandals and failures in corporate governance. These events have important implications for non-profit sector funding and may dampen some of the enthusiasm surrounding venture philanthropy according to Williams. She explores some of the key trends of the US non-profit sector. In 1999, a total of 170 000 organisations were reported to exist. In percentage terms, revenues do not necessarily match the actual number of organisations. For example, the healthcare segment only represents 17 per cent of the total number of operating non-profit organisations, but is dominant in terms of revenues. This is because funding largely comes from fees-for-services. However, the healthcare sector has been undergoing a major transformation since the 1980s. Many for-profit entities have acquired the assets of non-profit organisations, notably through the establishment of foundations. The cash generated through these operations is then held in those grant-making institutions for further distributions to other non-profit organisations. Williams argues that foundations have played and will continue to play a key role as providers of loans and grants to non-profit organisations. In recent years, not only have foundation assets grown, but their number has increased too. New charitable gift funds that allow individuals to make tax-deductible contributions to foundations have subsequently emerged, turning foundations into the "aggregators" of capital from individuals. This is also the case of Community Development Funds (CFDIs), who while not new, are playing an increasing role as aggregators and providers of non-commercial capital. In comparison to these sources of finance, the new financing methods that surround venture philanthropy and social entrepreneurship – earned-income strategies, socially responsible venture capital, or charitable giving from the "new wealth" – are not as widespread or targeted on non-profit organisations as is commonly thought, and may not justify the hype. Williams finally suggests that in the future, funding sources for the non-profit sector are more likely to be shaped by the emerging activism among institutional shareholders.

The chapter by Marguerite Mendell, Benoît Levesque and Ralph Rouzier (*Chapter 6*) begins with the view that any discussion about how to finance the non-profit sector must be informed by an unequivocal definition of its nature. The authors prefer to opt for the broader concept of "social economy" that includes non-profit organisations and co-operatives, but also private enterprises with a strong social remit (see glossary). These authors stress that organisations operating in this sector face many barriers; they are often considered as representing a high risk and hence find it difficult to attract investment. They do not generate competitive rates of return and require small grants on which transaction costs are high. Moreover, their leaders tend to be unknown to the business and financial communities and their mission-related objectives restrict the participation of traditional institutional investors. Traditional sources of funding have included donations and gifts from foundations, government grants and programme funding, and self-financing such as individual savings, "love money" and fundraising activities. The new financing instruments that have more recently emerged include community-based funds, hybrid funds, workers funds, co-operative funds and state funds. These tend to rest on mechanisms such as financial and social intermediation, leveraging, integration in territorial planning strategies, and innovative governance. The chapter reviews each of these instruments, focusing on the extent to which they can meet the needs of the social economy. Community-based funds are initiated by civil society organisations: they are often provided by community economic development corporations or may be autonomous loan circles and community loan funds. Hybrid funds involve state participation either in their capitalisation or in the financing of their operating costs. Worker funds – the capitalisation of which is often drawn from pension funds – are also a major instrument of social economy funding in that they commit firms to socio-economic objectives such as maintaining or creating jobs. State funds have purposefully been created by the government of Quebec to respond to the need for venture capital. Co-operative funds such as those provided by the Mouvement Desjardins – a major financial institution in Quebec with a membership of 5.3 million – have supported a variety of housing, educational and cultural projects in the past twenty years. These authors conclude that the tendency towards mixed funding in Quebec should not be interpreted as state retrenchment, but rather as the re-engagement of the state as a partner of socio-economic development. They suggest that a new social contract is being constructed in which civil society actors are increasingly playing a decisive role, notably through a national platform, the Forum on the Social Economy. However, the financial needs of the non-profit sector are still far from being met, especially with regard to the fragility of small community-based funds.

In contrast to Mendell *et al.*, Benoît Granger (*Chapter 7*) uses the "European" concept of "third system" (see glossary) and examines how it has been financed drawing on several surveys conducted in the second half of the 1990s. These have highlighted the barriers towards the access to financial services. Banks are extremely selective and refuse customers that are too small. As in the case of Quebec, the chapter reports that banks consider social economy projects as too risky both because of their geographical location and the profile of their holders. They tend not to understand the rationale behind the social economy where shareholder value is not the driving force. Moreover, the fact that macroeconomic benefits and social return cannot be established with certainty represents a major hurdle. However, many individuals and institutions are willing to invest their savings in projects with a social mission but are prevented from doing so because of legal restrictions. At present, three types of financial instruments prevail in Europe. The first of these instruments is micro-credit. This has spread quite significantly to respond to the problem of inadequate credit supply and combat social and labour market exclusion. Some micro-credit programmes seek to co-operate with banks, but others prefer to remain autonomous as they feel that banks have failed to engage with local communities and the social exclusion agenda. Granger illustrates this approach through the example of micro-credit programmes from Portugal and Belgium. The Portuguese example shows the importance of additional professional support in the form of mentoring. On the whole, the demand for micro-credit is much higher than the level of support that programmes can provide. This raises the issue of how these practices can be generalised and mainstreamed. Partnerships with government and banking institutions will prove particularly important. Secondly, the example of Community-Based Economic Financial Instruments (CBEFIs) shows that it is possible for institutions such as credit unions to engage in credit activities without having the status of banks. CBEFIs have been created within the third system, but are still very young. They provide integrated packages including loans, guarantees and advisory services. Advisory and counselling activities tend to represent half of the production costs so that the levels of profitability of these services cannot be compared to those achieved by banks. Moreover, CBEFIs are increasingly establishing co-operative links with large banks. Granger shows that changing practices within traditional retail banking institutions can also provide a useful answer. In fact, many co-operative banks have recently been established. Co-operative banks, mutual banks and savings banks hold of quarter of the market share in most EU countries, although de-mutualisation has also been observed notably in the United Kingdom. These institutions tend to be much more decentralised and have a strong local presence, which makes them highly relevant as a source of finance for the non-profit sector. According to Granger, the major challenge in the European context would be to achieve an extension, generalisation and mainstreaming of these innovative tools and practices. But this will require stronger and more assertive regulatory intervention from government.

Finally, this book seeks to shed light on the current state of evaluation of the non-profit sector. There is a strong demand for evaluation linked to the recent growth of the sector and the increasingly wide spectrum of stakeholders it has brought together. In particular, public and private sector investment in non-profit organisations depends upon the ability to show that there is a return. However, there have been very lively debates, not only about the nature of that return, but also about whether traditional evaluation tools can be applied to the non-profit sector. Here the chapters point to the central problem of *value*.

Xavier Greffe (*Chapter 8*) provides a European perspective on this theme. He argues that evaluation must be conducted against the value added and innovation generated by this sector. The profit motive seems to be a limited criterion given that the non-profit sector addresses multiple values and has both tangible and intangible impacts. Following a review of the nature, size and structure of this sector of the economy, Greffe investigates the extent to which it generates innovation. Innovation is explored at both the macro and micro levels of activity. At the macro-social level, the non-profit sector has been a model for a new form of social organisation, in which co-operation and solidarity have helped in moving beyond role specialisation. Three principles (the market, redistribution, and reciprocity) have however been present to varying degrees according to the chosen structure. The sector has thus been regarded as a hybrid form of organisation, "dovetailed" in society. However, this interpretation appears to be flawed as one cannot establish with certainty that trading principles are fully absent from the production of social ties. Greffe thus recommends turning to economic interpretations such as cost differences linked to economies of scale and socio-demographic characteristics. For example, the non-profit sector can be regarded as part of a new mode of public management whereby governments are increasingly calling upon non-profit organisations to discharge some of their duties or to ensure provision at a lower cost. It can also be seen as a tool for local development as it can engender new dynamics based on alternative approaches to employment demand. Here the non-profit sector may produce new services that the market economy either cannot or does not know how to introduce. The "interdependence theory" holds that the development of the non-profit sector is due to the inability of public sector agents to identify new needs and to provide appropriate responses. Other reasons for its emergence is the decisive role of new social entrepreneurs. Greffe reviews some other important factors for innovation such as a favourable legal environment, the presence of suitable financing mechanisms, as well as supporting institutions. He then attempts to establish ways in which social innovation – what he terms an "evaluation protocol" – could be measured, bearing in mind that many of the non-profit sector's impacts are intangible. One suggestion is to use a conformity indicator, which would help compare the activities, and services provided by the non-profit organisations to those provided by other agents. Productivity indicators may also be used to gauge the ability to disseminate an innovation. These may include, for example, comparisons with success rates of training schemes or variations in rates of accessibility to service users. Lifetime indicators would facilitate the assessment of vulnerability and survival, investigating amongst other things the ability to diversify resources and activities. However, these many instruments are predicated upon the assumption that monetary valuation is the sole type of added value. Greffe proposes to resort to horizontal and vertical evaluation, the former involving comparisons with similar commercial organisations, and the latter, comparisons with a leading institution through benchmarking procedures. He concludes that the actors concerned must be fully integrated in the evaluation process to facilitate data collection and analysis and successfully serve the three purposes of monitoring, learning and mediating.

In her chapter on Quebec, Nancy Neamtan (*Chapter 9*) argues that the contribution of the non-profit sector to economic development is still under-estimated. Like Greffe, she points to the added social value that this sector bears upon local economic development. She reports that evaluation that has been carried out in Quebec has been at the micro level (enterprise) and at the macro level (society), and then gives an overview of the state of development of the non-profit sector in Quebec notably through the Chantier de l'économie sociale, a major independent umbrella organisation that brings together the major actors active in this field. Neamtan identifies a number of obstacles towards evaluation. A major challenge is the attempt to trace an accurate portrait of the non-profit sector and overcoming the problems of defining the legal status of the organisations involved. Moreover, while many studies have been conducted, these tend to be of a piecemeal nature and often exclude the actors involved in the creation of the initiatives that are being studied. However, in recent years, funding bodies have tended to specifically support evaluation practices that require an active participation of practitioners. This makes evaluation carried out in this field very distinctive from evaluation of traditional enterprises or public policy initiatives. Neamtan argues that since the role of the non-profit sector is much broader than merely creating jobs, it becomes essential to identify its impacts beyond job creation. In particular, it would be important to assess the extent to which the non-profit sector is contributing to transforming the economy into a "pluralist" model, notably through its effects on the creation of networks of local, national and international solidarity. This author stresses that the analysis must not be confined to output measurement and social impact on local populations, but must also include global impacts, especially on institutional behaviour as this will indicate changes in the current model of development. But heterogeneous, or even conflicting, concerns and the lack of consensus on the methodologies to be adopted makes this task difficult. A first important experience of multi-sectorial evaluation brought together a variety of stakeholders, including the Quebec government and the Forum on the Social Economy. This work which was carried out in two stages sought to assess whether the activities of non-profit organisations had reached their original goals and achieved sustainability. Through the creation of further networks, evaluation will be developed even further. For example, the University-Community Alliance was created in January 2000. It brings together academic researchers and practitioners, and is a major element for the development of new methodological tools.

Wolfgang Bielefeld's view from the USA (*Chapter 10*) first recalls the interdependence between the non-profit sector and the other sectors of the economy as well as the important function of this sector in bringing people together, especially given the country's strong individualistic culture. The author thus finds it surprising that concern with impact evaluation is relatively recent. However, in the last twenty years, evaluation has become an "obsession", first for the conservative government of the 1980s, and more recently among the plurality of public and private funders. Academic interest has also been aroused and has recently focused on evaluation of sub-sectors. Bielefeld points to the complexity of evaluating the non-profit sector because of its diversity, and underlines that the term "evaluation" itself is problematic as it entails differing approaches. His concern is with impact analysis, with questions including the priorities that should be given to allocating public resources among the different sectors and how effectively, efficiently and equitably public interests are being addressed by the sector. But as in Quebec, there are numerous conceptual and methodological disagreements. A central point of contention is the desirability of using monetary valuation as opposed to other measures of value. Many social scientists have stressed that values are not always based on instrumental economic preferences. Bielefeld suggests that a closer examination of axiology, the branch of philosophy dealing with values, might well contain interesting and useful ideas that could advance non-profit studies. He also finds that the emphasis has been exclusively on positive aspects of the non-profit sector and that its potentially negative effects have been neglected, and that this bias should be redressed. From a methodological perspective, the factors to be measured should include at least inputs, outputs and outcomes, and possibly wider impacts. Among the difficulties identified are the lack of causal models, the lack of data, the lack of clear goals, services to anonymous beneficiaries, and intangible outputs and outcomes. Moreover, costs and benefits are almost impossible to measure in the absence of actual payments and market valuation. And if social factors such as quality of life and community cohesion can be measured through qualitative techniques, the results of studies cannot be easily compared as there are many variables involved and investigation techniques. Nonetheless, the various studies that have been conducted have addressed either functional sub-sectors, such as healthcare, the arts, community development, social capital and religion, or specific target groups, including women, religious, racial and age groups. Drawing upon the latest research in those fields, the chapter identifies some of the benefits brought by the non-profit sector. These include the minimisation of information asymmetries, the offer of a wider array of services when compared to other sectors (particularly in health care), higher educational attainment, increased self-esteem, the reduction of drug and alcohol use, suicides, neighbourhood disorders, and more generally improved well-being and community life. Whilst this chapter certainly illustrates that a vast array of projects are conducted in the field of non-profit evaluation, it concludes that this activity remains partial and fragmented.

The final chapter by Anheier and Mertens (*Chapter 11*) provides a constructive proposal on how to proceed to an evaluation of the non-profit sector, namely through the inclusion of a non-profit satellite account within national statistical datasets. Once again, these authors argue that welfare state reform has increased the economic clout of non-profit organisations, particularly as providers of welfare services, so that systematic and up-to-date information is greatly needed. Yet it is only since the late 1990s that rigorous studies have been conducted. An important step has been the Johns Hopkins Comparative Non-profit Sector Project, which covered 22 countries. Using this source of information, the authors provide a comparative profile of the non-profit sector. Taken all together, the countries covered by the Johns Hopkins project employ almost 30 million full-time staff, although only two-thirds are paid employees. Moreover, the non-profit sector is larger in the more economically advanced countries, and less so in Latin America and Central Europe. These studies also show that employment tends to be concentrated in specific fields of activity. For example, in Western Europe, a significant concentration of employment is in welfare services, whereas in the United States or Australia, the non-profit sector is more heavily represented in the health sector. Even if it is possible to draw some stylised facts, the authors point to the current limitations in establishing further evidence due to the shortcomings of the official statistical datasets, i.e. the System of National Accounts (SNA) and the European Systems of Accounts (ESA). Under current guidelines, these statistical series only include a small sub-set of Non-profit Institutions (NPIs), as the majority tend to be merged either in the business or in the government sectors. Those that do not have a legal status or do not employ paid staff are merged into the household sector. National accounting systems, therefore, lead to distortions and under-estimation of the non-profit sector's true significance and thus need to be improved according to Anheier and Mertens. In addition to the described shortcomings, a further problem concerns the low statistical coverage across the OECD. Among 160 countries that produce national statistical accounts, only 30 report some, yet incomplete data on the non-profit sector. A focus on the case of Belgium illustrates the sectoral distribution of the non-profit sector according to SNA and ESA conventions. It is argued that many of the economic flows generated by NPIs are either implicitly or not registered in national economic accounts, especially those that cannot be ascribed a monetary value. The adoption of a separate set of statistics on NPIs, i.e. a satellite account that would cover various features relating to the structure and size of the non-profit sector, would help provide a more accurate picture and in turn have a positive impact on the evaluation of other sectors of the economy. The recent production of a Handbook on Non-profit Institutions in the System of National Accounts (by the Johns Hopkins Center for Civil Society and the United Nations Statistical Division) will help national statistical agencies to provide consolidated data, some pertaining to paid and unpaid work, and thus will facilitate the conduct of both cross-sectional and longitudinal analyses on the significance and evolution of the non-profit sector. The satellite account is of course not an end in itself but a methodological tool that would help respond to a set of research questions on organisational choice, internal composition and the contribution of NPIs relative to other for-profit or public organisations.

In summary, this collection of essays on the non-profit sector strikes both in terms of its unity and diversity. Whilst there are many variations in terminology, definitions, actors and tools that characterise the non-profit sector, as well as varying concerns and suggestions for future developments, the authors all agree that the non-profit sector is now indispensable and that its set goals and the challenges it is facing are very similar across the countries reviewed. In particular, the key challenges for the foreseeable future will be *how to ensure its sustainability and improve its visibility*. Innovation in the field of finance is essential to facilitate the establishment of pilot projects and to ensure that well-established ones continue to play their essential role in building competitive and inclusive societies. So is evaluation and research to provide further evidence of the benefits that accrue to individuals and communities. The nature of non-profit studies, which Anheier and Mertens describe as an "interdisciplinary social science speciality at the intersection of economics, sociology and political science" implies that only a strong dialogue between policy-makers, practitioners and academics of various disciplines will improve our understanding of the difference the non-profit sector makes to the strength of our economies and the cohesion of our societies. This publication is an attempt to take up this challenge and to explore some of the possibilities that lie ahead.

PART I

# The Non-profit Sector Today

ISBN 92-64-19953-5
The Non-profit Sector in a Changing Economy
© OECD 2003

PART I

*Chapter 1*

# New Trends in the Non-profit Sector in Europe: The Emergence of Social Entrepreneurship

by

Carlo  Borzaga,
Department of Economics, University of Trento, Italy

and

Alceste Santuari,
University of Trento

## Introduction

In European countries, there was little, if any, interest in the non-profit sector until the end of the 1970s. The few papers written up to then by sociologists and political scientists were exclusively concerned with the contribution of voluntary or civic organisations to public social policies, since these, mainly advocacy organisations were deemed forms of direct democracy. The only non-profit form approached by economists was the co-operative (mainly worker co-operative).

From the end of the 1970s onwards, the interest in the non-profit sector started to grow. The interest of researchers, academic centres, the general public, the European Commission and national governments in the sector steadily increased, particularly due to its ability to provide new social services, its job creation potential – especially in favour of long-term unemployed – and its capacity to promote social cohesion.

The first systematic studies on the dimensions of the non-profit or third sector in Europe date back to the early 1990s and have developed throughout the decade (see Salamon and Anheier, 1996; Salamon and Associates, 1999; CIRIEC, 2000). These studies stress the fact that the non-profit sector also has its own specific weight in Europe as to the number of organisations, added value and employment. In several countries this importance is by no means marginal, in some cases it is the same as or even higher than in the United States. This means that the non-profit sector was well established in most European countries even before its recent discovery by researchers and policy makers. However, it remains to be explained why, after being ignored for decades, the non-profit sector has now become of general interest.

The reasons for this rediscovery are numerous. The most important ones are to be identified with the crisis of the European welfare systems built up during the nineteenth century and with the innovative characteristics taken on by non-profit organisations that have developed since the 1970s.

The European welfare systems were established on a division of tasks between the state and the market and pushed the non-profit sector aside. In some countries during the nineteenth century, many non-profit organisations were even eliminated, whereas in others they were made heavily dependent on public policies. However, the crisis in these welfare models, which began in the 1970s and has grown progressively, has made more room for private initiative, especially in the production of social services, where most European welfare systems were failing. And it is exactly the dissatisfaction with the insufficient supply of social services that explains the development of the new non-profit initiatives.

As some studies have demonstrated (EMES, 2000), the non-profit experiences developed after the 1970s are more autonomous and entrepreneurial than traditional non-profit organisations.

To stress these new characteristics of the non-profit sector the term "social enterprise" was introduced (EMES, 2000; OECD, 1999).

These new trends in the third sector were at first underestimated by researchers and policy makers, who rather stressed the voluntary and precarious dimension of the new organisations. Since the 1980s, the sector has been increasingly taken into consideration. Accordingly, it has become the object of a growing number of research projects and of several supporting policies at the European, national and local level. However, the interpretation of this development is still uncertain,[1] and the supporting policies have, to date, been indecisive, occasional and often uncoordinated. The outcomes of these policies are still controversial.

This chapter reviews the evolution of the third sector in Europe. In order to comply with this task, it is necessary though to move from a prevailing static and statistical approach (Salamon and Anheier, 1996; Salamon and Associates, 1999) to a historical dynamic approach to the sector under consideration. This shift will also take into account the evolution of the welfare state. Indeed, the strong interdependence between the welfare state and the non-profit sector is one of the most important features of the non-profit sector in Europe. In this respect, both the size and the characteristics of non-profit organisations in Europe depend on the way in which the welfare state is devised.

It is nonetheless necessary to state clearly that the analysis carried out herewith can be little more than introductory and, therefore, incomplete. The differences among the European welfare models are indeed remarkable and have increased over the last twenty years according to the diversities in the reforming policies accomplished. The legal systems are also different, accordingly, so are the characteristics of the non-profit sector in the different countries and its recent evolution. Notwithstanding these shortcomings, the authors believe that it is useful to carry out an analysis at the European level, at least as a first insight for future studies, which will necessarily be held in each country.

This chapter is divided into two main parts. The first is aimed at tracing briefly the historical evolution of the non-profit sector in Europe and at providing a synthetic classification of the role assigned to the sector by the different welfare state models during the late 1960s to early 1970s. The second part of the chapter begins with a brief analysis of the causes of the crisis of the welfare state, especially of the space that this crisis has opened up for the development of the non-profit sector; paragraph five will deal with the development of the new non-profit initiatives by highlighting: *i)* their main characteristics, etc; *ii)* the main fields of activity; and *iii)* the evolution of the relationship with public authorities and for-profits; paragraph six will focus on the contributions of the non-profit sector to European societies and economies. In paragraph seven a comparison with the United States will be made and, finally, the concluding paragraph (para. 8) will include some insights into supporting policies.[2]

## Historical background

Let us now try to place the evolution of non-profit organisations within the historical context in which they have developed over the centuries in Europe.

Until the end of the eighteenth century, charities, mutual organisations and co-operatives freely developed according to the changing social needs of the community. Social work, health care, alms housing and education were all areas in which charities and mutual benefit societies evolved.[3] Human and material resources were invested in non-profit organisations, which in turn would distribute them to the community or a significant part of it. The Governments would mainly ensure that charities carried out their objectives according to their original spirit and purposes. As long as a charity was established to achieve a beneficial purpose it could live on without being checked or hindered. In England, for instance, the relations between charities and the Government were mostly defined by co-operation and mutual support rather than conflict or antagonism. It was in the Government's interest to sustain charitable organisations and to help them to grow and develop, not only because such intervention would take a certain number of responsibilities away from the Government itself but also because this approach was perfectly in line with the liberal culture of the time. Charities then performed their activities in several areas, such as education, care of the elderly, poor relief, and so on, especially in the big towns during the Industrial Revolution.[4] In France, on the other hand *"while part of the community of associations arose from a philanthropic desire for social peace, the dominant philosophy was a republican egalitarianism reflected in a broad-based appeal to a multifaceted concept of solidarity. This solidarity principle eventually led the country beyond the dichotomy between liberalism and statism"* (CIRIEC, 2000, p. 108).

From the end of the eighteenth century, non-profit organisations were seriously affected by three external events, which affected the sector in different ways depending on the country involved:

● The occurrence of the French Revolution, which exerted a huge influence, especially on France and Italy.[5]

● Fascism and Nazism, which brought with them a deep fight against any expression of civil society and forms of local autonomy. These regimes affected mainly Germany and Italy.

● The formation of universalistic welfare state systems, which influenced, though to a different extent, all the European countries.

Starting from the end of the eighteenth century, when the French Revolution broke out in Europe, except for England,[6] a kind of suspicion of and aversion to charities began to grow. They were mainly regarded as belonging to extraneous powers, especially the Catholic Church, which were to be reduced because they represented a third party between the Government and individuals. Indeed, these were the only two subjects that the ideology of the Enlightenment recognised: the state was the highest and supreme interpreter of the people's will and no other established body could exist because citizens had to strengthen the authority of the state in order to widen and protect their individual rights. The liberal form of the state, which the French Revolution affirmed, implied the isolation of individuals. Accordingly, the legitimacy of intermediate bodies was to be denied, the only freedom thus being that referring to single individuals and not to social groups such as corporations, foundations and associations, which were consequently excluded a priori from any active role and welfare function. In continental Europe, therefore, the authorities of the state replaced that which had been always peculiar to charities and voluntary organisations.[7] In any case, such an approach was often characterised by an ideological bias. In France, as well as in Italy, the rules that the Government imposed on associations, especially on their carrying out of economic activities, was rooted in the intention of preventing the Catholic Church from consolidating its power (CIRIEC, op. cit., p. 109). For example, in Italy, the Government did not hesitate to pass acts that prevented religious and charitable organisations from owning property, from developing their resources and from carrying out activities without a specific state authorisation.[8] The suspicion directed at not-for-profit organisations has contributed to fostering the isolation of these organisations, which were regarded as a residual aspect of social and economic relations. Where this was not the case, the authorities of the state carried out some statutory acts aimed at incorporating the functions of private charitable organisations into public bodies that were directly controlled and managed by the Government.[9]

Fascism and Nazism were based on a strong centralised state. It followed that all existing non-profit organisations, including in particular co-ops, were either to be incorporated within the bureaucratic mechanisms of the state or suppressed altogether.[10] In Germany, the co-operative movement was twofold. On the one hand, the insurance mutual and credit co-operatives, representing mostly the interests of the middle classes, proved to be very successful. These co-ops expanded during the Weimar Republic, survived quite well during the Third Reich and eventually recovered easily after the end of Nazism. On the other hand, the co-operative movement linked to workers, especially housing co-ops, was hindered during the Nazi period (Bode and Evers, 1998).

The building of the modern welfare state started at the beginning of the twentieth century. It is, however, from the late 1940s that policy makers began to move towards a conception of a universal welfare state, i.e. a system in which the authorities of the state were to play a major role in the delivery of collective and public goods and services. With the evolution of welfare state systems, non-profit organisations were forced to change their basics.[11] Therefore, those private non-profit organisations that had survived until then became less important and increasingly began to concentrate their activities in fields in which any economic or distributive implications were to be excluded.

The impact of these three important events has varied from country to country. Some countries, like Italy, have been affected by all three factors, though with varying intensity. Others, like the United Kingdom, have suffered only from the last one.[12]

According to the nature and intensity of the shocks the following has taken place:

- In some cases, non-profit organisations, or large parts of them, were "transformed" in their original nature by being placed within the public sector.[13]

- In other cases, non-profit organisations were incorporated into the welfare system: they formally and legally remained private organisations but they were to be subject to administrative and bureaucratic checks, thus losing their autonomy.

- In almost all countries, the non-profit organisations that were not part of the welfare system were prevented from developing productive activities, that is, business. It followed that non-profit organisations were left with the possibility of carrying out only advocacy functions.

The ensuing civil and tax legislation is consistent with the foregoing trend. Indeed, from a tax point of view, with respect to the US, tax deductions are much more restricted both for donors and for non-profit organisations, which generally cannot benefit from these deductions when they carry out commercial activities.

## The non-profit sector in the European welfare models until the 1970s

The outcome of the combination of the three different shocks and their intensity can be outlined by depicting three main welfare models. These correspond to different ways of conceiving the non-profit sector and, accordingly, its different functions and dimensions. Although not all countries fit closely into one of these groups, the classification helps to explain the differences in the spread of non-profit organisations at the beginning of the 1970s.

The first group consists of countries with a well-developed, universal welfare state engaging both in public services provision and in cash benefits (pensions, unemployment benefits, vital minimum, and so on). Sweden, Denmark and, though to a lesser extent, Finland fall within this group. Until the reform that led to quasi-markets, England too belonged to this group. In these countries, non-profit organisations were confined almost exclusively to playing an advocacy role. Accordingly, this means a wide-spread third sector (in which there is strong citizen participation in associations) with little significance in the direct provision of social and collective services.

The second group consists of countries that also have a developed and universal welfare state, although largely based on cash benefits, with a limited commitment on the part of the government to direct supply of social services. Here both the family and the traditional third sector play an important role in the social and community care services provision, mainly funded by public authorities. Germany, Austria, France, Belgium, Ireland and the Netherlands fall within this group. In these countries, the non-profit organisations were widely involved in the provision of social services with well-established financing rules. This has caused a strong dependence on public authorities not only for funds, but also as to the sectors of activity and with regard to the specific organisation of services. The above-mentioned countries are those in which the welfare system has frequently been built up by incorporating non-profit organisations into the public welfare policies (though without making them public) and more generally in the supply of public services (see the school system in Ireland and Belgium and the system of mutual associations in Germany).

The third group includes countries with a less developed welfare state, especially until the early 1980s, largely based on cash benefits, with a limited public provision of social and community care services confined to few sectors (education and health). Since the welfare state was less developed than in other countries advocacy organisations were not widespread either. Italy, Spain, Greece and Portugal belong to this group. As the provision of social and community care services was mainly entrusted to the family and informal networks, the non-profit organisations providing social services have developed only to a certain extent.

In concluding this paragraph, it is possible to state that only in the second group of countries did non-profit organisations have some real weight. However, when compared to the US model, this group appears to be scarcely independent of, and often different only formally from, public services.

## Some features of the crisis and the evolution of the European welfare models

From the 1970s, the European welfare systems began to crumble under the burden of financial and organisational difficulties. The decline in the rates of economic growth and the rise of unemployment were the main contributors to this crisis, which at the beginning, was mainly of a fiscal nature and led to growing public deficits. While public revenues grew at a slower rate than in the past, public expenditures increased faster, especially in countries with generous subsidies for the unemployed and for the retired and pre-retired.

In the first stage, most European countries reacted against the fiscal crisis both by reforming employment subsidies and by restructuring, slowing down or blocking the growth in the public supply of social services. However, the increasing inability of traditional macroeconomic and employment policies to reduce unemployment, and to respond to an ever-swelling demand for social services, which proved to be increasingly differentiated and attentive to quality, gave birth also to a legitimacy crisis in European welfare regimes. In fact the crisis of the welfare system coincided with a decline in the informal provision of social services by the family, mainly due to the growing participation of women in the labour market and to the reduction in the size of families.

When European policy makers realised that the economy was undergoing strong structural changes, they tried to implement a wider reform of welfare systems. With regard to public services provision, action was undertaken in order to steadily reduce its impact on the public budget, and to tailor, at least in theory, the supply of services to users' needs. This was done by decentralising to local authorities some power in deciding and implementing social polices, by introducing prices and tariffs, by privatising some services, and by shifting from passive to active labour and employment policies. However, the introduction of prices and tariffs often affected the more needy, thus reducing social cohesion.

Policies for privatisation of social services provision were implemented both by separating financing responsibility, which was kept by public authorities, from services provision, which was contracted out to private enterprises, and by ceasing the production of some services. This set of changes has allowed for both a growth in the demand for private providers of social services by local public authorities, and for a wider range of needs opening new spaces to the non-profit action. Moreover, the supply of services has been made more dynamic by de-centralisation and policies aimed at separating purchasers from providers. De-centralisation and the consequent shift of responsibility to local authorities, closer to citizens' needs, has allowed for a better acceptance of civil society's initiatives and has made their public funding more viable. The separation of purchasers and providers has stimulated supply and especially boosted the establishment of new initiatives in a sector that for-profit enterprises regarded as of little interest to them.

A more specific reduction of the public policies, though important in explaining the development of the non-profit sector, can be found in the failures of traditional labour policies and in the difficulties in shifting from regulatory, and mainly passive, policies to active ones. These difficulties are associated with workers who find it hard to enter or re-enter the labour market, and whose number and duration of unemployment have progressively increased over the years, especially in France, Germany and Italy.

## The emergence of the new non-profit sector

The evolution of the crisis and the reforms of welfare systems have been accompanied by a revitalisation of the non-profit sector.

Since the 1970s, in almost all European countries some of the existing advocacy organisations and several new groups of citizens started providing social services, especially for groups affected harder by the economic crisis and not covered by public social policies. Their action was, at the beginning, autonomous from and often in open contrast with the public policies and largely based on voluntary work.

During the 1980s and the 1990s the collaboration with the public authorities grew as a consequence of the changes in the public policies. The more systematic funding policies established during the 1980s and the 1990s contributed to strengthening the role of the new non-profit organisations. However, the growth in numbers and economic size of non-profit organisations is only one aspect of this evolution. The new organisations differ from the traditional non-profits in several respects. In this paragraph we try to summarise the most important of these differences.

## Main characteristics of the new non-profit organisations

The new non-profit organisational typologies that emerged from the 1970s display the following main characteristics:

- They are characterised by productive and entrepreneurial behaviour: since their aim is the provision of services to meet needs often not recognised by public authorities, and not simply to advocate, they must organise a productive activity and find the economic resources. Since the beginning, most of the new non-profit organisations have based their activity on a mix of resources (donations, volunteers, and public funds) and are market-oriented.

- They show a high propensity to innovate the supply of social services from several points of view: in the types of services provided, in the target groups (often the more marginalised) and in the organisation of services provision (great attention to active policies and to the empowerment of users).

- They pay particular attention to the creation of new jobs, especially for hard-to-place people (long-term unemployed youth, for example).

- They stress the local dimension of their activity, the strong link with a well-defined community and with its needs.

- Although they do not distribute profits, they do not always assume, as the main or distinctive characteristic, the non-profit distribution constraint. However they give more importance to the clear definition of the social goal, to the different stakeholders' representation, and to democratic control and management.

Compared with the traditional European non-profit organisations the new organisations are:

- Less interested in advocacy or interested in it as a secondary purpose.

- More autonomous: they derive resources from a plurality of suppliers and they enter into relations with the public authorities as independent parties, often on the basis of contracts.

- More attentive to employment creation, especially for disadvantaged people and, consequently, more interested in collaborating with for-profits.

- Attentive to defining an ownership structure, capable of guaranteeing the participation of the stakeholders and self-management.

- Locally-based and generally small-sized, though the traditional non-profit organisations were often large and operated at the national level.

- Oriented to the creation of new services not provided by other organisations, and to new ways of answering the social needs.

One of the most interesting organisational innovations is probably the creation of the "multi-stakeholder" form, in which the membership and the executive board are shared among volunteers, workers, consumers and public authorities.[14] This organisational innovation can be seen as a way of taking into account the different interests characterising the production of social services.

However, the new non-profit organisations have profoundly changed not only the goals of the traditional non-profit organisation, their management and operational methods,[15] but in many cases, also the legal forms. At the beginning of their development, the legal forms available for the new organisations were associations and co-operatives. These forms were not deemed fully compatible with activities, which simultaneously were to be socially oriented and productive.

Largely spread in the civil law systems, especially in France, Belgium and Italy, the association was born as a "moral entity" for idealistic purposes, originally even hampered by the authorities of the state[16] and rigidly separated from companies at large. Accordingly, the association was, at the beginning, explicitly forbidden to carry out commercial and productive activities, thus being distinguished by the absence of a continuous productive or "speculative" activity. Although progressively, with the change in the activities carried out, associations have been allowed to manage the production of services of general interest, they were never granted a full entrepreneurial status.

Unlike the association, the co-operative society is considered by all European legal systems as an enterprise. And with the association, it shares the social purpose. Indeed, since co-ops were often established by groups of people who were prejudiced by the market, they were generally regarded as enterprises with a specific social purpose. For this reason, in Europe they have been generally limited in the distribution of profits.[17] However, co-operatives were characterised by the meeting between member and beneficiary and by a membership consisting of only one category of stakeholder.

The new organisations used both these legal forms, often even beyond the limits permitted by the law, to organise their activities. In some countries, the organisational changes introduced by these organisations have been recognised by the legal system, as in the case of the Italian "social co-operatives", the "social solidarity co-operatives" in Portugal, the "co-operative of general interest" in France, and the *entreprise à finalité sociale* in Belgium. To summarise this complex evolution and to provide a better identification for these new non-profit organisations, the term "social enterprise" has been introduced (EMES, 2000). The definition of what social enterprises are helps to summarise the recent evolution of the European non-profit sector.

As regards the entrepreneurial side, four elements are considered as the most relevant: 1) a continuous activity producing goods and/or services; 2) a high degree of autonomy; 3) a significant level of economic risk; and 4) the presence of paid work. A possible fifth parameter might be added: a market orientation, which means that a significant part of the organisation's income has to be derived from the market (services sold directly to users) or from contractual transactions with public authorities.

Five indicators depict the social dimension of these organisations: 1) an initiative undertaken by a group of citizens; 2) direct participation by the people affected by the activity; 3) power not based on capital ownership; 4) limited profit distribution; and 5) an explicit aim to benefit the community. The level of innovation of the service produced, with regard both to the typology of the services supplied (which also meet needs not traditionally addressed by the public welfare systems) and to the productive processes, can be seen as another specific, if not essential, characteristic of these organisations.

### The fields of activity

The new non-profit organisations are engaged in various activities. However, it is possible to break these activities down into two main fields: work integration and social and community care services provision.

Work integration non-profit or social enterprises are present in almost all European countries. They partly stem from the foregoing experiences of sheltered employment workshops, but with at least two important differences: firstly, they are generally less dependent on public funds and pay more attention to market dynamics; secondly, they pursue the objective of ensuring that employed disadvantaged people earn income comparable with that of other workers. Moreover, several of these organisations have the explicit aim of providing disadvantaged workers with job training, and they increasingly organise employment services with the ultimate aim of helping workers to integrate into the open labour market. In some countries, work-integration initiatives employ very specific groups of workers, mainly not supported by existing public employment policies (as in Spain). In other countries, social enterprises encompass a broader range of people and employ thousands of workers (as in Italy).[18] Whereas the traditional sheltered workshops fall within passive labour policies, the new work integration organisations are fully innovative tools of active labour policies for the same groups of workers.

A large part of work integration non-profit organisations is autonomous from the public sector and open to market relations. Some of them operate in new activities; generally labour intensive, disregarded (at least during the

1970s and the 1980s) by for-profits (see the case of recycling activities). Several of them also cover all the expenditure for training disadvantaged workers, supplying goods and services to private consumers or to for-profit enterprises. Often, the only public subsidies are the employment subsidies on which any enterprise employing the same types of workers can rely.

The second field of activity of new non-profit or social enterprises is represented by social and community care services provision. These non-profits are also present in almost all European countries, but with major differences with respect to work integration social enterprises both in the number of enterprises and in the types of service supplied.

Their diffusion largely depends on the organisation of the national welfare state.

In the countries with a well-developed welfare state, classified as belonging to the first model (para. 3), the new non-profit organisations developed only in specific sectors: normally, those in which the government or local authorities voluntarily reduced their own presence as providers, but maintained the role of financing; or those in which there was not an organised public supply.

In the countries belonging to the second model, the presence of new non-profit organisations is uneven: they have developed more in some countries (France and Belgium) or in some regions than in others and often operate in niches, mainly in the provision of new services and exploiting public resources not specifically geared to the production of social services (*e.g.*, employment subsidies). The wide involvement of traditional non-profit organisations in social services provision and the well-established financing rules that characterised these countries explain this uneven development and the fact that, more than in countries belonging to the other two models, the new non-profit organisations derive from an evolution of the traditional ones. In some countries (such as Germany) traditional non-profit organisations have more or less resisted the emergence of the new.

In the countries belonging to the third model, characterised by a limited public supply of services, the new non-profit organisations could develop in a larger set of activities since they were set up to bridge the increasing gap between needs and supply. However, their potential development was restricted by the limited amount of public resources for social services, especially in countries with the lowest *per capita* income (see Greece and Portugal).

Yet the distinction between different fields of activity is somehow artificial. In fact, many non-profit organisations combine production of social services and work-integration activities. This overlap has different explanations. It can be due to the fact that some social services are suitable for work-integration of disadvantaged workers, as they are labour-intensive and appropriate for skills acquisition. It can also be a way to provide a full social and economic integration of some disadvantaged groups, like drug addicts, for which service provision and work-integration activities cannot be separated. However, in some cases, this overlap has been caused by the lack of clear public funding policies for the new social and community care services, forcing new non-profit organisations to recruit unemployed people benefiting from employment subsidies in order to develop those services. They have accordingly been able to create actual and innovative social and community care services, by integrating public social and labour policies and without having adequate guarantees of survival in the medium-term because of the limited duration of the employment subsidies.

Beyond the direct beneficiaries of their activities oriented towards work integration or social and community care services, new non-profit organisations also operate for the development of local economic systems. In some cases, as for the Irish credit unions, the Finnish village co-operatives, and the UK business communities, such contribution to local development is among the explicit objectives of the organisations.

Finally, the analysis of the different national experiences indicates that new non-profit organisations are not confined to the services they have provided so far. In most countries, they are already enlarging their activity to other services, such as environmental and cultural services, less linked to social policies and more generally of interest to the local communities.

## Relationships between non-profit organisations and public policies

Since the areas of intervention of public social policies and of non-profit organisations are basically the same, it is clear that the evolution of the former, and accordingly of the relevant welfare models, has a great deal of influence on the evolution of the latter. And this is especially true in the European countries characterised by universalistic welfare systems.

Whereas, until the crisis of the welfare system of the 1970s the non-profit sector seemed to have been charged with a precise role, though marginal, that crisis opened up to new development perspectives. As has been already pointed out, there have been many such perspectives. New non-profit organisations have evolved either as open critics against the deficiencies of welfare systems or, at least independent of public policies by using the resources that were not generally devoted to the production of social services.

In the years following the crisis, and particularly during the 1990s, there were many attempts to reorganise public social policies. Decentralisation, privatisation and separation of funding and provision of services have been the main lines of the reforming action. However, this rearrangement of public social policies has not been pursued to bring the non-profit sector within the original boundaries set by the welfare systems. Rather, the strengthening of the non-profit sector has been the consequence. Decentralisation and the separation between the funding and provision of services have enabled the non-profit organisations established after the crisis, and mainly engaged in the production of social services, to consolidate their position. New organisations have also been created.

Less clear and less stimulating to date have been the policies in favour of non-profit organisations dedicated to work integration. In fact, it seems as though European policy makers have not yet come to realise the particular mission of these initiatives and their potential for the development of active labour policies benefiting the most disadvantaged groups of people.

The recent evolution of social policy has not only favoured the development of the non-profit sector; it has also partly changed its characteristics. Indeed, public policies have mainly been influenced by the aim of reducing or rationalising public expenditure and this has been achieved by attempting to reduce the costs of services. Accordingly, there has been an increase in tenders for the supply of single social service inputs, which are little interested in the quality of services and projects. This has had the effect of reducing the independence of non-profit organisations, their capacity to innovate both the products and the production processes, and their capacity to network with the other resources of local communities. Such an approach has favoured the development of organisations that are more oriented towards the creation of professional job opportunities rather than towards the pursuing of social aims. The risk connected to the spreading of these contractual policies in the future is the change in the nature of the new non-profit organisations. They might lose their particular characteristics and go back to being, as before the crisis, a group of organisations ancillary to public policies. In this case, though, these organisations would be even more precarious than in past welfare models, since they would be more dependent on short-term contracting.

### Relations between non-profit organisations and for-profit enterprises

Unlike the US, in European countries non-profit and for-profit organisations have traditionally represented two separate worlds. This separation came about because of the different cultures of these two worlds, the universality and extension of the welfare systems, the different levels of regulation relating to businesses and the different tax laws. Moreover, in recent years, after the start up of the reforming process of welfare policies, and especially after the creation of quasi-markets, the emphasis has been put on the advantages deriving from competition between non-profits and for-profits in the supply of social services and on the dangers of unfair competition which supposedly would stem from the tax benefits granted to non-profit organisations.

The investigation into the real relations between these two worlds is today still very slight. Nevertheless, according to the few analyses carried out to date, some new factors seem to be emerging. Above all, there are very few distinct circumstances under which unfair competition between non-profits and for-profits can be detected. This is why the social services sector does not appear to attract the interest of companies, particularly in those countries in which the non-profit sector is well developed and dynamic. Indeed, social services are characterised by a low profitability, especially in the short term, and they often require the capacity of activating both personal (volunteers) and financial (donations) resources, which are less accessible to for-profits.

Moreover, in Europe as well as in the US, forms of co-operation between for-profits and non-profits are developing. Mostly, such collaboration is concerned with work integration of disadvantaged people, which can take on different forms:

● Productive partnerships: for-profits purchase semi-manufactured or finished products from non-profit organisations dedicated to work integration, thus giving stability to the productive activity of non-profit organisations.

● Co-operation of disadvantaged people during the training process: for-profits temporarily employ disadvantaged people from work integration non-profit organisations so as to favour the completion of the training process.

● Collaboration in the creation of stable jobs for disadvantaged people: some systematic collaboration between work integration non-profits and for-profits has been developing over the years in order to favour the definite and stable integration of trained disadvantaged people in the open labour market. Some experiments of joint action for the creation of placement services for disabled workers are particularly interesting.

These forms of co-operation, though experimental, seem to be destined to develop in the near future, especially in those countries where companies are required by law to employ disadvantaged workers. Yet the development of these initiatives is often hindered by labour policies at the national level. At present, these still regulate excessively, if not impede, the collaboration between for-profits and non-profits as regards both the training and placement activity. In fact, the most innovative experiments so far have been made possible mainly within the actions funded by the European Community (see, for example, Integra, Horizon, and so forth).

## Contributions of the non-profit sector to European societies and economies

Both experiences and research demonstrate that a well-established and dynamic non-profit sector can contribute not only to social cohesion, but also to the efficiency and dynamics of the whole economic system. Therefore, the lessons derived from recent European experience are summarised as follows:

### Transformation of the welfare systems

The outcomes of the policies implemented to tackle the difficulties of European welfare systems, and especially of the attempts to privatise social and community care services provision, are still uncertain. Indeed, transaction and contract costs have often increased more than expected, thwarting cost containment efforts. Furthermore, at least in some cases, the quality of services and jobs has deteriorated. These negative outcomes have emerged mainly in those countries in which governments have particularly relied upon market simulation and for-profit enterprises.[19] The nature of quasi-markets often favours tough contracting out by tending to use prices as a major criterion to discriminate among providers when calling for tenders. At the same time, existing regulations are often not sufficiently well defined to guarantee the desired level of quality.[20]

In this context, non-profit organisations could contribute to the reform of European welfare systems in several ways, such as: by making the income distribution closer to the desires of the community and the supply of services closer to the demands for them; by helping cost containment; by providing a greater volume of supply and, in many cases, by helping to maintain or to improve the quality of services and jobs.

Autonomous non-profit organisations, though privately owned and managed, can pursue a redistributive function, thus contributing to modifying the resources and income distribution provided by the joint action of the market and the state. Non-profit organisations are often created to serve groups of people with needs not recognised by the public policies and base their redistributive action on a mix of free (donations, volunteers) and low-cost (motivated workers) resources, some of which are not available to either for-profit or public providers.

The studies carried out over the last few years (EMES, 2000) present several examples of this redistributive function. In some cases, non-profit organisations and social enterprises have replaced public authorities in their redistributive role. In Belgium, for example, new non-profit organisations provide housing services for marginalised people who are unable to pay the increasing rents and to satisfy the conditions required for social public housing. In other countries, non-profit organisations have autonomously taken up redistributive action in favour of groups of people with needs not recognised by public authorities, as in the case of work integration of people with major difficulties in finding a job. In countries where the supply of services organised through public policies is insufficient to satisfy demand, non-profit organisations contribute to the creation of an additional supply. This is the case for social services that governments are willing or able to fund only in part. In this context, non-profit organisations can increase supply through a variable mix of public, market and voluntary resources.

However, non-profit organisations, like other third sector organisations, also influence redistributive public policies. By providing services to new groups of people with needs not fully recognised by public policies, they can move public resources toward these services.[21] Moreover, non-profit organisations often mix their productive role with more traditional advocacy activities in favour of the same or other groups of users.

In creating new services, not only do non-profit organisations develop a redistributive function; they can also innovate with regard to services provided. They can make new services available, but they can also use new ways of producing traditional services, mainly through innovative forms of involvement of consumers (such as co-producers), of local community (volunteers) and of workers themselves. The new non-profit organisations created throughout Europe and the changes of both the associative and the co-operative forms are good examples of this innovative behaviour.

Another important possible contribution of non-profit organisations to the improvement of European welfare systems occurs in the context of the privatisation of service provision. The effectiveness of privatisation policies depends on a competitive supply of social services, and there are several difficulties in establishing contractual relations between public authorities and service providers. Because of their nature, non-profits can contribute to the creation of a competitive environment and to the development of contractual relations based on trust. Since the aims of non-profit organisations often converge to some extent with the aims of public authorities, this makes negotiations easier for the provision of the services for which effective quasi-markets cannot be established. They can also contribute to the reduction of production costs since they do not strive for profits and can mediate between non convergent interests of public authorities, consumers and workers, thus singling out, more effectively than other organisational forms, the right mix of customer satisfaction and worker guarantees.[22]

### Employment creation

Non-profit organisations also contribute to the creation of additional jobs. This is clear for the work-integration non-profit organisations that employ workers with few prospects of finding a job in traditional enterprises However, non-profits providing social and community care services can create new employment too since they make a sector with a high employment potential more dynamic, especially in countries in which the level of employment in the sector is still low.

The interpretations of slow employment growth and of high unemployment rates in most European countries have recently shifted their emphasis from the rigidity of labour markets to the rigidities of the product markets. These latter are seen as being responsible for the slow growth of employment, especially in the service sector, mainly (by assuming the US as a benchmark) in commercial and tourist services, in business services and in "communal" or social and community care services.[23] The level of employment in communal services is particularly low in European countries with a welfare state mainly based on cash benefit (like Italy, France and Germany) and a low public provision or public financing of social services. Moreover, this public expenditure composition is a possible cause of the insufficient employment growth in the sector, especially if combined with the constraints on public expenditure that occurred after the 1980s. Public expenditure composition is also at the origin of the increasing gap between demand and supply of services to people and communities, which is now being experienced in several European countries.

However, the potential increase in employment in social and community care services cannot currently be achieved simply by increasing public expenditure. The pursuit of such a policy is impeded both by the constraint of reducing the public deficit and by the necessity of using savings on public expenditure to reduce fiscal pressure and indirect labour costs, in order to face increasing international competition. An alternative policy can be pursued by changing the composition of public expenditure from cash benefits to services provision or services founding and by encouraging the growth of private demand. However, this is not likely to be fully accomplished by for-profit organisations either. They have, at least for the time being, little interest in producing these services, due to their low profitability and to information asymmetries that affect market relations both with consumers and local authorities.

Non-profit organisations, especially the new and more dynamic, on the contrary, may help in developing both demand and supply, as well as in reconfiguring public expenditure composition. They present several advantages. Since they do not aim at profit maximisation, they can easily be involved in productions entailing low profitability and, if they rely on volunteers and on resources derived from donations, they can reduce production costs, especially in the start-up phase.[24] Cost reduction is also possible when non-profit organisations attract workers and managers interested in working in the sector and for wages that are lower than in comparable activities.[25] Moreover, by involving consumers and by being rooted in the local community, they can quickly adapt supply to demand and can rely on fiduciary relations to overcome the difficulty for consumers of monitoring the quality of services.

Non-profits can contribute to job growth even if they are fully or partially financed by public funds. When non-profits are financed with public money, it is because the services supplied are considered to be for the common good. Normally, the higher the redistributive effect is, the greater the public funding. However, non-profits should not be considered a mere substitute for public authorities. Many of them started their activity without, or with negligible, public subsidies and only after some time was their activity recognised by public authorities. As a consequence, they have contributed to increasing the public expenditure directed to services provision and, along with it, the related employment.

### Local development

Since new non-profit organisations are mainly locally-based organisations they are among the actors involved in local development. Close links with the local community in which they operate are, for new non-profit organisations, a condition for development and efficiency, because they facilitate the understanding of local needs, the creation and exploitation of social capital, and the working out of the optimal mix of resources (from public authorities, donations, users and volunteers).

The globalisation process and the diffusion of new technologies have spearheaded productivity growth in manufacturing sectors, but also the increasing instability of employment. They have also weakened the link between enterprises and territory. An increase in demand for goods no longer produces increases in production and employment everywhere. The new jobs are generally created in areas different from those where demand arises in the first place. These processes mainly discriminate against the less developed or declining areas, thus creating vicious circles. To tackle the problems of these areas, traditional incentives to localisation are often ineffective. Conversely, new social and community care services, requiring proximity between supply and demand and organised by small local non-profit organisations, can help to create a more stable local source of labour demand.

Some of the projects recently supported by the "Third System and Employment" Pilot Action Programme of the European Community demonstrate that non-profit organisations operating in the field of social and community care services:

- Can transform informal and often irregular provision of personal services into regular jobs, especially in areas (like rural areas) in which the demand of labour for some groups (i.e. women) is weak.

- Change the nature of some services from a redistributive to a productive one, as in the case of public social housing, some non-profits employ the unemployed users to manage them and make improvements, enabling them to earn an income and to enjoy better housing at the same time.

Work integration non-profit organisations, which are probably among mostly locally-based non-profits, also contribute to local development. The contribution of non-profits to local development through the creation of new jobs for people within local communities could increase in the future, if non-profits expand their action from social to other services, such as environmental improvement, cultural services, and transportation. The creation of non-profit networks by local authorities and private, cultural organisations and a joint use of several small amounts of private and public resources have, in some experiences, allowed for an economically viable exploitation of unused or inefficiently used cultural and environmental resources, thus creating stable jobs.

## A comparison with the United States

If we compare the US system to the European experience, two different models can be clearly distinguished. Indeed, whereas in the former an individualistic tendency prevails,[26] in the latter it is the state authorities that are still presently in charge of the provision of many social services (Salamon and Anheier, 1994). These two different approaches towards the role of the state have brought with them two different roles for non-profit organisations. In the US, these organisations are deemed to be at the same level as companies, that is they are subject to the same rules and competition laws, except for the fact that they are compelled to invest any profits in the organisation and not to share them among the managers or owners. In Europe, as the state authorities began to accept that private agencies could play a role, though limited, in the provision of welfare services, non-profit organisations necessarily underwent a sort of institutionalisation process.

Accordingly, two consequences may be pointed out. Firstly, whereas in Europe there is a universalistic welfare system, though not only public, and a system of public policies, in the US there exists only an *ad hoc* collection of compromises between the reality of the economic necessity and the pressures of political tradition and ideology. Secondly, with regard to the non-profit sector, one can state that in the US any type of non-profit organisation is recognised and fostered, thus advocating the prevalence of the concept of sector.[27] In Europe, instead, the statutory provisions of the sector under consideration and the judgement of the utility and the opportunity of supporting the sector itself can be derived only from the public policies system, which implies the presence of the state as an independent actor. This role has caused, on the one hand, less attention to be paid to the non-distribution constraint, because of the more stringent public checks and a more similar type of governance (democratic principle) and, on the other hand, the growth of different legal and organisational forms.

Consequently, from a theoretical viewpoint, there remains a wide variety of definitions of non-profit organisations depending on which features are deemed distinctive. However, the prevailing tendency has been to reduce complexity through the use of the concept of "sector" (non-profit sector, third sector). The intention has been to stress the distinction between these organisations taken as a whole and the sectors of for-profit firms and public organisations. As a result of the influence exerted mainly by American scholars (economists in particular), the distinctive feature of these organisations and of the sector to which they belong has been identified with the non-profit distribution constraint. However, although this definition has been useful in determining the quantitative dimensions of the sector and of its evolution, while affirming the importance of studying these organisational forms, some scholars, especially in Europe, have stressed its shortcomings (Hansmann, 1995, p. 6) and the necessity of replacing it. Closer analysis of the phenomenon reveals that the studies carried out to date have tended to neglect at least two other aspects distinguishing these organisations in recent years: the change of their role and the birth of new organisational forms. The evolution towards organisational forms different from those traditionally studied in this sector is also of interest in the light of ongoing debate in the United States on the effective ability of the non-distribution constraint to differentiate satisfactorily between these organisations and for-profit ones (Hansmann, *op.cit.*; Frank and Salkever, 1994). The changes outlined above warrant more detailed study, for at least two reasons. Firstly, they refocus debate on the specificity of the European case and more generally on experiences different from those of the United States. Secondly, they reopen the theoretical debate on what are, may be or should be the distinctive features of private organisations producing or delivering welfare services. In other words, the issue may be stated as follows: on the basis of the recent European experience, could organisations with characteristics substituting or supplementing the non-distribution constraint prove equally efficient or more suitable to carry out public services?

## Development prospects and conclusions

The re-emergence of the non-profit sector in Europe and its development during the 1980s and the 1990s prove that a large, autonomous and well-developed non-profit sector is an essential component of any society. The constraints imposed on the autonomy of the sector during the predominance of public welfare models did not prevent its re-emergence, when these welfare models started to crumble under the weight of the crisis. After some years of uncertainty, this re-emergence has been recognised and strengthened by the reforms of the welfare systems, which have referred a specific role to the private, non-profit supply of social and personal services.

However, the future development of the non-profit sector in Europe still remains uncertain. Neither internal weaknesses nor external barriers allow the forecast of a return to a situation similar to the one existing in the 1970s, nor do they guarantee that in the future the non-profit sector will maintain the autonomy and innovative capacity that it has had over the last twenty years. These weaknesses and barriers have been examined in several documents (European Commission, 1999; CIRIEC, 2000, Chapter 6). The most important of them are summarised hereafter.

Despite its success, the organisational model of most non-profits remains fragile, based on a few well-defined rules and on a high degree of trust among members.

New non-profit organisations present high governance costs, which derive from their character as organisations without well-defined owners or which are owned by a plurality of stakeholders. Their advantage, *i.e.* the involvement of various categories of stakeholders (clients, volunteers, representatives of the local community) in the production and in the decision-making processes, can in fact be an element of inefficiency when conflicting interests limit the capacity of reacting quickly to a changing environment.

The awareness that non-profits, their managers and the movement as a whole have of their role in European society and economic systems and of their own specificity with respect to public, for-profit and non-profit organisational forms is still limited. In particular, there is a growing need for a well-established capability to manage the plurality of objectives that define non-profits and that bring together social aims with economic constraints.

These weaknesses reinforce the tendency towards isomorphism, that is, to evolve into organisational forms that are better defined, legally stronger and socially more acceptable while being unable to keep and develop the most innovative characteristics in the new organisational forms. Nowadays, one of the most widespread risks is that new non-profit organisations convert into associated workers' companies, consequently pursuing mainly the exclusive interests of those employed, and losing the linkage with the community and the capacity of fully using social capital. This risk appears to be related to the increase in the availability of public subsidies and the consequent decrease of the autonomous re-distributive role played by non-profit organisations.

Furthermore, the environment in which non-profits operate does not favour the strengthening of their organisational models. In most European countries, the belief that for-profit organisations together with active public policies can efficiently solve all social problems and satisfy overall demand for social and community care services still prevails. This belief led to an underestimation of the potential role of the non-profit sector. This is often regarded as being unnecessary or, at most, offering transitional solutions, useful as entities dependent on public policies or as organisations that should be active only for the problems that public policies cannot solve.[28]

Such a negative attitude, especially towards entrepreneurial non-profit organisations, is stronger in some countries, where a very traditional view of the enterprise is still the norm. According to this view, only those initiatives that derive their income from commercial activities and pursue the sole interest of their owners can be defined as enterprises. Accordingly, the concept of enterprise does not include those organisations capable of innovating and organising the production processes in non-market activities, of basing their income on market exchanges and furthermore does not include those who do not pursue the interests of their owners only. In this context, non-profit organisations are looked at with mistrust and suspicion, to the point of regarding workers involved in them as not fully employed. This attitude is also common in those countries where the competitive process is more emphasised, thus marginalising activities, such as social and community care services, for which competition is limited by necessity.

In addition, the relationships between non-profits, on the one hand, and social and labour public policies on the other, are still confused and often incoherent. The shift from direct public provision of social and community care services to the separation of financing responsibility from services provision, together with the autonomous development of private non-profit initiatives, has not been accompanied by a general and coherent change in contractual relationships and funding rules. Old ways of financing non-profit organisations have generally been maintained, while other new contracting-out rules have been established, especially for new services. More competitive practices were given an impetus by the introduction of quasi-markets in England and by the new European rules on contracting-out and public tenders. The result is an unclear mix of direct subsidies and contracting, more or less rigid and depending on the countries and the services. When contracting-out practices are applied, the specific characteristics of non-profits are very often not taken into account. As a consequence, non-profit organisations often have to operate in a precarious environment, relying on short-term contracts and without the possibility of planning their development.

Finally, in most European countries the legal forms suitable for organising non-profit activities are still inadequate. The legal frameworks are still designed so as to favour company forms. Furthermore, the process of drafting legal forms suitable for entrepreneurial non-profit organisations is still to be fully set in motion and it differs from country to country. This situation limits the workability and the possibility of reproducing the more innovative non-profit organisations.

However, some of these difficulties could be alleviated by a consistent set of policies.

The first policy that would facilitate the development of non-profits is the full legal recognition and regulation of the new organisational forms. Both are important for several reasons: i) to consolidate the most innovative organisational solutions; ii) to foster the replication process and the spread of new organisations; iii) to protect consumer's rights; and iv) to avoid isomorphism.

A second important aid to the development of non-profits would be a shift from today's predominantly fiscal policy, based on tax relief for organisations fulfilling certain organisational requirements, to policies seeking to foster the emergence and development of new demand for services. The emergence of private paying demand (by individuals and families) for social and community care services, and a change from the present informal provision, would be helped by reducing the costs of services through tax allowances in favour of consumers and through the provision of vouchers covering only part of the costs.

Another important policy would consist of better-defined contracting-out and quasi-market strategies. These could be more effective if they recognised the specificity of non-profits, and the redistributive component of the services produced. This entails acknowledging that non-profits are based on a peculiar mix of resources and have a local dimension. Both of these require the preservation of strong trust and community relationships, where they exist, or an effort to create them where they do not. Competition is important to achieve efficiency, but it should be balanced with the need to guarantee the continuity and development of already existing network relations that produce trust and social capital and allow the creation of the mix of human resources that help to maintain flexibility and low production costs. A local dimension could be applied to contracting-out procedures, so as to reduce the extent of competition for social and community care service provision.

Finally, the development of non-profits could be helped by a set of supply-side policies with the aim of: reinforcing their entrepreneurial behaviour; enhancing the managerial skills of their personnel; favouring the creation of second/third level organisations and increasing their natural propensity to spin off and create new and autonomous organisations.

The evolution of both the non-profit sector and of social policy in European countries is far from being well defined. As to the evolution of the non-profit sector, its re-emergence in the European arena does not simply consist of a revival of the traditional forms. The very nature of the sector has changed and with it so too have its role, the organisational forms and the strategies. The new non-profit organisations are looking for an autonomous space, not only among social organisations but also in the entrepreneurial sector. Yet the prevailing view characterising both contemporary economies and societies does not appear to accept this challenge. As to social policies, after the crisis of the established forms of partnership, there are many different attempts to find new forms. None of them, though, is well defined and accepted. While it is certain that the non-profit sector will play a major role in the future with respect to the "thirty glorious years" (i.e. 1940s-1970s), its future characteristics and its contribution to social policies are unsure. Indeed, much will depend on the capacity of the new organisations to find clear models of governance and development and on the capability of policy makers to comprehend the advantages of a pluralistic welfare system. The final picture of the ongoing process is far from being complete.

## Notes

1. Indeed, there coexist several different ways of defining the sector, such as "third sector", "third system", "social economy", "non-profit sector", each of which encompasses different groups of organisations. See the glossary contained in this volume.

2. The chapter privileges an institutional and economic approach. Nonetheless, it is largely consistent with other scientific contributions based on sociological or political approaches (see Evers, 1999; and Laville and Nyssens, 2000). In writing up this chapter, the authors have drawn heavily on the works carried out within the EMES network, in which they have taken part.

3. The English Charitable Users Act of 1601 read as follows: "Charity is (...) the relief of the aged, impotent and, poor; help for sick and mutilated soldiers and sailors; freeing schools and universities; repairing bridges, pavements, ports, churches, main streets and shores; educating and promoting orphans; help, relief and assistance to the prisons; marriage of poor householders; attention and rescue of prisoners; relief of any poor inhabitants as to the payment of taxes and rates (...)".

4. The urban population, which consisted of workers living in cities like London, Norwich and Bristol, was considered to be "a sort of wild, savage, unwelcome people, whom nobody knew and nobody visited" (Jones, 1967).

5. Since this analysis is limited to Western Europe, the effects of Socialism and Communism in Eastern Countries are not taken into account here.

6. The history of British charities and the voluntary sector has always been defined by the search for a partnership with the state. "In the late nineteenth century, the voluntary sector took the lead in establishing the nature of the partnership; in the later twentieth century it is Government that has proposed a new 'Compact' on relations between the two sectors (Home Office, 1998)". Lewis (1999).

7. Conversely, in Great Britain, the frontiers between the voluntary and statutory sectors have been mobile throughout the centuries. On the one hand, there have been parts of the British voluntary sector that have never been independent of the state, but rather have been linked by royal charter, patronage and networks of elite kinship, while others, such as universities or the Medical Research Council are linked to the state in ways that smack more of "fusion" than partnership (Lewis, *op. cit.*, p. 2).

8. It was only in 1997 that Section 17 of the Italian Civil Code of 1942 was repealed. This section provided for a specific authorisation on the part of associations and foundations should they intend to purchase a building or to accept donations or bequests in the form of assets.

9. In Italy, this process occurred with the passing of the Act of 1890 relating to Welfare and Benevolent Public Institutions by which the Government institutionalised benevolent and philanthropic organisations that traditionally were the expression of society. From a legal point of view, it is with the above-mentioned Act that the terms "state" and "public" started to be regarded as synonyms and were to be considered as such even later. Public, therefore, has been identified with state provisions of social services and not with the purpose that the organisations, both public and private, pursued.

10. In particular, Fascism intended to strike the second-level organisations, since they were fundamental in defining the behaviour of their members and were the real powers of the whole co-operative system. In this respect, the Italian Government of the time sought to crush local federations and to concentrate the control and co-ordination of activity of co-operatives in bodies at the national level. By Law No. 2288/1926, the Ministry of National Economy was entrusted with the supervision of all co-operatives, except for credit and insurance ones. Furthermore, by the same act, the National Agency for Co-operation was created, which was to act as a kind of administrative branch of the ministry for the control, development and co-ordination of co-operatives. The aim of such action was not either to paralyse or to destroy the co-operative movement, which represented a very important sector to the whole Italian society of the time, but rather to make the ideal motivations that supported the movement sterile. Such bias ended up violating the principles of free association that had always inspired the co-operative movement, so much so as to jeopardise the natural development of co-operation, the basic origin of which was turned upside down. For further details on the Fascist period and the co-operative movement, see Corelli (1979), Degl'Innocenti (1981), and Galasso (1987).

11. In particular, in England, with the development of major national social programmes, "*voluntary organisations no longer aimed to be the first line of defence for those in need as they had done in the early part of the century (...). Beveridge, while best known as a leading architect of the welfare state, was also a firm believer in voluntary action and harked back to the turn-of-the-century insistence on the importance of the 'spirit of service' and the ethical purposes of charity. The good society*

*could only be built on people's sense of duty and willingness to serve. The voluntary sector was in this sense a counterweight to both the 'business motive' and a necessarily rule-based state bureaucracy, albeit that it continued to be seen as supplementary or complementary to the state. Ethical purpose and public benefit (one interpretation of which is of course entrenched in English charity law) have continued to provide the basis for the case for voluntary action"* (Lewis, 1999, p. 260).

12. However, one is to acknowledge that it is not accidental that the current size of the non-profit sector is particularly limited in those countries, like Italy, which were hit by all three of the above-mentioned shocks.

13. It is the case of Italy where, for instance, the Red Cross was originally set up as a private non-profit organisation, which later on was subjected to public regulation, thus making it a paramilitary force of the state. The same occurred to ACI (the Italian Automobile Club) which was established as a private non-profit association to become later a branch of the public administration.

14. See CGM-CECOP (1995), CECOP-Regione Trentino Alto Adige-CGM-European Commission (1996), United Nations (1996), Pestoff (1994, 1996), and Spear (1995).

15. The changes brought about in British non-profit organisations by the introduction of the NHS and the Community Care Act are well documented in two works by Taylor, Langan and Hoggett (1994), and Langan and Taylor (1995).

16. In France, for example, it was only in 1901 that the legislature passed a statutory act by which associations were recognised as subjects at law, no longer to be suppressed or destroyed as they had been during the Revolutionary period.

17. Nonetheless, they are not considered, in international literature, as non-profit organisations.

18. For a wider presentation and a theoretical analysis of the work-integration initiatives, see Defourny, Favreau and Laville, 1998.

19. This seems to be the case of some social services, like home care services in the UK (see Young, 1999).

20. In some countries these regulations are improving. The Italian Social Care reform approved in the year 2000, for example, provides for new methods and criteria by which non-profit organisations are to be contracted-out social services. These criteria take into account the special nature and characteristics of non-profit organisations.

21. This is the case in countries with a limited public provision of social services like Italy where several services (day centres for handicapped or teenagers, services for drug addict rehabilitation, etc.) were initially created by non-profit organisations without systematic public support. Only after several years did national and local authorities decide to support fully the financing of these services and of the organisations providing them.

22. The few comparative studies on employment relations in social service provision (Borzaga, 2000) indicate that non-profit organisations tend to pay wages lower than public providers and higher than for-profit enterprises.

23. As demonstrated in several documents of the European Commission. See, among them, European Commission (1998).

24. A specific category of start-up costs faced by organisations willing to provide new social services are the entrepreneurial costs (Hansmann, 1996), *i.e.* the costs related to assembling sufficient volume of demand to sustain a stable and efficient production. By often consisting of users or their representatives, in many cases, non-profit organisations can evaluate the potential demand at low costs.

25. This specific advantage can be misused and can create perverse effects on the wage level of the employees. However, when correctly used, it represents an important advantage.

26. These authors argue that reliance on the non-profit sector reflects a long-standing American pattern of individualism and hostility to government. The American tradition of reliance on the non-profit sector has thus been the other side of a set of social policies that has kept governmental social welfare protections rather limited.

27. Nonetheless, whereas the tax-exemption of profits is common to all the organisations, the tax-exemption of donations, which are made both by individuals and by companies, is granted only to religious organisations or to those which supply services for the benefit of the public.

28. As suggested by the explanation of the non-profit organisations as "problem non solvers" (Seibel, 1990).

ISBN 92-64-19953-5
The Non-profit Sector in a Changing Economy
© OECD 2003

PART I

## Chapter 2

# New Trends in the US Non-profit Sector: Towards Market Integration?[1]

by

Dennis R. Young,
Case Western Reserve University, Cleveland, USA

## Introduction

Ever since scholars and policy makers began to study it, the non-profit sector in the United States has been a moving target, constantly adapting and responding to changes in the overall society. Prior to the 1960s and 1970s few even thought of non-profit organisations (also known as "non-profits") as a sector at all (Hall, 1992). Rather, attention was more narrowly focused on particular industries or fields such as social services, health care, education, the arts or perhaps "philanthropy" (Bremner, 1988). The concept of a sector linking organisations in these fields, distinct from business or government, driven by charitable purpose and relying on voluntary support, did not emerge until the 1970s. At the time, it was federal government's concern about the growing power of private, grant-making foundations that first galvanised the foundations and later other kinds of charitable and public purpose organisations into defining themselves as a sector and speaking with a unified voice in the realm of public policy (O'Connell, 1997).

The galvanising of the US non-profit sector in the late 1970s followed an era, born in the social programs of the Kennedy-Johnson administration, in which billions of dollars were poured into the economy to address issues of poverty, health care, education, community development, the environment and the arts. What may have been a relatively staid and stable charitable sector prior to that time became a dynamo fuelled by a government that chose to deliver its new portfolio of services largely through the financing of non-profit organisations rather than expansion of government bureaucracy (Salamon, 1995). Existing non-profits expanded, many new ones were created, and the non-profit sector became the fastest growing component of the newly recognised "third sector" economy (Hodgkinson and Associates, 1992).

With stagnation of the US economy in the late 1970s and the advent of the highly conservative Reagan administration in the 1980s, the picture changed again for the US non-profit sector. The Reagan administration failed to appreciate the degree to which non-profits were financed by government, and seemed to operate under the illusion that charitable support and voluntary effort could somehow fully substitute for the withdrawal of government funding. Federal programs in many areas were cut back dramatically, the non-profit sector's rapid growth was interrupted, and non-profit organisations scuttled around to find new sources of support (Salamon, 1995). Non-profits substantially readjusted and survived the 1980s intact, leaning more on state and local governments and private sources, for their support. But they also learned an important lesson in this era – that they needed to fend for themselves and that government was not a dependable source of sustenance in the long run; nor could the traditional sources of charity and volunteering grow quickly enough to make up for shortfalls in financing in their now expanded agendas.

The turbulence of the previous three decades helped prepare US non-profit organisations for the 1990s and beyond. Non-profits learned that they needed to earn their revenues and become less dependent on government or traditional sources of charity. Moreover, they were entering an era in which government was in decline and the free market ascendant in the US and in countries throughout the world. The welfare state was being discredited as an effective means of solving social problems and privatisation touted as a necessary avenue for nations to achieve efficiency and competitiveness in the global market economy. Non-profits found themselves to be part of both the problem and the solution. As part of the private economy, with unique access to volunteer energy, charitable impulse and socially focused entrepreneurial motivation, they were expected to find innovative and effective ways to address the social issues that the old welfare state could no longer manage. At the same time they needed to find new sources of support and to redefine their role *vis-à-vis* business in the private sector.

This is where non-profit organisations in the US presently find themselves. They have come to understand that they are embedded in a vigorous free market economy and must learn how to survive and prosper in that environment. They also understand that in some ways they have become the new embodiment of social aspirations in an era that stresses non-governmental approaches to social problem-solving. Non-profits are the trustees of much of the new "social capital" upon which society now wants to build its infrastructure of social welfare (Backman and Smith, 2000). In order to meet these diverse expectations, non-profits currently struggle to nourish themselves in the marketplace without becoming disenfranchised by behaving in ways indistinguishable from ordinary commerce.

The purpose of this chapter is to describe the various ways in which non-profits in the US are now accommodating themselves to the new environment of the marketplace. The picture is a mosaic consisting of several important interwoven strands or trends: a changing base of financial support, pursuit of a variety of new business ventures, new partnerships with business corporations, adaptation to a marketplace environment characterised by greater consumer and donor choice, and changes in the internal culture of non-profits themselves. At this point in time, the picture remains hazy and unfocused. In the end, however, non-profits in the US will be forced to embrace a fresh identity that somehow reconciles their new market orientation with the greater social expectations with which they are now charged.

## Changes in the mix of revenues

Of the three main sources of revenue for non-profit organisations – gifts and grants, governmental funding, and earned income – the latter has been fastest growing for US non-profits in recent years and has now become the chief source of non-profit revenue overall. According to Weisbrod (1998), reliance of US public benefit (according to section 501[c]3 of the tax code[2]) non-profits on fees for programme services (including fees paid by government but excluding government grants) increased from 69.1 per cent to 73.5 per cent of total revenues between 1987 and 1992. Such fee-dependence increased noticeably in education, health, human services and environmental and animal-related services, and was stable in the arts, over this period of time. Similarly, using a different combination of data sources, Segal and Weisbrod (1998) found that programme service revenue for all public benefit non-profits increased from 63.4 per cent to 71.3 per cent of total revenues, for the period from 1982 to 1993.

Alternative calculations by Salamon (1999), which classify governmental contract revenue under "government revenue" and not under "earned income", indicate that 54 per cent of the revenue of non-profit public-benefit organisations derived from earned income fees and charges) in 1996. Moreover, Salamon calculates that 55 per cent of the growth in non-profit revenue between 1977 and 1996 derived from fees and commercial income. By field, fees account for 69 per cent of the growth in social services income, 63 per cent in education revenues, 51 per cent in health care revenue and 43 per cent in arts and culture income.

Most earned income, as counted in the forgoing statistics, derives from fees and charges for the mainstream, mission-related services provided by non-profits in their respective fields – tuition in education, box office receipts in the arts, charges for hospital stays and services, fees for counselling in social services, and so on. Some of this income, however, also emanates from ancillary "commercial" fees and charges, not necessarily associated with essential, mission-related activities. For example, museums run gifts shops in shopping centres and airports, colleges offer travel services for their alumni, and YMCAs may rent out their facilities for private parties. Much of this fee-generating activity is presumably carried out primarily for revenue-producing purposes. One way to try and gauge such income is to measure how much of it is declared as "unrelated income" by non-profits on their tax returns. A non-profit must file a 990-T unrelated business income tax (UBIT) return if it receives at least $1 000 in gross unrelated business income in a given year.

Segal and Weisbrod (1998) found that the percentage of non-profits filing such a return varied between one per cent and 10 per cent over a wide range of non-profit fields.

Unfortunately, the data on unrelated business income is a poor indicator of non-profit commercial income incidental to mission, for several reasons. First, certain categories of earned income are excluded from UBIT, including passive investment income, and royalties and activities performed by volunteers or for the convenience of the non-profit's clientele (such as on-campus conveniences for students). Second, the rules on unrelated business income are liberal and allow non-profits to declare income as "related" rather than "unrelated" within very broad boundaries. Girl Scout cookie sales and on-premises museum gift shop sales of art reproductions are considered related income, for example, although one might argue that they are only peripherally important to mission. This may account for the relatively small proportion of non-profits that find it necessary to file UBIT returns at all.

Third, non-profits have broad discretion in allocating costs between related and unrelated activities so as to minimise their liabilities for profit tax on unrelated income activity. Thus, Riley (1995) found that in 1991, three of five returns reported losses rather than profits, and for UBIT filers as a whole, total expenses allocated to unrelated activities exceeded total revenues. Clearly UBIT data does not provide a full or accurate picture of non-profit commercial activity intended primarily to produce net revenue support for non-profits. Still, the data is of some interest. For the museum field, Anheier and Toepler (1998) found modest increases in the reliance on unrelated business income for the 1990 to 1992 period. These researchers reported that unrelated business income represented less than two per cent of total museum revenues, and that 76 per cent of museums were stable in this percentage over the 1990 to 1992 period. Some 16 per cent increased their unrelated business income during this period while another eight per cent decreased that percentage. Increases and decreases were all in the 10 per cent range.

While it is difficult to get a precise reading of the levels and changes in commercial revenue earned by non-profits, it is clear that interest in such income as a source of sustenance has risen over the past two decades. One of the earliest studies to document commercial ventures was carried out in 1983 (Crimmins and Keil). It was clear even then that non-profit enterprise was becoming a significant part of non-profit operations: "We found that enterprise contributes to the non-profit sector and has done so for a long time. What has changed recently is the scale and nature of the activities and the numbers of institutions engaged in enterprise" (p. 11). If anything, the pace has accelerated substantially since the 1980s.

## Promoting the non-profit agenda through commercial enterprise

The Crimmins and Keil (1983) and subsequent studies, such as Skloot (1987, 1988), Emerson and Twersky (1996) and Young (1998), strongly suggest that the growth of commercial enterprise in the non-profit sector is rarely completely unconnected to mission and is hence difficult to single out from so-called related earned income. While non-profits may take advantage of peripheral income opportunities that fall easily into their grasp (*e.g.*, renting their facilities, charging parking fees, etc.) or that manifest themselves as natural extensions of what they already do (*e.g.*, selling art reproductions, providing hospital laundry services to other hospitals), they usually conceive of commercial ventures as a direct means to achieving their mission objectives. This notion has helped to give rise to the concept of "social purpose enterprises" (Roberts Foundation, 1999):

> "*Social purpose enterprises are revenue-generating businesses that are owned and operated by non-profit organisations with the express purpose of employing at-risk clients in the business ventures*" (Volume 1, page 2).

Various other terms are compatible with the above definition, *e.g.*, "social purpose business", "community-based business" and "community wealth enterprises" (Reis and Clohesy, 2000). Using this definition, the Roberts Enterprise Foundation based in San Francisco has undertaken to support a portfolio of ventures by non-profit organisations that engage their clientele directly in business operations. These businesses are viewed partly as a means to generate revenue and partly as a means to serve that clientele in the most effective way. For example, Asian Neighbourhood Design employs low income individuals in its furniture manufacturing business, Barrios Unidos employs Latino youth in its screen printing business, and Community Vocational Enterprises employs people with psychiatric disabilities in its janitorial, food service, clerical and messenger service businesses.

Of course, some non-profit organisations, such as Goodwill Industries nation-wide, or Vocational Guidance Services in Cleveland, have long undertaken a "sheltered workshop" approach in their programming. However, the explicit practice of designing businesses as an effective means to address the needs of target clientele has become more widespread recently as a strategy both to sustain the organisation financially and to address its basic mission. Additional examples of this approach are found among cases assembled by the Pathfinder Project of Independent Sector and the University of Maryland (see *www.independentsector.org/pathfinder*). For example, the Greyston Bakery in Yonkers, New York, a for-profit subsidiary of the Greyston Foundation, trains and hires "hard-to-place" workers in its gourmet bakery business. The non-profit New Community Corporation in Newark, New Jersey provides job training and employment to inner city residents as well as needed retail services to under-served neighbourhoods through its various for-profit business enterprises such as franchised grocery and convenience stores, restaurants and print and copy shops. Pioneer Human Services, a non-profit based in Seattle, Washington, operates a variety of business enterprises including aircraft parts manufacture, food buying and warehousing services, and restaurants, in which it trains, employs and rehabilitates ex-offenders, drug-dependent individuals and people on probation or under court supervision. In such cases, business ventures are logically connected to the mission of the non-profit principally as a means to provide the work training and employment opportunities for their clientele, not because their particular products are especially relevant to that mission. The point of these ventures is to create commercial opportunities as the best possible environment in which to nurture client success and, at least incidentally, to generate resources to sustain the organisation.

However, the concept of social purpose enterprise can be extended beyond the Roberts Foundation definition to include business ventures that simultaneously contribute direct non-profit mission-related outputs, as well as revenues and mission-related employment. For example, the Orange County Community Distribution Center in Orange County, Florida serves an environmental conservation mission by warehousing discarded materials. It provides non-profits with new resources by providing local non-profits with donated materials, and it employs inmates on work release while training them in various skills and preparing them for subsequent employment. Similarly, Bikeable Communities in Long Beach, California promotes bicycle use to address community transportation and environmental objectives, by offering various services to cyclists, including valet bicycle parking, changing rooms and repair services (Pathfinder Project).

These various experiences with commercial enterprises by non-profit organisations are beginning to put non-profit commercial enterprise into a new light. No longer conceived as primarily a revenue generation strategy, these ventures suggest that market engagement may often be the most effective way to address a non-profit organisation's mission. It is based upon the belief that the best way out of poverty, homelessness, or even overcoming mental and physical disabilities may be to gain marketable skills and access to employment opportunities in the mainstream economy. Moreover, environmental or economic development issues may be addressed effectively through alternative services that are both sustainable in the market-place and which have direct impact on the environment or the local economy. This certainly seems to be the flavour of many of the new non-profit enterprise ventures that have emerged in recent years.

However, some in the "social enterprise" movement go even further than the position that commercial enterprise can contribute effectively to addressing non-profit organisational missions. In the US, and certainly in Europe (Borzaga and Santuari, 1998) there is an emerging stream of opinion that characterises the non-profit sector and its related business ventures as a continuum of activity between market and philanthropy, arguing for a more general understanding of social enterprise than a strict divide between non-profits and for-profits would comfortably allow (Dees, 1998). This argument is based on the observation that some socially focused enterprise activity takes place outside the formal non-profit realm, as well as through interactions and combinations of non-profit and for-profit activity. According to Reis and Clohesy (2000, p. 7): *"There are hundreds – and perhaps thousands – of examples throughout the US of organisations that are experimenting with enterprise or market-based approaches for solving problems... Some are new organisational models such as New Profit, Inc. and Share Our Strength that are weaving together profit-making activities with social change purposes."*[3]

## Closer relationships with business corporations

Much of the controversy in the US in the 1980s and early 1990s, surrounding enterprising behaviour of non-profit organisations, focused on the concern that non-profits may sometimes compete unfairly with small businesses. On the other hand, non-profits have lost market share to the for-profit sector in several fields. While this debate has been largely unresolved and seems to have ebbed in recent years, the gradual integration of non-profits into the marketplace is reflected in growing competition between non-profits and business.

Non-profit organisations operate in a variety of "mixed industries" in which both non-profits and for-profits, and sometimes government agencies, participate. In a number of those industries, non-profits have lost market share, mostly from incursions by the for-profit sector. Based on data from 1982 to 1992, these industries include individual and family services, job training, child day care, museums, radio and television broadcasting, and botanical gardens and zoos (Tuckman, 1998). On the other hand, non-profits gained relative market share in the nursing home field, and in elementary and secondary schools (presumably at public sector expense) during that period. The competition between non-profits and for-profits ebbs and flows over time. In the 1960s and 1970s non-profit nursing homes lost ground to for-profit homes, and in the 1990s for-profit hospitals and health maintenance organisations appear to have grown at the expense of non-profits. In other service areas, such as the arts, education and urban development, non-profits have gained relative market shares at the expense of for-profits since the end of World War II (Hall, 1998).

It is unclear whether for-profit/non-profit competition has become more intense in recent years. The debates over UBIT seem to have eased after the 1980s, for example. On the other hand, new areas, such as counselling, job training and placement services in connection with welfare reform, have opened up to for-profit participation in traditionally non-profit markets. In the field of charitable giving, financial services firms such as Fidelity and Merrill Lynch are now offering donor services similar to those originally developed by community foundations (Reis and Clohesy, 2000). Large corporations such a Lockheed Martin IMS have entered the social services market (Light, 2000) and other large corporations have become active in education, community development, and health care (Tuckman, 1998). In particular, the market for government contracts in a variety of public service areas is now more open to for-profit participation than ever before (Halpern, 1998).

Yet with all of the competition between non-profits and business, the forces of collaboration appear to be gaining strength. Non-profits and corporate businesses are working more closely together now than ever before. This relationship takes a variety of forms including corporate gifts and grants to non-profits, employee volunteer programs, event sponsorships, cause-related marketing, royalty and licensing arrangements, joint ventures and other initiatives (Austin, 2000). Over the last decade, the old stereotypes of corporate altruism on the one hand, and non-profit aloofness from business on the other, have all but evaporated (Burlingame and Young, 1996). It seems that the mutual benefits of co-operation have been acknowledged. Corporations have discovered the strategic value of working with non-profits, while non-profits have found ways to make their relationships with corporate business helpful to them both financially and programmatically. James Austin (2000) argues that the idea of "strategic fit" drives the formation of particular non-profit-business partnerships. Some of Austin's examples illustrate how this fit can manifest itself in a wide variety of ways:

- The Merck Corporation provides scholarship funds to The College Fund (UNCF) and mentors and internships to recipients of these scholarships. In return, Merck gains access to bright minority students with an interest in science.

- Ralston Purina provides support to the American Humane Association for the Pets for People programme whose purpose is to encourage adoptions of pets. In addition to gaining reputation within its industry, the corporation helps increase the market for its pet foods through this arrangement.

- Starbucks Corporation provides substantial financial support to CARE. The partnership assists the corporation in its expanding business relationships around the world, especially in coffee-growing countries.

● MCI WorldCom partners with the National Geographic Society to support the Marco Polo geography website, which promotes Internet content integration in the K-12 curriculum.[4] Both organisations stand to benefit from expanded use of the Internet in education.

● The Nature Conservancy works closely with Georgia Pacific to jointly manage wetlands owned by the corporation. Through this arrangement, the Conservancy is able to advance its mission of helping to protect large and important environmental resources while the corporation gains access to the Conservancy's expertise and improves its relationship with the consuming public.

The potential benefits to business corporations of collaborating with appropriate non-profit partners fall along several possible lines. Corporations polish their public images, gain access to special expertise or future talent, help expand demand for their products, and motivate their employees by providing opportunities for volunteering and community service. In turn, their non-profit partners gain access to substantial financial, personnel and other corporate resources, obtain wider forums in which to broadcast their messages and appeals, and in some cases influence consumers in ways that directly support the non-profit's mission. For example, when the American Cancer Society associates itself with the Florida citrus industry and offers the use of its name and logo on citrus products and commercials, it helps increase citrus fruit consumption, a contributor to cancer prevention. Similarly, the affiliations between the American Lung Association and the American Cancer Society with manufacturers of anti-smoking patches, and the affiliation between Prevent Blindness and makers of protective eye wear, directly contribute to the health-related missions of those organisations by influencing consumer behaviour (Young, 1998a).

In these latter arrangements, the exclusiveness with which non-profits associate themselves with particular products can become a difficult issue. Most of these arrangements involve financial transactions. The more closely a reputable non-profit is willing to identify itself with a particular product or company, the more it will be worth to that company and the more that company will be willing to remunerate the non-profit. The American Cancer Society receives substantial grants from the Florida citrus growers and from Smith-Kline Beecham in exchange for understandings that ACS will not identify itself with other producers of citrus fruit or anti-smoking patches. By comparison, the American Heart Association receives much more modest fees for attaching its "heart-healthy" seal to various food products that meet its nutritional standards.

These examples illustrate that the growing closeness of non-profits and corporations, while creating many benefits, is risky for participating non-profits. Non-profits must hence be cautious before entering partnerships with the private sector. In particular, a non-profit may be perceived as neglecting or harming its mission if it identifies itself with questionable products, with organisations that are disreputable, or exclusively with products that may not be the very best for its intended beneficiaries. In the recent case of the American Medical Association (AMA) and the Sunbeam Corporation, leaders of the AMA lost their jobs for entering an exclusive relationship that appeared to offer advanced endorsements of yet-to-be-tested medical devices. Similarly, AARP[5] has been questioned for entering special relationships with health insurers that may not always be able to assure the best coverage for older people. Along the same lines, the American Association of Museums recently found it necessary to issue a code of ethical standards for museums entering arrangements with owners and dealers of art collections, to protect against situations where private parties would stand to benefit financially from display of their art in a museum and where they might use financial incentives to inappropriately influence the museum's artistic decisions to exhibit their art.

In summary, while the phenomenon of non-profit-corporate partnerships has expanded from a trickle ten years ago to a virtual tidal wave today, the arrangements conceal a range of serious risks to non-profit organisations. Many non-profits, particularly smaller ones, remain wary of such involvement because they do not have the expertise or sophistication to avoid the pitfalls. Other non-profits have yet to identify corporations that provide the appropriate "strategic fit" with their own particular causes. For example, the National Kidney Foundation might consider makers of cranberry juice to be appropriate partners since cranberry juice is thought to benefit kidney function. However, those benefits are not proven and such a partnership would put the non-profit out on a limb if they turn out to be illusory. Finally, issues of organisational size influence the propensity to partner on both sides of the market. Smaller non-profits are wary because of their lack of sophistication in entering corporate agreements. Moreover, smaller non-profits may not be well enough known or may not represent large enough constituencies to be attractive to corporate sponsors. Non-profits with unpopular constituencies such as ex-offenders or people with mental illness might be similarly unattractive to corporations.

The uncertainties surrounding the benefits of non-profit-corporate partnerships constitute the principal reason why non-profits and corporations are often wary about them, and the reason why these parties are advised to think in terms of long-term relationships rather than one-shot deals. Austin (2000) describes a progressive process through which non-profits and corporate partners can move from arm's length charitable giving relationships, to contractual arrangements for particular programs, to an ongoing partnership in which both parties continue to explore multiple ways in which the corporation and the non-profit can work together. The latter may be the face of the future in business-non-profit collaboration, as such long-term relationships permit a building of mutual trust, reduction of risk, and a full exploration of the possible ways in which non-profits and corporate businesses can benefit one another.

## Accountability, transparency and consumer/donor sovereignty

By the mid-1990s, the market environment for non-profits had grown beyond the pursuit of earned revenue, commercial enterprise or corporate partnerships. It had permeated the overall environment in which non-profits operate. If non-profits were becoming serious competitors for societal resources, they needed to begin to measure up to the standards of business. Much of the impetus came from the funding community, both government and philanthropy. Funders began to talk about accountability and about measuring performance and results. Indeed, serious scandals in a few major non-profits had soured public attitudes towards non-profits. Non-profits no longer lived in a protected environment in which little was expected in exchange for financial support. Good intentions were no longer sufficient. Rather, non-profits were asked to demonstrate their impacts on society and their cost-effectiveness, and to justify their support and special benefits in public policy (Light, 2000). These rising concerns gave impetus to reforms that moved the non-profit sector further in the direction of the market.

The particular difficulties of United Way are of special interest in this connection.[6] Performance measurement and measuring social impact became a major theme for United Way during the 1990s, stressed by the national organisation for adoption by local United Way affiliates (Light, 2000). Moreover, heed was taken in the United Way system of demands by donors to have more say over the allocation of the funds they contributed through payroll deduction systems (Oster, 1995). "Donor choice" became a manifestation of consumer sovereignty in the realm of charity. So did the fact that the United Way monopoly was broken in the payroll deduction systems of many private and public sector employers. It is now almost accurate to describe charitable giving through payroll deduction as a choice among alternative charitable "mutual funds" which have assembled different portfolios of charitable investments for the donor to choose from, and which even offer donors choices of investments within those portfolios. More generally, with the development of the Internet and services such as Guidestar (*www.guidestar.org*), donors are being empowered to become active shoppers in the arena of charitable giving, requiring non-profits to sell themselves more forcefully in order to distinguish themselves from their peers. Overall, donor empowerment through choice is a particularly important manifestation of a growing, though long-standing practice in non-profit sector fund raising – identifying particular aspects of a non-profit's programme that can be "sold" to donors for a given "price". While general purpose-giving to favoured organisations still persists, non-profits are moving more and more to a product differentiation approach to solicitation, in which donors can designate their gifts, and often affix their names, to particular activities, initiatives or assets, that suit their preferences.

In addition to United Ways, grant-making foundations have also drawn criticism for practices deemed ineffective in achieving results. Much of this criticism has come from a new generation of philanthropists, these having become rich from the burgeoning technology-based economy of the 1990s, who wished to pursue their social interests in a more aggressive and dynamic way. This community has called for a new style of "venture philanthropy" in which donors take a stronger hand in the organisations they fund and nurture those ventures more intensively until they prove themselves or fail. The model for this approach is venture capital in the corporate sector (Letts, Ryan and Grossman, 1997). The venture capital approach has now been adopted by several foundations, including the Roberts Foundation (Roberts, 1999).

## Adopting business methods and perspectives

The deepening engagement of non-profits in the market environment mirrors important changes now occurring inside non-profit organisations. Management practices, organisational values, and the very language that non-profits use have been changing dramatically, signalling that non-profits are becoming very different kinds of organisations than they were in the past – much more embedded in the culture of the marketplace.

Twenty years ago, the term "entrepreneurship" was virtually unknown in the non-profit sector, and where it was applied, it was thought to be irrelevant or even pejorative. Entrepreneurship was seen as something that pertained to the for-profit sector, not to non-profits. However, as research on entrepreneurship revealed its generic character and as observers pointed out the key role of enterprising behaviour in non-profit organisational success, non-profits came to accept the importance of entrepreneurship as part of their own *modus operandi* (Young, 1983). Interestingly, however, people in the non-profit world never really fully separated the generic idea of entrepreneurship from its association with for-profit activity. Hence, the concept of entrepreneurial behaviour in the non-profit sector received a boost from the increasing interest in non-profit commercial ventures that began to take hold in the early 1980s (Crimmins and Keil, 1983; Skloot, 1988). As a result the rise of the "social entrepreneur" was increasingly seen as desirable.

Around that same time period, serious concerns were being raised about the quality and competence of the management of non-profit organisations. As previously noted, the early 1980s followed a period in which the non-profit sector had greatly expanded, largely as a result of federal government programs associated with the War on Poverty of the Kennedy-Johnson era. The sector was now facing a consolidation of those programs and a period of stringency and change in which federal largesse would decrease and more emphasis would be put on sustenance from local and private sources. Non-profits, which had proliferated and expanded for many years, now confronted a potential shake up. Good management, which could make the most efficient use of available resources and which could steer non-profits in productive new directions, was demanded. But strong management, using modern techniques, was also difficult to find in the non-profit sector, and perhaps it was even harder for non-profits to admit that it was needed. Traditionally, non-profits had not put much emphasis or great value on management, on hiring people with special management expertise or in educating people to the particular managerial requirements of the non-profit organisation. Non-profit managers were normally professionals in their various service fields – artists, social workers, doctors and nurses, teachers, and so on – who incidentally acquired and took on administrative responsibility as their careers evolved. Management specialists *per se*, or individuals educated specifically in management, were rare. The early 1980s witnessed the beginning of a change in these attitudes and practices, and the start of a new movement to educate professional non-profit managers through university programs (O'Neill and Young, 1988). Management was no longer a second-class vocation in the non-profit sector; it was becoming important. By the 1990s, although still somewhat controversial, non-profit management had become a respected career path and a legitimate profession (O'Neill and Fletcher, 1998).

The language of grant-making foundations is also changing. Some members of the social enterprise avant-garde have even written about an organised "non-profit capital market" (Emerson, 1999). In this conception, funders seethemselves as making investments in non-profits which are gauged in terms of their social returns, various grant and loan instruments are used to finance those investments, rating services are available for measuring those social returns, and funders manage portfolios of social investments with some degree of diversification for risk and return. Such an approach could potentially lead to a major change in the way non-profits are funded. Certainly, as Reis and Clohesy (2000) point out, the new generation of philanthropists is potentially very large and young, capable of ushering in a distinctly new way of doing philanthropic business.

In summary, the market culture is taking root in non-profit organisations in many different ways. The change in internal culture reflects important trends in the environment and changing practices of non-profits since the late 1970s. More importantly, the internal changes in language and perspective signal that there is no going back. The perspective therefore is for non-profits to become more and more integrated into the market culture for the foreseeable future.

## Concluding thoughts

The engagement of the US non-profit sector in the marketplace presents very substantial challenges as well as opportunities for the future of the sector and for the capacity of society to address social problems. It will also require a rethinking of the non-profit sector as we know it, and the public policies now underpinning that sector.

The potential opportunities are enticing if not yet clearly defined. By de-emphasising sectoral boundaries and engaging market forces and strategies in a more substantial way, "marketisation" offers the sector a greater resource base and enlarged productive capacity, and more combinations of solution strategies than it ever had before. No longer dependent primarily on the whims of government funding or the charitable impulses of citizens, the sector can make its own way with earned income, a source of sustenance much more under its control and with far more long-run potential than charity or tax support. Additionally, marketisation, in principal at least, makes the non-profit sector an ally and partner of the dominant business sector of the economy, rather than simply its supplicant.

But there are great risks and uncertainties associated with this trend as well. First, there is the distinct possibility that a market-embedded non-profit sector will lose its way and become just an instrument of business, driven by profits and neglectful of social mission. This fear has already arisen forcefully in several areas of non-profit activity, including health care and higher education. A recent article in the Atlantic Monthly talks about the "kept university", a reference to the fact that the research agendas of US universities are now being substantially driven by corporations which not only skew that agenda towards work of commercial value (to the neglect of other worthy research) but also influence long-standing mission-related practices and institutional values such as the public availability of research-generated knowledge (Press and Washburn, 2000).

Second, the marketisation of the non-profit sector is distinctly changing both its public image and internal identity in a manner that may be undermining the sector's public support. In an interesting legal analysis involving a Christian Science summer camp in Maine, Evelyn Brody (1997) points out that charitable non-profits have begun to recognise the substantially "business character" of their operations and have even begun to use that understanding to defend themselves in court. Brody questions the strategic wisdom of this position, which in the long run could undermine preferences granted to non-profits in public policy.

Perhaps the most perplexing aspect of the marketisation of the non-profit sector is that with the blurring of non-profit/for-profit boundaries, or the broadening of the "social sector" to include "social enterprises" which do not strictly conform to the non-distributional constraint of formal non-profit operation, one must ask what kinds of new governing mechanisms can ensure that a new social sector will behave responsibly with the resources entrusted to it? It is all well and good for socially responsible businesses to declare themselves as agents of social progress and as worthy vehicles for public support, but what institutional mechanisms are in place to assure that stance over the long haul? For example, will Ben and Jerry's Ice Cream continue to make its contributions to society now that it has been sold to Unilever, or will the new parent corporation exploit Ben and Jerry's reputation just to make more money? Is there really something different about a for-profit business created by socially progressive entrepreneurs to carry out some mix of public good and private profit that should justify public trust or special treatment in public policy, should we just let the market decide, or is there a need for new public policies to govern these so-called social enterprises?

The experience in Europe with social enterprise suggests that some rethinking of the American approach may be in order. The European approach would downplay the prohibition on profit distribution *per se* as a criterion for determining social merit worthy of public policy support, *e.g.* tax exemption. Rather, the two factors that are more important in this framework are intent and governance. Is the enterprise founded to address a socially defined mission? And is the arrangement through which "interest holders" govern the organisation sufficiently potent to ensure that such intent is pursued in good faith?

It has long been recognised in the US that the non-profit form *per se* does not guarantee responsible behaviour or effective performance by non-profit organisations. The non-distribution constraint must always be carefully policed to ensure that "self-inurement" is avoided, and even then it is difficult to ensure that non-profits are truly driven by mission rather than narrower and more self-serving goals.

However, the marketisation of non-profits and the concept of social enterprise raise the possibility that we may be looking in the wrong place to ensure socially responsible and socially effective behaviour – that not only is control of profit-distribution sometimes ineffective in ensuring such behaviour but that such control may actually diminish the performance of social enterprise by restricting its ability to engage market incentives and solutions.

Proponents of social enterprise do not argue against preferential tax treatment or other mechanisms for public policy to support non-profits. Rather they would probably broaden such support to include a variety of arrangements that engage market mechanisms in the cause of social good. This raises the issue of how public policy might be re-oriented to deal with a fully marketised, "no longer just non-profit", social sector. The seeds of such a policy may be found both in Europe's approach and in the new thrust in the US to focus on performance rather than form. The European approach would require a clear statement of organisational intent and conformity to a governance structure that could ensure that qualified organisations would maintain their social direction uncorrupted by excessive private gain. Recent American experience might add the notion of performance assessment whereby social enterprises are rewarded according to whom they benefit and how well they get the job done (Young, 1989).

Rethinking the basis of the US non-profit sector in light of its recent experience in becoming integrated into the market economy opens up a Pandora's Box at the very least. It is fraught with the danger that much good could be undone by threatening the infrastructure of many of our most valued and valuable charitable institutions. But it would also be unwise to ignore the changes now taking place in the sector and to assume that the present array of public policies is sufficient to deal with those changes.

## Notes

1. Acknowledgement: this chapter draws heavily from research undertaken by the author for the "The state of America's non-profit sector" project, supported by the non-profit sector research fund of the Aspen Institute and the Johns Hopkins University Center for Civil Society Studies

2. See On line Compendium of Federal and State Regulations for US Non-profit Organisations: *www.muridae.com/nporegulation*.

3. New Profit Inc. is a non-profit venture philanthropy firm operating a performance-based fund that helps grow proven non-profit organisations and encourages the development of a community of like-minded people willing to invest in social enterprise (see *www.nonprofit.com*). Share Our Strength is one of the US leading anti-hunger, anti-poverty organisations established since 1984 (*www.strength.org*).

4. This covers six to eighteen year old pupils.

5. Founded in 1958 by retired California educator, Dr. Ethel Percy Andrus, AARP (formerly known as the American Association of Retired Persons) today represents more than 34 million members. Over half of their members are working, either full or part-time, while the remainder are fully retired.

6. United Way is a major US fundraising organisation that operates through a devolved system of local agencies. See *national.unitedway.org*.

ISBN 92-64-19953-5
The Non-profit Sector in a Changing Economy
© OECD 2003

PART I

*Chapter 3*

# New Trends in the Non-profit Sector in Australia: A Greater Involvement in Employment and Social Policies

by

Julie Novak,
FACS – Commonwealth Department of Family and Community Services,
Australia

## Introduction

The non-profit sector has played a critical role in the sustainability of Australia's community life over the past two centuries. In recent times there has been a significant increase in the interest in the role and operations of the sector. A rapidly changing social and economic environment, resulting from changes such as globalisation, technological innovations, public sector reform and demographic changes, is propelling Australia's non-profit organisations into a period of fundamental transformation. These have created new demands on the non-profit sector to play a more influential role in shaping social and economic outcomes, particularly at a local community level. In addition, many organisations are adopting a more "entrepreneurial" focus to their growing suite of service delivery activities.

This chapter provides an overview of the Australian non-profit sector and examines recent trends impacting on the operations of non-profit organisations. First, the chapter defines the Australian non-profit sector, and provides a profile of its economic contribution. Next, it illustrates the major trends impacting on the recent development of the sector, including the growing contribution of non-profit organisations in the delivery of welfare and employment services, as well as the emergence of "social enterprises". It outlines some of the key opportunities and challenges likely to be faced by the sector. Finally, the chapter concludes by stating that the Australian non-profit sector has discovered a "new wave" of dynamism, and is well placed to continue to adapt effectively to the economic and social changes impacting on its operating environment.

## A profile of the Australian non-profit sector

### Definition and legal status

Throughout Australia's history, people have come together for the purpose of promoting social cohesion, serving the needy, or providing social goods and services not provided by either government or business organisations. Many of these organisations are motivated by altruistic concerns through their social mission. Their own rules prevent them from distributing any surplus income to their members,[1] focus on community action at a local level, and invariably rely on work performed without pay by their members. This collection of privately-controlled, social-purpose organisations, which are considered separate from the public or business sectors, has been variously referred to as the "independent", "voluntary", "non-government", "social" or "third" sector.[2]

A number of alternative legal forms at the Commonwealth and state levels of government control organisations within the Australian non-profit sector. In general terms, non-profit organisations may take on the form of an unincorporated association, a charitable trust, an incorporated association or a company limited by guarantee.[3] There are also non-profits created by specific acts of the various Australian Parliaments, or through Commonwealth legislation providing for a small number of specialist non-profit associations (such as indigenous councils and associations).

Significant variation in the legal definitions of non-profit organisations remains an issue of considerable interest in Australia, as policy makers look to ensure that the legal status of non-profit organisations properly reflects changing social and economic conditions. The Commonwealth Government announced an independent inquiry on 18 September 2000 into definitional issues relating to charitable, religious and community service non-profit organisations. The final Report of the Inquiry into the Definition of Charities was released in June 2001, and the government is currently considering the recommendations of this final report.[4]

## Economic contribution

The non-profit sector makes a significant contribution to the Australian economy. While data relating to the economic contribution of the Australian non-profit sector is not available on a consistent basis, data produced by the Australian Non-profit Data Project (ANDP)[5] for 1995-96 showed that.[6]

- There were 31 764 non-profit sector entities in June 1996. According to separate analysis by the Industry Commission, the size structure of the non-profit sector varies markedly, with the largest organisations possessing annual revenue well in excess of $100 million[7] while the smallest organisations receive less than $100 000 annually.[8]

- In June 1996, the non-profit sector employed 579 367 people, or 6.9 per cent of all people employed in Australia. In employment terms, the Australian non-profit sector was larger than the tourism sector, and also greater than the agricultural and mining sectors combined.

- In 1995-96, the non-profit sector contributed around $14.6 billion, or three per cent, to Australian Gross Domestic Product (GDP). This sector was larger than the accommodation, cafes and restaurants, communications, cultural and recreational services, or personal services sectors of the economy.

● The non-profit sector raised around $27.4 billion in revenue in 1995-96, with commercial sales, government funding and proceeds from fundraising accounting for 31 per cent, 30.3 per cent and 7.4 per cent of total non-profit sector income respectively.

● In terms of operating expenditure, the non-profit sector spent over $26.1 billion for the twelve months to June 1996. Labour costs accounted for around 51.3 per cent of total expenses, with other expenses accounting for the remainder.[9]

Table 3.1 provides a summary of the economic contribution of the Australian non-profit sector in 1995-96.

## Welfare services provision

The Australian non-profit sector has played a longstanding role in the delivery of welfare services to the community, and remains actively involved in many aspects of Australian life. It provides a wide range of services, including the distribution of food and clothing, education, health, accommodation, childcare, counselling, legal advice, and religious services. Non-profit organisations provide these services to a wide range of people including families, the aged, young people, people with low incomes, the unemployed, the homeless, and people with disabilities.

A key trend for Australian non-profit service providers over the past decade is the increasing willingness of governments to seek the wider involvement of the community to deliver welfare services. These reforms to the "welfare state" have broadly reflected a desire to reduce public sector monopoly provision of social services, and to exploit the inherent advantages that non-governmental organisations can bring to social service delivery frameworks in the form of diversity, innovation, flexibility and sensitivity to the task of providing services to local communities. At the same time there are debates about public sector accountability and whether the goals of non-profit organisations are always in alignment with government objectives. There is also a debate about whether flexibility in non-profit welfare services provision creates inequities in terms of access to services. In particular, governmental funding and support to the sector is being provided increasingly through outcome-based contractual funding agreements for the provision of defined services. This trend towards the use of the "purchaser-provider" model is reflected in recent Australian Institute of Health and Welfare (AIHW) data, which show that, of the $3.9 billion funded by the Commonwealth Government for welfare services in 1999-2000, only four per cent of Commonwealth funding (or $525 million) was directly provided to the community. Around 51.4 per cent (or $1.99 billion) of Commonwealth funding was transferred to the non-government community service organisations

Table 3.1.   **Key economic statistics – Australian non-profit sector, 1995-96**

In $ m

| | Community services | Health | Education | Education related | Other human services | Religion | Philanthropic intermediaries | Arts and culture | Sport and recreation | Interest groups | Other | Total |
|---|---|---|---|---|---|---|---|---|---|---|---|---|
| Organisations (nq) | 4 898 | 824 | 5 256 | 1 576 | 2 261 | 5 789 | 158 | 612 | 5 668 | 3 737 | 985 | 31 764 |
| Employment (nq) | 132 247 | 111 104 | 134 569 | 9 265 | 12 405 | 17 000 | 434 | 6 677 | 98 341 | 46 982 | 10 383 | 579 367 |
| GDP | 2 309.0 | 2 806.4 | 4 229.8 | 266.5 | 190.6 | 327.5 | 9.6 | 191.3 | 2 602.9 | 1 236.6 | 388.8 | 14 558.6 |
| Income | 3 870.4 | 4 382.5 | 6 033.9 | 947.7 | 376.1 | 659.5 | 12.0 | 466.0 | 6 491.2 | 3 251.1 | 902.2 | 27 392.5 |
| Government funding | 1 918.7 | 1 963.1 | 3 171.7 | 189.7 | 163.7 | – | 3.0 | 176.5 | 99.8 | 465.6 | 144.1 | 8 295.9 |
| Fundraising | 610.5 | 108.6 | 300.9 | 106.7 | 4.7 | 502.1 | 0.6 | 37.5 | 264.9 | 87.0 | 16.9 | 2 040.5 |
| Fees for service | 769.9 | 2 011.2 | 1 892.9 | – | 2.5 | – | 0.5 | – | – | – | 0.1 | 4 677.1 |
| Commercial sales | 325.0 | 81.7 | 382.3 | 443.5 | 190.6 | 157.4 | – | 212.5 | 5 430.8 | 848.4 | 439.8 | 8 512.0 |
| Membership dues | – | 5.2 | 41.9 | 158.5 | – | – | 0.5 | – | 584.6 | 1 321.5 | 155.3 | 2 267.4 |
| Interest income | 107.5 | 60.3 | 35.2 | 19.4 | 1.8 | – | 5.9 | – | 54.6 | 190.4 | 5.9 | 481.0 |
| Other | 138.8 | 152.4 | 208.9 | 29.9 | 12.8 | – | 1.5 | 39.5 | 56.5 | 338.2 | 140.1 | 1 118.6 |
| Expenditure | 3 699.8 | 4 191.8 | 6 137.6 | 870.3 | 362.5 | 550.2 | 14.5 | 433.7 | 5 941.5 | 3 001.5 | 905.6 | 26 108.9 |
| Labour costs | 2 204.6 | 2 734.6 | 4 229.8 | 266.5 | 190.6 | 327.5 | 9.6 | 180.6 | 1 656.7 | 1 236.6 | 356.0 | 13 393.2 |
| Other expenses | 1 495.2 | 1 457.1 | 1 907.8 | 603.7 | 171.9 | 222.7 | 4.9 | 253.1 | 4 284.8 | 1 764.9 | 549.5 | 12 715.7 |

*Source:* Lyons and Hocking, (2000, p. 51).

(NGCSOs)[12] to directly provide social services (with the remainder transferred to other levels of government).

The funding relationship between government and non-profit organisations has diversified to incorporate a range of funding instruments, ranging from grants through to competitive tendering processes.[13] This has created a "social economy" of welfare services with non-profits coexisting with other providers (particularly for-profit enterprises) in the provision of welfare services. ABS data on community services expenditure (see Table 3.2) illustrates that the non-profit sector has increased its share of expenditure[14] from 48.7 per cent in 1995-96 to 55.9 per cent in 1999-2000. Major contributors to the increase in non-profit community services expenditure include residential care and accommodation placements (up by 41.7 per cent to $3.59 billion) followed by personal and social support (up by 107.9 per cent to nearly $1.3 billion) and training and employment services for disabled people (up by 33 per cent to $496.9 million). In comparison, despite a significant increase in childcare expenditure (up by 58.5 per cent to $216.5 million), for-profit organisations experienced a reduction in their overall share of community services expenditure by 2.1 per cent in the three years to 1999-2000. The government sector experienced an even larger reduction in its share of overall community services spending (5.1 per cent) from 1995-96 to 1999-2000, in spite of increased funding in most areas of community services.

There is some evidence to suggest that increasing competition in the provision of welfare services has encouraged non-profit organisations to deliver these services in an innovative fashion (see Box 3.1), which will in turn help to effectively meet new community needs and to build local community capacity.

## Employment and labour market programmes

Another key shift in recent years affecting the non-profit sector has been the increasing participation of non-profit organisations in the delivery of employment services. In particular, Australia has embarked on world-first reforms in the form of the Job Network, a national network of around 200 private, non-profit and government organisations contracted by the Commonwealth Department of Employment and Workplace Relations (DEWR) to provide various employment services and labour market programmes.[15]

While the full impact and benefits of the Job Network are yet to be fully realised, analysis has shown that the Network is yielding positive results for people previously excluded from the labour market.[16] The non-profit sector has played a critical role in the success of the Job Network, increasing its share of the Job Network employment services "market" over time. Around 47 per cent of organisations that have won contracts in the current round of Job

Table 3.2.   **Expenditure on direct community services activities, 1995-96 and 1999-2000**

| | Non-profit organisations | | | | For-profit organisations | | | | Government organisations | | | |
|---|---|---|---|---|---|---|---|---|---|---|---|---|
| | A | B | C | D | A | B | C | D | A | B | C | D |
| Personal and social support | 625.1 | 7.4 | 1 299.5 | 12.1 | 24.9 | 0.3 | 50.1 | 0.5 | 806.2 | 9.6 | 820.8 | 7.6 |
| Child care | 392.0 | 4.7 | 412.6 | 3.8 | 370.0 | 4.4 | 586.5 | 5.5 | 229.0 | 2.7 | 157.2 | 1.5 |
| Training and employment for persons with disabilities | 373.7 | 4.5 | 496.9 | 4.6 | 0.2 | 0.0 | 1.5 | 0.0 | 0.2 | 0.0 | – | – |
| Financial and material assistance | 102.1 | 1.2 | 117.0 | 1.1 | 0.1 | 0.0 | – | – | 44.4 | 0.5 | 24.6 | 0.2 |
| Residential care and accommodation placement | 2 535.5 | 30.2 | 3 593.6 | 33.4 | 1 402.7 | 16.7 | 1 450.9 | 13.5 | 950.8 | 11.3 | 1 047.3 | 9.7 |
| Foster care placement | 30.1 | 0.4 | 55.6 | 0.5 | – | – | – | – | 82.4 | 1.0 | 134.2 | 1.2 |
| Statutory protection and placement | 10.8 | 0.1 | 14.0 | 0.1 | – | – | – | – | 185.3 | 2.2 | 218.8 | 2.0 |
| Juvenile and disability corrective services | 6.1 | 0.1 | 10.7 | 0.1 | – | – | – | – | 185.6 | 2.2 | 235.7 | 2.2 |
| Other direction community services activities | 15.1 | 0.2 | 10.1 | 0.1 | 13.6 | 0.2 | 9.4 | 0.1 | 4.9 | 0.1 | 0.9 | 0.0 |
| Total | 4 090.6 | 48.7 | 6 010.2 | 55.9 | 1 811.5 | 21.6 | 2 098.3 | 19.5 | 2 488.8 | 29.7 | 2 639.5 | 24.6 |

*Notes:* A = Expenditure, 1995-96 ($ m).
B = Share, 1995-96 (%).
C = Expenditure, 1999-2000 ($ m).
D = Share, 1999-2000 (%).

*Source:* ABS (2001, p. 15).

Box 3.1. **The Australian non-profit sector and innovation in social services: multi-purpose family centres in remote Queensland**

The non-profit sector is playing a crucial role in providing flexible childcare for Australians living outside the main capital cities. Several multi-purpose family centres, which are primarily non-profit based, have been established in remote indigenous communities located in North Queensland. These communities are socially and geographically isolated, and due to historical and economic factors many families in these areas experience periods of significant disadvantage. Multi-purpose family centres are jointly funded initiatives by the Commonwealth and State Department of Families, Queensland.

The family centres provide a range of services including childcare, playgroup sessions, vacation care, long day care and a family support worker. The centres assist the community with a range of family support services including child protection, prevention of domestic violence and, in some cases, overnight crisis accommodation. The centres can also provide a venue for a range of community meetings and parenting programmes, and some provide access to the Internet through the Rural Outreach Network as well as teleconferencing facilities.

Network (which commenced in March 2000) identified themselves as charity, community or non-profit organisations, up from 30 per cent in March 1998 and 25 per cent in 1996-97 (Eardley, Abello and MacDonald, 2001, p. 9). Some of the larger organisations within the Network are non-profit organisations and religious entities, including Mission Australia, the Salvation Army and Job Futures (a consortium of small community-based organisations). To examine various aspects of the government's employment assistance policy framework, the Commonwealth has recently commissioned the Productivity Commission to undertake an independent inquiry on the Job Network.

The non-profit sector is also actively involved in enhancing labour market opportunities for Australians through their participation in the following Commonwealth Government programmes:

● Work for the Dole (WfD):[17] The WfD programme provides work experience opportunities and activities for eligible job seekers. The programme funds community projects in activities such as heritage, environment, community care, tourism, sport, provision of community services and restoration of community facilities. Only non-profit organisations such as charities, religious groups and local associations are permitted to sponsor WfD projects.

- Regional Assistance Programme (RAP):[18] RAP provides seed funding for community-based projects that will boost business growth and create sustainable jobs. Funding is also available for projects that improve the skills base of a region or assist disadvantaged groups in the community. Under RAP guidelines project proponents will usually be non-profit organisations.

- Area Consultative Committees (ACCs):[19] ACCs are non-profit, community-based organisations funded by the Commonwealth Government under the RAP initiative. Each ACC brings community stakeholders together to identify opportunities, priorities and growth strategies for a given region harnessing the potential for jobs creation, skills development and small business profitability. There are 56 ACCs across Australia serving rural, regional, remote and metropolitan communities.

- Community Support Programme (CSP):[20] The CSP assists job seekers who have serious and/or numerous barriers (*e.g.*, drug or alcohol dependence, significant or debilitating personal development needs, and homelessness) to gaining employment. Initiatives under the CSP are delivered by private and non-profit organisations.[21]

## Social enterprises and social entrepreneurship

Australia's non-profit organisations are increasingly integrating social and commercial objectives to meet the needs of local communities. This practice is known as "social entrepreneurship", which is defined as any private activity conducted in the public interest, organised with an entrepreneurial strategy, but whose main purpose is not the maximisation of profit but the attainment of certain economic and social goals (OECD, 1999).

Many non-profit organisations have displayed a long history of engaging in social innovation and acting in an entrepreneurial fashion. However, in recent years the concept of social enterprises has been attracting greater interest. While larger organisations such as The Smith Family, Mission Australia, The Brotherhood of Saint Laurence, The Salvation Army and The Benevolent Society are remodelling themselves as social enterprises,[22] there appear to be only relatively small numbers of enterprises operating in both socially and economically entrepreneurial ways. Nevertheless, it seems that social enterprises will become an important participant in welfare services delivery in the future.

## Partnerships with government and business

There has also been an increasing tendency over the past decade for the Australian non-profit sector to engage in a wider range of partnerships with governmental agencies and business organisations. These partnerships have grown in response to the increasing desire of organisations to "... *engage in voluntary, mutually beneficial, innovative relationships to address common societal aims through combining their resources and competencies*" (Gribben, Pinnington and Wilson, 2000, p. 8). Partnerships are seen as a beneficial means by which to tackle the multi-dimensional, and increasingly geographically-based, sources of social disadvantage, such as unemployment, poverty and differential access to social services. They also represent a move beyond traditional interactions between the non-profit, government and business sectors such as philanthropic donations and tax incentives.

While purchaser-provider relationships between government and the non-profit sector have emerged over the past decade, the Commonwealth Government has increasingly introduced the partnership concept of the "social coalition" into its social policy framework. The social coalition is the means by which business and the community can join in partnership with government to enhance opportunities for social and economic participation, and ensure that disadvantaged people have fair access to the range of opportunities available to the wider community. The role of the non-profit sector in the social coalition also includes providing information and advice to government to assist in formulating policy initiatives and developing strategies for the implementation of programmes (see Box 3.2).[23]

Since 1996, the government's engagement of the social coalition in policy development and implementation, together with the work of non-profit organisations, has facilitated better targeting of assistance to families and communities to meet immediate and emerging needs. These cross-sectoral partnerships are likely to be an enduring feature of the operating environment of non-profit organisations. It is also likely that the central success factor underpinning these arrangements into the future will be their ability to build mutual understanding and trust of the partners (*i.e.* social capital), as well as to share resources, skills and expertise.

---

Box 3.2. **The stronger families and communities strategy: the social coalition supporting Australian families and communities**

The Stronger Families and Communities Strategy, announced in the 1999-2000 Commonwealth Budget, commits $240 million to prevention, early intervention and capacity building initiatives to support and strengthen Australian families and communities. The Strategy includes parenting and relationship education, community leadership training, the development of volunteering and support for local solutions to local problems.

The Stronger Families and Communities Strategy specifically engages the social coalition in policy development and implementation. A two-tiered advisory structure has representatives from government, the non-profit sector, academia and other experts in the family and community fields. It provides advice to the government on the Strategy's implementation and looks at how to forge better links between other government and non-government projects, programmes and services. The national advisory group, the Stronger Families and Communities Partnership, advises the Minister for Family and Community Services on the broad parameters of the Strategy such as targeting frameworks and funding envelopes. The State and Territory Advisory Groups use their local expertise to make recommendations to the Minister on funding specific projects.

---

## Looking to the future: opportunities and challenges for the Australian non-profit sector

Faced with a wide array of social and economic pressures, it is clear that the Australian non-profit sector is entering a period of considerable experimentation and growth. Participation in the burgeoning "social economy" provides the non-profit sector with the opportunity to acquire a reliable, and growing, flow of resources for the promotion of social objectives in local communities. Increasing competition against for-profit firms can provide incentives for greater efficiency, more targeted services and innovation within the non-profit sector, which in turn can benefit communities. Social enterprises can potentially attract new funds into the sector, while at the same time partnerships may encourage businesses to promote social goals consistent with the historical missions of non-profits. In other words, the marketplace may be utilised to advance social purposes, and consolidate the position of the Australian non-profit sector in wielding a significant and positive influence on social and economic outcomes and policy development.

On the other hand, recent trends also present challenges for Australian non-profit organisations. Concerns expressed include:

- Potential displacement of the social mission of the non-profit sector as competitive pressures shift attention away from the non-marketable (or "public good") aspects of non-profit operations, such as service to the needy and the building of community capacity. Similarly, government contractual requirements to deliver services more in accordance with the priorities of the "purchaser", may lead to a loss of independence on the part of non-profit organisations.[24]

- Pressures to increase the scale of operations,[25] which can lead to a loss of flexibility, responsiveness and closeness to the communities served.

- That larger non-profit groups are favoured in tendering processes for the provision of public sector welfare services contracts.[26] This is because larger organisations are claimed to have a higher profile, greater professionalism in negotiating and servicing contracts, and potentially lower service delivery costs due to greater economies of scale.

- Perceived shifts in the non-profit sector away from its distinctive social mission on the part of potential volunteers, the requirement for increasing staff professionalism within the sector, as well as changes in the legal environment impacting on non-profit organisations, may be leading to a relatively higher turnover (if not a reduction) in volunteer numbers.

While the impact of social and economic change on the Australian non-profit sector is still being assessed, the primary challenge for the sector is whether it can retain its distinctive qualities and characteristics, particularly its reputation for providing social services with sensitivity, innovation and flexibility and in a diverse fashion. There is a concomitant concern that social and economic pressures will lead to changes in the values held by non-profit organisations, with a consequent reduction in their involvement in local communities. Factors likely to influence the success of the Australian non-profit sector to meet this challenge, will include:

- The continuing capacity of the sector, particularly smaller organisations, to provide a range of "niche" services for local communities, particularly to address localised sources of social disadvantage and exclusion.

- The ability of non-profits to accurately "scan" the changing social and economic environment to pin-point new and unforeseen sources of community need, and to then successfully tackle social problems at source.

- The development of alliances within the non-profit sector to enable large and small organisations, and various combinations thereof, to pool their comparative skills, resources and expertise.

- The ability of non-profit organisations to build internal organisational structures that respond more quickly and flexibly in a more complex and faster-paced environment.

- Reconciling the need to tap into new and innovative sources of revenues (*e.g.*, subsidised loans, venture capital funds) to promote social ventures, whilst at the same time ensuring equal access to services and fair pricing structures.

- Meeting greater community demands for transparency and accountability by developing explicit outcome measures, performance indicators and consumer protection mechanisms.

## Conclusion

The Australian non-profit sector has played an important part in building Australia's economic, social, political and cultural foundations. Not only has the sector served human needs in a flexible, responsive and sensitive fashion, but its activities have served to strengthen civil society by combating social exclusion, promoting a sense of community and giving expression to citizen concerns. These activities have played a critical role in improving the quality of Australian life, including the development of "social capital" in local communities.

The social and economic environment in which non-profit organisations operate has changed in a number of fundamental ways over the past two decades. While these changes have the potential to provide non-profit organisations with further opportunities to influence community well-being and policy development, they will also require resilience and insightful agility to ensure that they effectively adjust to the pressures associated with change whilst maintaining their core ethos of providing benevolent community care. Given the demonstrated ability of the sector to prosper in response to historical shifts, combined with its longstanding ability to draw upon Australia's volunteer spirit, the future of the non-profit sector appears positive and is likely to remain a significant contributor to Australian social and economic life.

## Notes

1. However, some organisations, such as financial mutuals and trading co-operatives, may distribute a surplus to members but in proportion to members' use of the organisation.

2. For the purposes of this chapter, the aggregation of these organisations (with the exception of finance and insurance mutuals and trading co-operatives) will be referred to hereafter as the "non-profit" sector.

3. For a further discussion of legal concepts surrounding the Australian non-profit sector, see: Mark Lyons (1997), "Australia", in L.M. Salamon (ed.), *The International Guide to Non-profit Law*, John Wiley and Sons, New York; and M. McGregor-Lowndes (1999), "Australia", in T. Silk (ed.), *Philanthropy and Law in Asia*, Jossey-Bass, San Francisco.

4. The Inquiry into the Definition of Charities and Related Organisations was established by the Australian Prime Minister on 18 September 2000. In announcing the Inquiry, the Prime Minister spoke of the vital role such organisations play in the community and of the need to ensure that the legislative and administrative frameworks they operate in are appropriate to the modern social and economic environment. He went on to note that *"the common law definition of a charity, which is based on a legal concept dating back to 1601, has resulted in a number of legal definitions and often gives rise to legal disputes"*. See *www.cdi.gov.au*

5. The ANDP is a collaborative project between the Centre for Australian Community Organisations and Management (CACOM) at the University of Technology, Sydney, and the Australian Bureau of Statistics (ABS).

6. This data only incorporates those non-profit organisations that employ at least one person and are registered with the Australian Taxation Office (ATO) as a group employer. In addition, the data does not include the economic impact of voluntary work.

7. This chapter refers to Australian Dollars.

8. In 1993-94, the largest 50 organisations each had recurrent annual expenditures in excess of $10 million, and collectively spent some $1.6 billion. The total income for the largest 50 organisations accounted for one-third of the total income of the "community service welfare organisation" (CSWO) sector. On the other hand, most CSWOs (comprising 50 per cent of the sector) were small in size, generally employing fewer than five staff.

9. While ANDP data is generally regarded as the most comprehensive to date, the ABS provided the Commonwealth Government Inquiry into the Definition of Charities and Related Organisations with experimental data that show that:

10. The contribution of the non-profit institutions serving the households (NPISH) sector to gross value added (GVA) at basic prices (including volunteer services valued at market prices) in 1998-99 was $22 billion. In comparison, GVA of the agriculture, forestry and fishing industry was valued at $18.1 billion in 1998-99.

11. NPISHs employed on average 809 000 people during 1998-99 (including volunteer services valued at market rates and converted to a full-time equivalent basis), or 9.1 per cent of total employment.

12. This sector includes both non-profit and for-profit organisations providing various community services

13. Lyons (2001) describes five types of funding arrangements that currently exist, ranging from untied grants through to direct funding of consumers. These various funding instruments involve different levels of competition and autonomy impacting on the "provider".

14. Total of non-profit, for-profit, and Commonwealth and State Government sector community services expenditure.

15. Services provided through the Job Network include: Job Matching (the placement of suitable job seekers into suitable vacancies to meet an employer's requirements); Job Search Training (the provision of a programme of 15 days of assistance and training in job finding, interviews and placement); Intensive Assistance (an individually tailored programme of assistance over an 18 month period managed by the client's designated employment consultant); and New Enterprise Incentive Scheme (NEIS) (an individually mentored programme to assist eligible job seekers to establish and operate viable new small businesses).

16. According to DEWR data, in the twelve months to October 2001 alone, more than 72 000 long-term unemployed and at-risk job seekers who participated in Intensive Assistance had been placed into jobs for at least 13 weeks; more than 320 000 job seekers had been placed into jobs through Job Matching; Job Search Training commencements had increased to more than 76 000 in a year; and more than 6 500 job seekers had been assisted in commencing their own small businesses through NEIS. In a broader analysis, the OECD (2001) found that the Job Network has been at least as effective as former programmes in helping participants find work, at about half the net cost to taxpayers.

17. See *www.jobsearch.gov.au/w4d_cwc.asp*

18. See *www.acc.gov.au/rapguidelines.htm*

19. See *www.acc.gov.uk*

20. See *www.workplace.gov.au*

21. From 1 July 2002, the CSP will be replaced by the Personal Support Program (PSP), which improves upon the CSP and will encompass broader objectives to enable people to stabilise their lives and become more involved in their communities.

22. The transformation of larger Australian non-profit organisations as social enterprises has drawn criticism from some quarters. These include suggestions that the movement on the part of large non-profits in particular towards becoming social enterprises merely involves a branding and repositioning exercise. In response to these criticisms, The Smith Family has indicated that the transition towards a social enterprise has necessitated the development of a "… *new type of organisation that has the skills and competencies to innovate effectively in addressing problems of disadvantage and bringing about societal change*" (Simons, 2000, p. 1).

23. Other examples of non-profit sector participation in the implementation of Commonwealth Government programmes include the Prime Minister's Community Business Partnership, Youth Pathways Action Plan Taskforce, the Reconnect Program Development Reference Group, the Indigenous Community

Capacity Building Roundtable, and the Australians Working Together welfare reform package.

24. However, on closer inspection, there appears to be a relatively wide range of funding relationships between governments and non-profit organisations involving different levels of competition. See the discussion, including Endnote 11, above.

25. A number of Australian non-profit sector experts have claimed that the sector has entered a period of industry consolidation in order to effectively meet a growing suite of responsibilities, and to capture a greater share of newly developed welfare services "markets" from for-profit enterprises. Data attesting to this trend is not available on a comprehensive or consistent basis, and is indirect by nature. Evidence from ABS data for the period 1995-96 to 1999-2000 is mixed. While concentration (defined as the proportion of organisations employing 100 or more people) has increased markedly in the aged care and other non-residential accommodation services industries (by 4.7 per cent and two per cent respectively), and only slightly in the other residential accommodation and childcare services industries (by 0.7 per cent and 0.05 per cent respectively), the nursing homes industry enjoyed a decrease in the degree of concentration (by 3.9 per cent). In the case of the childcare services industry, the proportion of small organisations (i.e. employment of 19 people or below) also increased (by 4.7 per cent).

26. An assessment of this argument by the Industry Commission Inquiry into Charitable Organisations concluded that "... *there was no consensus ... about the relative advantages or disadvantages of large, newer or small providers in the tendering process*" (Industry Commission, 1995, p. 399). On a broader level, Commonwealth Government tender processes are undertaken on a competitive merit basis and do not unduly favour either large or small non-profit organisations

ISBN 92-64-19953-5
The Non-profit Sector in a Changing Economy
© OECD 2003

PART I

# Chapter 4

# The Non-profit Sector in Mexico: From Informal to Formal Recognition

by

Marco A. Mena,
SEDESOL, Secretaría de Desarrollo Social, Mexico

## Introduction

The consolidation process of organised citizenship and community participation in Mexico is very recent. It was only about 15 years ago that the public sphere within the Mexican society started to experience a rising and more consistent interaction with non-profit or non-governmental organisations. Although some philanthropic activity was initiated during the colonial period in the 16th century, mainly promoted by the Catholic Church, organised volunteering and giving only turned into a solid distinguishable trait of Mexico's society during the last decade.

There are at least three explanations for this development. Firstly, following the transition from a post-colonial to an independent Mexico in 1821, the most pressing and crucial issue for the country concerned its transformation into a nation-state. Other issues, such as the role of civil organisations in the political landscape were not addressed. Secondly, the origins of the Mexican nation, characterised by strong government control, hindered the establishment and operation of a participative democracy. Moreover, the government-led provision of public goods and services following the Mexican Revolution (1910-1917) further legitimised the omnipresence of the state in political life and slowed the emergence of civil society. Finally, due to the narrow and marginal participatory space left, especially up to the mid-1980s, the cultural and legal difficulties in opening and developing the non-governmental option within civil society had to be overcome.

Some of those problems have already been solved; others are still policy issues under debate. This chapter presents the recent trends in the situation of civil organisations in Mexico, as well as the most relevant achievements of their evolution as a sector, which are: change in prevalent focus of their role and activities, relationship with the government, public awareness of the importance of this sector, as well as civil organisations-related legal and fiscal issues on the national agenda.

## The relationship between government and civil organisations

As in many other countries, Mexico is not an exception when it comes to describing the relationship between government and civil organisations as promisingly collaborative but difficult at the same time. In fact, collaboration and partnership experiences have coexisted along with open disagreement and even conflict. Different degrees of reciprocal support to initiatives and projects have been combined with different degrees of distrust. This twofold interaction was the primary characteristic of the last few decades. Only recently, the July 2000 presidential election brought the defeat of the Institutional Revolutionary Party (PRI), which had been the ruling party for 71 years, in favour of the National Action Party (PAN). This brought major change to the functioning of the Mexican political system. The transition to a new political arrangement has raised new expectations for the achievement of more balanced and adequate governance. These expectations include the revision of the way in which the government relates to civil organisations.

The apparent contradiction between support and distrust was in fact the core of a relationship shaped by a constant attempt, on the one hand by the government, to direct and even control social and political participation, and, on the other hand by civil organisations, to defend and expand their autonomy and independence in order to gain moral and citizen recognition. Although many fruitful possibilities for partnerships are foreseen, they are also embedded in a complex, difficult and even conflictive framework. The problem is mainly explained by the prevalence of a governmental organisational culture and profile, as well as by the diversity of civil organisations that form the so-called third sector in Mexico (Aguilar, 1997).

Although the term "government" refers to a uniform entity and a structure of standardised collective action, a closer look at the way governmental agencies and public officials interact with civil organisations indicates a strong heterogeneity. The interest and willingness to collaborate with civil organisations varies enormously across the different bureaucratic hierarchies. Within the government there are many degrees of knowledge about civil organisations and perceptions about their role, work, and contribution to governance. The lack of this knowledge has caused, among certain agencies or public officials, either a discouraging attitude or a reticent position towards civil organisations. This is in contrast with the interest shown by an important share of the governmental sphere to promote closer collaboration with organised citizenship. It is also a task to which many officials have openly declared to be committed, in order to foster accountability and transparency in government actions. The result has been a manifold spectrum of reactions, ranging from disbelief to active partnership. To obtain a more balanced spectrum towards partnership is a challenging policy task, especially in a political transition environment, where many are still trying to distinguish between the governability of an authoritarian regime and the search for quality governance in a democratic society.

The composition of civil organisations in Mexico is very diverse and their relationship with the government is therefore dramatically different, depending on their influence, resources and willingness to interact with government agencies. The third sector is comprised of multiple organisations at various levels of institutional development, human resources and management professionalism, financing, and public recognition. Similarly to government agencies, civil organisations have multiple perceptions and degrees of trust in their official counterparts. In this sense, there is a relevant difference between the lack of homogeneity within the government and within the third sector. Civil organisations that have a fluent working relationship with the government are often questioned by others who strictly defend their independence.

These two different types of internal dynamics, both inside government and civil organisations, have determined, until now, their relationship in Mexico. The process of building a stronger, respectful, and collaborative interaction has been gradual and difficult. However, the current balance is positive. Concepts such as co-responsibility and stakeholders for development are now regarded, more than ever, as key elements for social progress. The painstaking Mexican way of achieving consistent citizen participation and a solid civil society organisation has evolved into a widely accepted recognition that working together is a necessity.

## Emergence of Mexican civil organisations

Starting in the post-revolutionary period, the Mexican government consolidated itself as the country's economic and social change engine. This governmental profile was necessary for Mexico to build up its national identity after the Revolution, and was made possible due to increasing financial resources generated both through augmenting the external debt and through petroleum extraction, especially during the 1970s. Besides the activities that may be regarded exclusively as governmental tasks, the government became responsible for deciding how society's problems were understood and defined, what the social priorities should be, as well as which solutions were most desirable.

During those years, the first social organisations emerged as incipient, simple mechanisms, which faced their most immediate needs or disseminated opinions about public issues. They were not in the position, however, to act independently from the governmentally-controlled framework. These few organisations may be defined as part of a "first generation" category (Korten, 1990) for they were intended to solve temporary needs or problems, and contributed in a very limited way to building up their beneficiaries' capacities or skills.

In the early 1980s, the crisis of the Welfare State undermined the government's legitimacy, as it was unable to sustain the production and distribution of benefits. This provoked the beginning of organised expressions of discontent. In fact, the Mexican government kept its legitimacy by directly benefiting selected groups of society. The capacity to produce and distribute benefits lasted until 1982, when the debt crisis caused the government to face the enormous fiscal deficit.

The "systematic" economic crises that were an unfortunate trait of Mexico's recent history (1976, 1982, 1988, 1994), especially when a president left office, generated the widely-spread belief that crises were provoked by the authoritarian regime itself. The claim for effective democratic mechanisms became very strong, and organisations found in this impulse a public audience willing to support their dissension with governmental decisions and discontent about the lack of capacity to deal with pluralism.

The link between authoritarianism and economic crisis, perceived by the active citizenship, was the origin of what could be called the rise of the Mexican organised society. Due to specific conjunctures, since the mid-eighties people have joined forces in order to demand from the government rapid responses to social problems and, in particular, electoral controversies, which were until the early 90s an inescapable topic regarding political stability.

Before some organisations showed their influence in the electoral issue, there was an event that proved that organised society was already a decisive actor in the public sphere. In September 1985, Mexico City suffered an earthquake that changed the whole of society's perception of its own civic strength and participation potential. The government's lack of capacity to face this emergency motivated citizens to organise and conduct the search for survivors, the healing of injured people, and the installation of shelters. When it was realised that society reacted more effectively than government, this tragedy served to stimulate the sense of solidarity and civic self-confidence in solving collective problems. The further expansion of civil organisations' activities has been continual since 1985. These may be considered to be "second generation" type of organisation, which not only demand action, but also actively participate in supplying the services or products they provide.

Similarly, after a presumed electoral fraud in the 1988 presidential election, civil organisations demanded a mechanism to guarantee transparency in elections. When the third sector in Mexico was born it focused primarily on electoral issues, and with great success. In 1989, the combination of the civil organisations movement and an aggressive lobbying routed by the opposition parties motivated Congress to reform the Constitution in order to create a regulatory law for electoral matters: the Federal Code of Institutions and Electoral Procedures (COFIPE). Later modifications of the legislative framework constituted the beginning of Mexican procedural democracy, as they were the basis that led to the creation of the Federal Electoral Institute

(IFE) in 1990, which is in charge of conducting and organising every federal election. The IFE is an autonomous agency directed by a Citizen Council. Previously, the Ministry of the Interior was responsible for this task.

Paradoxically, the emergence of organised society in Mexico was also catalysed by the government itself through some of its programmes. For example, during President Carlos Salinas' administration (1988-1994) many sectors of the population were neither ready nor adequately equipped to enter into and benefit from a healthier market structure that had been introduced. The government gave them benefits, mainly in-kind and cash transfers, through a major anti-poverty programme (National Program of Solidarity, PRONASOL, 1989-1995).

This programme's functioning was based on self-organised rural and semi-urban community groups. In order to obtain PRONASOL's funds, community citizens had to launch a Solidarity Committee (*Comite de Solidaridad*). Although this programme was also used as a tool to reinforce the political and electoral mechanisms of the PRI, its implementation and eligibility criteria of beneficiaries promoted organising skills in poor communities and indirectly fostered a culture of participation.

By the end of the 1990s, the experience and knowledge acquired by first or second generation civil organisations allowed several of them to achieve a more solid institutional development – a third generation. These revitalised organisations pursue comprehensive schemes of interaction with their institutional and organisational environment. They are willing to work with different government areas and are prone to exploring joint-action with other civil organisations. In fact, this type of organisation is currently bringing about the incipient formation of civil networking that may serve to consolidate their influence and effectiveness.

## Size and presence of civil organisations

Civil organisations have obtained increasing recognition within civil society for the collective value of their activities. First, as contributors to the consolidation of democratic governability in the 1990s, and recently as relevant participants in promoting better governance. Without a doubt this has been a radical change in the role civil organisations play in Mexico, compared to the early 1980s, when the very notion of non-governmental or non-profit organisations did not even exist. These concepts were at that time an analytic category among academics or a refined reference in the language of some professional policy analysts. Things are very different now. Although, theoretically speaking, the conceptual problem persists (*e.g.* non-profit organisations *vs.* civil organisations), they are currently perceived as key components of citizen participation and as legitimate actors in promoting issues of public concern (Pérez Yarahuán and García-Junco, 1998). Even among the most reticent public officials who do not feel comfortable working with these organisations, the prevalent opinion is that their contributions are desirable.

These perceptions, however, are combined with a lack of knowledge that both researchers and practitioners would like to improve upon. In Mexico, information and organised data regarding the number of civil organisations, their activities, the labour force they represent, the extent to which their projects are effective or at least the record of evaluation efforts, are scarce and incomplete. Besides, the quality and inter-temporal comparability of this information varies enormously.

Quantifying the numbers of organisations that currently exist in Mexico, for example, is not as easy a task as it may seem. Today, it is not possible to determine precisely how many civil organisations there are in the country. Several calculations have been made, especially since the late 1980s, but the available information is neither up-to-date, nor sufficient enough to describe satisfactorily the number or types of activities. Figures of approximately 4 000 organisations are suggested by several governmental records, but some researchers or independent records claim the existence of over 10 000. Of course, a reciprocal distrust (government-civil organisations), as it is mentioned above, is partly the cause of this difference, but there are other reasons to take into account.

One of these reasons is that national statistics do not take into account NPS organisations in their studies and publications. Not only is this a governmental fault, it is also in the interests of civil organisations to remain out of the reach of any signal of official intervention or control. This situation, however, affects both the civil society and the government. There is no agency or organisation, public or private, which systematically conducts statistical studies on the civil organisations sector. The most relevant efforts regarding this problem have been the initiatives of some organisations themselves, which combine their daily activities with the collection of data and statistical analysis. The reach of the available studies is, however, very limited and the quality of the information is questionable. There are also structural problems in the organisations that provide information. Most of them do not give accurate responses due to a number of incentives mainly related to the fiscal benefits they enjoy or the enhancement of their public recognition.

The scope of the analysis has also been insufficient. Many studies have focused their attention on the legal constitution of the organisations, which in Mexico can be either "civil association" (AC) or "public assistance association" (IAP). However, there are many other organisations that are not registered under either of these two forms. Due to distrust regarding the fiscal obligations of being an AC or IAP organisation or because their interests are in conflict with the responsibilities implied by these forms, a number of civil organisations actively avoid being registered. Studies carried out by universities and research centres are also incomplete. Most organisations refuse to answer questions that might compromise their interests or represent a possibility of external control. Researchers openly declare that obtaining accurate information on financing is a conflictive task.

There is a very positive perception about civil organisations within the higher levels of the government that should be complemented with proper information to match accountability expectations that are not yet fulfilled. This fact has been mainly realised and stressed by certain scholars (see, for example, Aguilar, 1997, 2001; Brito, 1997; and Méndez, 1998).

In Mexico, the most recent information is provided by three recognised civil networking organisations (Mexican Center for Philanthropy, CEMEFI; Mutual Support Forum, FAM; and DEMOS Foundation), a research centre of the Metropolitan University (Center for Information on Civil Organisations, CEDIOC) and a government agency (Information System for Civil Organisations, SIOS, at the National Institute for Social Development, INDESOL). Their results show important differences in their figures and they are evidence of the necessary heterogeneity in criteria in deciding the statistical samples and questionnaire designs.

In two research works carried out in 1998 by both DEMOS and FAM, the results showed that the presence of civil organisations in the states is minimal compared to Mexico City (Brito, 1997). Out of 3 451 organisations, 52 per cent are in Mexico City and the remaining 48 per cent are distributed all over the Mexican territory. In 2001, SIOS published a report in which out of 3 846 organisations, 31 per cent are in Mexico City and the remaining 69 per cent are spread over the rest of the country.

In 1999, CEMEFI and FAM accepted as valid a range from 5 000 to 6 000 organisations, but in 2001, SIOS and CEDIOC identified 3 846 and 10 852 respectively (PROCURA, 2001). The important differences among these results demonstrate that today it is still not possible to determine accurately the total number of these organisations in Mexico. Because almost all organisations are unable to conduct yearly research, carrying out inter-temporal analysis is extremely difficult. There is, therefore, an obstacle to measuring the growth rate of the third sector in Mexico. SIOS also reports that out of 3 846, 30 per cent work at local level, 10 per cent in municipalities, 16 per cent regionally, 16 per cent in states, 22 per cent at country level, and six per cent internationally. Although there is some data about Mexico City regarding funding, this type of information is scarce and incomplete.

Of course, it is unlikely that there are only 3 846 organisations in Mexico. This number was obtained from the detailed examination of 16 000 records (5 000 in Mexico City and 11 000 in the remaining states of the country). The detailed examination process implied important problems in the quality of information. Overcoming these problems is a necessary condition in determining the real magnitude of civil organisations in Mexico.

## Regulatory issues of civil organisations

Civil organisations in Mexico have two main legal forms: Private Assistance Institutions (IAPs) or Civil Associations (ACs). They are both comprised of individuals who share a non-profit purpose, subject to differentiated fiscal treatment. Even though these two legal forms of civil organisations are the most common in Mexico, the legal framework that regulates them presents uncertainties that impede clear distinctions of their characteristics. This causes problems for civil organisations in accessing privileges originally intended for their own promotion.

One of the main distinctions between these two types of legal forms is that they are supervised by different authorities. The IAPs must be registered by a Private Assistance Board (JAP), which acts as a representative intermediary between the IAP and the Ministry of Finance. They can be constituted as foundations or associations. There is a JAP in every state of the country responsible for the supervision of the IAPs' proper functioning, including the review of their activities and resource allocation reports. For this reason, IAPs are regarded as less autonomous. Contrary to IAPs, ACs are not accountable to any authority other than the Ministry of Finance. They enjoy a higher degree of autonomy, but are subject to a more rigid set of requirements to access the same fiscal privileges. The other primary distinction between IAPs and ACs is that the latter are regulated by the Civil Codes of each federal state instead of the Private Assistance Law, which determines the IAPs' responsibilities.

Federal and state governments provide fiscal incentives to ACs and IAPs through tax exemptions, subsidies and tax reductions. The activities eligible to receive these incentives are rigorously specified, according to criteria that are not suitable to the current spectrum of civil organisations' activities. It is for this reason that a large number of organisations are excluded from fiscal privileges and other benefits. The following table summarises the fiscal treatment for both Civil Associations and Private Assistance Institutions.

In addition to the fiscal treatment, the federal government has launched the Program of Public Debt Exchange to Support High Social Impact Projects, "Social Swaps". The objective is to promote the participation of civil organisations implementing projects of high social impact in education,

Table 4.1.   **Summary of similarities and differences in the fiscal treatment to Civil Associations and Private Assistance Institutions**

| Concept | Civil Associations (AC) | Private Assistance Institutions (IAP) |
|---|---|---|
| Similarities: | | |
| – Accounting reports presentation | Yes | Yes |
| – Pay the VAT | Yes | Yes |
| – IRS exemptions | Yes | Yes |
| – Emit deductible receipts | Yes | Yes |
| – Present tax retention declarations on wages, fees and leasing | Yes | Yes |
| – Tax exemptions in some states | Yes | Yes |
| Differences: | | |
| Procedure with the fiscal authority | ACs undertake the complete procedure | The Private Assistance Board (JAP) is in charge of the procedure |
| – Present accounting information to the fiscal authority | Yes | No, it is presented by the JAP |
| – Present a fiscal report of their financial situation to the fiscal authority | Yes | No, it is presented by the JAP |
| – Payment of rights and uses | Yes | No |
| – Present a declaration to the fiscal authority on the donations received | Yes | No, it is presented by the JAP |

Note:   Table based on information from "Las instituciones filantrópicas, asociaciones civiles e instituciones de asistencia privada", CEMEFI (2000), Legal, 1, Mexico.

health, poverty, agriculture or environment. The programme is designed to exchange foreign debt for internal debt in favour of civil organisations. An organisation may pay to a creditor a discounted amount of the government's external debt in dollars. This amount is then paid in full by the government to the civil organisation in national currency. Therefore, the amount of the discount goes directly to support the organisation's activities. In 2000 and 2001, the budget for social swaps was over 150 million dollars in each year.

## Challenges and final remarks

The democratic transition of Mexico has meant the emergence of valuable opportunities to solve policy debates that have been at the core of a difficult relationship with civil organisations. It seems today that the willingness to achieve collaboration between the government and the civil organisations has reached a positive momentum that had not been possible in the previous decades.

The first sign of this compliance took place during President Zedillo's administration, when the National Development Plan 1994-2000 officially recognised, for the first time ever, that civil organisations were important factors for the social development of Mexico. The Plan, which is constitutionally mandated and represents the most relevant government agenda at the beginning of each administration, identified civil organisations as autonomous entities contributing with high civic value to the design of public policies. The need for creating an adequate legal framework to regulate and promote third sector activities was also recognised. Today, however, this framework has still not been created.

In this sense, one of the main challenges for the Mexican government is to encourage a new institutional design that clearly defines formal and functional ways of interacting with civil organisations. Although informal links and occasional collaboration may help to build up a more solid public sphere, to consolidate a reliable relationship between government and civil organisations there must be certainty about the level of commitment. Regarding these pending tasks, the government agenda should include the following topics:

● Clarifying the fiscal regime of civil organisations.

● Consolidating formal schemes for collaboration in projects within government programmes.

● Assisting them to improve their own information quality.

● Regulating project evaluation standards that help to understand the degree of their social impact.

Regarding civil organisations, despite their interests to influence both the quality of citizenship and the policy process, they are still working in isolation from each other and are reluctant to face their accountability challenge. The deep public recognition that civil organisations currently enjoy implies the responsibility of overcoming conflicts among them, and consolidating the effectiveness of their practices. Therefore, organisations should consider the following:

● Fostering their collaboration with for-profit organisations.

● Publishing their financial statements to fulfil accountability gaps.

● Improving their effectiveness through the evaluation of their results and performance.

In summary, more efforts need to be engaged by both the government and civil organisations themselves so that their role and contribution to the social and economic development of Mexico be fully recognised.

PART II

# Financing the Non-profit Sector: Obstacles and Opportunities

ISBN 92-64-19953-5
The Non-profit Sector in a Changing Economy
© OECD 2003

PART II

# Chapter 5

# New Trends in Financing the Non-profit Sector in the United States: The Transformation of Private Capital – Reality or Rhetoric ?

by

Caroline Williams,
The Nathan Cummings Foundation, New York, USA

## Introduction

The non-profit sector in the United States is a diverse group of small and large organisations, covering a wide range of services and interests. Their funding sources range from small, individual contributions to multi-million dollar government contracts. Some have significant fee-for-service sources of revenue; most do not. A very few are able to access the commercial financial markets; most non-profit organisations, like small for-profit businesses, are too small or financially unstable to attract commercial funding. Almost all non-profit organisations rely to some extent on private capital, usually in the form of charitable contributions.

This diverse group of non-profit organisations is linked by several realities that have a substantial impact on their access to private capital.

The first is the strict definition under US tax law. While there may be some blurring of boundaries between the non-profit and for-profit sectors – by "social investors", tax law draws a much clearer line. Organisations that qualify under Section 501(c)(3) of the Internal Revenue Service Code as non-profit organisations are exempt from paying taxes. However, they are limited in their activities to charitable purposes that provide a public benefit. The tax law separates public benefit and private benefit, and provides very different incentive structures for charitable contributions and for investment. Donors to non-profit organisations can immediately deduct the contribution for income tax purposes. This is to encourage "investment" in public benefit activities. Investors in for-profit businesses do not get a tax deduction unless the business ultimately fails. The incentive is the potential for significant private benefit in the form of profits. These differences shape private funding sources and how non-profits, in turn, shape themselves in order to attract private capital.

The second is the amount and character of wealth in the United States. Federal government programmes were the engines for growth for the non-profit sector in the 1960s. However, as the government moved to downsize, the non-profit sector turned more of its attention to private wealth – to the industrial wealth created after World War II and most recently to the "new wealth" created in the "irrationally exuberant" stock market of the second half of the 1990s.

The new wealth became the new model for business development. Some saw a new paradigm, a new economy. Technology was fuelling change. Capital was readily available, particularly venture capital to fund new ideas. It seemed that entrepreneurship was the key to success and that private capital would easily follow. The non-profit sector took notice. Venture philanthropy and social entrepreneurship became heralded as the new paradigm for the non-profit sector even if these terms were not well defined. Venture philanthropy was originally coined by Christine Letts at Harvard to suggest that philanthropists should act more like venture capitalists, by funding organisational growth and development instead of restricted funding for specific projects and/or limited periods (see Letts *et al.*, 1997). The concept evolved, though, to suggest that venture capitalists and the newly wealthy entrepreneurs would adopt a new style of philanthropy. The term social entrepreneurship was adopted by the non-profit sector as well. The interpretation used in this chapter is that of a business model that seeks to incorporate social values and objectives into for-profit business operations (compare with Borzaga and Santuari in this volume). This evolved into a theoretical framework for evaluating social benefit as well as financial benefit.

The stage seemed to be set for a new model of philanthropic investing – one combining business and values, investment and philanthropy. The expectation was of an enlightened investor who, instead of giving a major gift to a museum and continuing to do traditional investing, would now consider total return. The new model could be applied to for-profit and non-profit organisations alike. This new investor might accept a lower financial return on an investment in a for-profit organisation in exchange for it generating demonstrated social returns. Similarly, he might fund a non-profit organisation's business-like venture. The organisation's tax status would not be as important as its mission.

The irrationally exuberant stock market ended in April 2000. Since then the United States has been hit by the "failure" of the dot.com industry, the terrorist attacks of 11 September, and major accounting and governance scandals in the corporate sector. There are significant repercussions from these events for both the non-profit sector and the for-profit sector:

- The "new wealth" is diminished, although not gone. Private capital is more cautious for now.
- Business methods and venture capital are no longer seen as "silver bullet" solutions. Perhaps not everything lends itself to market solutions.
- There is now a heightened attention to business methods themselves. Some are beginning to believe that the almost single-minded focus on near-term shareholder returns distorts some bigger, ethical issues.

What will this new caution and concern mean for the non-profit sector and the funding of issues traditionally addressed by the non-profit sector? The possibilities include:

- A continuation of the expectations of the late 1990s with private "capital" becoming a major source of funding for both non-profit organisations and for-profit entities that address social issues. In this scenario the mission of the organisation will be more important than its tax status.

- A continuation of the more traditional model of keeping philanthropy and investment separate. In this scenario, for-profit organisations seeking to be agents of social change at the expense of financial return will not be able to attract private capital and non-profit organisations will not attract substantial new funding by adopting business-like approaches.

- A more complicated blend of organisations and capital, one that seeks commercial and non-commercial sources of capital from a variety of sources and utilises new organisational structures to meet the objectives of each capital source.

- A new look at the ethical conduct of organisations.

In order to explore these possibilities this chapter will look first at overall revenue trends in the non-profit sector for indications of changes in funding sources. This will include trends in the growth of foundations, which are both recipients of private capital and funders of non-profit organisations.

The chapter will then look at sources of private investment capital both for non-profit organisations and for for-profit ventures that seek to address social issues. These sources include venture capital, commercial debt, and non-commercial debt. The chapter will look at what seem to be the emerging trends of aggregation of capital and use of intermediaries of sufficient size to access commercial markets. It is particularly interesting to note how these sources of private capital are increasingly being used in combination with non-commercial funding from foundations and government agencies.

The chapter raises questions about limitations and appropriateness of the basic business model that the new philanthropy seeks to adopt. Much of the new philanthropy language comes from venture capital and its focus on internal rate of return ("IRR"), the rate of return to investors. The language expands the concept to external rate of return ("ERR"), the external social benefit. The new philanthropy assumes that this societal benefit can be calculated and financial-like trade-offs can be made to maximise total return. However, this focus on financial calculus and rates of return, without a broader ethical framework of governance and accountability, may be too limited. A new trend now emerging in the United States, one that could have far reaching implications for both the non-profit and for-profit sectors, is to address these limitations through shareholder initiatives.

## Revenue trends in the non-profit sector

The full tax-exempt sector in the United States is a diverse group of small and large organisations, covering a wide range of services and interests. It can be characterised in four segments: public-serving organisations, foundations, member-serving organisations and religious organisations. Because public-serving organisations are the primary focus of this chapter, the term "non-profit" as used herein refers only to that segment. Foundations are also discussed because of the significant role they play in new trends in financing non-profit organisations. Of particular note is their substantial growth in recent years.

As of 1999 there were approximately 170 000 non-profit organisations (as defined above) with at least one employee (Urban Institute, unpublished data). Total revenue for these organisations was $685 billion. Social service organisations account for 40 per cent of the number of organisations but only 13 per cent of the revenues. Healthcare accounts for 58 per cent of the revenues, but only 17 per cent of the organisations.

### Health care organisations

The health care segment is dominant in terms of non-profit revenues, but it is often not thought of as part of the traditional non-profit sector. This is because its funding comes largely from fees for service paid for by private and

Figure 5.1.   **Composition of the non-profit sector, 1999**

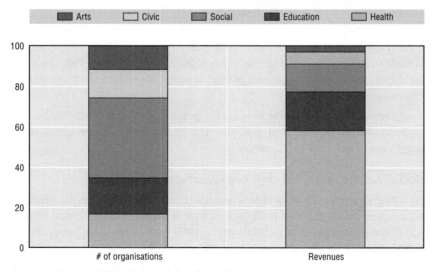

*Source:* Data is unpublished data from the Urban Institute. The data is an update to their published data series through 1997. See Lampkin and Pollak (2002), "The New Non-profit Almanac and Desk Reference."

government insurance programmes. The health care segment is of interest, though, because of its transformation over the last decade in order to access commercial capital.

In the 1980s and 1990s a combination of the need for substantial capital investment to update facilities and technology, the financial success of for-profit health care organisations, and the availability of commercial capital, resulted in a major shift of health care from the non-profit sector to the for-profit sector. For-profit organisations could raise the capital needed to buy non-profit health care organisations and to upgrade them. The result was a shift to for-profit activity and, secondarily, a transfer of non-profit assets into newly-created foundations.

Non-profit law states that assets held in the form of non-profit organisations cannot revert to for-profit status. Therefore, when a health care facility or organisation is purchased by a for-profit entity, the physical assets and operations may now be operated as a for-profit organisation for the financial benefit of the new owners, but the monetary value of those assets and operations must stay in the non-profit sector. These "conversions" have generally been accomplished through the creation of new foundations to receive the money paid for the assets.

Grantmakers in Health, an association of foundation officers, has identified 165 organisations that have received assets from conversions (Grantmakers in Health, "Assets for Health…" report). Most of these have been created since 1994. Total assets now exceed $15.3 billion. These organisations are now expected to distribute approximately $750 million annually.

The significance of this is that for-profit capital has been utilised to, i) fund a service usually thought of as part of the non-profit sector, and, ii) to transform physical assets in the non-profit sector into cash. This cash is now held in grant-making organisations for future distribution to other non-profit organisations.

These two concepts – accessing for-profit capital and funds accumulating in foundations for future use in the non-profit sector – now occur in other segments of the non-profit sector.

## Social service, arts and civic organisations

Social service, civic[1] and arts organisations are what are typically thought of as comprising the non-profit sector in the United States. These numbered approximately 110 000 organisations in 1999 with revenues of approximately $154 billion. This was almost a ten-fold increase in revenues since 1977 (see Lampkin and Pollak, 2002). The following figures and tables illustrate some of the trends in revenue growth from 1977 to 1999. The arts segment has had the

Figure 5.2.   **Indexed growth in non-profit revenues, 1977-1999**

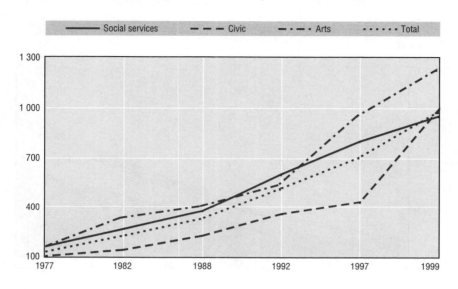

*Source:* All of the data is from the Urban Institute. The data for 1977 through 1997 is from Lampkin and Pollak (2002), "The New Non-profit Almanac and Desk Reference." The 1999 data is unpublished.

strongest growth over the full period, while civic organisations have shown the strongest growth in the late 1990s.

The Urban Institute data on sources of revenue is grouped into four categories: "Government"; "Fees and dues"; "Private revenues"; and "Other revenues". "Fees and dues" include fees for programme service. Because the categorisation of government fees changed in 1999, "Government", and "Fees and dues" are grouped together in the chart below, but are shown separately in the table at the end of the section. "Private revenues" includes contributions – "philanthropic capital" – to non-profit organisations, including new foundations. "Other revenues" includes earned income and investment income.

Overall the data shows growth in all of the revenue categories and seemingly little change in the mix of revenues. However, "Other revenues" almost doubles from seven per cent to 13 per cent of total revenues, which is significant in terms of incremental funding. This is confirmed by an IRS study which showed that in 1997, even after subtracting all exempted income, charities received $4.2 billion from outside business dealings – more than

Figure 5.3.   **Contributions to revenues, 1977-1999**

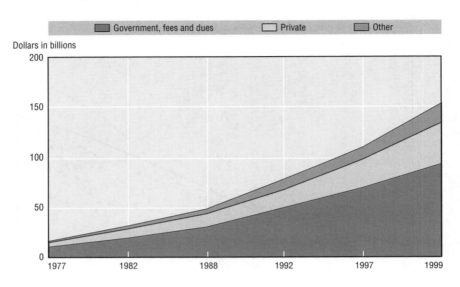

*Source:* All of the data is from the Urban Institute. The data for 1977 through 1997 is from Lampkin and Pollak (2002), "The New Non-profit Almanac and Desk Reference." The 1999 data is unpublished.

double the total in 1990 (Lipman and Schwinn, 2001). "Other revenues" has been particularly important for arts organisations, accounting for approximately 20 per cent of revenues throughout the period, reflecting the segment's early development of earned income operations.

The significant growth of "Other revenues" for civic organisations from 10 per cent to 22 per cent of revenues reflects the substantial growth of funds coming into foundations, which is discussed in the following section.

## *Foundations*

Foundations occupy a unique space in the non-profit sector. While we tend to think of foundations as funders of non-profit organisations, under US tax law they are, themselves, non-profit organisations as well. Dollars contributed to foundation endowments are permanently transferred from the private sector to the non-profit sector. Trends in the development of foundations may have future implications for funding of non-profit organisations.

Foundation assets were $486.1 billion in 2000, an 8.4 per cent increase from 1999. This growth was relatively modest, following five years of double-

Figure 5.4.   **Percentage of non-profit revenues, 1977-1999**

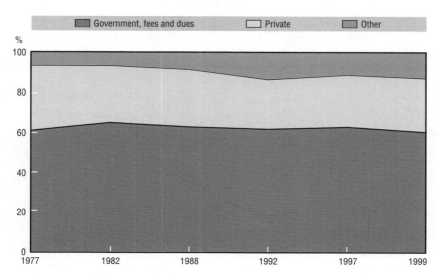

*Sources:* All of the data is from the Urban Institute. The data for 1977 through 1997 is from Lampkin and Pollak (2002), "The New Non-profit Almanac and Desk Reference." The 1999 data is unpublished.

digit growth, but substantial in light of the drop in the US stock markets in mid-2000 (see Foundation Today, 2001). Stock market returns until mid-2000 were a major reason for the growth in foundation assets. Another significant factor, though, has been the creation and funding of new foundations.[2]

● Over two-fifths (41%) of larger foundations were established after 1996.

● New gifts and grants to foundations slipped from $32.1 billion in 1999 to $27.6 billion (in 2000). Nonetheless, these new gifts from donors in 2000 totalled more than two and a-half times the $10.3 billion in gifts reported in 1995.

● The largest foundation in the United States, the Bill and Melinda Gates Foundation with $23.3 billion in assets, did not exist 10 years ago.

A corollary to the growth in foundations is the emergence of charitable gift funds, a non-profit sector version of the aggregation of investment capital into mutual funds (see Williams, 1998). Pioneered by Fidelity, the mutual fund management company, these vehicles allow individuals to make tax-deductible contributions to a foundation-like entity. The donor/investor controls how the funds are invested and can make grants to non-profit groups

Figure 5.5.   **"Other revenues" as a percentage of total revenues,**
**1977-1999**

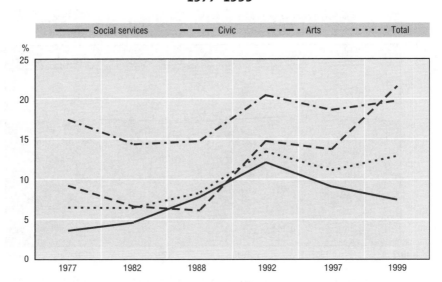

Source: All of the data is from the Urban Institute. The data for 1977 through 1997 is
from Lampkin and Pollak (2002), "The New Non-profit Almanac and Desk
Reference." The 1999 data is unpublished.

from these investment funds at their discretion. What is noteworthy is the
rapid growth of these funds. Fidelity launched the first such fund in 1992. It
now holds $3.5 billion in assets and received $735.9 million in donor-directed
grants in 2001. At least eight other funds have been started since 1997.

The sources of the private capital now coming into the new foundations
and gift-funds are individuals, from the post World War II industrial wealth
and "new wealth" created by the stock market boom of the late 1990s. As a
result foundations are serving as the "aggregators" of capital from individuals.

### Possible trends

Non-profit organisations are finding ways to access private, commercial
capital through structural changes such as health care conversions. Other
revenue sources such as earned income may be increasingly important. These
trends would seem to support the concept that more business-like approaches
are benefiting the non-profit sector. What does this mean for individual non-
profit organisations, and for-profit organisations with a social mission,
seeking private capital? What are the mechanisms for accessing capital and

Table 5.1. **The traditional non-profit sector in the United States**

| Revenue growth and sources of revenues | 1977 | 1982 | 1988 | 1992 | 1997 | 1999 |
|---|---|---|---|---|---|---|
| **Revenues ($ in billions)** | | | | | | |
| Social services | 10.3 | 20.4 | 32.2 | 55.9 | 76.9 | 92.0 |
| Civic | 4.2 | 5.8 | 9.4 | 14.7 | 17.9 | 41.8 |
| Arts | 1.7 | 4.8 | 6.0 | 8.2 | 15.4 | 20.0 |
| Total | 16.2 | 31.0 | 47.6 | 78.8 | 110.2 | 153.8 |
| **Government as % of total** | | | | | | |
| Social services | 54 | 55 | 48 | 50 | 52 | 24 |
| Civic | 50 | 50 | 48 | 33 | 30 | 16 |
| Arts | 12 | 17 | 15 | 15 | 10 | 11 |
| Total | 49 | 48 | 44 | 43 | 43 | 20 |
| **Fees and dues as % of total** | | | | | | |
| Social services | 10 | 15 | 19 | 18 | 19 | 51 |
| Civic | 12 | 14 | 13 | 20 | 21 | 24 |
| Arts | 29 | 29 | 30 | 24 | 28 | 30 |
| Total | 12 | 17 | 19 | 19 | 20 | 41 |
| **Private as % of total** | | | | | | |
| Social services | 32 | 25 | 25 | 20 | 20 | 18 |
| Civic | 29 | 29 | 33 | 31 | 35 | 38 |
| Arts | 41 | 40 | 40 | 40 | 44 | 40 |
| Total | 32 | 28 | 28 | 24 | 25 | 26 |
| **Other as % of total** | | | | | | |
| Social services | 4 | 5 | 8 | 12 | 9 | 8 |
| Civic | 10 | 7 | 6 | 15 | 14 | 22 |
| Arts | 18 | 15 | 15 | 21 | 19 | 20 |
| Total | 7 | 7 | 9 | 14 | 11 | 13 |

Source: All of the data is from the Urban Institute. The data for 1977 through 1997 is from Lampkin and Pollak (2002), "The New Non-profit Almanac and Desk Reference". The 1999 data is unpublished.

how widely are they available? The next section looks at various sources of capital for any organisation:

● Operating surpluses including non-profit organisations' earned income strategies and profits from for-profit subsidiaries.

● Venture capital for for-profit entities including subsidiaries of non-profit organisations and stand-alone for-profit entities with a social mission.

● Commercial debt.

● Non-commercial debt, particularly foundations.

● Blended structures that aggregate capital from various sources.

Another trend of note from the sector-wide data is the growth of new foundations. This would indicate that the new wealth is not yet funding social solutions through non-profit and for-profit organisations. Instead it is moving into endowments. As the new philanthropists define their interests and approaches, these new foundations may have increasing influence on programmatic and financing trends for the non-profit organisations. What do we know about these new philanthropists so far? The next section examines charitable giving in Silicon Valley, the area of California considered the centre of new technology, new wealth and new philanthropy.

## New financing trends

The preceding discussion of trends in revenue sources for the non-profit sector is meant to set the framework for considering new trends in financing for individual non-profit organisations. As such it identified possibly contradictory trends – use of commercial capital and more business-like approaches as well as capital moving into the traditional structures of foundations. We will now look at each of these in more detail and at examples of applications.[3]

### Business-like approaches – Earned income strategies and for-profit subsidiaries

Operating surpluses from earned income activities are the most flexible form of financing an organisation can have. There are no restrictions on the use of these funds, no repayment obligations and no issues of outside investors exercising control. However, they are typically not major sources of funding, not sufficient in size to fund new initiatives or capital requirements. They can, though, provide that extra margin of working capital to allow an organisation some operating flexibility.

The new paradigm of venture philanthropy and social entrepreneurship looks to business-like approaches and ways for non-profit organisations to generate operating surpluses so that they become more self-sufficient financially. In the past this usually meant a relatively small operation related to the core activity of the organisation, such as a museum gift shop, that could generate a modest net profit, i.e. "earned-income", to help support the non-profit. Today the concept is being applied more broadly to encompass establishing more sizeable business operations. These may or may not be related to the core activity of the organisation and the objective may be simply to generate a profit to be reinvested in the organisation. To protect the tax status of the non-profit organisation these new businesses may be incorporated separately as for-profit subsidiaries. The use of for-profit entities may also facilitate raising capital from commercial investors in order to launch and/or expand an operating business.

How widespread is this new approach? The 1999 data from the Urban Institute did not yet indicate major growth in this area. What then is the anecdotal evidence?

In the autumn of 2000, the Pew Charitable Trust commissioned a study of "the landscape of enterprise in the non-profit sector" (see Massarsky and Beinhacker, 2002). Carried out by means of a volunteer survey, the results likely overstate the level of activity because of the respondents being self-selecting. Nevertheless the results are informative if somewhat sobering. The overall finding was that the trend to venture has increased significantly over the past twenty years as more and more non-profit organisations explore revenue-generating opportunities. The movement toward income generation by non-profits continues to grow. Some of these ventures succeed, yet many more fail to meet either their social or financial goals.

Some of the facts and trends noted in the report on the survey include the following:

- Arts and culture organisations are more likely to operate earned-income ventures than other types of organisations. Among the organisations responding – the following percentages being operating ventures – 60 per cent are arts and culture organisations, 47 per cent are health organisations; 43 per cent are health services organisations, 43 per cent are public society organisations, 42 per cent are environmental groups, 33 per cent are educational institutions and only 26 per cent are religious organisations.

- Service-related ventures are the predominant type of earned-income ventures operated by the non-profit organisations responding to the survey. Seventy-four per cent of those operating ventures are currently running service-related ventures; 47 per cent are operating product-related enterprises; 26 per cent are renting and leasing properties; 15 per cent are running cause-related marketing projects.

- A greater percentage of non-profits that are renting or leasing properties are generating a surplus than those that are running service-related, product-related, or cause-marketing ventures.

- Budget size, the number of employees in a non-profit running an earned-income venture, and the age of the organisation appear to be important factors that influence the financial success of a venture. The majority of the non-profits operating ventures that are turning a profit have budgets of more than $12 million, retain more than 21 employees, and are more than 11 years old.

- Financial return – be it generating income for programmes, moving toward greater self-sufficiency or diversifying revenue streams – is the primary reason why more than half of the non-profits launch profit-making ventures.

● But financial return is not the only motivation. Thirty-nine per cent of those operating business ventures say their businesses also serve their constituents by providing employment, training, and therapeutic opportunities. Thirty-four per cent claim that the ventures generate positive community relations, and 23 per cent say the ventures help to revitalise the neighbourhood and community.

● The lack of financial resources to operate a venture and the lack of personnel resources to develop and manage the venture are the main reasons why organisations have never ventured, or shut down their operation.

### Examples of earned income strategies

The example often cited of a successful business enterprise owned by a non-profit organisation is the direct market catalogue business that was part of the Minnesota Public Radio organisation.

**Minnesota Public Radio (MPR).**   MPR built a direct marketing catalogue company originally based on selling items connected with its successful radio show. Over time it grew the business substantially by selling unrelated products. With revenues of almost $200 million the business generated several million dollars per year of operating surplus for MPR in the form of royalties and other income. When MPR sold the business in 1998, the $123 million sale price created an endowment for MPR. This example oversimplifies what is, in fact a large, complicated organisational structure with several layers of non-profit and for-profit entities. It evolved and grew to be a substantial unrelated business over time.

The following are three examples of more typical earned income strategies, all closely related to the non-profit's core activities.

**Exit Art.**   This small interdisciplinary arts organisation showcases new works by emerging artists and sells works in a small area of its cramped offices. This earned income operation generates approximately $25 000 per year. With the Internet e-commerce boom, Exit Art saw an opportunity to use technology to expand this operation through an on-line catalogue. Management estimated that with a $250 000 investment it could generate an operating surplus of $250 000. They sought a grant to fund this, which is a good example of venture philanthropy. However, this initiative has not gone forward, essentially because the end of the dot.com boom meant that efforts were concentrated on other matters.

**OperaAmerica.**   This service organisation was given the opportunity to purchase a for-profit company that sold opera videos. The seller agreed to payment over 10 years. OperaAmerica saw this as an opportunity to develop a net income stream of $100 000-$200 000 per year and, more importantly, to expand its educational services to the public. Changes in technology and the recording industry hurt the business model so that the for-profit operation has been dissolved. However, the experience gave the organisation experience of running a business. The remaining video sales business is now part of OperaAmerica's more successful on-line distance learning service.

**Independent Press Association (IPA).**   This organisation supports the independent press and the ability to express diverse views. It recently purchased a small distributor of independent magazines using a below-market interest rate loan from a foundation to finance the acquisition. This form of financing is discussed later in the chapter. It is too soon to judge the financial success of this deal done in 2001. IPA's current objectives for the business are to expand the number of titles it handles, an important part of IPA's mission, and to have the operation break even. Any operating surplus to help fund the organisation is yet to come.

Generating operating surpluses from earned income is not a new financing strategy in the non-profit sector. Its use has been mostly in the arts segment and the earned income operations have generally been relatively small in scale and closely related to the core activity of the organisation. One change is that this strategy is now spreading beyond the arts segment. The more notable change is the discussion of sizeable business operations, some in the form of for-profit enterprises. One of the issues this raises is management expertise. In each of the three examples above, a policy/service organisation had to run a product sales business and deal with inventory, receivables and payables. Each organisation would acknowledge that it was not well prepared to run a business.

This need for business-management assistance was also a conclusion of the Pew study. As a result of the study, the Pew Charitable Trust, the Yale School of Management and The Goldman Sachs Foundation launched the Partnership on Non-profit Ventures. The objective is to create "a marketplace to bring together the best of academic research and field practice to help support the efforts of non-profits in building new ventures". The Partnership is also launching a National Business Plan Competition for Non-profit Organisations. While business plan competitions have emerged in the entrepreneurship programmes of various business schools over the last five years, this is the first one for non-profit organisations. Its purpose is to "assist non-profit organisations in starting or substantially expanding successful profit-making ventures."

Another issue faced by non-profit organisations looking to establish or expand earned income strategies is the need for investment capital, money to invest in organisational structures and systems, to finance inventory and receivables, and to cover operating expenses until the enterprise turns profitable. The next sections, then, will explore the availability of investment capital, starting with commercial capital that is later transformed into non-commercial capital.

### Socially-responsible venture capital

Venture capital and socially-responsible investing were much talked about investment strategies in the late 1990s in the United States. This led some to think that there were substantial amounts of venture capital available for socially-responsible venture-stage companies. This concept fits with the new paradigm language of social entrepreneurship and venture philanthropy.

However, at the height of the venture capital market in the late 1990s there was not any meaningful overlap between these two spheres. Almost all of the venture capital was going into technology and the Internet. In contrast the case had not been made on any scale that venture-stage companies, which also focused on a social mission, would generate competitive investment returns.

Venture capitalists are financial investors who are in it for the money. They take big risks in exchange for the prospect of big financial returns. If problems arise, the venture capitalist may take an active – occasionally ruthless – role in management, changing business plans and replacing management. Investments that don't work are quickly sold or liquidated. Investments that do work are also sold, in whole or in part, so that the financial investors can realise their returns. This is not the model of venture philanthropy described by Letts et al. It does not hold the mission sacred and it means that the sponsoring non-profit organisation or social entrepreneur is likely to lose control in the future.

Socially-responsible investing in the United States has been limited primarily to individual investors. There is one group, Investors' Circle, which has worked for 10 years to promote this field. Investors' Circle is not an investment fund, but rather a network of approximately 150 individual investors. These are dedicated to facilitating the flow of capital to private companies that deliver commercial solutions to social and environmental problems. Behind each of the members' investments is the belief that business – not government or philanthropy – must lead the transition to a sustainable economy (see *www.investorscircle.net*). Since 1992, Investors' Circle has facilitated the flow of over $80 million to 120 socially responsible companies and small venture funds. This is less than one million dollars per company. Total funds invested over a decade are less than amounts invested by most venture capital firms in a single year or deal.

When discussing the concept of socially-responsible venture capital some point to several funds that have been established: Women's Growth

Capital: $30 million; Coastal Ventures: $5.5 million; Northeast Ventures: $15 million; and Sustainable Jobs Fund: $17 million. All of these funds are small by venture capital standards and all include some form of government programme capital, either Small Business Administration funds or the Community Financial Institutions Fund. The second is discussed later in this chapter.

In terms of stand-alone socially-responsible venture capital there are two. Solstice Capital was founded in 1995 with $23 million to focus on information technology, energy and medical opportunities. It has been successful, as were many technology funds during this period. The other is Commons Capital. With support from Investors' Circle members, Commons Capital raised $12 million in 2000-2001 for its first fund. Its target return rates of 15-20 per cent are below conventional venture funds' target rates, but respectable if met. Almost one and a half years later, it has invested only 25 per cent of its committed capital. As a result it may be another five years or more before initial investment results are known and a track record of successful investment returns on socially-responsible venture capital may be demonstrated.

### Examples of socially-responsible venture capital

Following are three examples of early-stage companies that did raise venture capital funds. Two were started and operated by non-profit organisations; the other is a stand-alone for-profit company that incorporates a social mission into its business.

**Big City Forest.**   This business recycled wooden shipping pallets into flooring, panelling and furniture. Founded by a 20-year old community development organisation it offered environmental advantages and provided employment in the Bronx. The founder served as the president and driving force of both entities. Originally funded with loans from the non-profit parent organisation the for-profit subsidiary sought five million dollars of expansion capital through the sale of 50 per cent ownership. However, when the founder became ill, investors would not provide financing for a young organisation without top management. The outcome was that the foundations that had long supported the non-profit parent organisation decided to liquidate and shut-down both the for-profit and the non-profit organisations.

**Production Designer.**   This for-profit entity was formed by a non-profit theatre company to commercialise multi-media technology that it had developed. The target market was small and medium-sized theatre companies. It found, instead, that there is a potentially large commercial market for use in trade show exhibits. With the change in the business model, it has been able to raise venture capital funds. The outcome was that the product is still offered to small theatres at a discount. However, the objective now is to grow the company as quickly as possible and to sell it. This will allow commercial investors to realise a return on investment and the founding non-profit theatre to create an endowment.

**Organic Commodity Products (OCP).**    This organic chocolate company incorporates sustainable agriculture and fair trade practices in its for-profit business model. It has been able to raise two million dollars of venture capital funding, primarily from individual investors and one million dollars in the form of a non-commercial loan from a foundation. This unique blending of capital serves the objectives of all parties. Like most venture-stage companies OCP has found that market development is usually slower than projected and some management changes were required. Not yet profitable, it is finding it difficult to raise additional capital.

Just as we saw in the earned income area, business management skills are needed in the for-profit, socially-responsible venture capital market as well. Again business schools are beginning to focus on this. Similarly to Yale co-sponsoring the first business plan competition for non-profit organisations, the Haas School of Business at the University of California, Berkley recently held the first Social Ventures Business Plan Competition.

There is also the need for investment capital. In the late 1990s it seemed that venture capital was readily available for almost any entrepreneur with a good idea. However, socially-responsible venture capital is, in fact, a very small segment of the commercial capital universe in the United States. In recent years traditional venture capital has gone almost exclusively to the "hot" areas of technology and the Internet. Today the professional venture capitalists are faced with triage, deciding which of their existing investments to support and which to simply close. The net result is that there has been little private capital for any new venture-stage companies for the past two years.

As far as the new paradigm of trade-off investing (investors who would recognise the social returns and factor them into the total return calculation) is concerned, three obstacles can be identified:

- Individual investors have learned that start-up enterprises are not easy after all. The IRR or financial return part of the total return calculation is uncertain because financial projections may not be realised.

- The ERR or social benefit part of the calculation is even more difficult because it is mostly theory. Work has been done to develop an analytical framework for social returns (see Emerson, 2000). However, little has been done to actually quantify these returns. Until standard methodologies are developed, tested and broadly accepted, total return will not be a meaningful investment concept.

● Even if investors had confidence in the components of the total return calculation, there is still the tax law, which sharply divides the non-profit and for-profit sector. The reality for the individual investor is that grants are tax-deductible, but poor performing investments are not. Making a grant (with the related tax benefit) and a separate traditional investment will usually result in a greater total (financial and social) return than making a lower return socially-responsible investment (Williams, 2001).

In the aftermath of the venture capital technology boom – and bust – with little venture capital funding now available in general, it is highly unlikely that substantial commercial venture capital will emerge to fund social missions. After looking at commercial debt markets the next sections of this chapter, then, will explore the availability of non-commercial capital.

### Commercial debt markets

In the United States there is a well-developed bond market that provides debt capital for large tax-exempt organisations. Hospitals, large educational institutions and large cultural institutions obtain financing in this market. However, the complexities and cost of accessing it are prohibitive for the vast majority of non-profit organisations. New approaches are being developed, though, to provide access to this market for the other non-profit organisations. Two organisations illustrate this new approach, both based on aggregating capital and expertise.

**National Housing Trust/Enterprise Preservation Corporation.**   NHT/ Enterprise is a national non-profit joint venture that develops and preserves affordable housing for low-income people. Its focus was on "Section 8" housing projects, a federal government programme that provided financing and rent subsidies for the development of apartment projects. Because of low commercial interest rates and the strong market demand for housing, many owners of Section 8 proprieties are now opting to refinance the federal loans and sell their properties into the commercial market.

NHT/Enterprise works with local non-profit organisations that will preserve the availability of housing on offer to low-income households. It assists them in negotiating and structuring tax-exempt bond financing to purchase and renovate the projects, sometimes aggregating several projects into one financing. In addition to expertise, it has also begun to provide capital directly, in some cases as subordinated debt to enhance the credit of the bonds being issued to the public and in some cases buying the property directly. During its first two years of operation NHT/Enterprise has assisted in the preservation and improvement of 2 600 housing units (see *www.nhtinc.org*).

In March 2001, NHT/Enterprise acquired Royal Oak Gardens Apartments, a 100-unit Section 8 subsidised property in North Carolina. The acquisition was financed with a HUD-insured mortgage, supplemented with financing from the John D. and Catherine T. MacArthur Foundation. The residents of Royal Oak endorsed NHT/Enterprise's purchase of the property and its application to HUD for assistance to keep their homes affordable.

During October 2001, NHT/Enterprise completed the largest-ever, multi-family bond transaction in the state of Texas. NHT/Enterprise acquired nearly 1 800 apartments in Dallas and Houston via a 501(c)(3) bond transaction. The Texas Affordable Housing Corporation issued $83 million in bonds for the transaction.

**Public Radio Capital (PRC).**   In 2001 over 1 000 radio stations were bought and sold in the United States as part of a major consolidation of radio ownership in recent years. This has led to a standardisation of content and lack of richness and diversity. Owner/operators of local "public" radio stations, typically 501(c)(3) organisations, have not had the capital to compete for these properties or to upgrade existing properties with state-of-the-art digital equipment.

Public Radio Capital (PRC) works with public broadcasters and educational institutions to evaluate and pursue opportunities for acquiring radio stations and for accessing tax-exempt financing. In some cases it will act as an intermediary by acquiring stations and entering into agreements with local stations to operate them. Its purpose is to expand public broadcasting services and, thereby, increase the radio format options in local communities. In its two years of operation PRC has worked with bond rating agencies to develop their understanding of the credit-worthiness of public radio operations and it has facilitated several transactions (see *www.pubcap.org*).

PRC helped Colorado Public Radio achieve the first ever investment grade credit rating in public broadcasting and obtain $6.5 million in revenue bonds for expansion of its two-channel state-wide system resulting in more service to more listeners. Furthermore, PRC represented Johns Hopkins University in the sale of its radio station for five million dollars to a newly-formed community group solely focused on the operation of public radio in metropolitan Baltimore. Finally, it also represented Nashville Public Radio in the acquisition and financing of an AM station and the refinancing of bonds issued for their construction, a total transaction of $5.5 million, and in the inauguration of a 24-hour public radio news service for listeners in Nashville.

The use by non-profit organisations (other than hospital and universities) of intermediaries to access commercial debt financing is a new development, but one with limitations. Both of these examples focus on providing commercial capital to non-profit organisations that are fairly sizeable and that have a fixed asset base. Smaller organisations, particularly service providers with few assets, will still not be able to access the commercial debt markets on this basis. Also, both of these pioneering organisations are themselves non-profit organisations. While they are developing market solutions, they are themselves dependent on non-commercial funding. The next sections then, will explore the availability of non-commercial capital.

### Non-commercial capital – Community development financial institutions

The primary vehicles in the United States for providing non-commercial capital to organisations dealing with social issues are Community Development Financial Institutions (CDFIs). These are private sector, for-profit and non-profit financial intermediaries that seek to meet the local communities' financing needs. There are over 500 CDFIs currently in the United States including over 200 loan funds, approximately 200 credit unions, 50 venture capital funds and approximately 40 banks (see *www.communitycapital.org*). While not new, CDFIs are playing an increasing role as both aggregators and providers of capital.

CDFIs are specialised financial institutions that work in market niches that have not been adequately served by traditional financial institutions. These CDFIs provide a wide range of financial products and services, including mortgage financing for first-time home-buyers, financing for needed community facilities, commercial loans and investments to start or expand small businesses, loans to rehabilitate rental housing, and financial services needed by low-income households and local businesses.

These organisations are defined as CDFIs by their being certified by, and qualifying for funding from, a federal government programme, the Community Development Financial Institutions (CDFI) Fund. The Fund's purpose is to provide financial incentives to increase private investment in these communities (see *www.cdfifund.gov*). The Fund provides relatively small infusions of capital to institutions that serve distressed communities and low-income individuals. The Fund's activities leverage private-sector investments from banks, foundations, and other funding sources. The Fund invests in CDFIs using flexible tools such as equity investments, loans, grants, and deposits, depending upon market and institutional needs. These needs are demonstrated by the applicant CDFI in its business plan and in its ability to raise comparable non-federal matching funds, both requirements of the application process. Since its creation, the Fund has made more than $534 million in awards (grants, loans and equity investments) to community development organisations and financial institutions.

Many of the organisations referred to as CDFIs were in operation before the federal certification and funding programme began. Recent data indicates, though, that CDFIs have become a major source of financing since the mid-1990s. National Community Capital, the association of these organisations, reports substantial growth in membership and in members' capital. Total capital was $1.794 billion at the end of the fiscal year in 2000, up 54 per cent from $1.168 billion in 1999. This represents the fourth year in a row of growth of over 50 per cent.

The following statistics are based on National Community Capital's 2000 statistical survey. The 2000 survey included 97 CDFIs ranging in capital size from less than $160 000 to more than $700 million. All figures are as at the fiscal year end in 2000:

- Total capital under management:               $1.8 billion
- Total cumulative financing:                  $2.9 billion
- Total financing outstanding:                 $1.3 billion
- Housing units financed cumulatively:       $121 194
- Businesses financed cumulatively:          $15 820
- Jobs created or retained cumulatively:      $141 122
- Community service organisations financed cumulatively:   $2 256

Of the $1.3 billion of financing outstanding, 91 per cent is in the form of relatively low cost loans. Housing is the major sector financed (see Table 5.2).

CDFIs are dependent on debt funds for their own capital. Of the total capital of $1.8 billion, $1.3 billion is borrowed. The sources are as follows: financial institutions: 33.3 per cent; foundations: 21.5 per cent; government: 5.6 per cent; religious institutions: 11.9 per cent; individuals: 6.6 per cent; corporations: 4.2 per cent; other: 7.0 per cent.

These figures indicate that the CDFI Fund has been successful in leveraging other sources of capital, particularly from banks and other financial institutions. A major reason for this is another federal programme, the Community Reinvestment Act (CRA) (see *www.ffiec.gov/cra*; see also Chapter 7 in this volume). The *www.ffiec.gov/cra* Community Reinvestment Act, enacted by Congress in 1977 and revised in 1995, is intended to encourage depository institutions to help meet the credit needs of the communities in

Table 5.2. **Breakdown of the loans by type of borrower, end of 2000**

| | Per cent of total | Average loan size (in $) | Interest rate (in %) | Term (months) |
|---|---|---|---|---|
| Housing | 43 | 120 660 | 6.3 | 113 |
| Business | 26 | 75 299 | 8.7 | 78 |
| Community services | 19 | 117 441 | 7.7 | 79 |
| Consumer | 8 | 2 181 | 8.5 | 31 |
| Micro-enterprise | 3 | 10 154 | 10.4 | 46 |

*Source:* National Community Capital Association (2002).

which they operate, including low- and moderate-income neighbourhoods, consistent with safe and sound banking operations. Loans, equity investments and grants to CDFIs generally qualify as required CRA credits.

The newest programme of the CDFI Fund is the New Markets Tax Credit (NMTC) Program. This is particularly aimed at raising equity capital for for-profit CDFIs by giving tax-credits to the investors. Under the NMTC Program the CDFI Fund will allocate tax credits to qualified CDFIs, which will then provide the credits to taxable investors who purchase equity interests in them. The Fund is authorised to issue tax credits to investors in connection with an aggregate of $15 billion in new equity raised. The tax credit provided to the investor will equal 39 per cent of the cost of the investment over a seven-year credit allowance period. Investors may not redeem their investments in Community Development Entities (CDEs) prior to the conclusion of the seven-year period. Financial institutions will likely be the major target market/ beneficiary of this government tax-credit programme.

As noted, CDFIs are the primary investment vehicles in the United States for providing non-commercial capital to non-profit and for-profit organisations dealing with social issues. Their growth has been the result of federal government programmes in the form of the relatively new CDFI Fund and the longer-standing Community Reinvestment Act. Through regulatory requirements and tax incentives they have used small amounts of government funding to leverage substantial funding from banks and other financial institutions. This has encouraged collaborations among for-profit and non-profit organisations and between commercial and non-commercial capital.

Foundations are also significant funders of CDFIs. Some foundations such as the John D. and Catherine T. MacArthur Foundation, which has been one of the leaders in this area, are now increasing their focus on CDFIs. There are two reasons for this: the community focus of the organisations, and also the increased leverage and impact the foundation can have by funding sizeable intermediaries.

### Non-commercial capital – Foundations

Foundation funding accounts for only about 10 per cent of total revenues of non-profit organisations, but it can make a critical difference in the operating flexibility of, and programmatic experimentation by, many non-profit organisations. Foundations may be the fastest growing providers of finance to the non-profit sector. The following information from the Foundation Center (Foundation Growth and Giving Estimates, 2001 Preview; and Foundation Today, 2001) illustrates this:

- "Giving by the nation's more than 56 000 grant-making foundations grew from $27.6 billion to an estimated $29.0 billion between 2000 and 2001."

- "Foundation giving has more than doubled since 1996, outdistancing growth in (direct) giving by individuals and corporations."

### Programme-related investments (PRIs)

While grants are the predominant form of funding by foundations, they are not the only form. As indicated in the earlier discussion of earned income, socially-responsible venture capital and CDFIs, foundations may also provide debt funding. In fact foundations can make non-commercial loans and equity investments to further programme objectives. This is a very small part of programme-related funding by foundations; $266.5 million in 1999 or approximately one per cent of foundation funding overall. However, it is a non-traditional form of funding both in structure and purpose.

The ability of foundations to make programme-related investments was established in the Tax Reform Act of 1969. To qualify, the investments must be shown to have a charitable purpose and effect and not to have financial return as an objective. In other words a PRI must have the same programme objectives as a grant and cannot be structured on commercial terms. In fact PRI loans typically carry below-market interest rates of one to three per cent. The few equity PRIs done – probably less than five per cent of all PRIs – are usually structured with a low fixed rate of return.

Grants and PRIs are made across a wide variety of programme areas, but with different areas of concentration. The most recent data on giving by the large foundations for 2000 shows that the major recipient categories are traditional ones, led by health and education ("Chronicle of Philanthropy", 4 April 2002). Information on PRI funding for 1999 indicates a different pattern

Table 5.3.   **Comparative use of grants and PRIs by programme area**

| Programme areas | Percentage of total dollar amount | |
| --- | --- | --- |
| | Grants (in %) | PRIs (in %) |
| Arts and culture | 12 | 10 |
| Education | 25 | 14 |
| Environment and animals | 7 | 8 |
| Health | 20 | 13 |
| Human services | 14 | 5 |
| *of which:* Housing | NA | 9 |
| International | 3 | NA |
| Public benefit | 11 | NA |
| *of which:* Community development | NA | 31 |
| Religion | 2 | 6 |
| Science and technology | 3 | 2 |
| Other | 3 | 2 |

Source: "The Chronicle of Philanthropy", 4 April 2002; Brody and Weiser (2001).

of funding with community economic development being the dominant category (Brody and Weiser, 2001).

**Examples of creative PRIs.**  We have seen how foundation funding in the form of both grants and PRIs is being used creatively to finance CDFIs. Below are a few examples of more "non-traditional" uses of PRIs. Each is a unique situation, not easily replicated. Therefore, they are not meant as indications of trends in non-profit finance. Instead they are meant to illustrate the potential for creativity.

- **Loan to a Non-Profit Organisation for Working Capital.** TechnoServe (see *www.technoserve.org*) provides technical assistance to small agri-businesses in Latin America and Africa. Amounts due under a contract with the World Bank and the Government of Ghana had not been received for 14 months because of paperwork procedures. Banks were not interested in a $300 000 working capital loan secured by these receivables. Instead the organisation was able to get an unsecured PRI working capital loan.

- **Loans to a Non-profit Organisation Providing Non-Commercial Venture Capital for Renewable Energy Projects.** E&Co provides consulting services and early-stage investment capital for renewable energy projects in developing countries. The capital is in the form of non-commercial loans and equity in amounts of up to $500 000. The purpose is to provide the initial funds needed to prepare early-stage projects for commercial investors. Established in 1994 and originally funded with grants from a major foundation, E&Co has obtained PRI loans from several foundations and "near-commercial" funding from the Multi-lateral Investment Fund of the Inter-American Development Bank.

- **Loan and Equity Investment in a For-Profit Company.** Organic Commodity Products, the venture-stage company discussed earlier, produces organic chocolate ingredients for food manufacturers. It can also be described as an organisation dedicated to sustainable agriculture, environmental preservation and fair trade practices. The company was able to raise two million dollars on commercial terms from private investors, but given the limited funds in this market, no additional capital. However, it did get a one million dollar loan and a two million dollar equity commitment from a foundation. The contractual return on the foundation's funding is three per cent with an investment period of six years. In addition the initial use of proceeds was limited to the purchase of organic cocoa from small-scale farmers, thereby meeting the charitable purpose and effect conditions for PRI investments.

Foundations have long been recognised as an important funding source for non-profit organisations. What has not been recognised is that in addition to grants, foundations can also provide capital in the form of debt financing for non-profit organisations and also in the form of debt or equity financing for some for-profit companies. One would expect PRI financing to be a growing area of activity in this supposed age of new philanthropy. However, even though they are on non-commercial terms, PRI financings still require knowledge of financing techniques and legal issues that most foundations and non-profit organisations do not have. Therefore, it is not clear whether this will emerge as a growing trend in non-profit finance.

Among foundations that do make PRIs there is a new trend to concentrate them. The MacArthur Foundation, which along with the Ford Foundation has done the most in this area, has recently decided to limit future PRI funding to intermediaries. This is consistent with their approach to CDFIs. In this way MacArthur can make larger transactions and can leverage its funding to serve multiple non-profit and for-profit organisations whose missions meet its programme objectives.

But what of the new foundations being created by the new wealth? It is too early too see any data about their possible use of PRIs. However, some studies have been done on their patterns of grant making. The next section looks at whether there are indications of creativity in the approaches of the new philanthropists who are establishing the new foundations.

### Charitable giving in Silicon Valley

Silicon Valley is the name given to the area of California that has been the centre of technological development for 30 years. It is, in fact, an area of approximately 1 500 square miles and a population of 2.3 million. Silicon Valley has become prominent over the last decade with the emergence of digital and Internet technology, the venture capitalists that funded the "new technology", and the resulting "new wealth."

The expectation has been that this "new wealth" would also foster a new paradigm of philanthropy, one based on the concepts of venture philanthropy and social entrepreneurship. Their direct charitable giving would be different, as would the foundations they establish.

The Community Foundation of Silicon Valley (CFSV) has conducted a series of research projects since 1994 to look at patterns of philanthropy in this community and to see how they differ from national patterns (see Hero, 1998 and *www.cfsb.org*).[4]

The report, "Giving Back, The Silicon Valley Way", includes several statements that would seem to indicate a new philanthropy:

> *"When we began we knew that the philanthropy fostered by the technological revolution at the turn of the 20th century differed significantly from the charitable giving fuelled by the industrial revolution at the end of the 19th century"* (p. 1).

*"There appears to be a strong investment culture in Silicon Valley. It pervades not only the region's economy – an economy of world-class companies financed by some of the world's most innovative, demanding and successful venture capitalists. It also appears to have a strong influence on our attitudes and patterns of charitable giving"* (p. 10).

*"There is an emerging philanthropic sector that is being led by people who have participated in business and industries that have had a transforming effect on society. ... Based on their experience, these individuals have confidence that what they do in philanthropy can have similar effects. When they get involved they like to think big and expect significant results"* p. 4).

The statistics on giving in Silicon Valley do indicate a few significant differences from national giving patterns, but they do not seem to be as transforming as it may be thought. There is a higher percentage of households giving to charity, but not a higher percentage of household income given to charity. Education is a higher priority and a high percentage of giving goes to organisations outside the region. These would seem to be related, reflecting the belief that education is perhaps the most important investment in the future.

*"There is a strong ethic to support education. Many Silicon Valley residents are beneficiaries of a good education; for many of them it has allowed them to relocate to the region and secure a well-paying career"* (p. 11).

*"In fact, this ethic is so strong that education as an investment in future success seems to be a higher priority than charitable giving to address immediate needs. Twice as many households give to education (36 per cent) than human services*

Table 5.4.   **Comparative giving patterns: the new philanthropy**

| Comparable statistics | Silicon Valley (in %) | National (in %) |
|---|---|---|
| Giving as per cent of household income | 2.1 | 2.2 |
| Per cent of households giving | 83.0 | 69.0 |
| Per cent of those 35-44 years old who give | 91.0 | 69.0 |
| Per cent of households contributing to: | | |
| – Religion | 36.0 | 48.0 |
| – Education | 36.0 | 20.0 |
| – Health | 28.0 | 27.0 |
| – Youth development | 24.0 | 21.0 |
| – Human services | 18.0 | 25.0 |
| – Environmental | 17.0 | 12.0 |
| – Arts and culture | No statistically significant difference in either category | |
| – International | | |
| Giving outside region | 40.0 | 20.0 estimated |

*Source:* Hero (1998).

*(18 per cent), compared to the nation in which giving is more evenly balanced"* (p. 11).

*"People focus on contributions that are easy and organisations that they have confidence in – like university alma maters and children's schools"* (p. 15).

The "new wealth" is different in its approach towards philanthropy and there is anecdotal evidence that it is more focused on fewer organisations and on building the capacity of these organisations. However, the patterns of giving by individuals in Silicon Valley do not differ significantly from national averages except for the higher percentage going to education, a very traditional form of philanthropy. As such they do not support, or at least not yet, the expectation that the new wealth will be innovators in providing financing for non-profit organisations and/or for-profit organisations that address social issues.

## Conclusions

The promise of much of the late 1990s in the United States was that capital and business-like approaches would generate market solutions to social concerns. Similarly, capital and business-like approaches would make non-profit organisations more self-sufficient financially. The corollary was that the new investor/philanthropist would invest in such organisations on the basis of total return whether the organisations were non-profit or for-profit entities. This was to be the new paradigm of venture philanthropy and social entrepreneurship.

To date there is little evidence of this happening. Socially-responsible venture capital is talked about, but there is very limited capital in this field. Current patterns of giving by the "new wealth" do not appear significantly different from established national patterns. This transformation of private capital appears to be rhetoric, not reality.

Instead the major trend we are seeing in the financing of non-profit organisations is the aggregation of capital in financial intermediaries. This aggregation is taking two very different forms:

- Intermediaries created to gain access to sources of capital.

- Examples of this are the CDFIs and the newer models such as NHT/ Enterprises and Public Radio Capital. These financial intermediaries have the benefit/advantage of size and financial sophistication. This will better enable them to access commercial capital markets. However, the bulk of the funding for non-profit and for-profit organisations addressing social issues will continue to come from non-commercial sources of capital – from government programmes, from foundations and from private capital that is "encouraged" by regulations or tax incentives.

- What the new financial intermediaries will add in this arena is the creativity and scale to bring these commercial and non-commercial funding sources together. They will then, in turn, be the creative sources of financing for traditional non-profit organisations.

- Private capital moving into foundations.

- Substantial amounts of capital are being transferred into the non-profit sector through the creation of new foundations by individuals. These new philanthropists are using the rhetoric of the new paradigm, of venture philanthropy and social entrepreneurship. However, there is little indication as yet that they will be substantially different from traditional philanthropy in their issues or approaches.

It remains to be seen whether these two very different trends of aggregation into intermediaries will come together, whether the new foundations will adopt collaborative approaches to leverage commercial and non-commercial capital as some of the older foundations and government programmes are doing.

What happened to the expected trend of the new paradigm of venture philanthropy and social entrepreneurship? Why is it not materialising? Arguably, it was an interesting concept that was a product of the late 1990s. Since then the financial markets have changed substantially. The "irrational exuberance" of the stock market is gone. The expectation of easy availability of capital, which was not widely true, is gone. The belief in market solutions has been shaken by recent corporate governance and accounting failures. In this environment it is hard to see new private capital flowing to creative market solutions for social issues.

The concept of the new investor – who can analyse social as well as financial return, who is willing to make trade-offs in order to maximise total return, who will "invest" without regard for non-profit or for-profit status – was also problematic. There is not an accepted methodology for calculating social benefit and including it in a total return equation. Also, the concept ignores the very different tax incentives for making charitable contributions *versus* financial investments.

A broader issue is the appropriateness of the basic business model that the new philanthropy seeks to adapt. It is a model that limits the considerations to quantifying returns. Some will argue that corporations that take into account environmental and social issues will generate better financial performance and, therefore, greater returns on investment in the long run. However, most observers believe that the US stock markets and professional investors simply do not care about the long term and do not factor long-term issues into investment analysis. Even if they did consider long term performance, there is still the problem of demonstrating that organisational behaviour does, in fact, positively impact investment performance.

What are missing from this discussion of markets and investment returns are the broader questions of ethics and of corporate practices and responsibility. Yet, it is in this area that we are seeing a very significant trend emerging in the United States.

Investors are mobilising to impact social change, not so much with their investment dollars, but with their shareholder votes. This year's proxy season in the United States saw an unprecedented number of shareholder resolutions and increasing percentage votes in support of them. While the religious communities have long been proxy activists, public and union pension funds are now getting involved in shareholder activism.

This emerging trend of addressing social issues through institutional shareholder activism on social and governance issues is likely to have an impact on social issues substantially beyond anything imagined for the new philanthropy. And this transformation of private capital is already real, not rhetoric.

### Notes

1. Non-profit organisations are classified by type under the National Taxonomy of Exempt Entities, or NTEE. This divides non-profits into 26 major groups under ten broad categories. The category "civic" corresponds to Public, societal benefit. This includes the following major groups: R: Civil rights, social action, and advocacy; S: Community improvement and capacity building; T: Philanthropy, volunteerism, and grant making; U: Science and technology research; V: Social science research; W: Public and society benefit.

2. The following statistics are from Foundation Growth and Giving Estimates, 2001 Preview, and Foundation Today, 2001 Edition.

3. For a discussion of the various sources of capital for non-profit organisations see Williams (2000), "Financing Alternatives – Sources of Capital".

4. The most recent results publicly available are from 1998. Results of the most recent survey were due to be made public in the summer of 2002, at the time this publication was going in print.

ISBN 92-64-19953-5
The Non-profit Sector in a Changing Economy
© OECD 2003

PART II

# Chapter 6

# New Forms of Financing Social Economy Enterprises and Organisations in Quebec

by

Marguerite Mendell,
Concordia University, Canada,

Benoît Levesque,
Université du Québec à Montréal, Canada,

and
Ralph Rouzier,
Concordia University, Canada

## Introduction

This chapter examines new forms of financing social economy enterprises and organisations. Before turning to the case of Quebec, we begin with a more general discussion in which we identify the issues involved in funding the social economy. These differ from the private sector and present new challenges. The examples we will present include those funding initiatives that are themselves part of the social economy, despite a diversified clientele that may or may not include social economy enterprises. The funds range from community-based funds to state funds, and include hybrid funds and workers funds. Still, they may all be considered part of the same social dynamic and institutional context.

Compared to the other Canadian provinces, Quebec's cultural, political and economic situation is distinct; it stems, among other things, from the fact that over 75 per cent of its population speaks French and that its government has always demanded greater autonomy in areas that come under its jurisdiction. The Quebec economy is also characterised by the strong presence of collective enterprises: state-owned corporations such as Hydro-Quebec, and co-operatives such as the "Mouvement Desjardins". In the area of economic and industrial policy, Quebec has promoted an approach that calls for dialogue among social actors, especially between unions and management (Bourque, 2000).

In 1996, the Government of Quebec, under the leadership of the "Parti québécois", convened a social and economic summit. Representatives of different sectors of Quebec society were invited to debate how to simultaneously reduce the deficit and create employment, two objectives that were generally seen as contradictory. In contrast to previous summits, this included community groups and women's groups for the first time. A variety of civil society initiatives, some of which date back to the early 1980s, such as the "Forum pour l'emploi" (Forum for Full Employment) and others that were more recent, such as the "Marche des femmes contre la pauvreté" (Women's March on Poverty) in June of 1995, had already laid the groundwork for the participation of new actors at the Social and Economic Summit of 1996. This not only increased the public visibility of the social economy, but it also permitted those socio-economic actors not normally engaged in the social economy, to position themselves on this issue.

These new participants in the Social and Economic Summit of 1996 were particularly active in a committee called the "Chantier de l'économie sociale" (Forum on the Social Economy) whose president, Nancy Neamtan, was recognised as one of Quebec's leading figures in the field of community economic development. This forum helped establish the conditions for institutionalising inter-sectoral collaboration. Among the key steps that were decisive for the future of social economy initiatives, the creation of special targeted funds deserves special mention. These include the "Fonds d'économie sociale" (FES), under the aegis of the "Centres locaux de développement" (local development centres, or CLDs), the social economy development fund (the RISQ, or "Réseau d'investissement social du Québec") whose objective was to accumulate $23 million[1] primarily from the private sector ($19 million). At the same time, reforms proposed by the Government of Quebec in the field of regional development – especially in the field of health and social services – paved the way for recognising the importance of community-based initiatives and the social economy.

Since 1999, the Forum on the Social Economy has become an independent and permanent organisation for the promotion and the development of the social economy in Quebec. As a non-profit organisation, it is a national network of social economy actors and those working to develop the social economy. Its organisational structure consists of a general assembly and a 29-member board of directors, representing various sectors in the social economy (environment, social services, communications, recreation, housing, natural resources, child and family services, culture, etc.), local development participants (*e.g*,. the "Association des centres locaux de développement du Québec", "Réseau des sociétés d'aide au développement des collectivités-SADC", "Inter-CDEC"[2]) and major social movements (unions, community groups, co-operatives and women's organisations). The Quebec government, however, covers the operating costs of the Forum. To carry out its mandate, the Forum has established a permanent and close relationship with the "Comité sectoriel de la main-d'œuvre de l'économie sociale et de l'action communautaire" (Sectoral Labour Market Committee for the Social Economy) and with RISQ (Fund for Social Economy Enterprises) and co-manages the "Alliance de recherche universités-communautés en économie sociale" [a consortium of universities and organisations (such as Forum on the Social Economy and labour federation) in Quebec] (Lévesque *et al.*, 2000).

## The challenges of financing the social economy

In recent years, there have been competing definitions of the social economy, which vary between and within countries (Lévesque and Mendell, 1999; OECD, 1999). In Anglo-American countries, for example, it is most commonly associated with the non-profit or third sector. In continental

Europe, the social economy referred, until the 1970s, to the co-operative and to the mutual organisation, almost exclusively (Defourny and Monzon, 1992). In 1997, the European Commission designated the "third system" to include the panoply of co-operatives, associations, voluntary organisations, non-profits, etc., thereby recognising both market and non-market elements of the social economy. In France, a "Secrétariat de l'économie solidaire" was established under the Jospin administration. Among its objectives was the promotion of dialogue and exchange with colleagues in Quebec.[3] This initiative marks an important step in France as it bridges what was a long-standing division between the "old" social economy – co-operatives, mutual associations, etc. and the so-called "économie solidaire" – civil society associations, non-profits, etc.

Increasingly, all countries are focusing on the third sector or on non-profits as solutions to problems of social exclusion and unemployment and to respond to unmet social needs that the market economy is unable to fulfil. While the non-profit sector does indeed represent the social economy, it is too restrictive a designation. Despite the growing recognition that the social economy includes the non-profit sector, it is still considered the principal location for most social economy activity. As such, the social economy is perceived as being synonymous with the social service sector, especially by its detractors.[4]

In Quebec, the increasing provision of social services by non-profit enterprises opens up important debates and controversies regarding the transfer of what were formerly public responsibilities to civil society organisations. These debates must take place, as, indeed, there is an ongoing reconfiguration of state responsibilities. However, there are ways in which the displacement of many social services from the public to the non-profit sector, as well as the provision of new social services, can maintain the commitment of the state and result in better social provision and generate new jobs in the process. For this to occur, the non-profits in the social economy providing services in the public interest must be redefined as a new hybrid organisational structure with significant public participation. In most cases, these non-profit organisations, when limited to social services, cannot be self-financing. If the services are to be provided by well-paid employees at low cost and offer high quality services, financing this component of the social economy calls for recurrent public support. This will be discussed later.

In our view, the social economy is broader still. It includes the production of both goods and services. Moreover, it not only includes co-operatives and non-profit organisations, but also, in some cases, private enterprises with shareholder agreements[5] that force majority shareholders to agree to social objectives undertaken by the firm. What distinguishes the social economy is the decision-making capacity of stakeholders in contrast to the dominance of shareholders in private enterprise. Those firms, in which the role of shareholders is reduced, should also be included in a broad definition of social enterprises.

These introductory remarks summarise briefly, some of the important debates and discussions in recent years concerning the social economy throughout industrialised countries. Fortunately, there is a growing literature that documents these debates and experiences. Whatever our selected nomenclature to capture the firms engaged in the social economy, they are all social enterprises, subject to different laws governing their behaviour, which vary from country to country. Company law governing private enterprise, is itself complex, permitting the socialisation of firms required to comply with non-market criteria. In our view, there is insufficient research in this area because until now, the private sector has been excluded from any definition of the social economy.[6] This is still controversial among social economy actors; however, if we interpret the increasing pressures placed on some firms to operate under different principles as the outcome of the successful experiences in the social economy, a closer look would be necessary.

A great deal of effort has been placed in demonstrating that, contrary to common belief, social economy enterprises are, for the most part, less risky and, in some cases, potentially more profitable than private sector firms. The role played by stakeholders in the social economy contributes additional resources which are not easily accountable in financial terms, but which greatly diminish risk and increase profitability. Major difficulties result less frequently in bankruptcy than in the private sector, due to non-market factors operating within these enterprises.[7] In some cases, investment in the social economy is as profitable, if not more so, than in the private sector.[8] In other cases, as noted above, financial contributions by the state are warranted given the nature of the service offered by a social enterprise. These are offered at low cost as an ongoing commitment to the availability of affordable services. For this commitment to remain, public subsidies are essential. This said, the problem of financing the social economy remains, because many of the enterprises concerned are very small, new and engaged in less profitable activities. The increasing complexity of the social economy requires, however, that a full portrait be available so as to dispel the prevailing view that all is new and high risk in this field.

In this chapter, we have identified four difficulties faced by social economy enterprises:

- For the most part, social economy enterprises do not generate competitive rates of return on investment. This is not their primary objective. The first difficulty, therefore, relates to the commitment to social goals, thereby compromising purely economic returns. This reduces the number of individual or institutional investors who seek high rates of return, generally in the short term.

- A second difficulty arises for most social economy enterprises, especially for the new generation of small non-profits or co-operatives. For financial institutions, the banks in particular, the transaction costs for what are generally small loans are too high. Moreover, these enterprises are considered high risk due greatly to a misunderstanding of the nature of these enterprises and their long-term potential.

- A third difficulty in social economy enterprises is the presence of new actors unknown to the business and financial communities. Many of these individuals have extensive experience in community activism but little exposure to the market economy. This contributes to the difficulty in attracting investment or in securing loans from traditional financial institutions.

- A fourth difficulty relates to those firms in the private sector that we have included as social economy enterprises. The complex shareholder agreements in these enterprises, which limit, by definition, the participation of individual and/or institutional investors whose primary interest is the rate of return on their investment, pose complications for financing.[9]

Traditional sources of financing those social economy activities more closely associated with social objectives have included donations, gifts, government grants and programme funding, loan guarantees and self-financing. Donations have come largely from foundations, religious communities and charitable organisations. Government funding has supported both social service provision as well as economic activity in those social economy enterprises deemed to be in the interest of the public. This support has most often reflected the priorities of governments in power and not necessarily the social objectives of the enterprises involved. Loan guarantees have included mortgage guarantees on housing, leasing arrangements or government guarantees on loans. Self-financing has relied on three sources: individual savings, "love money" and community fund-raising activities. These traditional sources of funding are, in fact, not generally available to those individuals and enterprises that are part of the new social economy. They are considered high risk and therefore have very limited access to these sources of finance. For these reasons, the co-operative sector and non-profit enterprises have tried to develop non-traditional sources of finance over the last twenty years, which includes, in some cases, combining traditional and new sources of funding to accumulate the necessary capital. This often requires a great deal of time and effort as the eligibility, amounts available etc., vary for each of these funding sources. This

**144**

seems to be the fate of non-profit organisations, accustomed to investing much time and energy in fund raising. The stakes are different today as these organisations in the social economy participate in the market. It is also the fate of many newcomers in the social economy who learn very quickly that multiple sources, new and old, must be tapped to mount the necessary finance.

In recent years, new financial instruments have emerged to meet the growing needs of small enterprises, not only in the social economy. In particular, we refer to venture capital and local development funds that are distinct from the speculative capital market. In the best cases, these instruments include some and/or all of the following characteristics:

- Long-term and/or equity finance (financial intermediation).
- Counselling and follow-up (social intermediation).
- Partnerships (financial and social intermediation).
- Leveraging (permits entry into traditional capital markets).
- Integration in the community, local or regional planning.
- Democratic participation; innovative governance.

These characteristics vary according to the nature of the financial instrument. In our research in Quebec, we identified five principal types, all of which provide finance for the social economy:

- Community-based funds.
- Hybrid funds.
- Worker funds.
- Co-operative funds.
- State funds.

In the following section, we will evaluate the capacity of these funds to meet the financial needs of the social economy.

## Community-based funds

A clear distinction between community-based funds and those that are state supported is difficult to make because the state intervenes either directly with financial support or indirectly through employability programmes that enable these funds to hire their personnel. Therefore, our understanding of community-based funds is of those that were initiated by civil society organisations. In Quebec, the community economic development corporations established in the mid-1980s[10] are among the most important in this regard. Today, many community-based financial instruments are located in these corporations; autonomous loan circles and community loan funds have also emerged, especially in the last decade to serve the growing need to develop initiatives to counter poverty, unemployment and exclusion. They include a large variety of financial instruments, established to fill the gap created by banks unwilling to serve this clientele.

Community economic development was initiated and consolidated in Quebec by the first generation of CDECs established in the city of Montreal.[11] The objectives of these corporations were three-fold: job creation, local economic development and urban renewal. In order to respond to this new socio-economic mandate for what were previously community-based organisations engaged primarily in social intervention, it was necessary to create financial instruments. The first community-based development fund, "le Fonds de développement de l'emploi de Montréal" (FDEM) was formed and funded by a partnership between the municipal and provincial governments and the "Fonds de solidarité de travailleurs du Québec"[12] (worker fund). At the time, the focus was not on the social economy, *per se*, but on the revitalisation of neighbourhoods hard hit by the recession in the early 1980s and economic restructuring.

In important ways, these events set the stage for the emergence of community-based initiatives, including new financial instruments. For the labour movement, the involvement of the "Fonds de solidarité" in the FDEM signalled the need for small investment funds; in 1993, in partnership with civil society actors, the "Fonds" created SOLIDE throughout the province.[13] In their early phases, these initiatives responded not only to economic decline but also to a growing dissatisfaction with government approaches. In the 1990s, however, these initiatives also had to respond to the savage cuts in public spending. The history of community economic development in Quebec over the last twenty years provides a backdrop for much of the socio-economic innovation under way today in regions and localities, especially in the social economy. For those familiar with the history, it was not always harmonious, as social movements – the women's movement in particular, which is recognised for putting the social economy on the political agenda – collided head-on with community activists engaged in economic initiatives. The historic separation of social and economic concerns and strategies, with community organisations and women's groups primarily involved in social intervention, was played out in this period when, in fact, the opportunity to capture control of economic decision-making at the local level and integrate social needs into economic development, became possible for the first time. We might say that this struggle is now being played out in the social economy, where economic actors – businesses, banks – have to be persuaded that investment in the social economy is a good thing.

In the last decade, Quebec has witnessed the emergence of various community-based funds including loan circles and loan funds, to respond to the persistent unavailability of small loans. The best known among these is the Montreal Community Loan Association (MCLA), which was established in 1990.[14] Support for the first loan circle in Quebec was among its early initiatives. The activities of these two instruments are limited. The MCLA and loan circles provide micro-credit: in the case of loan circles, the loans are between $500 and $2 000. In the case of the MCLA, the maximum loan is $20 000. The capitalisation of the MCLA has reached approximately $650 000 in ten years; for loan circles, the amount available for loans is approximately $20 000 per loan circle. These funds are themselves part of the social economy, given their broad socio-economic objectives; however, they provide finance not only to social economy enterprises. Until recently, these funds were not part of any established network. Today they are represented by "le Réseau québécois du crédit communautaire".

### Montreal Community Loan Association (MCLA)

The MCLA was the first community-based loan fund in Canada. Its influence has been very important in this area; its ongoing challenges reveal a great deal about the changing environment in Quebec, where unlike other provinces in Canada, or for that matter, unlike many experiences elsewhere, the government has embarked on a programme of decentralisation that includes the establishment of local development funds throughout the province.[15] The verdict is not out yet, as these events are unfolding as we go to print, but the situation has become extremely precarious for organisations such as the MCLA, which struggle in this new political environment.

From the beginning, the MCLA distinguished itself from a financial institution in that its objectives were to serve a marginalised population unable to access loans from banks and to support only those projects that could demonstrate both economic viability and social utility. The Association recognised the vulnerability of its clientele; still, it insisted that its role was not to manage poverty, but to leverage loans so that those excluded from bank finance could approach financial institutions once the Association had given them an opportunity. To achieve this, all loans include training, counselling, technical assistance and follow-up as part of a loan package, thereby greatly reducing the risk associated with small loans. While the commitment of the MCLA was to promote the establishment of co-operatives, non-profits and community enterprises, many of its clients are small private firms. Of the almost 50 projects which have been financed by the MCLA, only sixteen are non-profit organisations, including two loan circles. However, all enterprises must comply with the socio-economic criteria established by the Association.

Investors in the MCLA include foundations, religious organisations, individuals, the labour movement and the private sector. Government support for the Association at all three levels – municipal, provincial and federal – has been scattered at best. In addition to three full-time employees, approximately 40 volunteers assist the Association in its daily operations. Its volunteer board of directors has, over the years, included individuals drawn from the community, private and academic sectors. The governance of the Association is broad-based and democratic.

We begin with this example because of the important role that the MCLA has played, not only in Quebec, but across the country as well. Also, its ongoing work and difficulties capture the challenges faced by those involved in the community sector and in the new social economy in Quebec. And so, in some ways, the MCLA is a prototype for community-based finance from which we continue to learn. Its capacity to finance social economy enterprises is only limited by its strange position, as the political deck gets reshuffled in Quebec. The support of the Quebec government for social economy initiatives is, perhaps, too focused on institutional responses, at the expense of community-based organisations with the experience and knowledge to undertake this activity as well. Rather than a mixture of state-based and community-based initiatives, the pendulum is leaning towards more structures created by the Quebec government, for better or for worse.

In the *mêlée* of the emergence of new financial instruments in the 1990s,[16] the MCLA would not yield on its principles of serving a marginalised population, who, in most instances, despite the numerous funds around, could still not access loans. Instead, the Association formed partnerships with existing organisations that shared its objectives, to establish new funds. These partners include a community economic development corporation, the co-operative movement, and a youth fund created by the Mayor of Montreal.[17] Despite these attempts to remain autonomous and grow through partnerships, the Association suffers the fate of most non-profit organisations; it is not yet self-financing and therefore struggles to meet its operating costs. At approximately $150 000 per year, this represents almost 25 per cent of its loan capital.

If we return to the characteristics we set out to describe what might be the best-case scenario for new financial instruments, the Montreal Community Loan Association scores very high in all six categories. In the first case, it provides debt finance over a period of up to three years. With respect to leveraging, the Association will extend a second loan to a client still unable to get bank funding despite good credentials, in the hope that it will succeed in the next round. The repayment rate, 94 per cent, is also high. The Association has convened three national conferences and has recently initiated a national network of community loan funds that met for the first time this year. Together, they may find a solution to the ongoing difficulty many such funds face. Together, they may be able to lobby their respective provincial governments and the federal government to subsidise operating costs and to introduce fiscal advantages to attract more investors.

## Loan circles

The loan circles here and elsewhere have been inspired by the Grameen Bank in Bangladesh. In general, they provide small loans to groups of four to seven individuals who collectively share the responsibility for repayment. While we cannot say that they provide funding to social economy enterprises, the circles themselves are part of the social economy; their objective is to assist those who have been left behind by mainstream institutions.[18] The social culture of the loan circle model is certainly an influence on future business development by those involved in circle training programmes before a loan can be issued. Training is an essential component; members of a loan circle agree to ongoing training sessions for up to two months before the loan is issued to the group. In most instances, the individuals in a loan circle do not know each other; establishing confidence in strangers is the first challenge. The socialising process here is innovative; a financial need is addressed in an environment that brings individuals into contact with larger objectives and common concerns. In this light, the values of the social economy are potentially transferred into the work environments these people subsequently find themselves in.

In Quebec, there are 22 organisations in which loan circles are located, some of which belong to the "Réseau québécois du crédit communautaire". In all, close to 1 500 individuals have participated in loan circle training sessions throughout the province. Of these, 406 have set up small enterprises and another 344 are in a pre-start-up phase. Over 160 individuals have found a job, 76 have returned to school and just over 350 individuals have been referred to further training and assistance programmes in their communities. A total of $478 708 has been invested in 750 enterprises by member organisations, for an average of $638 per enterprise.

In many cases, the success of the loan circle model is also due to the support it receives from other community organisations. As stated above, the MCLA has provided funding for loan circles. The credit union movement in Quebec has also been involved (Malo and Ignatieff, 1997). Training is also offered according to need, by individuals and groups outside the immediacy of the loan circle. Without government support, however, these loan circles cannot exist. Once again, it is impossible to cover operating costs, which greatly exceed the loan portfolios of these circles. Loan circles in Montreal recently succeeded in renewing their government funding for the next three years. The uncertainty surrounding this reminds us how precarious these alternative sources of funding are. They do not fit into the current restructuring in Quebec; they must continuously renew their request for financial support.

## Hybrid funds

We have designated a number of funds as hybrid in that they are either quasi-public – the state finances the operating costs of these funds but transfers management and decision-making to organisations and/or public intermediaries – or the state is a partner in the capitalisation of the fund. Examples of such funds serving the social economy involve both the federal and provincial government. In this section, we introduce the role of the "Sociétés d'aide au développement des collectivités" (SADC) which were created by the federal government in rural communities, the "Centres locaux de développement" (CLD) established by the government of Quebec (the CLDs manage two local development funds, one dedicated to the social economy) and the "Réseau d'investissement social du Québec" (RISQ), a fund in which the capitalisation comes from both the private sector and the state.

### Sociétés d'aide au développement des collectivités (SADC)

At the beginning of the 1980s, the federal government embarked on a programme to support community-based initiatives in low-income regions across the country. The Community Futures Development Program was the result, in 1994, of the merger of several earlier programmes designed to revitalise poor rural regions. These corporations, known as "Sociétés d'aide au développement des collectivités" (SADC) in Quebec, are under the responsibility of Economic Development Canada. In Quebec, there are 96 "Municipalités régionales de comté" (MRCs), which are regroupings of small municipalities. Of these, 55 are considered eligible for an SADC.

Table 6.1.  **Les Sociétés d'aide au développement des collectivités – SADC**

| Status | Non-profit organisation |
|---|---|
| Capitalisation | $140 million ($2.3 million per investment fund) and $17.6 million ($320 000 per youth fund) |
| Source of capitalisation | Government (federal) |
| Objectives | Creation or maintenance of jobs; economic development |
| Clientele | Small enterprise |
| Eligibility | Local development, educational projects, economy projects, health, environment, cultural projects |
| Nature of investment | Shares, equity loans, negotiated interest rate, conventional loans etc. Up to $125 000 (investment fund) or $5 000 to $15 000 (youth fund) |
| Number of projects | Over 4 000 |
| Jobs created or maintained | 19 436 |

*Note:* These figures refer to 2000.
*Source:* The tables contained in this chapter have been elaborated by the authors on the basis of data obtained from the various organisations described herein.

SADCs have become of great interest as a model of local governance. They are financed by the federal government but the state support they receive does not have many restrictions, permitting a great deal of autonomy. Also, the operating costs of SADCs are assumed by the federal government. In 1999, the operating costs for the SADCs in Quebec were $12 million. The operating cost per SADC is approximately $230 000 per year (about 12 per cent of their capitalisation). This resolves the problem that we mentioned above, with respect to community-based funds. Each SADC has a development fund that is available for investment in local enterprise development, including the social economy. The boards of directors of the SADCs consist of representatives from all social and economic sectors – business, labour, community organisations and the community itself. The SADCs belong to a provincial network that provides non-market resources to its members.

Each SADC has a development fund that is available for investment in local enterprise development, including the social economy. The investment may be as much as $125 000 but rarely exceeds $75 000. Approximately 4 400 files were examined in 2000, representing approximately 80 projects per SADC, 50 per cent of which are new requests. According to one study, 75 per cent of the requests involve technical or financial assistance; 25 per cent are concerned with what might be called the collective interest of the community concerned (EvaluAction, 1999). The average loan issued by the SADCs is for $32 800. Two-thirds of these loans are issued without guarantees. The sectoral distribution of the loans and/or technical assistance is as follows: 63 per cent in the service sector, 29 per cent in manufacturing, five per cent in the primary sector and three per cent in the so-called "*secteur quaternaire*" or social services. Up to the year 2000, the SADCs created or maintained a total of 19 436 jobs. The average investment per job was about $7 000. Together the SADCs in Quebec employ approximately 350 individuals and mobilise 1 250 volunteers.

SADCs play several critical and innovative roles in the regions in which they are located. In addition to the services and funding they provide, the SADCs are strategic locations for economic planning, in collaboration with local socio-economic actors. The presence of a variety of such actors also permits the transfer of knowledge and expertise to personnel employed by the SADCs, an important externality that contributes considerably to the long-term social benefits provided by the SADCs. SADCs also provide financing and counselling for projects that may not necessarily receive immediate funding. Although the majority of enterprises supported by the SADCs are in the private sector, the objectives and broad mandate of the SADCs place them firmly within the social economy in Quebec. Projects in all sectors are launched to limit youth exodus, to update Internet installations in poor regions, to promote sales of local or regional products, to consolidate local assets, etc. While the SADCs do also fund social economy enterprises, information on the amount specifically dedicated to the social economy is not available, nor is there data on the success of these projects as yet.

### The Centres locaux de développement (CLD) and their funds

The CDECs and the SADCs have inspired the establishment of local development centres (CLD) by the Quebec government throughout the province. In effect, these centres have the same objectives as the SADCs but do not distinguish between urban and rural areas or between regional disparities. The mandate of the CLDs, created at the end of 1997, is to promote local entrepreneurship, including social economy enterprises. Each CLD must develop a strategic plan for its region within the context of the strategies, orientations and objectives adopted at both regional and national levels. ("Assemblée nationale", 1998, p. 258).

There are currently 108 CLDs in the province of Quebec.[19] In Montreal, the CDECs are mandated to carry out the activities of these local development centres. In effect, the CDECs now find themselves with greater responsibilities, but also with new political and economic legitimisation as local intermediaries between the state and civil society, with clear responsibilities and accountability. This institutionalisation of the CDECs, which is by and large positive, as they now have greater resources at their disposal, also implies a loss of autonomy. In our view, the availability of these additional resources and policy instruments at the local level, however, is a radical break with top-down programme funding, the legacy of community-based organisations. The CDECs and the CLDs now have funds to support local initiatives, including the "Fonds d'économie sociale" (FES), designated for social economy enterprises – co-operatives, non-profits, and associations. With the availability of these FES across Quebec, the CLDs/CDECs will not only assist the social economy financially, but they will play a decisive role in how the social economy evolves in Quebec. The governance of the CLDs and the CDECs, its board and its many committees, requires broad representation of the community. Decisions are, therefore, undertaken by groups of individuals who reside in the territory represented by the CLDs/CDECs and who understand the potential and limits of initiatives in their communities, including those in the social economy. The "Fonds d'économie sociale"[20] provides support for start-up and more importantly, for pre-start-up or feasibility studies. This is critical, as pre-start-up funding is generally very difficult to secure. While social economy enterprises must produce goods and/or services with demonstrated social utility, they must also demonstrate the capacity to become self-financing. As we noted above, this is currently the subject of much discussion, as some social enterprises are less able to achieve this status than others, especially those providing low cost services. The FES provides subsidies of $9 000 per job created, up to a maximum of $75 000 per social enterprise. Each CLD/CDEC also manages a "Fonds local d'investissement" (FLI) which extends micro loans between $1 000-$50 000. Access to the FES makes it possible to seek further finance from the FLI, which is available for social economy enterprises as well, but not exclusively. As with SADCs, it is not yet possible to know exactly how many jobs have been created in the social economy, because data for the CLDs is only now being collected. But we do know that the social economy projects supported by the CLDs are mostly in services (tourism, day care centres, etc.) and that about $26 million was available from 1998 to 2000 for the FES.

### Réseau d'investissement social du Québec (RISQ)

The "Réseau d'investissement social du Québec" (RISQ), a non-profit organisation, was established in 1997. It is considered a hybrid fund because of the multi-sectoral composition of its principal investors, its board of directors and partners which is an extraordinary mix of all social actors in Quebec society committed, by this engagement, to the promotion of social economy enterprises.[21] The original objective of RISQ was to raise $23 million in capital; to date, it has not increased its initial capitalisation of $7.3 million, $4 million of which comes from the government of Quebec. Raising this additional capital remains a challenge given the necessity to convince the private sector – the financial institutions in particular – to increase their participation. Among the current partners are the "Groupe Jean Coutu", major corporations, banks and the "le Mouvement des caisses populaires et d'économie Desjardins", Quebec's large credit union which has financed the offices of RISQ until now.

For the time being, RISQ is the only investment fund designated exclusively to social economy enterprises, co-operatives and non-profits. It provides both loans and loan guarantees of up to $50 000. In addition, RISQ

Table 6.2.   **Le Réseau d'investissement social du Québec – RISQ**

| Status | Non-profit organisation |
| --- | --- |
| Capitalisation | $7.3 million |
| Source of capitalisation | Mixed |
| Objective | Funds social economy enterprises |
| Clientele | Non-profits and co-operatives |
| Eligibility | Start-up, expansion, consolidation |
| Nature of investment | Unsecured loans (up to $50 000) Pre-start-up repayable technical assistance up to $5 000 |
| Number of projects | 47 loans and 82 technical assistance loans |
| Amount invested | $1 974 200 in loans and $467 713 in technical assistance |
| Jobs created or maintained | 1 344 |

Note: These figures refer to April 2001.

offers technical assistance, often in the form of pre-start-up support. The amount designated towards this assistance is added to the loan; only if a social enterprise is unable to launch its activities is this amount written off.

Since 1997, RISQ has retained 129 projects. Of these, 47 projects received funding immediately; 82 received technical assistance. In the first case, a total investment of $1.97 million in loans subsequently leveraged $19.5 million, significantly multiplying the initial investment in these enterprises. Similarly, the total investment in technical assistance, $467 713, leveraged an additional investment of $1.1 million. The investments by RISQ, in this short period of time, have created or maintained 1 344 jobs; including individuals who have been placed in training businesses. The average investment per job created or maintained is approximately $3 247 (RISQ, 2001). The types of enterprises supported are diverse. They encompass culture, funeral co-operatives, tourism, recycling, day care centres, theatre, agriculture, computer businesses and community restaurants.

## Workers funds

The "Fédération des travailleuses et travailleurs du Québec" (FTQ), Quebec's most important labour federation, established a workers fund in 1983 to respond to the loss of jobs during the recession in the early 1980s. The Quebec National Assembly passed legislation in June of 1983 to create the "Fonds de solidarité". The remarkable performance of the "Fonds de solidarité" has become a model for other workers funds established throughout Canada and for a second such fund in Quebec, "Fondaction, le fonds de développement de la Confédération des syndicats nationaux pour la coopération et l'emploi" established by the "Confédération des syndicats nationaux" (CSN). The "Fonds de solidarité" is considered one of the most important sources of risk capital in Canada and the most important worker fund internationally.

Today, the "Fonds de solidarité" has 426 592 subscribers, 59 per cent of whom are unionised workers whose pension funds are invested in the "Fonds"; 41 per cent of its investors are from the general public. The total assets of the "Fonds de solidarité" have reached $3.86 billion. From its inception, the growth of the "Fonds" has been greatly assisted by extremely attractive fiscal advantages offered to investors from both the federal and provincial governments.[22]

Why do we include the "Fonds de solidarité" in this discussion on the social economy? In our view, the objectives of investment funds themselves must be evaluated, not only the clientele they serve. If, for example, investments by funds in the private sector are conditional to compliance with social goals, an inventory of funds in the social economy must, in our view, include those funds that, in important ways, commit firms to socio-economic objectives. This not only increases the inventory of social economy funds, but it demonstrates the capacity of social actors, the labour movement in this case, to influence private enterprise to pursue both economic and social objectives, without compromising profitability. Because the "Fonds de solidarité" subjects its clients to a social audit before investing and insists that firms adhere to a series of practices – these may include participatory management, employment practices, environmental considerations, etc. – investment decisions are tied to non-market criteria in the private sector. The "Fonds" has in fact done more than this. It has been an active player in economic development and job creation strategies in Quebec for almost twenty years. The "Fonds de solidarité" was a partner in the FDEM, which, as we noted above, was the first community-based investment instrument targeting job creation and economic development in local communities. It has also responded to the critical need for job training and re-skilling by developing innovative educational programmes. Employees of the "Fonds de solidarité" and investors have access to a learning environment promoting public understanding of financial markets. As such, the "Fonds" is recognised for the democratisation of knowledge, de-coding complex financial and economic phenomena, often inaccessible and therefore intimidating.

The "Fonds" has created over 90 000 jobs and has provided education and training in all firms in which it invests. As we noted above, over the years, the "Fonds" has been instrumental in economic planning, both sectoral as well as territorial. Its role is respected in Quebec as it is increasingly seen to be acting in the general interest of Quebec society, while always supporting the collective interests of unionised workers and the individual interest of investors.

Table 6.3.   **Le Fonds de solidarité des travailleurs du Québec – FTQ**

| Status | Venture capital fund |
|---|---|
| Capitalisation | $3.86 billion |
| Source of capitalisation | Worker contributions (facilitated by fiscal incentives) |
| Objectives | Protect workers' retirement income while financing the growth of small and medium-sized enterprise and creating permanent jobs |
| Clientele | Small and medium-sized enterprise in almost all sectors except retail. Investment in both unionised and non-unionised enterprises. |
| Eligibility | Pre-start-up, start-up, expansion, consolidation, mergers and acquisitions, public offerings, and sectors with high value added |
| Nature of investment | Minority equity investment from $750 000; membership on board of directors |
| Number of projects | 123[1] |
| Amount invested | $372.4 million |
| Jobs created or maintained | 90 919 (since 1983 including direct, indirect and maintained) |

Note: These figures refer to 2000.
1. An additional 1 477 projects are added if we include all those supported by the different funds controlled by the "Fonds de solidarité" – regional funds, the SOLIDE, technology funds, etc.

In response to the growing need for small investment funds, in 1991, the "Fonds de solidarité" and the "Union des municipalités régionales de comté" (UMRCQ)[23] created a holding, SOLIDEQ, to establish SOLIDE, a new financial instrument providing investments between $5 000 and $50 000. The initial capitalisation of $30 million (today it is $40 million) came from the "Fonds de solidarité". SOLIDEQ would match every dollar invested in a SOLIDE by the milieu (civil society) in the form of a gift or a loan with no interest, with an unsecured loan at five per cent interest, up to $250 000 for a period of 10 years (at least in the first round).

The launch of a SOLIDE requires a resolution passed by the board of the "Municipalités régionales de comté" (MRC) or an eligible municipality as well as a business plan. These must themselves be preceded by the establishment of a "Corporation de développement de l'économie et de l'emploi" (CDEE). The delegate from this CDEE will subsequently become a member of the board of directors of the SOLIDE which consists of a minimum of five administrators (one each from the "Fonds de solidarité", the MRC and the CDEE) and which sets the objectives and orientation for the SOLIDE. Local intermediaries are contracted to manage the daily affairs of the SOLIDE.[24] Finally, the "Fonds de solidarité", through SOLIDEQ, assists the SOLIDE not only with financing but also with ongoing support.

SOLIDE provide primarily equity loans for start-up, purchase of equipment, consolidation of enterprises, etc. Only those enterprises in the primary, manufacturing and the new economy located in a given MRC are eligible. There are currently 86 SOLIDE in Quebec, located in MRCs. In 2001, 1 166 projects were supported through the SOLIDE. The average investment per project was $30 479. These investments permitted the creation or maintenance of 10 329 jobs, for an average investment of $3 441 per job.

The SOLIDE instrument added to the many socio-economic innovations emerging in the early 1990s in Quebec. In particular, the partnership between social actors, on which many of these innovations were and continue to be based, mark what we consider to be important steps in developing an

Table 6.4.   **SOLIDE**

| Investments | 30 June 1998 | 30 June 1999 | 30 June 2001 |
|---|---|---|---|
| Number of SOLIDE | 75 | 76 | 85 |
| Number of projects | 616 | 797 | 1 166 |
| Authorised finance | $17 561 679 | $22 810 684 | $35 538 523 |
| Average investment per project | $28 509 | $28 621 | $30 479 |
| Total value of project investment | $148 962 103 | $195 137 507 | $354 110 995 |
| Jobs maintained or created | 5 172 | 6 784 | 10 329 |
| Number of jobs per project | 8.4 | 8.5 | 8.9 |
| Average investment per project | $3 396 | $3 362 | $3 441 |

alternative financial market in Quebec that does not correspond with the behaviour of capital markets as they have developed in the last twenty years.

The SOLIDE, in our view, is also part of the social economy, not only because they are non-profit organisations, but also because they are responding to needs not met or inadequately met by existing financial instruments, namely the need for micro-credit. Additionally, the SOLIDE are also embedded in local economic development strategies. We have provided a great deal of detail regarding their decision-making structures to demonstrate the innovation in democratic and participatory governance. All sectors are represented in various governing bodies; the capitalisation of the SOLIDE, likewise, must come from the public sector and the milieu as well as from SOLIDEQ. Finally, the links between the SOLIDE and the municipalities again demonstrate their commitment to the wider general interest of the community in which they are located. Nonetheless, it is also true that to date, the SOLIDE have not invested directly in the social economy.

## Fondaction, le fonds de développement de la Confédération des syndicats nationaux (CSN) pour la coopération et l'emploi

In 1995, the "Confédération des syndicats nationaux", the second largest labour federation in Quebec, established the "Fondaction, le fonds de développement de la CSN pour la coopération et l'emploi".[25] Although the experience of the "Fonds de solidarité" was certainly influential, the initial mission of "Fondaction" was to invest only in the social economy. The actual involvement of "Fondaction", however, in the last few years, has been in the private sector and only indirectly in the social economy, by investing in intermediaries that finance the social economy. This does not compromise the objectives of "Fondaction"; on the contrary, it will only invest in those enterprises which practice some form of participatory management and whose objectives are linked to sustainable development. It is obliged to invest 60 per cent of its total assets, more than $133 million, in this type of enterprise.

"Fondaction" is fully controlled by the CSN; similar to the "Fonds de solidarité", the capitalisation of "Fondaction" is largely drawn from worker pension funds. Subscribers receive the same fiscal advantages as those investing in the "Fonds".[26] Firms in which "Fondaction" will invest, are subject to an extensive evaluation concerning their potential to create or to maintain jobs, the competence of management, governance and decision-making, working conditions, as well as a full evaluation of the market for the goods and/or services produced by these firms, including, obviously, its financial situation and its profitability. It is too early to evaluate "Fondaction" in terms of the social economy. Its potential collaboration with community funds such as the MCLA or with RISQ, or with the eventual creation of a fund dedicated to the development of co-operatives, will determine the extent to which "Fondaction" will become a partner in community-based or social economy finance. For now, its willingness to explore these possibilities and its presence in many social economy networks and organisations affirms its initial commitment to support, promote and consolidate the social economy in Quebec.[27]

Recently, "Fondaction" launched a new fund called "Filaction, le fonds pour l'investissement local et l'approvisionnement des fonds communautaires". This fund has the same objectives as "Fondaction" except that the amount invested is between $50 000 and $150 000. This fund is available to social economy organisations as well as other types of enterprises. The capitalisation of this fund will be $8.5 million: $7 million from "Fondaction" and $1.5 million from the "Ministère des régions" ($300 000 per year over the next five years).

## State funds

The government of Quebec, as part of its economic development strategy, created a number of public or state funds to respond to the need for risk capital, for example, "la Société générale de financement du Québec" and "la Caisse de dépôt et placement du Québec". Currently, "Investissement Québec", is the one public fund that offers finance for social economy enterprises, co-operatives and non-profits. It offers both loans and loan guarantees. "Investissement Québec" was first established in 1971 (as the

Table 6.5.   **Fondaction – CSN**

| Status | Social investment fund |
|---|---|
| Capitalisation | $133.4 million |
| Source of capitalisation | Worker savings (26 762 subscribers) |
| Objectives | Protect worker retirement income and invest in enterprises to maintain or create jobs |
| Clientele | Small and medium-sized enterprises demonstrating participatory management, social economy enterprises and those which protect the environment |
| Eligibility | Expansion of production, development of new products and/or new markets, consolidation, mergers, acquisitions, and increased participation of workers in management |
| Nature of investment | Shares, unsecured loans, guarantees, from $ 250 000 to $2 750 000 |
| Number of projects | 36 (from 01 June 1998 to 30 May 2000) *of which* 11 in the environment-related field, 10 in the social economy, and seven in co-managed enterprises |
| Total invested | $30.2 million |
| Jobs created or maintained | 940 |

Note: Financial year 1999-2000.

THE NON-PROFIT SECTOR IN A CHANGING ECONOMY – ISBN 92-64-19953-5 – © OECD 2003

"Société de développement industriel") to finance small and medium-sized enterprise. While "Investissement Québec" falls within the mandate of the "Ministère de l'Industrie et du Commerce" (MIC), it is governed by an independent board on which the social economy and the labour movement are represented. Its current assets total one billion dollars.

In 2000-2001, 141 enterprises received financial assistance; $41.6 million was invested in co-operatives ("Garantie coop", $17.3 million) and in non-profit enterprises performing commercial activities ("Garantie OBNL, économie sociale", $24.3 million). These investments must, according to the by-laws of "Investissement Québec", be in those enterprises that "promote participation as well as individual and collective responsibility" ("Investissement Québec", 1999, p .25). The objective of the fund is to create or maintain 5 119 jobs over the next three years ("Investissement Québec", 2000).[28]

The government of Quebec also facilitates the promotion of the social economy indirectly, through a series of fiscal advantages targeting social economy enterprises. We have already noted the significant tax benefits associated with investments in the "Fonds de solidarité" and "Fondaction". We now add to these fiscal incentives to encourage investment in co-operatives.

In 1985, "le Régime d'investissement coopératif" (RIC) was launched to permit co-operatives to benefit from the same fiscal advantages offered by the "Régime d'épargne action" (REA)[29] to those investing in Quebec-based firms.

Table 6.6. **Investissement Québec – Vice-president to the development of co-operatives and the social economy**

Investments only in the social economy

| Status | Division of a public (state) enterprise |
| --- | --- |
| Capitalisation | $113 million (1998-1999) |
| Source of capitalisation | "Investissement Québec" (state enterprise) |
| Objectives | Develop the social economy |
| Clientele | Co-operatives and non-profit organisations |
| Eligibility | Collective enterprises or those with a collective vocation |
| Nature of investment | Loans or loan guarantees from $50 000 ("Garantie coop" and "Garantie OBNL, économie sociale") |
| Number of projects | 141 |
| Amount invested | $41.6 million ("Garantie coop", $17.3 million and "Garantie OBNL, économie sociale", $24.3 million).[1] |
| Jobs created or maintained | 5 119 (over the next three years) |

Note: Financial year 1999-2000.

1. There are two programmes designated for social enterprises. "Garantie coop" provides loans and loan guarantees to co-operatives – producer, consumer, and worker – worker shareholder co-operatives, and solidarity co-operatives. "Garantie OBNL économie sociale" provides funding for all non-profit enterprises considered part of the social economy on the grounds of their productive activities.

As in the case of the REA, additional advantages accrue to those who fold their RIC into a registered retirement savings plan. This demonstrates the commitment by the Quebec government to direct capital into co-operative enterprises through state subsidised private investment. In addition, "Investissement Québec" finances the formation of worker shareholders' co-operatives. Worker shareholders' co-operatives are formed by workers who collectively own shares in the enterprise in which they are employed (Comeau and Lévesque, 1993). This appears to be a unique arrangement, which exists only in Quebec. It is distinct from the better-known ESOP model in that purchased shares are managed exclusively by these worker co-operatives and not by an independent trust or holding. Moreover, the shareholders' agreements in such firms require the presence of workers on the boards of these enterprises as well as a right to purchase additional shares in the event that the enterprise is sold. Finally, "Investissement Québec" may also provide funding for the purchase of a block of shares. In all cases, loan repayments are deducted directly from workers' salaries over a period of five to ten years. However attractive, this model is not as widespread as it could be; there are currently 50 such worker shareholders' co-operatives in Quebec (some in large enterprises).

## Co-operative funds

The "Mouvement Desjardins" is recognised as the most important financial institution in Quebec (Lévesque, 1997). Moreover, with its 5.3 million members, 18 000 volunteers and 1 150 *caisses populaires* (credit unions), the "Mouvement Desjardins" plays a significant social and economic role throughout the province. Although not all of the local credit unions support social economy enterprises directly, the accounts of the majority of non-profit organisations in Quebec are held here. Certain *caisses* have created so-called social or community funds from non-distributed surplus. Others have initiated specific programmes, such as "Sois ton propre patron" (STPP), launched in 1989, which provides capital for young entrepreneurs (Van Kemenade, 1999). In 1996, 196 out of 312 *caisses populaires,* which belong to the "Fédération des caisses populaires de Québec" (regional federation of *caisses populaires*), inspired by the STPP, launched "Travailleur autonome", a programme offering assistance to the self-employed (*ibid.*).

There is one exceptional credit union within the "Mouvement Desjardins", the "Caisse d'économie Desjardins des travailleuses et travailleurs (Québec)",[30] which has specialised in the financing of social economy enterprises. In fact, it is easily the single financial institution in Quebec that has been involved in supporting these enterprises. Its members are largely unionised workers, associations and individuals who share common objectives. Among the 5 000 members of the "Caisse" which has several

Table 6.7.   **Caisse d'économie Desjardins des travailleuses et travailleurs (Québec)**

| Name | "Caisse d'économie Desjardins des travailleuses et travailleurs (Québec)" |
|------|------|
| Status | Credit and savings co-operative |
| Capitalisation | $ 243.9 million |
| Source of capitalisation | Labour unions |
| Objectives | Support economic and community development and social entrepreneurship |
| Clientele | Labour unions, co-operatives, community and cultural groups and organisations |
| Eligibility | All projects associated with social entrepreneurship |
| Nature of investment | Secured term loans, lines of credit |
| Number of projects | 29 |
| Total invested | $4.4 million to the community sector in 2000) |
| Jobs created or maintained | Unknown |

Note: Financial year 2000.

local branches, 1 000 are associations which hold 60 per cent of the current liabilities. With total assets of $243.9 million, the "Caisse d'économie des Travailleuses et Travailleurs (Québec)" is the third largest *caisse d'économie* among 120 in Quebec. After two decades of financing the social economy, it has certainly demonstrated the financial viability of this "clientele". Between 1985 and 1995, the "Caisse d'économie Desjardins des travailleuses et travailleurs (Québec)", was one of the most profitable within the "Mouvement Desjardins" (Lebossé, 1998, p. 100). The many projects which it has financed over the years include, co-operative housing, the renovation of buildings to house training centres, a co-operative association in the North, funeral co-operatives, recycling enterprises, cultural enterprises (theatre, circus schools, etc.), day care centres, etc.

## Conclusion

In this chapter, we have introduced the many sources of finance available to meet the increasing needs for investment capital in the social economy. We have classified these as community-based, hybrid, worker, co-operative and state funds. As we have pointed out, these funds have distinct investment criteria, sources of capitalisation as well as their own histories. We have also noted the advantages and disadvantages of these various investment instruments. As tempting as it is to draw up a scorecard and evaluate the positive and negative aspects of these funds to develop a model of sorts, the reality is mixed, with positive and negative elements characterising each of these funds. We have outlined these above. This shows that a normative model of social economy finance is premature. However, autonomy and proximity are undoubtedly confronted by a number of trade-offs. These include the high operating costs in the case of community funds, the established and well-capitalised workers funds with their potential and their hesitation to invest in the social economy, or the much-needed involvement of the public sector at the cost of centralised decision-making. We have acknowledged the vital role played by the state in all these funds, and the vulnerability of small community-based funds that lack the necessary state support to operate. We have also gone one step further in our analysis to include in our list several funds that may not necessarily finance the social economy directly, but are themselves part of the social economy. And we have included fiscal advantages offered by the Quebec government that contribute to the accumulation of risk capital in the social economy.[31] This may invite controversy, but as we have pointed out, an accurate picture of the social economy must include both the direct and indirect engagement in the social economy. It must, therefore, also include those economic actors who have challenged the way in which business can or must be conducted.

For those interested in supporting social economy initiatives, demonstrating the success of social economy enterprises financed by some of the funds we have identified should dispel the myth that investing in non-profit enterprise and/or co-operatives implies only high risk.[32] Nonetheless, we have also insisted on the necessity for mixed funding for those social enterprises that are not self-supporting.

As we examine the many initiatives under way in Quebec and elsewhere, it is increasingly evident that the post-war social contract, which many governments have buried, is, in fact, being reconstructed in new ways. Within the interstices of the market economy is a great deal of social innovation and experimentation that can be interpreted as an emergent social contract, in which civil society actors play a decisive role. This has no resemblance to neo-liberal strategies to disengage the state and transfer responsibility to citizens. Quite the contrary: it represents the re-engagement of the state as a partner in socio-economic development strategies. Part of this re-engagement includes the financial participation in new debt instruments to respond to a gap that neither financial institutions nor private investors are willing to fill, for the most part. The growing need for small long-term investments has forced the creation of new debt and equity instruments. For the banks, the transaction costs of small loans are considered too high; for capital markets still focused on short term and largely speculative activity, this is out of their reach.

Although the financial market for small loans and investments is considered part of the larger market for venture or risk capital, the instruments and the institutional settings in which they reside, represent, in our view, more than simply a new source of finance. In every respect, the funds we have identified must be considered innovative and distinguished from typical financial institutions. Whether we examine these funds from the perspective of i) their target clientele (eligibility criteria, the selection process, the technical assistance and support provided), or ii) from the perspective of the investment "product" (the various types of debt/equity instruments available), or iii) if we look closely at the governance of these funds (the composition of its boards of directors), or iv) the institutional context in which these funds are located (e.g., the CDECs, the CLDs or the SADCs), these are all innovations. In many cases, these funds are integrated into strategic plans at local and regional levels. Their influence is clearly demonstrated by the current negotiations in Quebec, between actors in the social economy and the government, to introduce new funding sources for the consolidation of social economy enterprises. This is a critical step as it recognises that enterprises in the social economy need three phases of financing: pre-start-up, start-up and consolidation, before they can subsequently approach financial institutions.

To summarise, funds that may be considered part of the social economy fall into two broad categories:

- The first includes those that rarely invest directly in the social economy, but impose social criteria on the enterprises in which they participate.
- The second is designated for social economy enterprises – non-profits and co-operatives.

In Quebec, these two types of funds maintain close ties and share certain characteristics. These common characteristics include:

- A strong commitment to partnership, in particular, with the state, but also with the private sector.
- A focus on long-term investment reflecting the priorities of the local development plans of intermediary organisations.
- Financial investment combined with technical assistance and follow up.
- A leveraging effect of approximately 8.5 for small loans, demonstrating the capacity of social enterprises to approach financial institutions.

Quebec presents a particular case because of the extensive involvement of civil society and the state and especially because of the existence of a national network, the Forum on the Social Economy ("Chantier de l'économie sociale"). Still, the financial needs of the social economy are far from being fully met. Finally, we must recognise that the small investments sought by many social economy enterprises are costly, given the necessity for non-financial support and technical assistance that accompanies these investments in most cases. For example, the operating costs of a loan circle may represent from 150 per cent to 200 per cent of the loans issued; this cost falls sharply in a community-based fund such as the MCLA, but still represents 25 per cent. In the case of an intermediary such as the SADCs, this falls to 12 per cent and to two per cent for worker funds, where the volume of activity is substantial. This clearly demonstrates the fragility of small community-based funds and their incapacity to be self-financing.

We have been following the evolution of this alternative financial market in Quebec for several years now and continue to study its development. As we noted above, there are currently discussions in the National Assembly to create a "consolidation fund" for the social economy. Earlier this year, the Minister of Finance announced his commitment to financing the creation of sectoral networks in the social economy.[33] The many funds available in different ministries are not as visible to the public.[34] Moreover, they are generally in the form of programme funding. Still, they increase the possible sources that can be tapped by social enterprises.

Since we began our research in the early 1990s, there is a great deal more collaboration among social economy actors, no doubt largely because of the existence of the "Chantier de l'économie sociale", but not only because of this critical institutional location. We have discussed the importance of partnerships among different social actors within existing social economy funds and particularly within new intermediaries, such as the CDECs, SADCs and CLDs, in which economic strategies are conceived and implemented. In this chapter, we have not discussed another important form of partnership that has emerged and is not, as yet, institutionalised.

Increasingly, those involved in financing the social economy collaborate to assist social economy enterprises in mounting investment capital, drawing on several sources of finance. This is not necessarily to accumulate larger investments; it is more often undertaken to pool the risk involved and to share the expertise of many investment providers in considering the viability of projects. In some cases, for example, RISQ will require the participation of the MCLA, a FLI, the FES or some combination of these funds, before agreeing to go ahead. This does not only reflect caution in undertaking an investment. A bad investment is a bad investment and is recognised as such rather quickly. Rather, an informal partnership has emerged between a new group of social economy actors, who are fast developing a collective expertise. And, if we recall the partnerships on which all social economy funds are themselves based, including, in some cases, the financial community, and the large number of volunteers present in these funds, the cast of characters is indeed large. The transfer and exchange of knowledge sharply contrasts with the closed environment in which financial institutions operate. A new financial sector has emerged in Quebec in which principles of competition have been replaced by collaboration. We continue to watch these events unfold.

### Notes

1. Note that the currency unit throughout this chapter is the Canadian Dollar ($).

2. "Corporation de développement économique communautaire" (Community Economic Development Corporation).

3. This is an important initiative as it takes place in the policy domain. The critical work by Jean-Louis Laville and others on *"l'économie solidaire"*, which referred primarily to associations and non-market activity, has inspired the establishment of the *secrétariat* (Laville, 1994; Laville and Sainsaulieu, 1998). This marks a recognition that associations providing primarily non-market services, co-operatives, and mutual associations belong together and require a policy environment.

4. The Quebec government defines social economy enterprises as fulfilling the following objectives: *i)* Financial viability; *ii)* Capacity to create stable employment; *iii)* Response to social needs; *iv)* Produce goods and services which correspond to unmet needs; and *v)* Contribute to improving the quality of life of workers in local communities.

5. For example, worker funds may invest as a minority shareholder in a capitalist enterprise and, by virtue of a shareholders agreement, press certain social conditions upon the enterprise in question. A group of individuals may, likewise, invest in a firm and accept a shareholders agreement that complies with a variety of what we may call "social" objectives.

6. The participation of the private sector in the social economy in Quebec has been largely in the context of partnerships in social economy enterprises or in partnerships with the state and local actors in new local and regional political intermediaries created by the Quebec government.

7. A comparison of co-operatives and private enterprises by the Ministry of Industry and Commerce in Quebec (1999) has found that the survival rate of co-operatives after five years of existence is six out of ten in comparison to four out of ten for the private sector.

8. In Quebec, the "Caisse d'économie Desjardins des travailleuses et travailleurs (Québec)", a credit union, which has financed social economy enterprises for almost twenty years is more profitable than over 1 200 credit unions in the province which are not necessarily dedicated to supporting the social economy (Lebossé, 1998).

9. We will not, in this chapter, discuss the importance of the ethical or social investment movement. Some of these firms may, indeed, be attractive to those investors whose portfolios consist largely (or exclusively) of so-called ethical or social investment. We are, in a sense, pushing the boundaries even further by suggesting that we look closely at those firms which may not as easily be included in those selected by ethical and social investment analysts, but, indeed, should be, given the nature of the restrictions placed on their shareholders. In Canada, there is an Ethical Guide to Investment that lists all firms considered eligible for this designation. More work needs to be done in this area to look at all aspects of the firm – not only what it is producing – the more typical manner in which its social engagement is evaluated, but also to the roles given to majority and minority shareholders on issues of social concern. We must add a caveat here. It is also true that today the list of firms with so-called ethical objectives is very extensive and sometimes so broad as to make it difficult to distinguish them from other firms.

10. There are currently nine such community economic development corporations in Montreal (CDECs) and 14 throughout the province.

11. For a history of community economic development in Quebec, see Favreau and Levesque (1996). The role of community activists in Quebec is critical to the

recent history of the social economy. See also Mendell (2000), and Lévesque and Mendell (1999).

12.  Now called "Le Fonds de solidarité FTQ".

13.  In 1993, the "Fonds de solidarité" diversified its investment portfolio to establish the SOLIDE, which are now located in local development centres (in some CLDs but also in some SADCs) throughout the province of Quebec. We discuss these in Section Four of this chapter.

14.  For a history of the MCLA, see Mendell and Evoy (1997)

15.  In 1998, the "ministère des Régions" established local development centres ("Centres locaux de développement" or CLDs). There are currently 108 such centres in the province each with funds dedicated to economic development and the social economy. While we will discuss these in this chapter, we note this here to illustrate how the political environment we are observing is very new.

16.  See Lévesque and Mendell *et al.* (2000).

17.  FACILE ("Fonds ACEM CDEC CDN/NDG pour les initiatives locales d'entrepreneurship") is a partnership between the MCLA and a community economic development corporation in Montreal; FONCOOP is a partnership between the MCLA and the "Regroupement québecois des coopératrices et coopérateurs du travail" (RQCCT) and works in partnership with the "Fondation du maire de Montréal", a fund established by the mayor of Montreal. In this latter case, non-financial resources such as personnel and premises are shared with the MCLA.

18.  Loan circles are not considered part of the social economy; although they operate in group setting, they promote individual entrepreneurship. Still, for the reasons we state above, they are broadly part of the social economy, in our view.

19.  The Quebec government has dedicated $60 million to the CLDs throughout the province. The municipalities were expected to invest an equal amount; to date, they have contributed approximately $30 million.

20.  The total amount available for the FES across Quebec is approximately $11 million. This includes the administration costs of the fund.

21.  Investors in RISQ include the Royal Bank of Canada, the "Confédération des caisses populaires et d'économie Desjardins du Québec", "la Banque Nationale du Canada", Bank of Montreal, Alcan Aluminum Ltd., "le Groupe Jean Coutu (PJC) Inc.", "la Fondation Marcelle et Jean Coutu" and the Quebec government. Its partners include, alphabetically, the Association des CLDs (the network of CLDs in Quebec), the "Caisse Desjardins des Travailleuses et Travailleurs (Québec)", the "Chantier de l'économie sociale", the "Comité sectoriel de la main-d'œuvre en économie sociale et de l'action communautaire", the "Co-opératives de développement régional" (CDR), the "Corporations de développement communautaire" (CDCs), "Corporations de développement économique communautaire" (CDECs), "Fondaction, Investissement Québec", and "Réseau des SADC".

22.  If investments in the "Fonds" are folded in registered retirement savings plans, for example, the savings are very high. An investment of $1 000, can, in fact, cost as little as $200.

23. Since October 1999, the UMRCQ has been replaced by the "Fédération québécoise des municipalités" (FQM).

24. In May 1999, these consisted of: 46 managed by CLDs (54.7 per cent); 24 by SADCs (27.9 per cent); six by MRCs/municipalities (7 per cent); four by MRCs in partnership with either a CLD or an SADC (4.6 per cent); two by a partnership between a CLD and an SADC (2.3 per cent); two by a community economic development corporation (2.3 per cent) and one by a credit union (1.2 per cent).

25. See the website: *www.fondaction.com*

26. In Quebec as in Canada, workers' retirement programmes consist of two parts. One is a universal retirement plan administered by the state ("la Régime des rentes du Québec" in the case of Quebec); the second is complementary and voluntary and is in the private sector. "Le Fonds de solidarité" seeks this portion of discretionary retirement savings from workers and from the general public. In a way, the "Fonds de solidarité" socialises this private component of retirement funds.

27. Such a fund was recently announced by the director and president (CEO) of the "Conseil de la coopération du Québec". See Pierre Théroux, "Création d'un fonds de développement pour les co-ops", *Les Affaires*, 26 August 2000, p. 22.

28. As we go to press, the Quebec government has just released its budget (1 November 2001) in which it has announced the creation of a new financial product "la Financière du Québec" that will be part of "Investissement Québec". The amount available for loans and loan guarantees is $100 million for the next two years. Of this amount, $15 million will be dedicated to the social economy.

29. In Quebec, the government offers a tax credit for the purchase of shares in Quebec – owned firms. This is called the "Régime d'épargne action" (REA). The objective of the REA is to provide equity finance to those firms that are undercapitalised and demonstrate potential. The REA was not previously available for social enterprises because they do not have shareholders.

30. The distinction between a *"caisse d'économie"* and a *"caisse populaire"* is that the former serves a prescribed territory, and the latter serves a collective organisation – for example, a trade union, an ethnic community, etc.

31. At the time of writing, the Quebec government had just introduced significant fiscal advantages for a new social economy fund – "Capital régional et coopératif Desjardins", a $1.5 billion fund (capitalization of $150 million per year over the next 10 years) created by the "Mouvement Desjardins" for investment in the regions. Fifty per cent of investment in this fund is tax deductible. In our view, this is equivalent in importance to the creation of worker funds in the early 1980s and the critical role they have played in economic development and job creation in Quebec since that time. Clearly, the portrait is widening as the state now recognises the need to attract investment into the social economy. With "la Financière du Québec", this demonstrates a clear commitment on the part of the Quebec government to create more investment opportunities in the social economy.

32. According to the Ministry of Industry and Commerce, the average survival rate of co-operatives is 64 per cent after five years and 46 per cent after 10 years in contrast with private enterprise with rates of 36 per cent and 20 per cent respectively. In 2000, the total number of co-operatives and not-for-profit

enterprises was 4 764 (more than 1 000 since 1996) employing 49 450 individuals (a 15 000 increase since 1996) representing $4.2 billion in economic activity.

33. In April 2000, Bernard Landry, Minister of Finance, Quebec, committed $3 million to a programme to achieve this objective: "Programme de soutien en regroupements sectoriels en économie sociale" (Document distributed by the "Chantier de l'économie sociale", 2000).

34. Among the many programmes, we note only one example. The "ministère de l'Environnement" will provide financial support for the development and consolidation of social economy enterprises involved in the recovery, enhancement, recycling and resale of waste material, and the expansion of existing firms through the development of new projects or niches. The assistance is in the form of non-repayable grants.

ISBN 92-64-19953-5
The Non-profit Sector in a Changing Economy
© OECD 2003

PART II

# Chapter 7

# Financial Tools for Third System Organisations: A European Perspective

by

Benoît Granger,
Association MicFin, France

## Introduction

Recent research on "third system" organisations[1] has demonstrated that a variety of new financial tools are being developed. For example, the 1996 survey by INAISE, the International Association of Investors in the Social Economy[2] resulted in a book entitled "Banquiers du futur" ("Bankers of the Future") which provides an overview of these initiatives (see Granger *et al.*, 1998). It shows that the bulk of the new financial tools is being developed within the third system, and that most of them are not connected with the "old families" of the social economy such as co-operatives and mutual associations, which sprang up in the 19th century.

Furthermore, the European Commission (DG Employment and Social Affairs) developed a capitalisation operation on the "financial and legal tools" within the framework of the Third System and Employment pilot action.[3] The programme raised a number of important issues such as the identification of the specific features of these initiatives, their relative effectiveness, know-how and modes of development compared with other sectors and the appropriateness of the legal and financial tools. The means by which these tools were to be replicated and disseminated and the criteria for evaluating them were further crucial research questions (Granger, 1999).

In the meantime, several studies have been conducted to explore some of these aspects in greater depth. For example, in 1998, the International Labour Office (ILO) launched a series of studies on enterprise creation by the unemployed and the role of micro-finance (see ILO, 1998). Other studies have focused on the problem of access to financial services and the responsibility of banks. In particular, the possibility of introducing a Community Reinvestment Act (CRA) mechanism in Europe[4] was discussed by a cross-national team of experts (see Evers and Reifner, 1998).[5]

A closer examination of some common features of the various financial tools in this field indicates that the issue of access to financial services has gained increased awareness. The financial initiatives that have emerged appear to have three common features:

● They are always launched by the social sector, but take a variety of forms. In northern European countries, they are often created by churches or related groups. In southern European countries, co-operatives and mutual associations more often take the lead.

- Today, they increasingly represent a reaction against the trend towards exclusion. Traditional banks are excluding certain types of customers more and more ruthlessly; consequently, the concern of the promoters of these community-based economy financial instruments (CBEFIs) is to make available basic services that banks no longer provide.

- They finance complex, low-profit activities. Whether the applications are for professional micro-credit, payment facilities or consumer credit, they are always complex to process, which means that banks, which are under the continual pressure of competition, prefer to eliminate these applications rather than devote time to trying to understand them and find innovative solutions.

In addition, the legal status of the third system poses a number of complex challenges. From a legal point of view, the financial tools created by third-system projects can either adopt the status of an organisation belonging to the third system or of a bank or financial company with a limited licence. In the first case, the usual conduct of the organisation's activities is clearly restricted due to the financial and fiscal regulations imposed upon it. In the second case, some disadvantages could arise as a "bank" status is tied to a profit aim and thus clashes with the social and environmental objectives of the non-profit organisation.

Whilst this chapter does not provide a full survey of the new financial tools created within the third system, it will highlight various initiatives and practices that could be disseminated or mainstreamed.

## New financial needs

### Basic services for all citizens or for all customers?

The fundamental issue in the current debate on basic financial services is whether these services should merely address the needs of the "customers" or those of the citizens at large. Indeed it could be argued on the one hand that they should be restricted to the customers of banks in virtue of their ability to pay, but on the other, they could be extended to all on the grounds that they contribute to developing citizenship and inclusive society.

However, banking trends suggest that small customers have been increasingly discounted. From North to South Europe, traditional banks are eliminating whole segments of their former customers, preferring to finance large corporations to make high profits in market activities or take high risks in new activities (such as real estate in France).

Between 1989 and 1997, during which time some 5 000 bank mergers and acquisitions took place in the United States, the average return on capital was roughly 14 per cent. The figure was 18 per cent in the United Kingdom, and

4 per cent in France, where the major players have set an objective of 15 per cent. Overall, these rates of return seem unrealistic, or at least unsustainable in the long term, since they have little to do with the rates of growth of the real economy.

In addition, banking is changing significantly. Financing large corporations is not always profitable, since the recent development of direct market access has introduced cut-throat competition in the cost of services provided by banks. There is also increasingly fierce competition for market activities and capital management, including for third parties, since the new entrants (insurance companies) do not have the same commercial constraints as banks. This is spectacular in the case of distance or Internet banking which, according to Tim Sweeney, Director of the British Bankers Association, can literally cream off the best customers, who are looking for high-quality services and who are very profitable for traditional banks. As a result, bank mergers are increasing, employment is declining, and the criteria for return on capital is rising yearly in this sector at the expense of retail banking activities.

Lastly, the various scandals associated with Banesto in Spain, Barings in the United Kingdom and Crédit Lyonnais in France have presently discredited the profession in the eyes of the public.

### Lack of understanding of the social economy amongst banks

The 1994-1996 INAISE survey which investigated the creation and development of the new community-based economy financial instruments (CBEFIs) found that banks are overly selective and refuse customers who are too small (see Granger and INAISE, 1998). They find it difficult to understand the rationale behind third-system initiatives and, more broadly, behind initiatives that have both social and economic content.

The INAISE survey established a list of the reasons why traditional banks turn away customers who then look for CBEFIs:

● The financing is requested by people in groups that do not fit the profile required of entrepreneurs, such as women, immigrants, etc.

● Applicants lack training or experience in managing traditional SMEs.

● Banks do not understand the rationale behind the social economy, in which project promoters deliberately choose to forgo some of their profits.

● Projects are in overly innovative segments of the service sector, which are too difficult to understand.

● Projects are located in zones that banks consider risky.

The accumulation of what tends to be seen as handicaps in the traditional culture of bankers explains why those involved in socio-economic initiatives connected with a social movement are strongly tempted to "replace banks".

At the same time, proposals for reform are being studied, to make the European Commission (and the member States) more aware of the inadequacy of financial regulations that are concerned only with internal profitability and the distribution of dividends to shareholders. Some proposals are seen as threats, such as the idea of a "European" CRA if banks are unable to agree on methods of "community investment" (Evers and Reifner, 1998). Other proposals call attention to the unfairness of certain rules. For example, in some EU countries, CBEFIs are prohibited from adopting non-profit legal status despite the fact that, given their objectives, it is impossible for them ever to make a profit. However, they are taxed as if they did.

### Some common features of projects within the third system

The survey carried out on behalf of the European Commission (DG Employment and Social Affairs) concluded that the projects in the programme had certain common characteristics (Granger, 1999). Projects managed according to the standards, concepts, methods and objectives of the third system are by nature complex, and therefore generate numerous financial and legal difficulties.

### Between the public service and the marketplace

The representatives of the recent, often experimental, projects gathered together by DG Employment and Social Affairs agree that third-system organisations steer a course midway between the public service, which is responsible for the general interest, and the market sector, where private companies are active, geared to profit and above all private gain.

Thus, third system bodies share the objectives of both. They have avowed economic performance objectives, but they are also concerned with the common good and the general interest.

This trend is consistent with the hypothesis that a "new social economy" is being created to fill the vacuum left by the decline of the public service and, in many respects, that of the private sector as strictly defined (Westlund and Westerdahl, 1997).

### Economic or financial activities with a high social content

All projects financed through the third system involve economic activities, inasmuch as they produce and sell goods or services, but most of them are also directly or indirectly involved in the creation of jobs for the disadvantaged. If this is not the case, then they have objectives linked to preserving the environment or promoting citizens' rights. Although employment and combating exclusion may be secondary goals, they are major determinants of their activity.

Moreover, these bodies are managed according to the rules of internal democracy, which is not the case in traditional firms. Their promoters often pursue ethical objectives (respect for the environment, etc.), which is also unusual in traditional firms.

In addition, positive externalities tend to be emphasised by managers. For example, developing an economic activity that will create jobs is not, in itself, an extraordinary objective. But they see the organisation of an economic activity aimed at creating jobs for particularly disadvantaged groups as a social objective as well as a managerial one. Consequently, the following four characteristics can be considered to be the common features shared by third-system bodies, and especially those in the DG Employment and Social Affairs sample.

- They set social objectives for their economic activity.
- Their management reflects internal democracy principles.
- They take ethical criteria into account in strategic decision-making.
- They target and try to measure positive externalities, in the macroeconomic sense of the term.

### The problems of measuring macroeconomic benefits and social externalities

Two examples can help to explain why traditional bankers find it difficult to enter into these kinds of projects.

Firstly, the French *"entreprises d'insertion"*[6] are not profitable according to the traditional criteria, *i.e.* they do not create "value for shareholders", and more generally do not seek to maximise the rate of return for investors or the entrepreneurs themselves. Instead, their activity is maintained by their turnover supplemented by subsidies amounting to between 20 per cent and 30 per cent of their "total income".[7] It is the combination of both these components that enables them to pay salaries to people who were formerly dependent on various welfare payments that were costly to society. Because this kind of macroeconomic profitability is difficult to measure, it is often dismissed all together.

A second example of other discernible macroeconomic benefits could be mentioned. It is often argued that the long-term unemployed and other particularly disadvantaged groups are prone to sickness and depression, and consume disproportionately large amounts of medical and social assistance. These social ills will engender macroeconomic losses.[8] If each excluded person was in paid employment and consumed "normally", the point could be made that there would be significant macroeconomic effects through increased social contributions from wages, VAT on consumption, and of course income tax.

This type of reasoning makes it possible to arrive at the figure of 18 500 euros per year as the annual overall cost of an "average" unemployed person. Consequently, in view of the proponents of macro-microeconomic tradeoffs, any job creation subsidy that is lower than this figure or, that is less than the social minima, such as the social minimum income (RMI) in France, which is approximately 5 200 Euros per year, would still be "profitable" for society as a whole.

This argument is certainly open to criticism, but it is very prevalent among the promoters of third-system initiatives, who see the heavy toll taken by the most serious forms of unemployment and social exclusion worsen every day.

### Savings with a social return on investment

In many European countries, there are savers and various types of institutions that wish to use their savings or manage their reserves and capital in a more meaningful way, and neither the market nor traditional banks can meet their needs.

On the other hand, there are many third-system projects that are seeking to attract savings to fund their projects, against security and rates of return that are naturally not the same as those prevailing on the market.

This is why the regulatory authorities, which are responsible for protecting savers, are very reluctant to approve these operations when they take the form of public offerings.

Furthermore, they also tend to prohibit any attempt to carry out financial activities outside the highly restrictive legal framework that defines the status of banks.

## Responses of the third system

The responses formulated within the third system to address the problems of exclusion can be divided into three categories: micro-credit, credit activities without a banking status and changes within traditional banking institutions. This section discusses each of these responses in turn, using examples from the aforementioned field surveys carried out during the second half of the 1990s. The experiments described in this section are often small and relatively recent, but they are exemplary since they show the energy and imagination that the third system has shown in developing this form of combating exclusion.

## Micro-credit to finance micro-projects

Micro-credit is undoubtedly the field in which the most spectacular progress is currently being made. Micro-credit programmes are developing throughout Europe, on very different legal and institutional foundations. Several countries have well-established programmes. Some notable examples are ADIE ("Association pour le droit à l'initiative économique") in France, WWB ("Fondación Laboral Women's World Banking") in Spain, "Kwinnenbanken Norgesnett" in Norway, PYBT (Prince's Trust) in the United Kingdom and First Step in Ireland. Other programmes also have a marginal involvement in micro-credit activities such as credit unions in the United Kingdom and Ireland (Nowak, 1999).

Micro-credit is not merely a matter relating to the amount involved. Members of the European Commission point out informally that most banks are no longer interested in business loans of less than 100 000 euros. Consequently, any loan below this amount can be considered as micro-credit, although ADIE loans averaged just 3 400 euros until 1999.

Micro-credit programmes seek to fulfil various objectives: First, they endeavour to respond to the problem of inadequate credit supply faced by those who lack expertise. Indeed, it appears in retrospect that from a macroeconomic standpoint the enterprise creation market (VSEs and SMEs) is a profitable one, but most banks have been unwilling to invest the time and develop the resources necessary to supply credit to this market. This has had disastrous consequences, for businesses are created in difficult circumstances by people who lack training and are poorly informed about what running a successful business entails, which has a negative impact on overall performance. A broad range of initiatives have developed in recent years based on the values and methods of local economic development, such as Business in the Community and the Prince's Trust in the United Kingdom and the community development corporations in the United States.

A second explicit objective of micro-credit is to combat social and labour market exclusion. Giving personal loans to long-term unemployed people who wish to go into business for themselves lies totally outside banking practices. Consequently, it requires specific tools and resources, not only because complex partnerships (with government, with support and advice networks, etc.) must be built to make this activity feasible, but above all, because the goals are social rather than economic. For example, restoring autonomy to the disadvantaged is seen as the defining characteristic of ADIE's work.

The third objective of micro-credit is to target excluded minority ethnic groups. Tontines[9] and other experiences such as the "Cigales" in France and credit unions in Ireland, Austria and Poland, are often started by immigrant communities, which show great solidarity in business, more or less out of necessity since it is difficult for them to gain the trust of bankers in their host country.

This raises the issues of moonlighting and the development of unregulated financial practices. For example, SEON an organisation founded in 1994 which deals with business support and entrepreneurship development in the Netherlands[10] is taking an interest in projects ranging between 25 000 to 50 000 euros, which is much higher than the average amount of credit granted by ADIE. But SEON is only interested in projects for people with an immigrant background or refugees, including illegal immigrants, who cannot work legally.

A striking feature of micro-credit programmes lies in their two alternative approaches. They either seek to co-operate with banks, or prefer to work independently, on the grounds that banks have disavowed their responsibilities towards local communities. These approaches are illustrated below with the examples of two small programmes, ANDC in Portugal and "Crédal" in Belgium (see also Nowak, 1999).

### The example of ANDC: a public-private partnership

This recent Portuguese project provides an interesting example of public-private partnership in the field of micro-credit. The creation of ANDC by the National Association for the Right to Micro-credit in Portugal was based on a thorough study of previous achievements in this field, including the experience of ADIE (see Fundacao Calouste, 1998). Furthermore, ANDC owes its success to its partnership approach – it has managed to involve the country's biggest commercial banks, BCP (Portugal's central bank) and the government through two agreements formally concluded in March 1999.

ANDC's micro-credit method consists of an initial screening of the projects by the local associations that are members of Animar[11] – the umbrella group for over one hundred local development and socially oriented organisations – which can verify whether projects are sound or individuals trustworthy through their local networks.

The loan applications are then examined by the ANDC team, and once approved the loans are released by the bank. Under the agreement with ANDC the bank relinquishes part of its decision-making power. Loans average 4 500 euros, at a rate of approximately five per cent (the interbank rate plus two points) over an average period of three years.

Furthermore, the traditional collateral mechanisms that usually apply when securing a loan do not come into consideration here. This is because at ANDC's request, the bank agreed not to require collateral guarantees (on the borrowers' assets). The bank is not barred from taking legal action against a borrower who does not repay the loan, but it has agreed to notify ANDC before doing so. A major requirement however is for ANDC to make a deposit in the bank's accounts from savings schemes open to its supporting groups. This deposit is to amount to five per cent of the funds committed and will be used to repay losses. Finally, there is a ceiling on the funds committed: the bank agreed to provide 450 000 euros for the first year of operation (which straddles 1999 and 2000), i.e. 100 loans averaging 4 500 euros, and to provide four times this amount the following year.

Nonetheless, as in other countries, the best insurance against failure is the quality of the support provided to loan recipients outside the bank. The ANDC-BCP agreement ensures that each entrepreneur is advised by a mentor, appointed and paid by the ANDC through government subsidies (under the ANDC-government agreement), and the mentors receive training from the ANDC.

The loans are primarily intended for the groups assisted by the organisations that belong to Animar, i.e. people who are disadvantaged or live in depressed regions, who have sound, realistic and well-designed micro-creation or self-employment projects.

In fact, many of these people currently work in the informal economy. Direct government subsidies to this type of micro-activity have a perverse effect in that they force the recipients to join the formal economy immediately. This means that to receive a government subsidy, fledgling entrepreneurs must relinquish the social benefits that they receive (unemployment, etc.), complete the complex and costly formalities required to create an enterprise and pay social contributions immediately. This seems to discourage some applicants.

With the loan described above, the constraint is more flexible. Since the lender (the ANDC and the bank) has no direct link with the government, the applicant can receive the funds without being forced immediately to complete the legal formalities necessary to create a business. The transition is more flexible and better attuned to the development of turnover. Of course, the ANDC has made a commitment to the government to urge borrowers to repay their loan before it expires.

Consequently, this programme is clearly intended to involve the banking system, through a private commercial bank well known for its stringent management. This is the alternative solution to creating a specific financial tool, as was done in France by ADIE in its initial stages, and by the FIR platforms ("France initiative réseau"[12]).

### The example of Crédal: Combining socially-oriented micro-credit with a co-operative micro-bank

"Crédal" (Co-operative for Alternative Credit) has over ten years of experience in social lending (this financial co-operative created by the associations "Vivre ensemble" and "Justice et paix" has been active in Belgium since 1984) and did not have a single "bad debt" during its first 12 years of existence. But "Crédal's" financing was long limited to its own kind, i.e. co-operatives and associations, which can explain to some extent, the total success in repayments.

"Crédal" provides a complete system of savings and credit, since it receives deposits from co-operative members and savers who wish to invest their savings in socially oriented activities. "Crédal" then lends to and invests in small enterprises in the social economy (400 loans over 10 years), and provides management consulting services. Before launching this new micro-credit programme, "Crédal" waited until it was operating stably and gave thought to possible directions for development, such as extending its sphere of operations or establishing closer co-operation with other financial tools, etc.

"Crédal" has made an important contribution to financing the third system through the creation, in the autumn of 1999, of a tool for micro-investment in social enterprises that lack capital. Furthermore, in addition to its activity of lending to co-operatives, it has recently launched micro-credit schemes with much smaller amounts targeting marginalised people. Seven banks contribute to the fund, the largest of the investments being one million Euros over five years, under the aegis of the "Fondation Roi Baudouin", which pays for the support provided by independent consultants (Granger and INAISE, 1998).

The key to securing these loans – which average 6 150 euros for projects costing 9 000 to 12 000 euros – is the instruction and follow-up, that is to say, the quality of the support provided. This is costly: "Crédal" has to spend 3 000 euros in order to lend 6 000 euros – 1 500 euros before the loan to examine and prepare the project, and 1 500 euros after the start-up of the small business to monitor its progress. The donors required this rule and the facts have shown that it is indeed necessary.

Even with all these precautions, the failure rate is relatively high at 35 per cent after the first two years. The non-repayment rate is somewhat lower, for an enterprise that goes out of business after twelve months has repaid a share of its loan during this twelve-month period.

### Expanding micro-credit

First Step in Ireland, "Fundusz Mikro" in Poland and ADIE in France are probably the most firmly established and best-known micro-credit programmes. Nevertheless, they grant only a few hundred to a few thousand loans each year, despite the fact there is a long list of prospective customers waiting for this service.

The issue of how these practices can be generalised must therefore be addressed. However, micro-credit activities allow for few, if any, economies of scale and scant productivity gains if their essential aspect is to be preserved, i.e. the fact that the loans are combined with personalised counselling and follow-up.

Consequently, the expansion of micro-credit raises two questions:

- How is it possible to identify the costs of all components outside the loan itself? And how can the related advice, training and follow-up be financed? This further raises the question of what can be done to involve the government?
- How is it possible to take advantage of the productivity gains provided by banks through their logistics base, their extensive network of branches, etc.?

The section below focuses on the latter point and discusses possible forms of co-operation with banks.

### Credit activities without a banking status

The development of new tools not only concerns micro-credit, but also all "retail" financing activities, although the underlying trends are very negative. We know that the Basle Committee, which is made up of representatives of the banking profession and advises the regulatory authorities, is trying to make the rules for establishing financial companies and banks even more restrictive. Of course, the reason given is the need to better protect savers, but it would be a serious mistake if no distinction were made between the various types of financing tools and their objectives and public confidence in them. Is using the same criteria to treat a socially-oriented bank, created by a church or a co-operative movement, and an ordinary case of attempted fraud the best way to restore savers' confidence in traditional banks?

### Is it useless to resist banks?

The title of a meeting organised by INAISE on 10 May 1999 – "It is useless to resist" – illustrates that given the current macro-economic trends, the pressure of competition and the profitability rates required, it is useless to "resist" by trying to introduce a different approach to banking. However, a series of case studies show, instead, that much has been learned, and that financial activities based on trust and community ties can provide services that traditional banks no longer do (see Sattar, 2000).

### The good practices established by Community-Based Economy Financial Instruments (CBEFIs)

These "micro-banks" and other financial tools invented by and for the third system have several common characteristics that will be summarised very briefly, but which are consistent with the ethical content of the projects:

- These tools are very recent and very modest in size. Of 47 monographs prepared for the INAISE study in 1996-97, only four CBEFIs were more than ten years old and managed more than 10 million Euros of capital in 1996.

- Half of them are aimed at fostering job creation, in particular for disadvantaged people. The others have different main objectives: the environment or the promotion of biodynamic farming, etc.

- All CBEFIs interviewed argued that they always provided several services to their target customers: money, of course, in the form of loans, guarantees, capital, etc., but also development assistance services, and especially training and advice.

- Advisory services are essential for the long-term operation of these tools. The cost of services associated with micro-credit generally represents 50 per cent of the loan amount. Services such as counselling and training provision are an integral part of the loan.

- Consequently, in terms of profitability, the production costs of CBEFIs cannot be compared with those of banks, since CBEFIs have expenses for counselling, training and support that banks do not. It should also be borne in mind that CBEFIs' customers are generally those that have been excluded by traditional banks.

This approach takes into account the macro-economic benefits, positive externalities and benefits to the community already mentioned.

### Changing practices within the "old" banks of the social economy

The numerous studies carried out by INAISE and MicFin[13] show that CBEFIs are increasingly seeking to establish partnerships and co-operation schemes with large banks. These studies also provide useful analyses of the diverging trends within the retail banking profession.

Different banks behave differently and even today may still be influenced by their history and the values that led to their establishment. It is, for example, known that Barclays was founded by Quakers to finance local development. In addition, NatWest, which has a community financing project, is one of the few banks in Europe to publish a yearly "ethics report".

Several examples show the differences between co-operative banks and others:

- Many private and public banks are managed in a highly centralised fashion, while co-operative banks, which are often the outcome of "field" initiatives, are often much more decentralised and focused on the regions in which they are established, and influenced by public opinion in these regions.

- Most banks are becoming selective, setting conditions for opening new accounts and trying to eliminate less profitable accounts. Savings banks claim that they are fighting against this trend, and the European Savings Banks Group (EGSB)[14] has published a charter whereby savings banks promise to take considerable precautions before closing a customer's account.

- The number of people barred from using cheques and credit cards is growing rapidly due to the fact that many bank customers are caught in the trap of unemployment and dwindling incomes.

- Although the building societies in the United Kingdom have been demutualised, this is not the case in the rest of Europe, where mutual banks, co-operatives and savings banks still have the confidence of the public (and significant market shares), since they have more than 25 per cent of retail deposits in Italy, Germany, Finland, the Netherlands and France.

- For the same cultural reasons, mutual or co-operative banks are often leaders in the financing of small businesses (the "Banques populaires" in France), and the associative and non-profit sector.

- With regard to the serious mistakes made on the real estate market during the early 90s, with just one exception, co-operative and mutual banks were not involved in the real estate crisis and did not make the gross and costly errors of conventional commercial banks.

- In the examples of partnerships between CBEFIs and banks, the vast majority of the agreements were concluded with mutual and co-operative banks.

- Banks mainly sponsor prestigious activities in the artistic and cultural fields. Social economy banks are virtually the only ones that sponsor solidarity-based initiatives.

Co-operative banks have been thriving in recent years, and are gaining market share in retail banking compared with banks in the French Banking Association ("Association française des banques"[15]). They are even engaged in the process of buying networks, even though some of the more militant third-system leaders fear that they are running the risk of losing their specific characteristics.

### Towards possible co-operation?

Within INAISE, the debate is currently focused on identifying the fields where co-operation between CBEFIs and traditional banks would be most fruitful. In broad terms, the challenge for CBEFIs is to take advantage of banks' logistics while applying social pressure.

Today, an initial pattern for this co-operation seems to be emerging with the experiments conducted in the United Kingdom and France.

In the United Kingdom, credit unions realised early on that it would be a mistake to deprive themselves of the logistics provided by banks, which are able to develop computer systems, a costly back office and absorb the management of new activities at a very small marginal cost. This led those CBEFIs to establish good relations with the Coop Bank.

In France, ADIE has changed from a system in which it handled all aspects of the financing to a system in which banks set up loans, although it remains responsible for examining applications and following up the borrowers' activity. ADIE has been working on what appears to be one of the most innovative projects to date.

This body is able to lend funds, as an exception to the banking monopoly introduced by the law on social lending. This is also the case for the component units of "France initiative réseau" and the "Fonds France active" network.[16] But this exception is very limited, since the association can only lend its own funds, and cannot, unlike banks, borrow in order to lend. ADIE is therefore supporting a project in which specialised organisations would be given a limited licence that would allow them to borrow in order to lend, provided that they were more or less closely supervised by the banks from which they would borrow part of the loan funds. Thus, to a certain extent, banks would delegate to *ad hoc* organisations, the micro-credit that they are unable or unwilling to process directly. The distribution of loans would be highly decentralised, so that lenders and borrowers would remain in direct contact in the field, although the back office would remain centralised.

## Conclusions

This chapter has reviewed some of the major features of the financial tools recently created within the third system. It seems that sufficient experience has been gained to make it possible to outline the general forms that the necessary mainstreaming should take. Moreover, the negative trends remain of concern, for the banking profession does not really believe in the significance of these innovations.

The main lessons to draw from this review are summarised as follows:

- The development of the financial tools created within the third system, especially micro-credit tools and CBEFIs, demonstrates that traditional banks are no longer fulfilling their role. Banks are indeed excluding a growing share of their former customers. This trend is all the more serious given that access to basic financial services is now seen as an integral part of citizenship.

- The development of CBEFIs and micro-credit tools is a response tailored to the financial problems of third-system projects.

- The main issue faced today is the extension, generalisation and mainstreaming of these tools.

- Many financial tools have benefited from sufficient experience for it to be possible to estimate what it would cost to double their size or expand their activities tenfold. This would entail the risk of losing one of their essential characteristics, i.e. the physical proximity and shared values of lenders and borrowers.

- Third-system projects have considerable job creation potential, as they give rise to many innovative concepts for future services, i.e. various types of personal services. There is general agreement that these jobs are among those least costly to create. The initial financing plan of ADIE entrepreneurs averages approximately 10 000 euros. Little large-scale investment is needed in these sectors, market access costs are low and the skills required are such that many disadvantaged people with low skills are capable of succeeding.

- Above all, creating jobs for the excluded with third-system methods is infinitely less costly than using traditional social policy methods.

- The operation is cost effective provided that the macro-economic gains derived from the creation of these jobs are taken into account. This type of job costs four times less than the average cost of an unemployed person in Europe.

- Fund providers of the social economy have demonstrated the operational feasibility of initiatives in which traditional banks did not believe. Banks have often preferred to merely follow their lead in the new paths opened.

The development of CBEFIs will never provide a full answer to the problem of social exclusion, but it will contribute to restoring the autonomy and the self-respect of marginalised people.

Furthermore, deregulation is gradually breaking down the barriers between social-economy financial institutions and private banks. This has had consequences, such as the demutualisation of building societies in the

United Kingdom that can enable shareholders to reap short-term gains, but only once every one hundred years at most.

Finally, regulatory changes – such as the Basle Convention on banking controls, which prevents any bank from entering into new activities for which it lacks adequate capital – raise the costs of market access. If the minimum capital required to create a new financial institution increases further, it will become impossible to create CBEFIs targeting VSEs and SMEs.

All the above reasons suggest that governments should become involved in the development of financial tools for the third sector. Their effectiveness cannot be determined merely by comparing their performance with the ratios of banks; it should further be assessed in terms of the common good.

## Notes

1. The term "tiers secteur" (or third sector) is also frequently used in French, as for example, in the report by Lipietz (2000) commissioned by the French Ministry for Employment and Solidarity to study the possibilities of introducing "a new type of community-based company".

2. See www.inaise.org

3. At the initiative of the European Parliament, the European Commission introduced, in 1997, a new pilot action entitled "Third System and Employment". The aim of this pilot action was to explore and enhance the employment potential of the "Third System", with an emphasis on the areas of social and neighbourhood services, the environment and the arts, and to disseminate the results throughout the European Union. The Commission's Directorate-General "Employment and Social Affairs" implemented the pilot action and selected 81 projects for support. For more details, see http://europa.eu.int/comm/employment_social/empl&esf/3syst/index_en.htm

4. The Community Reinvestment Act (CRA), enacted by the US Congress in 1977 is intended to encourage depository institutions to help meet the credit needs of the communities in which they operate. For more details see www.ffiec.gov/cra/default.htm

5. Further notable contributions are the "Étude sur l'intégration des exclus par le travail indépendant et le microcrédit en Europe – Identification du cadre législatif et réglementaire", ADIE report edited by Maria Nowak, November 1999, for DG Science, Research and Development, and the work of the New Economics Foundation (see http://neweconomics.org).

6. SMEs that have signed agreements with the central government to set aside a number of jobs for people otherwise excluded from the labour market; these jobs, whose holders receive work experience, training and social guidance, are government subsidised. See the website of the "Comité national des entreprises d'insertion": www.cnei.org

7. In France, entreprises d'insertion generally receive 20 to 30 per cent of their "total income" (i.e. turnover and subsidies, as well as other social income) from public resources to offset the low productivity and skills of workers in these programmes, and the need for greater supervision.

8. A more detailed analysis would make it possible to take into account other collective expenditures, such as the additional maintenance required in distressed neighbourhoods, the need for larger numbers of police, the extra investments in social, educational and medical infrastructure for people in difficulty, etc. ISEOR made a systematic analysis in terms of the "estimated hidden costs in a neighbourhood" stemming from problems of exclusion. It makes it possible to assess the cost of theft, physical damage, deterioration of the housing stock, the impact of drug addiction and alcoholism, underachievement in school, etc. (see *http://iseor.com*).

9. Tontines are fiscal instruments that allow several individuals to collectively acquire a good, asset or property. The contract stipulates that the asset will go to the last surviving person in case of the death of its partners.

10. See *www.seon.nl*

11. See *animar-dl.pt*

12. See *www.fir.asso.fr*

13. MicFin was an EU-funded project launched in December 1997. Its purpose was to identify and develop suitable financing mechanisms and to establish, in connection with local development, partnerships creating a multiplier effect between third sector operators and traditional social economy operators, the social partners and the public authorities. The project was managed by Ired Nord in Rome. See *http://europa.eu.int/comm/employment_social/empl&esf/3syst/en/MicFin.htm*

14. See *www.savings-banks.com/esbg/esbg.htm*

15. See *www.afb.fr*

16. See *http://franceactive.org* and *http://fir.asso.fr*

PART III

# Evaluating the Non-profit Sector: New Challenges

ISBN 92-64-19953-5
The Non-profit Sector in a Changing Economy
© OECD 2003

PART III

# Chapter 8

# Innovation, Value Added and Evaluation in the Third System: A European Perspective

by

Xavier Greffe,
University of Paris 1, Panthéon-Sorbonne, France

## Introduction

The importance of the third system is universally acknowledged, even though there is still debate over its boundaries and size. In Europe these issues are resolved by concentrating far more on the effective production of the bodies constituting the third system than on the existence and/or distribution of operating surpluses.

However, the importance of the third system is not based solely on quantitative benchmarks. It also stems from the recognition of the value added generated by third system institutions, compared with private or public companies, in terms of recognising and meeting needs, social integration, territorial improvement, greater democracy and sustainable development.

This value added – or potential for innovation – is evaluated either at the macro-sectoral level or at the level of individual institutions, and a large number of measurement tests are now starting to become available, each of which has its own advantages and limitations. However, in this respect it is difficult to make use of analytical instruments based on the unifying rationale of profit when the third system addresses so many values and can have either tangible or intangible impacts both within a given institution and in the territorial jurisdiction of that institution. In order to clarify the issues arising from this debate, it is therefore necessary to take account of the three possible functions of evaluation, namely monitoring, learning and mediation.

## The third system: preliminary definitions

The third system has always existed in European society, although it has gone under a variety of names. For many years treated as part of the co-operative or mutualist movement, it has benefited from strong growth in the number of different types of non-profit institution to the point that it now finds itself in the vanguard of efforts to promote employment, solidarity and sustainable development. The European employment strategy for the period 2000-2006 recognises the importance of the third system by expressing the hope that all parties will help to promote measures that will realise the potential of the perspectives offered by job creation at the local level and in the social economy, notably with regard to new services (European Commission, 1999). In view of this, evaluating the third sector is now in itself a priority, for which, as indicated in a recent Note by the OECD, there are a number of reasons: the need to secure funding of different types and from

**190**

different sources, the need to move away from the perception of the third system solely in terms of social integration, and the need to take account of all of its positive impacts at the territorial level (OECD, 1999a).

Inevitably, a precise definition of the third system remains elusive. While Europeans often start with the definition suggested by the Johns Hopkins studies, they have gradually started to distance themselves from this approach as a result of the programme of action pursued by the European Commission (Borzaga *et al.*, 2000). The difference between this European approach and the so-called "American" approach primarily lies in the fact that the former embraces all co-operatives and social enterprises – even if they distribute a share of their surpluses to their members, albeit under certain conditions – whereas the latter adheres strictly to the criterion of the non-distribution of profits. On the other hand, the European approach excludes those foundations or associations that are simply public agencies in all but name in that they are primarily financed through subsidies (universities, hospitals), *i.e.* the criterion of non state dependency is applied in practice and not simply for form's sake. The following table illustrates the differences between the two approaches (see Campbell *et al.*, 1999).

Table 8.1.   **Criteria for classification as part of the third system**

| European approach | Johns Hopkins approach |
| --- | --- |
| Formal organisation | Formal organisation |
| Independent organisation | Independent organisation |
| Self-managed organisation | Self-managed organisation |
| Limited redistribution of profits | Non-redistribution of profits |
| Production of social capital | Voluntary participation |

Despite these differences in approach, the indicators of the size of the third system, notably in terms of employment, are not that different. The most exhaustive European study to date – that carried out by the CIRIEC (CIRIEC 2000) – gives percentages for civil employment in the third system which are relatively comparable (8.8 million jobs, *i.e.* almost 6.6 per cent of civil employment in EU member states, of which 25 per cent in co-operatives, 71 per cent in associations and four per cent in mutual organisations) (see Tables 8.2 and 8.3). Despite these relatively consistent figures, the constituent elements of the third system differ quite sharply from one approach to another. This is important with regard to the definition of innovation where the Europeans place the emphasis on the "productive input" provided by the third system, but without this detracting from the importance of representation, expression and mobilisation, which are central elements in the Johns Hopkins approach.

Table 8.2.   **Employment in the third system in Europe**

| | Full-time equivalent | % of total civilian employment |
|---|---|---|
| Austria | 233 662 | 6.91 |
| Belgium | 206 127 | 5.85 |
| Denmark | 289 482 | 12.56 |
| Finland | 138 580 | 6.92 |
| France | 1 214 827 | 5.93 |
| Germany | 1 860 861 | 12.56 |
| Greece | 68 770 | 1.81 |
| Ireland | 151 682 | 12.57 |
| Italy | 1 146 968 | 5.88 |
| Luxembourg | 6 740 | 4.16 |
| Netherlands | 769 000 | 14.69 |
| Portugal | 110 684 | 2.51 |
| Spain | 878 408 | 7.45 |
| Sweden | 180 793 | 5.15 |
| United Kingdom | 1 622 962 | 7.32 |

*Source:* Based on data compiled by CIRIEC, 1999, pp. 17-18.

Table 8.3.   **Structure of the third system in Europe**

(as a % of civilian employment)

| | Co-operatives | Associations | Mutuals |
|---|---|---|---|
| Austria | 24 | 75 | 3 |
| Belgium | 17 | 77 | 6 |
| Denmark | 26 | 74 | 0 |
| Finland | 55 | 45 | 0 |
| France | 24 | 69 | 7 |
| Germany | 24 | 68 | 8 |
| Greece | 17 | 81 | 2 |
| Ireland | 21 | 78 | 1 |
| Italy | 42 | 58 | 0 |
| Luxembourg | 29 | 70 | 13 |
| Netherlands | 14 | 86 | 0 |
| Portugal | 44 | 55 | 1 |
| Spain | 46 | 53 | 1 |
| Sweden | 50 | 46 | 4 |
| United Kingdom | 7 | 90 | 3 |

*Source:* Based on data compiled by CIRIEC (1999), pp. 17-18.

By presenting itself as an alternative to the market and to public production, the third system has always claimed that it plays a pioneering role compared with these other two means of allocating resources. The very use of the term "system" rather than "sector" underlines this deliberately "alternative"

**192**

aspect. Obviously the third sector – which ostensibly presents itself as residual – could be interpreted as a kind of catch-all category for all those bodies that feel that they belong neither to the public sector nor to the market sector, or which cannot find solutions in the latter to the problems they wish to resolve. The third system would therefore very swiftly find itself transformed, in this case, into an indicator of unmet needs, a set of preferences that have not been taken into account, or a catalogue of social demands.

However, third system institutions (TSI) in Europe have often announced ambitious objectives and presented their modes of management as contributing factors in the transformation of society. They supply services that are new in terms of the way in which they are conceived and the processes they use; they express needs that have not been taken into account; they disseminate values that help to improve life in society; they set out to make social inclusion, employment and qualifications ends in themselves and not simply instruments related to a greater or lesser degree of activity; and they create social ties. The deliberate use of the word "system" rather than "sector" clearly indicates that they aim to function in terms of a given form of co-operation rather than play a palliative or complementary role. Emphasising the contrasts between systems in this way will make value judgements paramount and will result in innovation being conceived in terms of the differences between products rather than processes, which is unfortunate.

In more general terms, analysing the innovative capabilities of the third system for a variety of reasons poses many problems.

Innovation is generally defined as the development of something that is novel and is therefore related to creativity – indeed, to such an extent that initial efforts to measure innovation consisted of constructing indicators capable of determining whether or not products conformed to existing goods. However, there are many new products that are not considered to be innovations, in addition to which a product considered to be novel at a given point in time may not necessarily remain so.

Innovation may consist of the introduction of new products or processes; a system may therefore be innovative if it is able to find a different way of providing the same service by making use of other references or values.

Innovations may occur at the level of an agent, institution or system; the level at which the analysis is conducted will modify the field of innovation considered.

In view of the above, there are three questions that need to be asked:

- In what way is the third system innovative?
- What conditions encourage or discourage innovation?
- Can innovation be measured?

## The third system as a source of innovation

Since innovation can be produced both by individual institutions and by groups of institutions sharing common values, it is only logical to distinguish here between two levels of analysis:

- Analysis of the third system as a whole, in which case we shall talk in terms of systemic or macro-social innovation.
- Analysis of the constituent institutions of the third system, which will call for new responses to economic and social problems.

### The third system as macro-innovation

In Europe, the third system has been credited with achieving three types of innovation: developing a new social organisation matrix based on co-operation; serving as a new instrument for public management; creating development capacities at the local level.

### The third system as a model for a new form of social organisation

**Co-operation as a means of going beyond role specialisation.** Contemporary forms of the third system in Europe emerged in the course of the 19th century, primarily in the form of what is now termed the "social economy". The aim was three-fold, namely to ensure the right to work as opposed to a wage-earning system held to be "undignified"; allow workers access to consumer goods; implement the principles of solidarity, notably between producers and consumers, in order to correct the functioning of an unseeing market. Contrary to a popular misconception, such initiatives have not been limited to urban working populations but have also emerged in rural areas in the form of support for farming families, hence the continuing importance of the third system in rural areas in Europe.

The relative weight of these objectives varied according to the type of institution. "Co-operatives", aimed at establishing solidarity networks between producers and consumers such as the Rochdale co-operative, could therefore be contrasted with mutual societies designed to help resolve the most pressing social problems. However, while mutual societies have progressed in a wide variety of forms, co-operatives have never managed to overcome the dominance of capitalistic enterprises and the associated rationale of the market economy. Yet they offered references that were radically different, by fostering solidarity between producers based on mutual respect or by bringing together independent producers, be they farmers, craftsmen or traders, in networks of solidarity.

**"Dovetailing" as a contemporary interpretation of the third system.** With the emergence of a consensus on the market economy – underpinned by the

Welfare State – macro-social thinking on the third system has evolved considerably. The challenge it faces is no longer seen as the search for an alternative to the market economy but is in further development of the trading relationship. In addition to this will to establish a non-confrontational relationship with the market economy, the linkages to the sphere of public intervention have also been improved. In the tradition of Polanyi, some European experts felt that the third system enshrined the three basic principles of economic organisation (CIRIEC, 2000, p. 109, etc.).

- The **market**, which presupposes encounters between suppliers and consumers for the purposes of trade.

- **Redistribution**, which assigns responsibility for resource allocation to a central authority.

- **Reciprocity**, which sees, in the circulation of goods and services between individuals or groups, the manifestation of a social link, in which each donation calls for a counter-donation and every link is at once a debt. We are far removed here from redistribution, which would imply an obligation to do something or to return something, as in the case of a market transaction, which would imply planning related to an exchange of equivalents. What we have is therefore a non-monetary economy governed by reciprocal inputs of the type found, for example, in subsistence or household production.

The third system would therefore appear to embody these three principles to varying degrees according to the type of structure chosen. It would appear to be the area where the "donation/counter-donation" relationship is embodied. Rather than seeing this as an alternative form of organisation to the market and/or the state, it would be more appropriate to view it as a hybrid form of organisation that is "dovetailed" into society.

The flaw in this thesis of a dovetailed third system, however, lies in an inherent uncertainty. There are without doubt trading transactions that do not consist solely of the substitution of counterparts but also of production of a social link. The problem lies in determining where such links manifest themselves. Links that are forged between service producers would indicate a co-operative rationale, but if they are perceived as a new form of market operation then it makes matters more ambiguous because there are no grounds for asserting that relations between producers and consumers in the third system are systematically different to what they would be in the "mainstream". In order to understand the impact of mutual societies on agricultural co-operation institutions, it would be better to start with an economic interpretation in terms of cost differences, which are often linked to economies of scale or socio-demographic characteristics, than with interpretations of the "dovetailed" type.

## *The third system as a new system of public management*

In both Europe and the United States, the third system is now seen as a solution to the problems encountered by the Welfare State. Over the past two decades, the institutions of the Welfare State have fallen short in identifying new requirements or devising appropriate solutions (Smith and Lipsky, 1993; Greffe, 1999). While decentralisation, users' committees and quality control may initially have been able to provide tentative responses, the mobilisation of non-profit organisations by means of contracts was seen as a more innovative and acceptable approach. At that time there was even talk of a new form of governance. The contribution of these organisations transformed public action into a networking and team-working exercise. The concept of public action based on a vertical hierarchy and specialisation gave way to a concept of public action based on the association and mobilisation of all parties.

This concept is not new. By as early as 1830 Alexis de Tocqueville had demonstrated the role played by citizens' associations in expressing the wishes of the community and in providing solutions. Things have changed somewhat since then and nowadays the state is perfectly willing to entrust these organisations with assignments that for some of them had long been within their purview. Furthermore, states increasingly tend to entrust to organisations that are "accepted" within the community tasks which would be not be condoned were they to be undertaken by civil servants. This mobilisation of the third system is based on contracting or the introduction of new services. Social action is the priority area for this new form of public management, although training and social inclusion are other examples.

**The mobilisation of the third system poses many problems both for Third Sector Institutions (TSIs) and for society.** There is a strong likelihood that TSIs will be used to discharge duties that the state is unable to fulfil or, even worse, duties that it wishes to fulfil at lower cost. Faced with budget restrictions, governments are increasingly tempted to use arrangements deemed to be less expensive than the creation of new departments despite the risk, in certain cases, of depleting the availability of voluntary workers, a resource that largely accounts for this economic advantage. The situation is exacerbated by the growing financial weakness of such institutions that see their resources increasingly dependent on a single source, with the attendant risk of fluctuations and budgetary restrictions. The renewal of subsidy contracts forces these organisations to invest much of their time in such activities and, against their better judgement, to accept a status of customer that is at odds with their original *raison d'être*.

For society, the risk lies in entrusting private organisations, even non-profit organisations, with tasks in the general interest of the community.

Undoubtedly the contracts and codes of conduct are quite specific in this respect. The day-to-day management of such actions, however, is ensured by boards of directors whose representativeness or capacity for innovation may ultimately be challenged. Lastly, the transfer of public services to TSIs poses problems about the management of human resources in former government departments or regional administrations.

## The third system as an instrument for local development

Over the past twenty years European researchers have come to adopt the view that TSIs have a special role to play in local development in that the capacity for territorial development or redevelopment is linked to how much account is taken of the long-term interests of a territory, the emergence of new services and the creation of social links. These TSIs help both to enhance their environment and to strengthen the players with whom they interact in terms of production or consumption by:

- Creating forums for exchanges where alternative approaches to development can be compared and joint projects discussed.

- Considering employment not as an instrument but as an end in itself that by improving skills allows actors within a given territory to respond more effectively to the challenges posed.

- By taking as a starting point the needs felt at the local level, unlike trade-off or selective instruments, both public and private, based on centralised approaches in which local data are marginalised.

This role is analogous to that of the third system in the development of communities (Piore, 1994). The latter suffer from a lack of social bonding – such as that provided by the family or religious institutions – which cannot be compensated for by traditional organisations. Their demands emanate from groups which have no real place in economic life and which therefore cannot rely upon the types of body, such as unions, through which demands were traditionally conveyed. Lastly, the activities of their members are not coherent in economic terms and at best find a degree of unity in an informal production of mediocre quality. Unless there are clear vectors or procedures for channelling efforts, the best way for groups or the individuals who constitute communities to organise a minimum degree of social life, express their needs and implement the means to satisfy those needs is through organisations in the third system. In this area, the TSIs are therefore superseding older organisations, some of a religious nature and others the outcome of government initiatives. Indeed, it is essential for territorial authorities that wish to meet the needs of communities to have a local body to relay information and thereby ensure that the choices made – and the resulting constraints – are more readily accepted by the local population (Smith and Lipsky, 1993).

### The third system as a forum for micro-innovation: renewal of processes and production

Third system institutions produce new services that the market economy either cannot or does not know how to introduce. They add to these services social values that have either been forgotten or discarded by other production mechanisms. They put into place mechanisms for social inclusion that are sustainable in the employment market, etc. A more precise definition of such institutions might be to say that they pursue several objectives which can never be reduced solely to the pursuit of profit and which embrace the pursuit of social, environmental, etc. values, both for users and for producers or their territory.

Third system institutions are innovative in that they make it possible to:

- **Produce new services that the market economy either cannot or does not know how to introduce.** Because they embody a wide range of aspirations, are not subject to pressure to make short-term profits and can mobilise capacities for social innovation, these institutions are able to see where the response of the market economy to existing needs is inadequate, identify those needs, design relevant responses and put in place funding networks that will ensure those needs are met. Recent examples of this include the role played by the Danish association FMI which for over 15 years now has endeavoured to develop sport for everyone and to make it possible for people who are either out of work, socially marginalised or disabled, or people who are usually excluded from sports clubs and the sports they practise, to participate in such activities. There are many reasons for which people do not take part in sporting activities: long-term unemployment, night workers, lack of the means needed to practise sport in clubs no matter how low the fees charged (although they generally tend to be high). In providing access to sport for such people the association attempts not only to provide them with recreational activities and allow them to improve their fitness but also, for many of the people targeted, to restore access to the social links from which they are excluded. The service provided therefore has a two-fold purpose: first it provides an opportunity to practise something that may be beneficial; secondly, it creates and strengthens a social tie with other members of the community. In the minds of those responsible for directing these efforts, these two aspects cannot be dissociated because they combine to ensure better social integration: 10 per cent of those who have taken part in these programmes currently find a job within six months, a new job clearly being the most obvious material manifestation of the formation of a social tie.

**198**

- **Draw attention to economic or social values which market production fails either to take into consideration or to capitalise upon.** Associations or small co-operative type firms can help to secure the social inclusion of young people through the development of public works projects, such as the restoration of old buildings or historical properties. In performing such work these associations do both a conventional economic good for which there is market demand and a social good in the form of a capacity for inclusion with regard to the young people involved in such projects.

- This "production of social ties" can acquire an even more collective, or even territorial, dimension. Through the production of cultural services the Marcel Hicter Foundation in Brussels intends to create forums for socialisation in territories that have experienced the three-fold handicap of long-term unemployment, environmental damage and haphazard migratory movements. Reconstituting areas for social exchange, which had suffered from the disappearance of all kinds of micro-instruments such as shopkeepers, public markets and local cinemas, creates a favourable environment in which new projects can be developed and undertaken. Culture can satisfy a number of individual or collective aspirations at the local level if it can take the form of cafes where music is played, cyber cafes, local theatres, street performing arts, libraries, etc. (EU TSEP Summary Booklet, 2000).

- This approach is more generally based on the type of innovation that prompts TSIs to go beyond the simple rationale of "professionalisation" that often lies behind the introduction of services to incorporate additional social or long-term approaches (Greffe, 1998).

- **Transform new services into sustainable sources of employment**. Third system projects all have objectives with regard to employment but address a wide variety of potential job-creation mechanisms. Some projects aim to create jobs, either directly or indirectly, in order to deliver new services. Others attempt to give rise to or disseminate new skills, particularly in the area of social services. There is yet another type of project that aims to develop mechanisms that will allow individuals to return to the labour market. The "Escale Solidaire" project in the Hérault (France) seeks to set up groups of employers in rural areas so that individuals, who often only have access to part-time or seasonal work in rural areas, by working for several employers, can have a proper full-time job.

- **Realise the potential impacts of new technologies as a source of social progress**. The development of new technologies is routinely perceived as a source of productivity gains, although primarily from an economic standpoint. Third system institutions, however, have often attempted to use such technologies as a source of social productivity. The cyber-cinema initiative in Babelsberg (Germany), for example, uses digital cinema to create a dialogue between communities in different regions of Europe confronted with the same type of problem, *i.e.* the socially excluded (long-term unemployed), immigrants (people from Turkey or the former Yugoslavia), groups traditionally living on the margins of society (gypsies), former prisoners, etc. By enabling them to share the problems they face, but also the solutions they may have found, the project aims to create a link that will extend to the communities or municipalities alongside which they live.

● **Update informal activities and improve their functioning.** This dimension of the third objective is more original. In many service activities, and more particularly those subject to seasonal fluctuations, their informal nature tends to make employment more precarious and to compromise the quality of jobs due to a lack of innovation, training and a stable and firmly-rooted organisation of procedures for commercialising products. The Rioja Foundation has been successful in transforming marginal craft activities into genuine jobs. Obviously there is a danger that such improvements may lead to higher prices, but this a condition for the transformation of "disparate" activities into sustainable employment and for achieving a significant improvement in the quality of goods by improving the ways in which training and employment are organised.

## The conditions for innovation

A distinction may be made between two types of conditions:

● Those relating to the environment of the economic and social system; they require a response to be given to the problems posed by market and public modes of regulation.

● Those relating to the effective emergence of institutions and actors in the third system; they implement practical responses to the problems posed.

### Environment-related conditions for innovation

Work carried out in Europe on the potential for innovation of the third system highlights a certain number of factors.

The will to ensure access to basic services irrespective of income level. This desire to correct social inequalities in a decentralised manner is paramount to the emergence of the third system. This argument has been advanced in two directions, the first concerning the limits of public intervention and the second, those of the market:

● With regard to public intervention, the argument decries the way in which majority rule operates in that it favours the needs of the median voter and denigrates preferences that are far removed from the former.

● With regard to the market, the argument challenges the informational gaps it creates; this interpretation is not without relevance in that information on the quality of services is not readily available, which can be a disincentive to consumers.

One of the most common interpretations in Europe (the so-called "interdependence theory") holds that the development of the third system may be explained by the functional shortcomings of public intervention, notably its limited ability to identify new needs and to provide appropriate responses. This explanation would seem to fit in the areas of aid and social action. In addition, it supports the analysis of the third system as the "source" of a new form of public management.

Another factor in innovation would appear to lie in the weakness of sectors such as social action, training or culture. Initiatives are hampered by major economic risks inasmuch that the cost of the services provided may prove to be very high and in which case cannot be borne by users unless public subsidies or private donations are made available. This henceforth traditional analysis is the outcome of the tradition imbued in the cultural economy by Baumol's law whereby "service" sectors do not benefit from productivity gains comparable to those in the rest of the economy, in which case its costs are driven upwards. Firms in the sector therefore find themselves caught in a dilemma: either they raise their access prices, in which case they are faced with decreased demand; or they do not raise their prices so that they can continue to mobilise demand, in which case they operate at a loss. It is here that we find the *raison d'être* for the third system since its institutions make it possible to mobilise public funds without being subject to a bureaucratic style of management or to produce at low cost through the use of voluntary services and thus generate higher demand by charging lower prices.

Building and expanding upon the above analysis, a fourth interpretation explains the presence of the third system in terms of the will of the latter to realise indirect profits and/or social values that are not taken into consideration by the market and disregarded by private operators. These values are only of benefit to society in the long term, whereas market mechanisms derive value solely from the spin-offs from short-term activities. The third system would therefore serve here to make good the "telescoping" defect in both the market and individuals, a defect that in fact is becoming worse.

### Conditions for innovation related to organisations and actors

A second series of conditions for innovation is related to the emergence of new actors or favourable institutional or financial mechanisms.

## Third system entrepreneurs or "civic enterprises"

Innovations produced by the third system are often the outcome of the mobilising of specific people or institutions, which then play the role of civic entrepreneurs or innovators:

- They innovate by helping to put in place new forums for decision-making or project implementation.

- They are civic in that they attempt to "optimise" the prospects for sustainable development of benefit to all in a given territory by making use of the satisfaction relating to economic and social values (Borzaga *et al.*, 1998).

Intermediary firms, local public/private bodies, associations, and co-operatives are types of structures that are often used by actors combining economic and social values, *i.e.* the reintegration of long-term unemployed, aid to marginalised groups, environmental protection, development of services in the home, etc. These entrepreneurs (Henton *et al.*, 1996) make use of innovative approaches to problems, act as catalysts in the forging of links between private and public resources and produce a social capital. A civic entrepreneur is not necessarily a single individual but may consist of a group of people exhibiting mutually complementary capabilities, or even better, people involved at different stages of innovations within the third system. There are three stages that can be distinguished here:

- Initiation: the civic entrepreneur changes the way in which the members of a community perceive themselves, makes them accept new challenges, motivates them in favour of change, and instigates networks – he is both motivator and mediator.

- Preparation and implementation: the resolve to meet a challenge that has become apparent; the challenge must be transformed into a coherent strategy – here the entrepreneur acts as teacher and mentor.

- Adaptation and renovation: the civic investor must maintain a watch and act as an agent for renewal.

In Europe, such innovators were traditionally to be found in denominational organisations or unions for social action or workers' education. While these sources still exist, civic entrepreneurs are increasingly drawn from communities that are attempting to integrate into society. One last attribute should also be mentioned: these entrepreneurs frequently exhibit a life cycle. After spending a certain amount of time working within third system institutions, they either leave them or attempt to make them evolve into structures within which the institutions can grow, often to the detriment of their original uniqueness.

## A favourable legal environment

Despite the existence of many different types of status, some commentators feel that in many cases the legal form of TSIs inhibits their potential for innovation. The problem here relates not so much to status as to changes from one status to another as TSIs develop or to linkages between the status of institutions and that of the people who work in them:

- In order to grow, TSIs must change status over time, which is by no means easy. Many TSIs are therefore obliged to have several different statuses at the same time (commercial enterprises and associations), thereby creating an institutional "halo" that does not necessarily work in their favour.

- The fact that these institutions receive a large number of subsidies imposes severe constraints on those who work for them, particularly in terms of wages. Initially bearable, such constraints increasingly become less so over time, with the result that certain organisers or entrepreneurs ultimately have no other alternative but to espouse a commercial status.

Apart from the problem of status there is also the problem posed by the regulatory framework within which TSIs must operate. In some cases the rules are highly favourable; for example, the provision made under French law for several employers to set up an association to manage in their name a full-time occupation, itself composed of a variety of activities pursued by the entrepreneurs involved, makes many innovations possible. On the other hand, the omission of social clauses in public contracts stymies the potential for innovation of the third system. These so-called "social clauses" made it possible to give preference to third system firms that set up re-insertion programmes for people in difficulty but are now considered to adversely affect the operation of the single market.

## The presence of suitable financial mechanisms

Apart from mutual institutions of certain co-operative movements that have access to their own financial institutions, TSIs find it difficult to secure financing. There are many reasons for this: low financial returns, the slow gestation of projects, the lack of personal guarantees from borrowers, and in some cases the lack of managerial capacities. Innovation in the third system is thus highly sensitive to innovations that affect its own financing structures. Examples of this include (INAISE, 1997):

- The development of micro-credit provided that those who grant it could, in practice, deduct all losses from their taxes.

- The conversion of passive resources (budgets providing compensation or coverage for social problems) into mechanisms for financing new activities (Vitamine W in Antwerp) provided that the law affords some degree of flexibility in adjusting status.

- Micro banks or "business angels", which make it possible both to draw upon unused local savings and to provide funding for projects with the greatest utility.

### The presence of supporting institutions

Irrespective of their merits, TSIs often experience difficulties with regard to expert services, negotiating or even management, hence the importance of providing support structures. Such structures have always existed and have even assumed major importance in some countries (FEFECO-OP in Belgium, CEPES in Spain, PANCO in Greece). However, more often than not they address traditional sectors in the social economy rather than new associations that submit the larger share of requests for funding. With regard to the latter, organisations operate through horizontal networks that strengthen the sustainability of third system institutions:

- By allowing information to be exchanged and institutions to learn how to use it.
- By establishing franchising or brand-name systems to provide access to shared resources (WISE in the United Kingdom, ENVIE in France).
- By creating synergies between different local initiatives to allow them to mutually reinforce each other ("strawberry fields", see Campbell, 1999, p. 100).
- By organising "mothership" or umbrella schemes to oversee the development of an initiative.

All of these initiatives highlight the important role played by trust in consolidating such initiatives: trust between members of a TSI, trust between TSIs and their partners.

## Measuring innovation in third system institutions

For many years underestimated or reduced to macro-sociological interpretations, the economic measurement of innovation in TSIs needs to be carried out more systematically than it is at present, subject to the proviso, of course, that account is taken of the distinctive nature of their *raison d'être* and the way in which they function. A certain number of resources are siphoned off, either directly or indirectly, to the third system and it is perfectly legitimate to question whether the results are commensurate with the effort invested. In addition, the impacts of this third system are in many cases intangible, whether they affect the internal functioning of firms, by fostering a more democratic approach to working conditions or the environment within which firms operate, for example, by strengthening the capacities available within a given territory. The challenge here is therefore not to update evaluation mechanisms that are totally different to those used for private firms, but rather to enlarge, if possible, the field of the most traditional indicators applied to intangible elements, as clearly proposed in the OECD Note mentioned previously (OECD, 1999a).

Two possible approaches are therefore open to us: we can either measure the efficiency of the third system *per se* or we can measure the efficiency of its different components. The first approach leads us back to the assumptions examined above regarding the emergence of TSIs. It would be more pertinent, however, to seek to determine how TSIs actually fulfil the innovative role they are supposed to have. Attempts to measure their efficiency and effectiveness, either *per se* or in relation to those in other sectors of the economy, have indeed been made but have not always been integrated. It would therefore be of interest to see whether an evaluation protocol in this respect could be employed on a more systematic basis. An analysis of these two points follows:

### Disparate evaluation efforts

Measuring the potential for innovation of the third system consists of measuring its capacity to provide new services or to supply them under better conditions than those prevailing in other public or market systems. This type of evaluation has always posed major problems. Whether constructed on the basis of results obtained or costs borne, it must contend with the following major difficulties:

- If the basis chosen is that of values, the problem is that of the intangible nature of some of the services supplied.

- If the basis chosen is that of costs, the problem consists of the complexity of their production function (acknowledged importance of voluntary work) and the difficulty in accounting for non-market elements (fiscal expenditure, advantages afforded under specific regulations, etc.).

After taking the above considerations into account, this problem is usually approached in one of three ways:

- Do TSIs actually differ from other private or public institutions? The aim here is to identify a "conformity indicator", an indicator that is not easy to construct but which could shed light on discussions over whether it would be appropriate to develop TSIs.

- Does the performance of TSIs improve over time? The construction of "productivity indicators" would be an easier approach to adopt, but one whose results would be of limited scope for statistical reasons.

- Can TSIs last over time or do they lose their distinctive features, thus compromising their innovative contents? The development of "survival indicators" attempts to answer this question.

## Conformity indicator

This procedure sets out to isolate the innovative nature of the third system by seeing whether or not it differs from other systems, usually in terms of the contents of the services supplied (Castaner, 2000). Other points of comparison might once again be considered here, such as the level of prices with regard to the service supplied. However, price differences might well be artificially created and are only meaningful if the services supplied are identical, which cannot be presumed at the outset.

This conformity indicator determines, for a given period of time, whether the activities of the third system are actually different to those of the public or private sectors in a comparable field of action (Heilburn, 1998). In the case of training institutions, for example, we shall see that differences exist in terms of the levels and types of qualification offered by these institutions. In the case of cultural institutions, it would be worth determining whether their programmes are the same, different, or on the contrary, convergent over time.

This analysis must overcome several difficulties:

- Innovation is not exactly the opposite of conformity. For there to be conformity, not only must certain things start again on a par with what might already have existed but there must also be a convention that will allow this fact to be both recognised and admitted as such. In other words, some things may no longer be absolutely novel but may not necessarily in conform to what was already known. Furthermore, this would presuppose that the existence of conformity or non-conformity is not the outcome of a variable that was not initially taken into account (Rogers, 1995).

- This method of proceeding may recognise product innovations but has greater difficulty in recognising innovation in terms of processes, which would call for detailed analyses on a case-by-case basis.

- Innovation does not necessarily imply a visible change in a product or process. New ways of establishing contact with users may be considered as social innovations without there being any change in what can most readily be observed in the basic approach.

- If it were assumed that these problems could be overcome, an analysis would still need to be made over the long term to see whether the conformity convention holds up or not. Far from being restricted to revealing variances, conformity indicators should also reveal differences between dynamic pathways.

Despite the major difficulties inherent in construction of a conformity indicator, devising such an indicator would be of great interest in that it would determine whether or not the existence of specific budgetary or regulatory arrangements in favour of TSIs is legitimate. It would indicate whether such exceptions should be kept in place – if not developed still further – or whether it might perhaps be more appropriate to put an end to them in order not to distort the conditions for social production.

### Productivity indicators

These are a more traditional form of indicator. While they cannot reflect novelty *per se*, they can at least provide an indication of ability to disseminate an innovation. Three types of indicator are used.

The first identifies the volume of services supplied, either *per se* or through comparison with the services supplied by alternative organisations to TSIs. Comparisons will be made, for example, with success rates in training schemes, variations in rates of accessibility for service users, etc.

The second attempts to measure the number of jobs created, and where applicable to highlight performances that are better than those of other organisations. There is no lack of analyses of this type, and the actions undertaken by the European Commission fairly routinely make use of such indicators:

- The Danish eco-centre Homeservice considers, on the basis of its own experiences, that the development of a service in the home by TSIs could at present create 20 jobs in a population of 20 000 inhabitants.

- The Spanish initiative VOVIS, which aims to create jobs for people over forty years of age in car parking and guarding services, has created around 800 jobs in a population of around six million inhabitants (although the rate of coverage is not uniform).

- The "Leg Standort" initiative, which aims to develop tourism services for elderly people with limited mobility, considers that introducing such a service in Germany could create some 5 700 jobs.

- The "Escale Solidaire" initiative in the Hérault *département* in France achieved a different type of result in that by organising groups of employers in rural areas it managed to convert seasonal jobs into 15 permanent jobs in a rural population of around 2 000 people.

The third and last type of indicators attempts to measure the production of "intangible value" such as production of a social capital, improvement of a local environment or better integration into the community. Use is made here of indicators such as growth in places where agents can meet, reduction in a given poverty rate, etc. The measurements are broader in scope and qualitative, such as those used in the INDE initiative in Portugal where the creation of a network of inclusion firms in Alhandra (Vila Franca), slowed the decline of the industrial zone.

The difficulty here lies less in the construction of such indicators (many of them are scarcely different to those used in private organisations or public policy) than in their interpretation. Two points are worth noting:

- Efficiency may be the outcome here of a large number of causes of which only a few can be attributed to the presence of the third system. If we consider the effects in terms of the indirect creation of jobs, an aspect that is frequently mentioned in impact studies of the third system, these effects will vary in scale according to the economic climate or the degree of integration of local economic activities, factors that are independent of the behaviour of TSIs.

- Measuring efficiency requires the precise determination of costs; these costs, however, partly depend on specific fiscal or regulatory arrangements. While not contestable, such schemes make cost determination an extremely complex exercise.

### Lifetime indicators

**Indicators of vulnerability.**   TSIs are subject to numerous risks, the most important of which are financial risks. Subsidies or donations, which account for a substantial share of their resources, may cease or decline, and their market resources are in many cases insufficient. The condition that will allow them to maintain their potential for innovation over time is therefore linked to their ability to overcome such shocks. There are four indicators that can be used to identify this capacity:

- Diversification of the sources of funding for a TSI. The greater the diversity of an institution's resources, the better placed it is to cope with unexpected fluctuations in one of its sources of funding and to continue its innovative activities. A good indicator here is the one used by Herfindal. The institution's sources of funding are determined as a percentage of the total amount; their weight is then squared and used to derive a concentration index. If there is only one source of funding, the index will be equal to one. The greater the number of sources, the more the index tends towards zero and the "best" institution is therefore the one whose index is closest to zero.

- The possibility for a TSI to have access to funding through shares or title deeds and/or large holdings of such deeds under such conditions that the deeds do not compromise the status of the institution; in order to simplify this approach, given the large number of possible types of status, such a possibility can be measured in terms of the difference between its assets and liabilities compared with income. This operating margin is not only a means of coping with external financial restrictions, but also a means of acquiring other forms of funding and of taking charge of non-solvent requirements.

● The scale of administrative and management costs. If the operating costs of a TSI are properly matched to its activity, the only way in which it can reduce costs and cope with sudden losses of income is to reduce its administrative and management costs. If a TSI has high administrative costs, it can cope with unexpected financial difficulties by reducing those costs.

● The scope for generating margins and reserves without all or part of these margins being distributed. If margins do actually exist (income – expenditure/income), a TSI will be capable of absorbing financial shocks. The use of such an indicator may be challenged on the grounds that the organisations are non-profit institutions, but this would constitute a mistaken view of management in that what is being determined here is not whether or not margins exist but the way in which these margins are distributed.

It seems that no significant study has been made at the European level in which these criteria (or criteria derived from them) are applied to third system organisations. However, as shown in certain studies carried out in various countries many years ago, and given the distinctive nature of the European third system, these indicators of vulnerability are usually powerful and linked to both the lack of resource diversification and lack of margins (intermediary associations in the labour market, local development organisations, and local non-profit cultural institutions). The criterion for access to funding bonds is paradoxically less negative than might be thought (co-operative and mutual organisations).

**Survival indicators.**   Increasing vulnerability will ultimately lead to the disappearance of TSIs. It can therefore be said that those institutions that exhibit unfavourable indicators of the type already mentioned are amongst the most fragile. These four elementary indicators can therefore be used to construct a composite indicator by modifying the weighting coefficients according to the type of organisation concerned. If we take the four vulnerability indicators:

$$I_{v,t} \, , \, I_{v,r} \, , \, I_{v,d} \, , \, I_{v,a}$$

where:

● $I_{v,t}$ represents the index of vulnerability with regard to ownership of deeds.

● $I_{v,r}$ represents the index of vulnerability with regard to *ex ante* balance.

● $I_{v,d}$ represents the index of vulnerability with regard to the diversification of financial resources.

- $I_{v,a}$ represents the index of vulnerability with regard to administrative costs; then we can construct the following composite indicator:

$$I_{survival} = \alpha I_{v,t} + \beta I_{v,r} + \delta I_{v,d} + \gamma I_{v,a,a}$$

The weighting coefficients can then be modified according to the type of organisation envisaged:

- For co-operative or mutual organisations, the $\alpha$ coefficient must be very high since the underlying rationale of such organisations is to attract new members.

- For intermediary or cultural associations, the $\delta$ coefficient must be relatively high since these organisations frequently benefit initially from resources that are exclusively supplied by the public sector and that they must therefore diversify.

A given type of indicator is therefore only valid for a given family of institutions, subject to prior analysis of their mode of operation and principal challenges.

Another indicator of survival is the lifetime of such organisations. Paradoxically, very few studies have addressed this aspect of institutions and the most common approach here is by analogy with very small enterprises whose rates of survival are known better. There are two reasons for this reticence, one of which is far from being valid:

- "Lifetime" does not mean the same for a non-profit organisation as it does for a commercial firm.

- The lifetime of these organisations depends upon external factors.

Neither of these two reasons is particularly convincing, since the very fact that a low survival rate has been observed is in any case an indicator of the limits encountered, whether they be external or internal. On the other hand, it is true that the very fact of survival may be linked to factors that have nothing to do with what is happening within the organisation concerned.

While uncommon, such analyses may nonetheless exist:

- A national survey carried out in the course of the Assizes on local development held in France has shown that the main reason for the non-survival of third system organisations in France, notably in the area of insertion into the labour market, was related to the growing scarcity of actors who were supposed to organise and guide such initiatives. This failure was therefore linked far more closely to the survival of these "social entrepreneurs" than to their organisations, since after a certain time these actors wanted to be able to move their institution forward in a different direction (which would require changes in status) or to secure legitimate improvements in their situation (which was not always easy given the way in which the organisation had been designed).

A recent summary report drawn up in the United States has shown that third system organisations overcame the difficulties they encountered by becoming increasingly commercially oriented (Weisbrod, 1998). They did this in many different ways:

- Sales of ancillary products that relate to the main activity but which might also be marketed by private firms (*e.g.* products sold in third system museum shops).

- Price increases.

- Creation of subsidiaries with private status operating without restriction in financial markets.

- Creation of joint ventures with private firms, etc.

Such diversification of activities poses few problems provided that it remains subject to the basic imperatives of the organisation and in particular to the production of social values or processes that create a social value added. On the other hand, if such commercialisation jeopardises the ranking of the values pursued by third system organisations, the conclusion may be drawn that it will ultimately lead to the demise of this system. A good indicator of such deviations here is that of changes in managers, which often reflects a reversal of the order in which the goals of an institution are ranked.

### Is it possible to define an evaluation protocol?

There are many instruments that can be used to analyse the performance of TSIs. So why is it that there is the feeling that evaluation tools are lacking or, at the very least, inadequate? There are several reasons for this:

- The vulnerability of TSIs, which precludes cross-cutting analysis.

- By presenting themselves as being systematically innovative (Rose-Ackerman, 1990), the TSI system relativises attempts to measure their efficiency that assume that stable benchmarks are available over time.

- It is hazardous to base analysis on indicators addressing a single type of utility when the distinctive attribute of TSIs is that they produce several types of values, which therefore cannot be integrated into a single criterion such as that of profit. If we take the example of an association working to promote the integration of young people we can see that it produces both marketable goods and services (*e.g.*, the repair or maintenance of household appliances) and an intangible good, namely the strengthening of the capacity for social integration of young people in difficulty. Obviously we could attempt to address this result in monetary terms, but that would scarcely make sense without recourse to "heroic" assumptions.

To overcome these problems we need to start with the objectives of such an evaluation, which are to:

● Identify the capacity of TSIs to be efficient or to meet needs under good conditions. The innovative nature of the third system makes determination of this capacity a difficult exercise in that, constantly modifying its "output" or adjusting production to a constantly changing context does not afford the product stability needed for us to be able to assess its development over time. It would therefore be logical to measure efficiency on the basis of the differences in results between TSIs and other institutions. This approach is that of horizontal evaluation.

● Identify the capacity of TSIs to be efficient or to optimise the management of the resources they need to meet such aims. Here comparisons might be made of third system institutions through the use, for example, of benchmarking. This approach is that of vertical evaluation.

*Horizontal evaluation*

The first stage in the evaluation of TSIs should consist of analysis of the ways in which their behaviour differs from that of other firms. Let us take the relatively straightforward example of institutions providing cultural services. One of the expected differences in behaviour lies in the composition of the public which uses their services, or the regularity with which their services are used, since TSIs are expected to address a wide variety of users who often have modest income levels, hence the financial support granted to them, unlike market institutions which concentrate on the most lucrative segments of the market.

To determine the efficiency of the third system, it is therefore necessary to:

● Compare the composition of the public for TSIs at any one given time with that of commercial institutions.

● Determine how this difference evolves.

Let us take the example of a museum managed by an association (M.A.) and a private museum, and then analyse the composition of their publics broken down into quartiles from $Q_1$ to $Q_4$ where $Q_1$ represents the highest income categories and $Q_4$ the lowest income categories. The hypothetical outcome illustrated in the following table shows a clear difference in behaviour from which it may be concluded that we are indeed dealing with an innovation meriting financial support or regulatory waivers.

If on the other hand what we find is a visitor profile of the kind illustrated in the following table then doubts arise as to the efficiency desired and financial resources. Now it is very easy to move from a Type one to a

Table 8.4. **Horizontal evaluation – Type one scenario**

|  | $Q_1$ | $Q_2$ | $Q_3$ | $Q_4$ |
|---|---|---|---|---|
| Museum managed by an association | 15 | 25 | 50 | 10 |
| Museum run on market principles | 20 | 40 | 35 | 5 |

Type two situation, which would therefore challenge the role of TSIs but would not necessarily lead to their demise (the change in behaviour could simply be a result of possible constraints on TSI funding).

Table 8.5. **Horizontal evaluation – Type two scenario**

|  | $Q_1$ | $Q_2$ | $Q_3$ | $Q_4$ |
|---|---|---|---|---|
| Museum managed by an association | 15 | 40 | 40 | 5 |
| Museum run on market principles | 20 | 40 | 35 | 5 |

This evaluation has several characteristics:

- It measures a value added by TSIs compared with other bodies.

- Its significance is based on a pre-defined criterion for value added which here consists of the difference in the profile of the visiting public (or the provision of equal access to cultural practices), although it would have been perfectly feasible to use others such as differences in theatre programming. If TSIs were to be compared with commercial institutions in the area of training (Van Laaroven et al., 1990), for example, consideration could be given to a criterion such as success rates by socio-professional category or a second criterion such as rates of insertion by socio-professional category.

- It must be performed at set intervals to be properly meaningful.

- It does not equate to a demonstration inasmuch as the presentation of the information produced must reflect the way in which institutions operate in practice.

One last implication concerns the issues at stake in the funding of TSIs. If subsidies are granted, they may be part of contracts containing objectives whose horizontal evaluation specifies and measures the terms under which they are to be achieved. Charters, statements of objectives, service projects and long-term development are all instruments that, to a greater or lesser extent, serve to achieve this end. The problem with such contracts is that they are often incomplete and implicit, which makes them less effective than might be desired. There are normally three risks that contracts might be incomplete:

- Some situations may not have been covered, including the characteristics of the people or groups involved.
- The actions of TSI managers may not be completed due to lack of funding.
- The quality of the product or services cannot be checked by third parties.

The risks with these "implicit" contracts are intrinsic, but they could doubtless be limited if contracts were regularly redrafted. Checking contracts is just as difficult over short periods of time as it is over long periods. In contrast, contracts comprising several different periods can serve only to encourage the parties to make clear their actions and improve their behaviour.

### Vertical evaluation

The fact that the efficiency of TSIs is of a different type to that of commercial institutions is not alone sufficient to pass judgement on the quality of their management. It is already enough if TSIs are able to manage themselves efficiently. In view of the distinctive nature of their production function, which may include linkage to resources differing from those of private firms *e.g.*, the sense that voluntary work can impart to production, it would be more instructive to compare institutions that are comparable in the knowledge that not all of their resources have a monetary value.

**Use of benchmarking.**   The required perspective is therefore that of the benchmarking of institutions, *i.e.* "comparisons and constant measurement of the achievements of an institution with reference to those of a leading institution in the domain concerned in order to the produce the information needed to improve its management" (Filgueiras-Rauch, 2000). The principle here is to arrange the various institutions into some kind of order by placing the emphasis on the least well placed, or to establish a cut-off for efficiency above which there is at least one TSI and then to see how the others are placed in comparison. A TSI will therefore be said to be efficient if it can no longer maintain its production by:

- Commensurately reducing all the resources it uses, in which case the economies of scale have been captured and what we will talk about here is radial efficiency.
- Reducing the quantity of one of the resources used, the levels of the others remaining constant (non-radial efficiency).

In the case of TSIs, benchmarking cannot be applied as systematically as it is in the sector, *i.e.* between competing firms. In such a situation, the starting point will be performance in relation to a reference activity, which will lead to a classification that in general is not particularly contentious. In the third system, the problem is a harder one to solve in that the product is rarely the same.

Let us take insertion associations as an example. We could use as a key criterion the insertion rate in the primary market on exiting the intermediary association, but unless the populations catered for and the labour markets are identical it is difficult to compare such associations on the basis of this criterion. It is therefore necessary to add other criteria for comparison such as the image of the association and the feelings that the beneficiaries of insertion programmes have towards it. The outcome is a set of criteria each one of which is given a rating between zero (least efficient institutions) and one (the most efficient institution). This approach can be applied to other dimensions of the activity of TSIs such as financing or marketing, provided that prior agreement is reached on evaluation criteria with regard to such functions.

The use of benchmarking therefore faces three problems:

● It is a cause for considerable debate over evaluation criteria and value judgements, even if it might be thought that the agreement would be possible on such value judgements.

● Interpreting the results is a complex exercise given the sensitivity of performance to the type of environment.

● The patterns of behaviour concerned may be contingent on imperfect information.

**Other measures.**   As part of such vertical evaluation a certain number of instruments for vertical evaluation have been developed, often by banks, in order to obtain an integrated representation of the functioning of TSIs:

● The Leuven University "Centre de recherche pour la solidarité" has studied the efficiency and effectiveness of work-based training enterprises. Most of the benefits and expenditure have been costed and various ratios are considered according to the length of the time horizon utilised (Gaussin, 1997).

● The "Banca Etica" has designed a model to evaluate social enterprises for the purposes of credit selection. This model, known as VARI (Values Requirement Indicators) uses a set of ten indicators and examines their interaction to see whether there are possible outcomes that might or might not be worth promoting (democratic participation, co-operation, transparency, equality of opportunity, respect for the environment, respect for working conditions, social quality produced, voluntary work, solidarity, links at the territorial level). The interest in using such criteria lies in the fact that they apply equally well to the type of resource used to that of the outcomes and products (Fuori Orario, 1999).

An approach comparable to the one above has been adopted by Human Resources Development Canada where a set of five criteria is used: production, worker training, working conditions, links at the territorial level, and match between processes and impacts.

The European Quality Foundation Model attempts to relate financial data to internal data on the functioning of the enterprises, such as staff morale, quality of social relations, etc. Although this instrument is aimed at all enterprises, it has the advantage of placing the emphasis on a primary aspect of the third system enterprise, namely its participatory mode of management (Connell et al., 1995).

The Training and Employment Research Unit at Glasgow University has made an evaluation of the Wise Group initiative in which an attempt was made to combine three aspects and different social utilities, namely urban renewal activities, the provision of social services and the scope for transferring such initiatives. The overall outcome is highly positive, but above all the analysis shows that the way in which needs are perceived can ultimately secure a significant reduction in the cost of satisfying those needs (McGregor et al., 1997).

### Composite evaluations

Other evaluations have attempted to combine inputs from both vertical and horizontal evaluations, usually for the purpose of devising a cost-benefit type analysis. Identifying differences between TSI products and those of other institutions is not seen as sufficient, so an attempt is made to express these differences in terms of relative costs over the long term. Evaluations of this kind are usually to be found in areas where efficiency can readily be identified, which is the case with regard to the capital cost of jobs created.

The committee set up by the European Commission to study the operation and prospects of the third system in Europe determined the amount of capital needed to fund creation of a job according to the type of funding used to create that job. The results are given in the table below (Campbell, 1999).

The "Agenzia del Lavoro della Provincia Autonoma di Trento" has monitored over time the progress made by a number of individuals in re-entering the labour market by comparing the results of re-insertion aided by social co-operations and those where direction was provided by other enterprises ("Agenzia del Lavoro della Provincia Autonoma di Trento", 1997). The rate of effective reinsertion of the people helped by social co-operatives was 52 per cent, a relatively high figure compared with the results achieved by the private sector, and the analysis concluded that the co-operatives were efficient on the basis of financial balances alone (Henton et al., 1996).

Table 8.6.   **Capital cost of job creation by type of institution**

| Type of financial intervention | Expenditure (euros) |
|---|---|
| Micro-credit (ADIE) | 3 400 |
| High-street bank | 9 000 |
| Conventional start-up | 15 000 |
| Structural funds (average) | 63 400 |
| Unemployment benefit (average) | 18 500 |

*Source:* Campbell (1999).

## Conclusion: the three functions of third system evaluation

In view of the challenges facing current public policy a considerable effort is currently under way to develop ways in which to evaluate the third system (OECD, 1999b):

● What is the added value of the third system?

● How can the existence of regulatory waiver mechanisms in common law or specific financial advantages be justified?

● How can action be taken to protect over time against changes in bureaucratic procedures and loss of expected value added while specific advantages are allowed to remain in place, thereby distorting competition and reducing collective welfare?

The instruments that have been described in this chapter are all relevant, even though individually they pose problems and have limitations. Rather than review them again in conclusion, it would make more sense to indicate the spirit in which they must be used, which is by far the most important point. Straightforward numerical indicators, often based on a rationale in which choices are one-dimensional and the behaviour of actors dictated by the sole motive of profit, will always fall short when exposed to a set of objectives in a context in which the demands of all actors must be taken into consideration. To this end it is worth recalling that evaluation serves three purposes here (Greffe, 1999):

● Monitoring.

● Learning.

● Mediation.

Monitoring refers to the collection and processing of the data used to support the implementation and development of a programme. The data collected will relate both to the products of third system institutions and to their economic, social and financial impacts. Monitoring or follow-up can therefore be viewed as an initial evaluation. The aim of such evaluation is not so much to identify causal links as to ensure that indicators are available to signal or give warning of deviations from what has been decided beforehand would be a desirable train of events. Monitoring data must therefore be collected on a regular basis and will primarily take the form of time series. These data will serve as a starting point from which the monitoring actions desired can address:

● The outcomes of actions, both over time and in space.

● The outcomes of actions, notably with regard to the expected impacts on target groups.

● The changes required in the behaviour of members of target groups.

An important aspect of the monitoring of third system institutions relates to their spatial impacts, which therefore calls for specific mapping and collection of data. A territorial area can no longer be assumed to be uniform and malleable and the cost of ensuring access to services must be taken into account on the basis of multidimensional analyses in which geographical distances and travel costs are simply additional elements. Furthermore, this would also require thought to be given to versatility or clusters of services, which are generally taken into account in official statistical systems which need stable and objective bases over time.

For many years it was thought that evaluation methods should provide direct access to a given number of results to decision-makers or their principal agents, in which case the latter would simply apply the results mechanically. However, policy-decisions by TSIs are not so much based on the scientific information thus obtained as on compromises and negotiated agreements. Scientific results therefore do not exert a direct influence but one whose impact is felt in changes to conceptual frameworks of actors. The issue at stake here is therefore not the production of pure knowledge but rather the capacity to integrate such knowledge at the local level and thereby modify behaviour.

The evaluation process will therefore gain from the actors' integration of these learning procedures. An evaluation made by the actors or an evaluation in which the actors are directly involved has a greater chance of influencing decision-makers than an evaluation that has not been designed from this standpoint. Those who are directly in charge of evaluation are better off not playing a central role and, on the contrary, leaving the leading positions to social actors. The evaluation team will not see its field of action reduced since it will always be called upon to provide expert services, apply procedures and identify topics on which there are conflicting views, acting in the role of moderator. In contrast, social actors in the third system retain the primary role with regard to the setting and selection of priorities and criteria, discussions of the strategy of evaluation in different stages, support for and approval of the results of this research. For this process to function properly:

- The person requesting the evaluation must agree to allow all functions to be delegated in the course of the research work.
- The actors concerned must be prepared to involve themselves in the process.
- Their minimum consensus must not necessarily relate to the values to be implemented, but at least to the instruments and procedures that are to be used.
- Technical skills must be brought together systematically and without fail.
- There must be a constant exchange of information between the actors and the environment with regard to the conduct and results of this evaluation, which primarily calls for networks to be available as well as people who know how to work in a network and thereby become genuine public entrepreneurs.

Evaluation is now perceived as a social and political process which creates its own reality and through which the assessor becomes a mediator who provides support and guidance for learning and negotiation processes. Mediation here is taken to mean a process of dispute settlement in which the opposing parties participate willingly and whose goal is to recognise their differences, find room for manoeuvre for future actions and arrive at a solution in the form of an agreement to which all participants will lend their support (Waterman and Wood, 1993). These mediation processes outnumber traditional conflict settlement processes in that they usually require a commitment from participants to resolve the issues they had been disputing up to that point. They make it possible to avoid the high costs and uncertainties that can lead to appeals.

Evaluation is often at the heart of existing mediation processes and cannot but facilitate them. Initially, these evaluation processes were not necessarily carried out from this standpoint and the most traditional forms of evaluation appear to have been carried out by independent experts, leading to one-way communication of information. The situation changes, however, if the evaluation process attempts to bring together all the actors concerned. It will therefore end with a consensus, even if that was not its original aim. The perspectives addressed by the criteria used are formulated jointly by the actors and their field of vision cannot but converge in the course of the process. In many cases the field of action of the third system lies in areas where there are major conflicts of interest. While it cannot make these conflicts disappear, evaluation may make it possible to convey a more accurate picture of the issues at stake and the scope for mutual support by virtue of its very approach. Furthermore, the initiatives taken by TSIs often take the form of partnerships in terms of both design and implementation. Their efficiency therefore primarily lies in matching the behaviour of the various social actors concerned to the objectives decided upon, which adds to the need for a process that will secure convergence between long-term goals and the sharing of constraints. This way of perceiving the role of evaluation as an instrument for mediation has, in fact, prompted some specialists to propose an approach that is typical of mediation evaluation. Evaluation does not open up scope for mediation "by chance", it is organised with this end in view from the very outset:

- In the first phase, the evaluation must identify the groups affected by tensions or disputes, specify the subjects to be debated, set out a schedule and procedures, and then ensure appointment of a mediator.

- In the second phase, information must be exchanged in order to create a pool of knowledge; it is then necessary to identify the room for negotiations and transactions and draw up proposals for an agreement.

- In the third and final stage, a timetable must be established and implementation monitored; where necessary, appeals procedures will also need to be put in place.

ISBN 92-64-19953-5
The Non-profit Sector in a Changing Economy
© OECD 2003

PART III

*Chapter 9*

# Non-profit Sector and Evaluation: The State of Play in Quebec

by

Nancy Neamtan,
Chantier de l'Économie Sociale, Québec, Canada

## Introduction

Since the Women's March against Poverty in the spring of 1995, the two major socio-economic summits held in Quebec in 1996 and the creation during that same year of the "Chantier de l'économie sociale" (Forum of the Social Economy), the social economy has been the object of considerable development in Quebec and has raised an important collective debate in which university researchers, the community and union movements, the women's movement and the Quebec government are active participants.

This rise of the social economy is the result of a long process of networking and building of partnerships on the local, regional, national and even international level, undertaken by the "Chantier de l'économie sociale" and the actors of the social economy over the past five years.

The interest that Quebec society has in the social economy no longer needs to be proven. Nevertheless, the contribution of social economy enterprises to the overall socio-economic development of Quebec is still strongly underestimated. Several reasons explain this phenomenon.

Firstly, despite the inroads that have been made, the social economy remains an unknown reality for a large part of the population. As a result, many have the tendency to reduce the contribution of the social economy to social and professional reinsertion of marginalised groups and the production of goods and services that have been left aside by the state and the marketplace. However, the added social value of the social economy has repercussions in other spheres such as the dynamism of local economies, the creation of social links, the establishment of a climate of confidence among local actors, etc.

Secondly, the potential of the social economy is far from being entirely exploited. Many economic activities that are not, cannot or should not be taken care of by the state and the private sector remain to be developed, in addition to the fact that social needs are far from being entirely satisfied.

Thirdly, only a few rare studies have presently attempted to account for the social and economic performance of this new sector of activity, on the micro level (the enterprise) and on the macro level (society). At this time, evaluation is a fundamental issue in the process of understanding and recognising the accomplishments of the social economy. The evaluative process is a crucial tool with which to understand the specifics of the social economy, to qualify at its real value the micro and macro impact of these activities and to identify the necessary conditions that will allow these initiatives to inscribe themselves in a new model of development whose aim is to make the economy and society at large more pluralistic and democratic.

Whilst the "Chantier de l'économie sociale" works on a wide scope of issues, this chapter will focus on the question of evaluation of the social economy, and more precisely the state of the dossier in Quebec. First, it will briefly review the latest events that marked the process of recognition of the social economy in Quebec. It will present the "Chantier de l'économie sociale" and introduce the definition of the social economy, which is the subject of a consensus among the principle social actors in Quebec. Secondly, the major issues concerning the field of evaluation of the social economy in Quebec will be discussed, from an academic, governmental and policy implementation perspective. Finally, the chapter will conclude by identifying the current major initiatives in Quebec in the field of evaluation of the social economy.

## The Quebec experience of the social economy

### The Chantier de l'économie sociale

The "Chantier de l'économie sociale" is an independent and permanent organisation whose mission is the promotion and development of the social economy. As a non-profit corporation, the "Chantier" regroups leaders of social economy enterprises in a wide variety of sectors (environment, personal services, communication, social tourism, recreation, housing, natural resources, family and childcare, and culture), local development organisations (Association of Local Development Centres, urban-based community economic development corporations, and rural-based community futures corporations) and the major social movements (unions, community groups, environmental networks, co-operatives, and women).

### Brief history

The "Chantier de l'économie sociale" was created in March 1996, in the context of the preparation of the Summit on Economy and Employment, which took place in October 1996, and brought together the main socio-economic partners. The partners at the Summit recommended that the "Chantier" continue over a two-year period to promote the concept, clarify the role and potential of the social economy, oversee the implementation of the various projects and contribute to the development of policies and measures necessary for the future development of this sector.

Additionally, they recommended that the Quebec model of the social economy be recognised as an integral part of the socio-economic structure of

Quebec. They also confirmed that on issues related to the socio-economic development of Quebec, the status of full partner be given to actors of the social economy by ensuring that they are adequately represented in all partnership structures and all processes of collaboration.

The social economy actors decided in 1998 to ensure the permanence of the working group responsible for the promotion and development of collective entrepreneurship. The "Chantier de l'économie sociale" thus became an independent corporation, with an organisational structure made up of a wide membership and a 29 member board of directors representing a diversity of actors of the social economy and the social movements that support it.

In order to accomplish its mandate, the "Chantier de l'économie sociale" collaborates closely with the "Comité sectoriel de main-d'œuvre et l'économie sociale et de l'action communautaire and the Réseau d'investissement social du Québec" (RISQ), a social economy investment fund (see Mendell in this volume), as well as co-directing the University-Community Research Alliance on the Social Economy.

### The retained definition of the social economy

In Quebec, the definition of the social economy that prevails is that proposed by the "Chantier de l'économie sociale". This definition is inspired by the "Conseil Wallon de l'économie sociale" (CWES, 1990) (*www.terre.be/gi/ economie_sociale.htm*) following work done by the Belgian economist Jacques Defourny, including essentially two aspects: one pertaining to the economy and the other to the principles inspiring it.

The concept of the social economy combines two terms that are sometimes considered to be opposed:

- "Economy" refers to the concrete production of goods and services; the enterprise as the organisational structure; and it contributes to a net increase in the collective wealth.

- "Social" refers to the idea that benefits are not automatically derived from economic activities, but that the latter are explicitly formulated to perform a social function. The social benefits are assessed in terms of the contribution to democratic development, the support of an active citizenship, and the promotion of values and initiatives for individual and collective empowerment. The social benefits therefore contribute to enhancing the quality of life and well-being of the population, particularly by providing a greater number of services. As with the traditional public and private sectors, the social benefits can also be evaluated in terms of the number of jobs created.

The social economy field covers all activities and organisations built on a collective entrepreneurship and operating on the following principles and rules:

- The primary purpose of a social economy enterprise is to serve its members or the community rather than simply make profits and focus on financial performance.

- It is not government-controlled.

- It incorporates in its bylaws and operating procedures a process of democratic decision-making involving users and workers.

- It places people and the work first before capital in terms of the distribution of its profits and revenues.

- Its activities are based on the principles of participation, empowerment and accountability of individuals and communities.

This definition is broad, embracing co-operatives, mutual benefit societies, associations and even all forms of organisations with accepted rules that allow them to conform to these principles. On the other hand, it confronts the practices of these organisations with the values and principles proclaimed in the definition. Finally, beyond its inherent qualities, the definition has the advantage of being a common reference point for all Quebec actors given that it was the subject of a consensus among the original steering committee of the "Chantier de l'économie sociale" and accepted at the Summit in 1996.

## Evaluation issues in the field of the social economy

Despite the fact that the reality of the social economy is not new in Quebec, its rise in the current context, the place it has begun to occupy in development strategies, the debates that have been provoked by this growth and the greater visibility which has resulted, require important efforts in the field of evaluation.

The challenge of evaluating the social economy is complex. Several obstacles emerge even before one can begin to discuss the questions of process or methodology. These obstacles are the reflection of the multiple realities of the social economy.

### The challenges

#### The need to circumscribe the reality of the social economy

The first challenge is to be able to circumscribe the sector. As is the case in several other countries, there are no precise figures based on statistical studies in Canada or Quebec that allow us to trace a clear portrait of the social economy in Quebec. This problem stems as much from the very recent interest in isolating this sector from other economic activities or the voluntary sector, as from a legal status that is lost in a much wider and diversified sector (with the exception of the co-operative legal structure), and the difficulty in distinguishing social economy enterprises involved in the production of goods and services from voluntary organisations involved in recreational or citizenship activities. The social economy is based on the association of people but it distinguishes itself from the voluntary sector in the sense that it is involved in the production of goods and services. In effect, the social economy calls on the contribution not only of volunteers but also of salaried workers, which is not the case, for example, for many volunteer organisations.

### The challenge of the micro and macro approach and the impact of models of development

To begin with, it is important to distinguish the different levels of evaluation of the social economy. On the micro level, the experience in the field of evaluation is without doubt much richer. In Quebec there are at least a hundred evaluative research exercises, sponsored either by government, academic instances, or by the private sector. For most of these, the evaluations did not include the civil society actors involved in the creation of these initiatives, which constitutes in itself a major shortcoming in the evaluative process.

At the same time, the field of social research in Quebec has been confronted for many years with methodological problems related to the evaluation of impact (cost/results) of health, education, socio-professional integration, primary and secondary prevention programmes.

For example, in the area of health, the compilation of these works has led researchers to realise that the mental and physical health of individuals and communities is directly related to social and economic determinants such as housing, employment, income, social networks, etc. The overall work has required soliciting the contribution and expertise of grassroots actors and communities, laying the basis for a new partnership to face the challenges of evaluation and the evolution of scientific knowledge. This has also led to a renewed production and a better adaptation of methodological tools.

These new research practices in evaluation, though imperfect, have incited funding organisations to create programmes allowing the financing of research that requires an active participation of practitioners. This has directly impacted on the development of a specific evaluation model for the social economy.

In fact, several research funds (Canadian and Québécois) now have very strict requirements for partnerships in the supervision of research projects, the diffusion and the appropriation of results by all the actors involved and not only the scientific community, of knowledge transfers in a mutual learning process.

These major changes are recent and the social economy has once again been challenged by the requirements of evaluation with these new tendencies on the level of economic viability as well as social profitability for these enterprises.

Several authors have already shown interest and begun to work on the various challenges of evaluation in the social economy. For example, Comeau *et al.* (2001) attempt to pin down the originality and complex specificity of the social economy in comparison with traditional enterprises and the market economy, which makes the evaluation of this sector more complex. The particularities of the social economy require an original methodology that they qualify as a "fifth generation", due to the strategic and highly participative characteristics of the sector. They argue that the evaluation of the social economy must contain three dimensions: the dimension of economic efficacy, social utility and the institutional dimension. The economic efficacy refers to the productive performance of the social economy initiatives: jobs, costs, benefits, cost effectiveness and relative performance in the sector are some of the major indicators; the dimension of social utility represents the added value characteristic of the social economy and can be found in indicators such as the structural effects, the mobilisation of communities, the partnerships with other social actors, policies of equity and redistribution, amongst other things, as well as certain economic indicators such as job creation; the institutional dimension refers to the power structure and significance of different actors (employees, users/consumers, society and the public) in decision-making. The presence of joint committees, rules permitting the presence of actors in decisional bodies, and various consultative measures reveal an intention of democratisation.

But for the social economy, it is not enough to measure the results of initiatives by isolating them from a broader range of factors, nor by cutting them off from the more global impact on the models of development of a society. The social economy claims to be able to influence relationships between economic and social factors, relationships between civil society and the state, relationships between different components of society on a local, regional, national and perhaps even international level.

The capacity to measure these impacts is even more important today when one can observe several changes in the conjuncture characterised by economic growth and job-creation recovery. It becomes essential to identify the impacts of the social economy beyond job creation. Drawing on an emerging body of literature in this field, Lévesque (2001) argues that the role of the social economy does not merely consist of creating jobs but that it performs a vast range of functions. First, it is a leading force in research to transform collective needs into social demands (Comeau, 1997). Second, it also responds to concerns from segments of the active population who desire democracy in their workplace and in the economy (Lévesque, 1997). Third, it makes up for deficits in citizenship by its professional or territorial proximity, its co-production of services by users and workers, its non-profitability, its horizontal and vertical partnership (Demoustier, 2000, p. 34), and by its political questioning of relationships between the economy and society (Laville, 1994). Finally it permits the emergence of networks of international solidarity (Favreau, 1999). Lévesque, (2001, *op. cit.*) adds that, more broadly, the social economy and local development contribute to an economy that is not uniquely capitalist. Variable according to each country, the combined forces of the public economy and the social economy can act as a counterweight to the global private economy, which does not take into account the territory where it settles. In doing this, the prospect of building a more pluralist, solidarity economy in the common social interest becomes plausible.

In Quebec, this question is clearly stated in the context of the debate on the "Quebec model". The rise of the social economy in Quebec is contributing to the renewal of its model of development, characterised by its public economy, the presence of networks of local development organisations on the entire territory, by the presence of the social economy in most sectors, and by the force of the social movements, including the movement for national affirmation. Lévesque (2001, *op. cit.*) underlines the place and the role of the social economy in a pluralist economy arguing that co-operatives and associations have often been called on to innovate, to stray from the beaten track in order to carry out changes which are part of a true small social revolution. This may be seen as "a quiet revolution", but it is also a profound transformation of the organisational cultures of many actors and the birth of new micro power relationships at the grassroots level both in the social and economic sphere.

A pluralist economy instead of an exclusively capitalist one, more visible in Quebec than elsewhere perhaps, has actively emerged. The critical and enlightened criticism by economic and social actors of the new social economy and the new local development can encourage the emergence of a "solidarity economy inspired by the common interest" to use the expression favoured by CIRIEC and by the publication of the "Économie et solidarités" association, which also participates in the debate on the social economy (see bibliography). This new perspective on the social economy and the strategies and programmes that have been set up contribute to the renewal of responses to the issue of development. These include the redefinition of social protection, the control of markets in the global context, the protection of the environment, the management of the urban crisis and the control of technological progress.

Evaluation in such a context is a major challenge. Not only must one measure the statistical impact of initiatives (number of jobs, contribution to the GNP, etc.) or the direct social impact (answer to non-satisfied social needs, impact on marginalised populations, etc.) but one must also evaluate the more global impacts on the behaviour of all societal actors and institutional behaviour (public administrations, local communities, social movements, and the private markets) and as a result, on the current model of development.

This requires evaluative approaches that are simultaneously multi-sectorial, multi-dimensional, comparative and longitudinal. It calls on the collaboration between experts in various fields such as economics, sociology, business administration and management, public policy, and governance. It demands scientific rigor allowing the debate on the social economy to escape an ideological stranglehold in order to open up a clearer debate on its efficacy and its efficiency in resolving economic, social and political problems that confront our modern societies.

This challenge has not yet been met in Quebec in a systematic way or in a manner accepted by all partners of the social economy. From the point of view of public officials, evaluation is still too limited to a function of management control and support for the decisional process concerning precise programmes. From the point of view of civil society actors, there is still much distrust concerning evaluation, for they fear an attack on their autonomy and a non-recognition of their accountability toward their communities and their members (when it concerns, as it usually does, governmental evaluation). For university researchers, it is difficult to arrive at a consensus on methodologies to be adopted. In other words, taking up the challenge of evaluating the social economy will have to be done in the spirit of social innovation and democratic debate.

## A first experience in a multi-sectorial and multi-dimensional evaluation

The report by the "Chantier de l'économie sociale", "Taking up the challenge of solidarity", presented at the Summit on the Economy and Employment was the impetus for the development of a range of initiatives, some leading to the creation of new economic activities and others leading to the creation of new transversal or sectoral training or financial tools, the adjustment of public policies or the creation of new networks and partnership structures. While it received enthusiastic support from many actors of Quebec society, it also attracted much scepticism and even mistrust from others. It became clear very early on that it would be important to develop instruments to measure the impact and the concrete results of this action plan. Therefore a process was initiated in order to evaluate the action plan for the social economy accepted by the Summit and the actions that stemmed from it.

The evaluation process distinguished itself in several ways from the typical evaluative process. Firstly, the committee responsible for supervising the process was jointly chaired by the secretariat of the Summit on the Economy and Employment of the Executive Committee of the Government of Quebec, and the "Chantier de l'économie sociale". In doing this, it distinguished itself from the traditional unidirectional process by involving a series of stakeholders in the process. This allowed a better participation by civil society, which perceived the goals of the evaluation in a more positive light. It also ensured that the evaluation would be well balanced, by taking into account the interests of all the stakeholders and in allowing the measurement of governmental behaviour and not only that of civil society.

A third major element of the process was the fact that the evaluation was carried out through scientific research structures, allowing a better scientific legitimacy for all partners. The call for proposals and the scientific evaluation was carried out by the Quebec Council on Social Research (CQRS) in order to validate the scientific aspect of the process.

Finally, this process was based on a multi-sectoral approach, since in addition to the "Chantier de l'économie sociale", several ministries such as Health and Social Services, and Employment and Social Solidarity, were involved in the supervising committee.

The first goal of the research was to determine if the commitments made at the Summit had been met during the implementation period. In addition, the evaluation also determined the presence, when applicable, of certain constraints that could compromise the development of the various projects.

The second goal was to identify the impacts of the projects and the extent to which they had succeeded in reaching their original objectives, such as responding to non-fulfilled collective needs, increasing production of goods and services, transforming the demand for goods and services into a solvable demand, using democratic entrepreneurial processes, and creating quality and durable jobs.

More specifically, the researchers were asked to respond to the following two questions:

- Have the means necessary to achieve the commitments made at the Summit contributed to the development of the social economy through the creation and the consolidation of functional and lasting enterprises?
- Has the creation of these conditions allowed the projects to have the desired impact on users, employees, communities and Quebec society as a whole?

These two central questions were accompanied by a series of sub-questions with the goal of creating indicators that would allow more permanent responses to the questions raised. The evaluative process was progressive and dynamic. The methodology was based on participatory evaluation, which inscribes itself in a process instead of constituting an *ad hoc* or isolated action. This methodology of evaluation is not new; it has been experimented in several sectors linked to the social economy, but principally in other fields (health and social services, education, etc.). The evaluation was carried out in two stages. The first was dedicated to the evaluation of the implementation process and the second was oriented toward efficacy and impact. The final report published in 2001 is based on data from before and after the action plan.[1] The data also allows comparisons with small businesses in the traditional economy. These comparisons help identify certain structural and distinct elements of the new social economy. Amongst other things, the evaluation process has brought out the various constraints related to institutional behaviour.

Moreover, this evaluation exercise was a first step in attempting to evaluate a multi-sectoral intervention in relation to public policy. Once again, the limits of the process are clear, particularly in relation to the time period that has been evaluated. Given the time requirements related to the process of renewal of certain government policies, the process was prepared too quickly, preventing the possibility of measuring some of the most important impacts, particularly the changes in development cultures as well as the durability and the solidity of the new partnership initiatives which have been created in the context of the action plan.

## Specific tools for the evaluation of the social economy in Quebec

### The University-Community Research Alliance on the social economy (ARUC)

The issue of evaluation is certainly one of the most important subjects that will be treated over the next few years in the context of a broad and in-depth partnership that is being built in Quebec between actors of the social economy and research networks.

The Canadian Council for Research in Social Sciences has created a funding programme that finances partnership infrastructures in research, dissemination and training. The funding is not given directly to research but to the support for close partnerships in the elaboration of research goals, methodological tools, and strategies for disseminating and appropriating useful knowledge for the development of communities.

Since January 2000, the field of the social economy has had access to such an infrastructure co-directed by practitioners and university researchers known as the ARUC-Social Economy.[2] This novel initiative faces many challenges in terms of putting together empirical knowledge belonging to actors of the social economy and the theoretical knowledge belonging to the university milieu in order to build a third level of knowledge specific to the social economy. All the work accomplished by ARUC is linked to different practices in the field of social economy *e.g.* housing, personal services, native communities, job creation, sustainable development, local and regional development, and tourism. Two working groups have taken on transversal subjects related to international comparisons and evaluation.

Other major issues being treated include the conditions for the emergence of the social economy, the dissemination and development of the social economy, the internal functioning of social economy enterprises, the place and the role of women and youth, relationship between the new social economy, the state and the market, mechanisms for collective learning, and evaluation and measurement of the socio-economic impact of the new social economy.

The University-Community Alliance is a major element for the development of new methodological tools designed for the social economy. In the same way that "total quality" processes taking place in the manufacturing sector demand a broad and diverse approach, the most advanced evaluation calls on the contribution not only of isolated experts or authorities, but of the entire personnel, supported by external experts. The participation of community-based actors and experts in the University-Community Alliance creates the continuation for this type of evaluation to take place.

The ARUC-Social Economy alliance represents an additional recognition of the role of the new social economy in Quebec. It will undoubtedly contribute to the diffusion of better evaluative tools and processes.

### The Social Economy and Community Action Labour Force Development Committee (CSMO)

As a strategic partner of the "Chantier de l'économie sociale" and the University-Community Alliance, the Social Economy and Community Action Labour Force Development Committee is an essential component for the development of the Quebec social economy. The Sectoral Committee was created in 1997 in the wake of the Summit on the Economy and Employment and its funding is possible in the context of the Quebec Government's employment policies which favours the creation of partnership structures to take on the challenges of labour power development and training in different sectors of the Quebec economy.

The mission of the CSMO is principally to elaborate strategies for the development and training of the labour force in the social economy, through the consolidation of partnerships and common strategies in various sectors. As in the case of the Alliance, the CSMO is also a partnership structure in which one finds all the major networks involved in the new social economy, including co-operatives. The CSMO also plays the role of tracking the development of activities in this sector, taking into account the volume, the quality and the diversity of jobs and enterprises, the qualifications for human resources in the various skills and professions, the identification of present and future skills required for the labour force in the new social economy.

In order to carry out its mission, the CSMO has produced a portrait of the new social economy in Quebec. This portrait will facilitate the task of circumscribing the sector for the first time in Quebec. A rapid review of this portrait points out clearly the diversity, the complexity and the dynamism of social economy enterprises: over 500 different skills and professions, operating budgets from C$25 000 to C$5 000 000, from a minimum of three to several hundred employees, the presence of wage policies and training in the vast majority of these enterprises, and a widespread presence in a variety of economic and social spheres. This information allows us to set up an evolutionary data bank on the characteristics of this sector, thus contributing to the development of new approaches, tendencies and tools in the field of evaluation. The CSMO has also carried out other studies in relation to the sectoral portrait, and the work being carried out by research teams in the context of the Community-University Alliance will allow us not only to enrich debates but also to build adequate and efficient tools for the development and the consolidation of the new social economy. Among the ongoing work, a team in the evaluation working group of the Community-University Alliance is in the process of developing a methodological tool with specific dimensions that identify the characteristics of the social economy at the level of economic viability and social profitability.

Work is also being done to define parameters for the management of the quality of services in social economy enterprises, which contributes to the definition of the sector's specificity as well as its development and consolidation.

### The Quebec government's new scientific policy

The Quebec Ministry for Research, Science and Technology adopted a new scientific policy in the autumn of 2000 (see ministère de la Recherche, de la Science et de la Technologie, 2001). For the first time, this policy integrates the question of social innovation as a strategic element. It defines social innovation in the following way:

> "By 'social innovation' we refer to any new approach, practice or intervention or any new product that has been created to improve a situation or to solve a social problem and that has been taken up by institutions, organisations or communities".

The scientific policy recognises that "economic growth, job creation, cultural vitality and prosperity for Quebec society, today and in the future, depends on our collective aptitude to take up the challenges related to innovation and to do it in the perspective of sustainable development".

In this context, it is important to underline that, contrary to technological innovations, which generally have as their starting point laboratory research, social innovations are usually produced on the grassroots level by practitioners and not by scientists. By trial and error, by learning in practice rather than in theory, by the confrontation of ideas in democratic bodies (for the social economy), new methods are thought up and experimented. As an experimentation, social innovation is made up principally of tacit knowledge and collective apprenticeship that has not yet been codified and organised for wide dissemination. That is why research and evaluation often begin after experimentation and proceed first of all by case studies. In this sense the process of evaluation must be on-going in order to evaluate the capacity for dissemination, as well as to show the specificity of the innovation.

The new scientific policy of the Quebec government, by foreseeing mechanisms adapted to social innovation, will become, in future years, an important tool for bringing to fruition Quebec society's capacity to evaluate the contribution of the social economy.

Quebec thus has – with the University-Community Alliance, the CSMO, and the new scientific policy – important instruments involving all the major partners, for developing new evaluation models that correspond to the complexity, the diversity and the dynamism of the new social economy.

## Conclusion

The social economy sector is constantly confronted with issues that will determine its future. These include the under-capitalisation of enterprises, the difficulty for public administrations to recognise the value of the work being done in various sectors, the challenge of the training of managers in the social economy, and the accusations of unfair competition by certain private sector companies. The very image of the social economy in society where unbridled competition is often considered a basic standard is also a major issue. So are the interface between the social economy and the public sector in the service sector, the challenges of trade on an international level, and now the evaluation of enterprises and the actions of the social economy.

Evaluation constitutes a fundamental challenge in the development of the Quebec social economy, for it should facilitate the measurement of the economic performance of social economy enterprises as well as their social impact. At the same time, it should promote a better understanding of the overall contribution of social economy enterprises to the economy and local communities, to clarify the basis for government support they receive and to legitimise their role in the dynamics of economic and local development.

However, the particular characteristics of the social economy make the evaluation process very difficult and the traditional ways of evaluating companies impracticable. It is necessary to innovate and create models adapted to this emerging sector. In order to do this, it is fundamental that the evaluation be carried out in partnership and in collaboration with public administrations, universities and the social economy actors. The latter, with their wealth of grassroots experiences, should furnish strong support for the identification of the indicators that will reveal the full potential of the Quebec social economy. International exchanges would be an important means to enrich this ongoing work.

*Annex*

# A Pilot Project by the Social Economy and Community Action Labour Force Development Committee (CSMO)

A first draft of a system of indicators was built according to specific objectives and territorial particularities. It is important to make clear from the outset that the indicators were elaborated with the aim of supporting the creation of a methodological tool that would help to draw the portrait of the social economy and the community action sectors. This portrait must identify the specifics of the social economy and community action as well as the "limits" of what can be called a hybrid "grey zone" between the two sectors. It must also answer the need to determine i) the type of jobs and qualifications and ii) profitability (social and economic).

The list of indicators does not aim to respond explicitly, and in the first instance, to the need to establish a portrait of these two sectors and how they are inter-connected. It does, however, maintain that a framework be established on which the pertinence of each of these indicators can be validated in order to trace the portrait. The validation will be based on the capacity of each indicator to take into account the specifics of the social economy and/or community action. This explains the operational characteristics of this exercise.

The process is thus a pilot project devoted to creating and applying a tool to a certain number of social economy and community action organisations. It consists of building a methodological tool based on the particular dimensions of the sector, the levels of employment and social profitability of the social economy and community action. Each of these dimensions must, in the course of its passage from a dimension to an indicator, be the subject of an operational process carried out in regard to the specifics of the sectors. The notion of "specifics" refers, in this context, as much to the characteristics of the sectors – and thus their "reality" – as to the territorial dimension – and thus their geographic location. This exercise, whose goal is the elaboration of a system of indicators, must thus be conceived as being and remaining *ad hoc*.

The dimensions were chosen on the basis of this anchorage in "reality". They reflect the characteristics of the social economy and community action sectors because they are the products of an operational process carried out on the basis of the defining elements of the social economy and community action sectors (see Bouchard *et al.*, 1997).

*"The development of the social economy is defined by a legal framework that assures the preservation of the specificity of co-operative and non-profit organisations.*

*The social economy enterprise is independent of government.*

*The social economy enterprise integrates in its bylaws and operating procedures a process of democratic decision-making involving users and workers."*

The first of these dimensions is the status and organisational information. It includes the goals identified in the charter, the legal status, principal areas of intervention, geographical territory, internal structure, and the degree of autonomy *vis-à-vis* government.

*"The social economy enterprise has as its finality the goal of serving its members or the community rather than simply to produce profits (…) its activities are based on the principles of participation, empowerment and individual and collective responsibility."*

The second dimension is that of the type of activities. This produces information on the type of products and services offered as well as the clientele. This dimension must also refer to the recognition of the organisation by the community or the group it represents, particularly when the activities are linked directly to social goals.

*"The terminology 'social economy' included two frames of reference. The first, economy, relates to the production of goods and services having the enterprise as its organisational form and contributing to the net increase in collective wealth."*

The third dimension involves classic financial information applied to businesses linked to forms of the traditional economy, such as accounting information and funding sources.

*"The organisation defends the primacy of people and work over capital in the distribution of surpluses and revenues."*

The fourth dimension seeks out employment specifics and characteristics. In this sense, it does not include the measure of social impacts linked to employment. It identifies more specifically the jobs offered in the organisations, the level of remuneration and on-the-job training. This has the advantage of shedding light on key factors such as the quality of working conditions, qualifications, durability, the proportion of jobs paid by the organisation and the participation in employability or integration programmes.

*"Social profitability of social economy organisations is measured by their contribution to democratic development, by the support for active citizenship, by the promotion of values and initiatives of individual and collective empowerment.*

*Social profitability thus contributes to the improvement of the quality of life and the well-being of the population (...) As is the case for the public sector and the traditional private sector, the number of jobs created can also measure this social profitability."*

The fifth dimension is social profitability. This involves taking into account economic and social impacts. The first type of impact is unavoidable in the economic and evaluative context of the social economy and community action. In the sphere of community action, economic impacts are considered as being linked to the recognition of the group by its milieu.

The second type of impact refers to what can be called collective wealth, concretised in the services offered which contribute to a qualitative improvement of the functioning of the community.

## Notes

1. The report, "L'économie sociale et le plan d'action du sommet sur l'économie et l'emploi" is co-authored by researchers from the "Centre de recherche sur les services communautaires" at the University of Laval and the "École nationale d'administration publique" of the "Université du Québec". The evaluative process was based on a collection of quantitative data (*e.g.*, number of jobs, number of members, number of people at annual meetings, percentage of women in the full-time and part-time labour force, the assets and liabilities of enterprises, income sources, percentage of self-generated revenues, etc.) and qualitative information (from interviews and group discussions).

2. The ARUC-Social Economy is co-directed by Benoît Lévesque, professor-researcher at the University of Quebec and outgoing president of CIRIEC Canada and by Nancy Neamtan, president of the "Chantier de l'économie sociale". The major partners are made up of four universities (University of Quebec in Montreal, Concordia, University of Quebec in Hull, University of Quebec in Chicoutimi) and four major civil society organisations, *i.e.* the "Chantier de l'économie sociale", Rural Solidarity, the Quebec Federation of Labour and its Quebec Solidarity Fund, and the Confederation of National Trade Unions and its fund, "Fondaction". The alliance brings together over one hundred researchers from various disciplines such as sociology, economics, management, industrial relations, social work, geography, accounting, and political science and an equal number of partners including the "Chantier de l'économie sociale", the major union federations and their investment funds, the "Comité sectoriel de main-d'œuvre de l'économie sociale et action communautaire", the Association of CLSC, the Coalition of Community Groups in the field of labour force development, the Quebec Association of Regions, the CIRIEC, the Association of Local Development Centres, the Quebec Network of Community Recycling Enterprises, the Housing Co-operative Federation as well as several other networks covering the entire territory of Quebec.

ISBN 92-64-19953-5
The Non-profit Sector in a Changing Economy
© OECD 2003

PART III

*Chapter 10*

# Non-profit Sector Impact Evaluation: The View from the USA

by

Wolfgang Bielefeld,
School of Public and Environmental Affairs,
Indiana University – Purdue University,
Indianapolis, USA

## Introduction

Interest in the evaluation of the impact of the non-profit sector is growing among practitioners, policy makers, and academics in the United States. A number of major initiatives focusing on evaluation have recently been seen, including the United Way's push for programme evaluation, the growth of performance-based contracting by government agencies, and the efforts of INDEPENDENT SECTOR.[1] This chapter will consider academic and research developments of the past few years.

Since the role and structure of non-profit sectors varies widely in different countries, we will start with a brief discussion of the sector in the United States. This will help frame the interests and debates that are considered in the remainder of the chapter. Non-profit organisations have traditionally been an important part of American life and have contributed to American individual and community welfare since colonial times. Alexis de Tocqueville in fact pointed out to the world in 1835 how important voluntary and collective action was to life in the United States. Many authors since then have described the multitude of impacts that the non-profit sector has had. What follows is a summary of ideas found in the writings of major American non-profit theorists (Van Til, 1988 and 2000; Salamon, 1999 and 2000; Smith, 1983).

The non-profit sector in the United States in inexorably intertwined with the public, for-profit, and household sectors. As such, its role involves both providing important services and relating to the other sectors. It provides services which neither neither the government nor the for-profit sector will provide, as explained by market and government failure theories. The non-profit sector also works in partnership with both the public and for-profit sectors. It is the recipient of government contracts to deliver public services, particularly social welfare. In addition, corporations have traditionally funded non-profit organisations, and co-operative arrangements between non-profits and corporate partners, such as cause-related marketing, are becoming increasingly common.

In addition, the non-profit sector in the United States serves as an advocate on behalf of those who criticise or seek to change either government or for-profit activity. It mobilises public attention to community problems or needs and allows people to be heard on issues that they consider important. On another level, the non-profit sector helps bring people together, an important function in an individualistic society such as the United States. It both counteracts the isolation that can be found in American society and allows Americans to share important values. Both those seeking to preserve old values, ideals, and traditions, and those seeking to change them or create new ones utilise non-profit organisations. In addition, the sector facilitates the development of bonds of trust and solidarity that make joint community action possible.

Given its importance and range of activities, it is surprising that sector-wide research and concern with impacts are relatively recent agendas. The first major systematic nation-wide consideration of the non-profit sector was the Filer Commission, whose results were published in 1977 (Commission on Private Philanthropy and Public Needs, 1977). Widespread interest in the evaluation of the sector became a concern in the 1980s, sparked by a conservative government, funding cutbacks, recession, privatisation of government spending, commercialisation and marketisation of welfare, sector blurring, and non-profit scandals. These factors combined to produce a crisis atmosphere in the sector (Estes *et al.*, 1989) and the perception that the sector needed to defend itself, including more clearly demonstrating its role and contribution.

The trend that started in the 1990s featured an improved economy, sector growth, increasing and new wealth, an increased market focus, continued government cutbacks and privatisation, and a new breed of givers with a philanthropic focus on social entrepreneurship and venture philanthropy (see also Williams in this volume). These factors have meant continuing challenges for the non-profit sector. Local governments are pushing to impose property taxes; for-profits are claiming unfair competition; and there is anecdotal evidence of fraud, corruption, and excessive executive salaries. The results of these trends have led to a current obsession, among both public and private funders, with the evaluation of the outputs of individual non-profit organisations.

There is also increasing interest in non-profit evaluation among academics and researchers. Previously, debates in these circles had been about performance and programme evaluation in single organisations, such as the benefits and drawbacks of process *versus* outcome evaluation. In the last several years, a new interest has developed for the evaluation of the sector and its sub sectors. In line with this, INDEPENDENT SECTOR held a research conference in 1996 on sector impact and also initiated a major measurement project (see the organisation's website at *www.independentsector.org*). A number of books on the topic have also recently been published (Flynn & Hodgkinson, 2001; Foster *et al.*, 2001).

Everyone writing on the topic agrees that evaluating the impact of the non-profit sector is an extremely complex task (and an impossible one according to some). One problem, illustrated in the descriptive material above, is the diversity of the sector. The National Taxonomy of Exempt Entities (NTEE) classification, for example, consists of 26 major categories of non-profit services, each broken down into a multitude of subcategories. This, however, is not the only issue. In the sections to follow, we will summarise the state of thinking among scholars and researchers in the United States about conceptual and methodological issues.

## Conceptual issues

The first question that needs to be addressed is what it is that we are trying to measure and assess. We will not consider the question of what the non-profit sector itself is. There is vigorous debate about what should be included in this notion and great variation in the legal definitions of the sector found in different countries. In the United States, the sector comprises the private organisations, which are registered as tax-exempt with the Internal Revenue Service. The central question for us in this chapter is: "What is impact?". Wyszomirski (2001), presents a useful distinction between evaluation/assessment and impact analysis. The former deals with the operations and programme activities of individual organisations and is useful for planning, management, and reporting. Impact addresses different, often external, audiences and may have political and policy implications. Questions can include the priorities that should be given to allocating public resources among the different sectors and how effectively, efficiently, and equitably public interests are being addressed by the sector.

There is an intense debate about how objectively impact could be assessed. Cobb (2001) examines a range of possibilities. On one extreme are positivistic academic social scientists, who stress the necessity of value-free indicators (as all values are held to be arbitrary). Somewhat less extreme are those who claim to be value free while using taken-for-granted monetary valuation. Republicans are cited as exemplars. A third camp relaxes things further by allowing values such as compassion, tolerance, and economic and social equality in their assessments. Democrats (even though they currently also favour hard data) are given as an example. A fourth camp is explicitly and pervasively value based. This is the home of activists dealing with social problems and seeking to change the status quo. Indicators are multidimensional, including social and alternative economic measures, such as non-monetary indicators of development.

At the heart of much of the current debate is the desirability of using monetary valuation as opposed to other measures of value. When assessing multiple dimensions of non-profit activity, monetary valuation can provide a common measure with which to evaluate diverse activities. Critics, however, claim that it has a serious limitation by forcing everything into an economic framework. It presumes that money and market dynamics can, even hypothetically, be used to assess the value placed on things. The question becomes how to deal with aspects of non-profit functioning that are not reducible to a market metric, particularly the non-quantitative dimensions of non-exchanged, non-market activities or outputs (Reed, 1994). This leads to the speculation of what other bases might be used to assign values and the larger question of what values are. For instance, what other bases could be used to derive instrumental/rational standards and how might standards based on psychological, social, and cultural factors be formulated?

It is important that sector evaluation efforts confront these questions in order to avoid the charge of bias. The same issues have been strongly debated in the environmental field between environmental economists and those advocating alternative views of the value of the environment (Guy, 1999; van Kooten et al., 2000; Posey, 1999). Non-profit evaluation could benefit from a closer consideration of this material.

In addition, there has been vigorous debate in a number of social science disciplines about the limits of economic analysis and the role of values in economic models. For example, Brockway (1995) argues for economics as a moral science, involved with the proper conduct of life and people acting in a free way to express and promote a wide range of values. Mansbridge (1990) presents a number of essays by social scientists, including economists, which argue that individual behaviour and social organisation are influenced by the motivations of duty, love, and malevolence. Etzioni (1988) describes a paradigm struggle, pitting the entrenched utilitarian, rationalistic-individualistic, neo-classical outlook against a social-conservative paradigm that sees individuals as morally deficient and irrational, and requiring authority to guide action (p. ix). He advocates an alternative viewpoint – individuals acting rationally to advance themselves, but significantly influenced by their attachment to sound communities and moral and personal underpinnings. Blinder (1987) points out that even in areas where economic analysis is sound, it is often ignored by policy makers representing narrow interests. What is needed is economic policy that includes both economic efficiency and concern for the needy in society. Also discussing policy, Gillroy and Wade (1992) contend that the role of the citizen is distinct from that of the consumer and that public policy should recognise values that are not based on instrumental economic preferences.

For other discussions, see Lutz and Lux (1979), Ben-Ner and Putterman (1998), Phelps (1975), Hausman and McPherson (1996), Dworkin and associates (1977), Clark (1995), and Tool (1986). This body of literature should also be more explicitly considered in discussions about non-profit evaluation. Economics has developed rationales and models to assess impacts (discussed below). The critics of these approaches in the non-profit field, while pointing to the limitations of these models, have not systematically developed alternatives.

It would, moreover, be interesting to see the non-profit field initiate discussions of even more fundamental considerations of value. Axiology, the branch of philosophy dealing with values (Rescher, 1969; Handy, 1970; Frondizi, 1963), might well contain interesting and useful ideas that can advance our thinking about the non-profit sector. Non-profit literature has not explored any of the points from this branch of philosophy.

Finally, there is the issue of the negative effects of the non-profit sector, which is both conceptual and methodological. From the very inception of its study, it has usually been assumed that the non-profit sector provides numerous benefits to individuals, communities, and society. These actual or presumed benefits have often been the focus of discussion and research. On the other hand, there have been a few suggestions that non-profit contributions may not all be positive. The idea of NIMBY (Not In My Back Yard) implies that some, at least, might object to non-profit activity in their area. In addition, some types of social capital (bonding, as opposed to bridging) have recently been held to have potentially negative consequences for group relations (Putnam, 2000). Recent scandals and mismanagement have also raised doubts. For ideological and/or programmatic reasons, non-profit research in general and non-profit evaluation in particular, have tended to focus on or seek to demonstrate positive aspects of the sector or particular organisations. This is a bias that should be redressed. It leaves the sector unprepared to respond when real or alleged negative consequences are uncovered. A good example is the criticism levelled against secular non-profits by proponents of religiously-based service provision (to be discussed below).

## Methodological issues

The conceptual issues raised above are usually considered in research. Of more immediate concern are methodological factors; specifically, what should be measured, how it should be measured, and the adequacy of the data that is available for measurement. The conclusion by all writing on this is that there are significant difficulties to be overcome, which might, in fact, be insurmountable depending on the standards.

A list of the factors that have been suggested for measurement (for example, see Land, 2001; Wolpert, 2001; Young and Steinberg, 1995) includes at least: inputs (such as money and labour), outputs (the volume of services provided), and outcomes (changes in the state or conditions of programme participants). In addition, evaluation should seek to assess impacts, which are broader programme results than outcomes, involve the criteria of external audiences, and include political or policy implications. In addition, evaluations can include side effects (changes to other areas not directly tied to programme activity), opportunity costs (the other things that cannot be done), distributional effects (how benefits are distributed to various social groups – who benefits and who doesn't), and multiplier effects (effects on other parts of the economy due to non-profit financial activity, such as purchasing and employment). Wyszomirski (2001) also notes that we need to calculate benefits and costs, be concerned about both direct and indirect effects, allow for positive as well as negative effects, and recognise intended as well as unintended consequences.

An equally long list of difficulties has been cited. A basic problem, which will influence all parts of the assessment process, is that we usually lack a causal model (DiMaggio, 2001). This problem also applies to the operations of for-profits and government agencies. For non-profits, the situation is exacerbated, however, by factors such as the heterogeneity of the sector, the influence of for-profits and government on non-profit actions, and the influence of opportunity costs and unobservables. DiMaggio also discusses how the multiple and often ambiguous goals of non-profits complicate the situation further. These goals are often easiest to express in technical, quantitative terms, with the real goals remaining unstated, and, therefore, unassessed. There are, moreover, political disincentives to providing information for performance assessment. Finally, to the extent that ambiguity may be useful to them, managers will not see it in their interest to release data for evaluations.

Others echo these points. Stone and Cutcher-Gershenfeld (2001) point to the non-market and mission-driven quality of non-profits, the possibility of intangible outputs, competing constituencies and the necessity of adopting vague goals to deal with them, and the loose coupling between donors and beneficiaries who have different objectives. In the absence of clear means-ends relations, its not surprising that political factors are often the determinants of the performance measures used or demanded. Land (2001) points to the lack of clear goals, services to anonymous beneficiaries, and intangible outputs and outcomes.

If effects beyond single organisations are sought, the need to aggregate makes things even more difficult (DiMaggio, 2001; Land, 2001). Effects can be measured at the client, programme/organisation, community, or sub-sector level. The lack of direct measures at higher levels and aggregation difficulties may lead to the temptation of observers to impose goals on a sub-sector. DiMaggio also points out that, even if organisations were willing, there are likely to be constraints on the data that would be available. Organisations lack the capacity to gather extensive outcome or impact data. Cost considerations will necessitate the use of existing data, which is poor. In addition, there is great variation in data availability across sectors.

In spite of these difficulties, however, work on evaluation is being done. We can distinguish between economically derived methods and those employing other techniques. Among the former, one technique that has received much attention in the policy field and is being advocated in non-profit research is cost benefit analysis. Young and Steinberg (1995, pp. 211-242) present a useful discussion of this mode of analysis. Their main points are summarised below.

Cost benefit analysis is used in situations where profits are an inappropriate measure, for instance when externalities are present, public goods are being provided, or information problems are present. Cost benefit analysis seeks to provide an equivalent to profit, based on social costs and benefits as opposed to market costs and benefits. For a given course of action, economic benefits and costs are computed (regardless of who actually benefits or pays) and these are discounted for opportunity costs. If alternatives are being considered – after subtracting costs from benefits for each – the alternative with the highest benefit is chosen.

While conceptually simple, considerable difficulties can be encountered in the implementation of cost benefit analysis (see also Foster *et al.*, 2001, pp. 11-18). One issue is the consideration of the distribution of costs and benefits. To assess distributional consequences, transfer payments, secondary effects, and political and ethical considerations may need to be considered. Measurement of costs and benefits can also be very difficult. In situations of market failure, market prices are not reflective of social costs and benefits. It may be possible in some cases to use comparable market costs/benefits if they exist; in other cases this might not be possible.

Economic cost includes the opportunity value of resources used. For non-profits, this will include the other uses that beneficiaries and donors could have made of a given amount of money, the cost of replacing volunteers with paid workers, and the use that government could have made of forgone taxes (Foster *et al.*, 2001). Economic benefits are conceptualised as the value of resources that people are willing to pay (WTP) for something. That "something" however, that people can get from non-profits can involve both direct benefits as well as indirect benefits such as altruism, warm glow (impure altruism), private benefits (acquired contacts, skills, etc.), externalities, and options (benefits to be used later) (Foster *et al.*, 2001).

The basic question is how to measure benefits in the absence of actual payments. In these situations, WTP has been estimated using indirect approaches such as private sector equivalents or opportunity cost.

Alternatively, direct approaches such as contingent valuation or choice modelling (hedonic analysis) are available. Contingent valuation is based on using survey methods to ask people what they would be willing to pay for certain benefits. Some of the problems with this technique (see also Weisbrod, 2001) involve people's ability to make judgements about goods or services they are not familiar with, or not being honest even if they are familiar with the services. In addition, for services to the poor, it is unreasonable to ask people who have no money how much they would pay for services.

In the hedonic approach, models are built to predict the price of a good, which is assumed to be the result of multiple factors (Dowling, 1984). The component parts of the good are then broken out in the analysis. This approach has been used in housing studies (Rothenberg, 1991), urban economics (Man and Bell, 1996; Muth and Goodman, 1989), and environmental economics (Markandya and Richardson, 1993). When applied to house prices and neighbourhood quality, "Goods that are not explicitly valued in the market, such as clean air, could be valued implicitly by comparing parcels or dwelling units with different air qualities. Housing demand could be decomposed into demand for the various components of the housing bundle, including neighbourhood." (Goodman, 1989, pp. 59-60).

In this way, through incorporating any variables which may influence the sale price, hedonic modelling allows us to derive a value for those things which are tangible and easily observable, such as the characteristics of the house itself, as well as the value (shadow price) of those things which are not, such as neighbourhood quality (Young and Steinberg, 1995, pp. 217-19). In terms of the presence of non-profits, positive impacts could be due to services that are available to neighbourhood residents, increased social capital, positive spill-over effects on other organisations, well-kept and/or highly visible facilities, or even just the presence of a prestigious or respected organisation. Negative effects may be due to the presence of clients that residents perceive as unpleasant or dangerous, the provision of services not favoured by residents, or facilities that are unsightly, or generate traffic, noise, or pollution.

When we move beyond these economic-based techniques, we don't find other major agreed-upon models, techniques, or variables. A number of factors have been held to be important, such as the quality of life, justice, equity, community cohesion, community development, integration, and inclusion. Their measurement is sometimes made with questionnaires or qualitative techniques. Measurement is usually restricted to documenting the existence of these factors or whether there is more or less of the factor. Given the diversity of variables and ways to measure them, it is difficult to compare the results of studies.

In spite of the conceptual and methodological issues and problems outlined above, sectoral assessments are being made. There are a number of reasons for this. The sector must respond to external and internal pressures and as mentioned previously, demands for evaluation are coming from funders, government agencies, the media, and the public. In addition, decisions need to be made, both by agencies and policy makers. In the attempt to improve decision-making and policy, the perception among influential actors is likely to be that any information is better than none. While this conclusion may be highly questionable, non-profits must, nevertheless, respond and gather information.

There are, in addition, a number of other reasons for sector evaluation. DiMaggio (2001) considers the symbolic and ritual nature of evaluation and the benefits that can come from this. These include legitimisation, as the sector signals its commitment to the "rationality" of assessment (joining the for-profit and public sectors in this regard). The process of evaluation can also stimulate changes that improve the sector as well as promote useful dialogue about the sector and its role. This can involve clarifying objectives, focusing attention, negotiating shared identities, and generating research. But, given that no scientific "bottom line" can be assessed, the results could become politicised.

DiMaggio contends that two dimensions will determine the degree to which impact assessment is possible, including, i) the homogeneity of structural features and organisational forms in the activity area, and ii) the degree to which goals and missions are shared in these areas. In homogeneous areas with low mission-sharing, there are likely to be incentives to conceal information and passive resistance to impact analysis. In heterogeneous areas with low mission–sharing, there is likely to be goal conflict, resulting in poor prospects for assessment. In areas where there is strong mission sharing the prospects for impact assessment are improved. If these are homogeneous areas, however, there is a potential for self-censorship. The best prospects for impact assessment are in heterogeneous areas characterised by mission-sharing.

Weisbrod (2001) outlines a number of reasons for evaluation from a policy standpoint. Problems, criticisms, or challenges to non-profits may lead to greater regulations or restrictions in the sector. Consequently, it is important to evaluate the role of the sector both for public policy as well as for non-profits themselves as they seek to reduce the uncertainty about their social contribution. The goal of evaluation, therefore, should be to assess if it would serve us better if non-profit resources were used in the other sectors (in light of the limitations of those sectors).

Weisbrod also considers the difficulties of measurement. Many of the things non-profits do are difficult to measure. When they don't get measured, they do not get valued well or at all. For example, to value public or collective goods that are provided to everyone, one would need information on the total WTP of all people. In addition, non-profits avoid opportunistic behaviour and this is also likely to be undervalued. Sector assessment should include: efficiency, productivity, output quality, access by consumers regardless of ability to pay, collective goods complementing government, alternatives to government, the encouragement of altruism, promotion of expressions of socially-oriented motivations, and mechanism for shaping and adding variety to the political system.

Weisbrod also advocates assessment of how the non-profit sector affects other parts of the economy. Decreasing government funding has led to increased non-profit commercialism, leading to competition with for-profit organisations. On the other hand, co-operation between non-profits and both government and for-profits is also increasing. The impact of both of these should be evaluated. These could lead to a number of consequences (some of them unanticipated). In terms of non-profit co-operation with for-profits, for example, each party may gain, but the economy could end up worse off. The impact of commercialism on non-profit mission and priorities also needs to be examined.

Weisbrod reviews evidence that non-profits do, in fact, behave differently than for-profits or government and provide economically valuable functions that the other do not. Evidence includes higher output quality, trustworthiness, access to services, volunteering and, in some cases, lower managerial compensation.

## Areas of inquiry

In this section, we will consider the areas where assessment of the impact of the sector is being carried out or proposed. The discussion includes current assessment activities, the kinds of evidence being used for them, and the prospects for future assessments. We will include the sector as a whole, key subsectors, and major subgroups.

### The sector as a whole

A number of sources provide descriptive, overview information about the sector in the United States. This information does not go into extensive detail, but it does provide some measures of the dollar value of inputs and outputs as well as some key organisational factors, primarily employment and volunteering. Recent works include Boris (1999) who presents the number of organisations, recent changes in numbers, employment, types of services provided (subsectors), geographical distribution, and sources of income. In addition, Salamon (1999) presents the numbers of organisations, revenues and expenditures, employment, and volunteers for the sector and key subsectors. He also considers the relative scope of government and for-profit sectors. Another source of information is INDEPENDENT SECTOR's new almanac (Weitzman *et al.*, 2002), which contains information on numbers, geographical distribution, share of national income employment, expenditures, revenues, and financial trends.

A long-time source of information on philanthropy is "Giving USA" (AAFRC Trust for Philanthropy, 2001) which presents yearly levels of giving by individuals, foundations, and corporations. It also includes the uses of contributions. In addition, INDEPENDENT SECTOR also publishes "Giving and Volunteering in the United States" (Kirsch *et al.*, 1999) which presents findings from periodic household surveys. These are useful for understanding the philanthropic inputs the sector receives.

### Functional sub-sectors

#### Health care

Given the economic and social importance of health care, it is not surprising that much attention is currently focused on this area. Gray (2001) considers a number of difficulties occasioned by the current state of affairs in the field. There are many types of health care provided in many kinds of settings and the relative presence of non-profits differs in each subsector. Most importantly, the health care field in the United States is rapidly changing. This includes changes in ownership, operations, and the lines of separation between the non-profit and for-profit sector. This makes the health care industry very complex and difficult to study.

The biggest challenge is what should be counted as "impact"? In terms of the work currently going on, Gray notes that many measures pertain to volume (such as the number of beds) perhaps combined with yield measures such as occupancy rates. A major problem in interpreting these kinds of measures is the lack of standards as to what constitutes "good" care. Payments for services are also frequently used, although this measures activity as opposed to performance or outcome. A number of improvements are needed to interpret this type of information, including measures of quality, inefficiency, fraud, and abuse. In addition, an assumption common in the field is that more is better. This assumption should be more critically examined.

Besides individual, private benefits, health care is also assumed to have community and public benefits. Non-profits are held to be important for redressing information asymmetries, and some evidence exists that some health non-profits are perceived as more trustworthy. In addition, people may lack the ability to pay for needed services and have to rely on charity care. Finally, non-profit organisations may be leaders in addressing community needs. Gray proposes 30 dimensions of community benefits, including positive externalities, minimising negative externalities, provision of public goods, and minimising information asymmetries.

In terms of the evidence of community benefits, attention has recently been focused on the uncompensated care provided *versus* the taxes exempted. These are difficult to measure. On other measures, the non-profit sector scores high, including having local governance, being located in urban areas with poor populations, providing more research and education, having a greater array of services, and less ownership change.

### Arts

Arts is an area which has received much attention and many types of impacts can be assessed (Wyszomirski, 2001). For artists and patrons, notion of impacts include individual transformation and inspiration, and the degree of public access. Artistic and aesthetic impacts also include creativity and performance. Other suggestions for impacts have included economic, educational, medical, political, technological, and social factors. Finally, personal, community, and national identity could be communicated and embodied and political values like freedom of expression could be reinforced. In addition, there are many possible recipients on which to measure impacts; these include individuals, organisations, fields, and professions. Impacts could also be local, national, or international. Effects could range from immediate to long term. Given these alternatives, the development of indexes to assess impacts at organisational, economic, or community levels may be useful.

Wyszomirski discusses sources of information. Field-level aggregate information is collected by national arts service organisations, funders, and government. This information, however, is fragmented and incomplete. It is not used to consider redistribution effects or cost/benefit ratios. There is also a need to increase the comparability of data and to co-ordinate data gathering. Numerous types of more specific data are also gathered. Surveys are used to measure audiences, primarily for marketing purposes. Public surveys, including both attendees and non-attendees, yield information about the reach of the arts and factors that might promote or inhibit attendance. Public opinions about actions, preferences, attitudes, intentions, and expectations relative to the arts are also gathered.

Economic impact studies are frequently developed and used, usually to gain funding. Wyszomirski cites a number of good examples from New York,

New Jersey, and California. Suggestions for improvement include the measurement of net impacts, human capital development, quality of life, and community cohesiveness and engagement, as well as the use of contingent valuation and hedonic modelling techniques. Also, more work on the definition of the "cultural industry" is needed (see for example O'Connor, 1999).

The educational and social effects of the arts have been studied. Measurement of educational effects has included impacts on achievement, motivation, school attendance, content knowledge and skills, self-esteem, cultural awareness and attitude towards the arts. Numerous positive effects have been documented. Measurement of the social utility of the arts has included health, impacts on at-risk youth, drug and criminal rehabilitation, quality of life, better product design, and community revitalisation and integration. Some anecdotal evidence of positive effects has been obtained.

*Human services*

Human services is a very diverse category. The NTEE lists seven major categories of services under the term. Services may be delivered to a wide range of beneficiaries, who vary by factors such as race, gender, age, income, and place of residence. Given its extent, diversity and importance, much work is being done in this area.

Greenway (2001) cites a number of problems in evaluation trends and prospects in the human services, including the fact that: i) improvement in people's conditions will depend on many things besides the specific services they might receive, ii) impact has ambiguous meanings, and iii) outcomes need to be considered for both individuals and communities. A number of approaches to measuring outcomes are currently being pursued at national or local levels.

The most rigorous work has involved national studies that have used experimental or quasi-experimental designs to assess participant outcomes. Local programmes are used as study sites. Studies have focused on child welfare, including alcohol use, sex, educational interests, and attitudes. In most of those that Greenway cites, positive effects were found. There are also rare locally developed experimental evaluations that have become national models. Greenway cites an evaluation by a Family Service affiliate in Wisconsin that found positive results and subsequently became a national model.

Other national initiatives have used less rigorous techniques and have had other focuses. A number of national studies of local programmes used survey techniques and focused on current or retrospective participant perceptions (for example, Red Cross client satisfaction studies). Again, positive results are reported. Other efforts have involved outcome evaluation assistance from national organisations to local human service affiliates and national certification. Organisations such as the Girl and Boy Scouts, Big Brothers/Sisters, and the United Way have produced manuals and workbooks to help local affiliates monitor, measure, and assess their programmes.[2] Certification that requires outcome measurement is increasingly being dictated by managed care providers, for services such as counselling and home health care. These, however, are often based on little solid evidence about what good outcomes should be.

Greenway reviews a number of indicators that are commonly used. Measures of volume and participant satisfaction are common. Good outcome measures, however, will be hard to obtain, given that outcomes may be hierarchical, occur in sequence (for example, first knowledge and then behaviour), and be short or long term. The lack of benchmarks is also a problem.

Studies, moreover, are usually limited to individuals and measuring outcomes at the community level imposes an additional set of problems. It is not a simple matter of aggregating individual results, since community outcomes may also be driven by more than individual outcomes. Community outcomes, for example, can be due to collaboration across programmes/ sectors and be affected by public policy, the local economy, and informal support systems. In this way, positive programme outcomes may be swamped by negative contextual factors. In addition, evaluations often look for direct impacts on community factors, ignoring individual outcomes that may affect community outcomes more indirectly. Both better theories of change and better ways to link programme and contextual information are needed.

A number of recent studies of impact have been carried out using economically-based models. Ottensmann (2000) computed the economic value of selected social services provided by the Catholic Diocese of Cleveland. Work is also being done using hedonic modelling to test the hypothesis that the presence of non-profit organisations in neighbourhoods affects property values (Ottensmann, 2000; Bielefeld *et al.*, 2002). Ottensmann (2000) carried out a study of the value of the facilities of the Catholic Diocese of Cleveland and found that proximity of church facilities had a positive impact on the value of both owner-occupied and renter-occupied housing in Cleveland (2000, pp. 14-18). Ottensmann cites two previous studies of the impact of church facilities on house prices. Their findings were contradictory. Do, Wilbur, and Short (1994) found that the presence of churches has a negative effect on housing prices in one community and Carroll, Clauretie, and Jensen (1996) report that the presence of churches has a positive effect on housing prices.

Work is also currently being done in Indianapolis (Bielefeld *et al.*, 2002) using geo-coded housing house sale data and non-profit locations. The results show that for all non-profits, proximity increased house sale price. For non-profit subsets, this positive effect is found for arts and culture, education, health, public benefit, international, and mutual benefit. The opposite pattern is found for environment, human services, and religious non-profits.

### Community development

Non-profit organisations have played, and continue to play, prominent roles in community development efforts and are usually seen by analysts and researchers as critical for success. According to Felkins (2002), community building includes activities that promote alliances and coalitions. Increasing social capital and trust also facilitates co-ordination and co-operation among different organisations and agencies. Non-profits, in their roles as mediating structures, can be key actors in these processes. Felkins examines six social service organisations whose missions include community building. He concludes (pp. 6-7): "*The non-profit sector also serves a valuable function in linking corporations and neighbourhood groups in co-operative projects.*" Besides providing services to meet specific needs, they were also concerned with issues of social justice, were active in local and national networks and alliances organised to help build community at the neighbourhood level, engaged in advocacy, and provided training and resources to neighbourhood people.

Simon (2001) points out that local non-profits can use a number of advantages, including relational density and synergy, a geographic focus, and face-to-face interactions. Community organisations can pursue a variety of community goals, including overcoming market limitations, building social capital, and representing interest group outlooks and agendas. One of their contributions can be to lower the conventional boundaries between levels of government and types of enterprises (Musso *et al.*, 2002).

Chaskin and colleagues (2001) examine community capacity and capacity building. Community capacity involves (p. 12) resources, problem-solving ability, and commitment. These can be found in individuals, organisations, and networks. Capacity enables a community to provide goods and services as well as organise, plan, and make decisions. It can be developed through leadership, organisational development, and organisational collaboration. Non-profits can be involved in all of these. Three case studies are examined. The authors found (p. 62) that the non-profits provided goods, services, access to resources, and opportunities; leveraged and brokered external resources; developed human capital; created and reinforced community identity and commitment; and supported community advocacy.

Wright (2001) gives an overview of the results of the Pew Charitable Trust's Neighborhood Preservation Initiative in working-class neighbourhoods. Community foundations in nine mid-sized cities partnered with neighbourhood-based organisations and community actors. The evaluation concluded (p. 161) that the programme was a success. Much of the success is held to be due to successful collaborations among local organisations (p. 167): "... *promising organisational model that emerged stresses shared capacity: enabling a constellation of partner organisations linked on strategic joint projects, strengthened in turn by technical and financial support from foundation and intermediary partners, to act collectively on neighbourhood goals. As a model, the shared capacity approach proved to be effective and durable and appears to offer solid promise as a replicable approach in other neighbourhoods.*"

## Social capital

The concept of social capital is currently of great interest among academics from numerous disciplines and much theoretical and empirical work is being produced. While not a distinctive service provided by a set of non-profit providers, no discussion of the non-profit sector is complete without considering social capital. Its creation is held to be pervasive throughout the sector, as is its influence.

The concept was popularised in sociology by James Coleman (1988) and then more generally by Robert Putnam in a series of publications, primarily and most recently, "Bowling Alone: The Collapse and Revival of American Community" (2000). At this point, social capital is also an interest among policy makers and practitioners. Definitions of social capital differ and this is an issue in academic literature (Lin *et al.*, 2001; Baron *et al.*, 2000). Most research work, however, uses Putnam's definition (p..19), "*Social capital refers to connections among individuals-social networks and the norms of reciprocity and trustworthiness that arise from them*". Most research has focused on looking for the positive benefits of social capital. These benefits have been held to accrue to individuals, organisations, and communities. There have been theoretical discussions of possible negative aspects of social capital, but these have not been the subjects of much research. Besides its definition, the measurement of social capital is also an issue. Even among those using Putnam's definition, there is not an agreed-upon way to measure social capital. This makes it difficult to compare the results of different research studies and evaluate their contributions.

In 2001, Putnam, in conjunction with the Saguaro Institute at the John F. Kennedy School of Government at Harvard University, carried out a major study to measure the extent of social capital in American communities. In all, nearly 30 000 people in over 30 sites were interviewed. Ten dimensions of social capital were considered, including social trust, inter-racial trust, diversity of friendships, conventional politics participation, protest politics participation, civic leadership, associative involvement, informal socialising, giving and volunteering, and faith-based involvement. The overall results of the study have not been published, but a summary is currently available on the website of the Community Foundation of Silicon Valley (*www.cfsv.org/ communitysurvey/*). The results showed that the strength of resident's social ties to their communities predicted the quality of community life and resident's happiness better than other measures, such as education or income levels. In addition, communities varied widely on many of the measures.

Most other research does not consider the range of measures that Putnam's study did. Non-profits are usually seen as settings where social capital can develop (through people interacting with each other) and as vehicles where social capital can be used (through carrying out collective actions). Therefore, communities with larger and more diverse non-profit sectors have the potential for developing more social capital, which in turn, will result in smoother community functioning (Eastis, 1998; Stolle and Rochon, 1998). A number of areas are currently the focus of research, including neighbourhood disorder (Ross *et al.*, 2001), housing and community development (Lang and Hornburg, 1998), and economic growth and democratic governance (Ashman *et al.*, 1998).

Future research should incorporate other definitions and measures of social capital and what these might mean in terms of non-profit organisations. Also, the negative consequences of social capital should be explicitly included (DeFilippis, 2001). In addition, much work on social capital is currently being done by the World Bank, as well as several programmes by groups in Canada and Europe that examine social cohesion. This work should be more closely examined in the United States.

## Religion

The comments below will pertain towards religion and religious organisations in general. The activities of particular religious groups will be considered in the Subgroups section to follow. Widespread considerations of religion are relatively recent in the non-profit literature in the United States. McCarthy (2001, p. 166) points to a "... *vigorous debate during the past decade: should religion be included in non-profit research? Are sectarian functions of 'public benefit' and, if so, should they be included in our definition and statistical analyses of the non-profit sector? ... can we develop testable hypotheses about the relationship between religion, philanthropy, non-profits, and civil society?*". As the review below shows, the answer to this question at this point is a resounding "yes".

One of the foremost investigators of religion, Wuthnow (2001), reviews the history and current state of research on religion. While religion has been an important part of the voluntary sector since the founding of this country, the lack of interest and research on the link between religion, philanthropy, and the voluntary sector until the 1980s is due to academic specialisation and institutional arrangements. INDEPENDENT SECTOR and Lilly Endowment began research on the topic in the late 1980s (for example, in "Giving and Volunteering").

Much of the data gathered to date has been survey data, and Wuthnow notes a number of data limitations. While the higher generosity of the religious has been well measured, the more important factor of religious participation has not. In addition, distinctions are seldom made between specific types of religious involvement. Beliefs and motivations (involving understandings and factors such as guilt or gratitude) are even harder to measure. Congregation variables such as size, length of involvement, and orientation need to be included and these data are also hard to obtain. Finally, the service activities of congregations need to be linked to community characteristics in longitudinal research designs.

Other important topics that Wuthnow notes include the civic dimension of religion and volunteering (for example advocacy) *versus* service activities. Also of interest are the changing organisational forms through which religion is carried out, including partnerships, interfaith coalitions, and referral networks. The relations between religious and non-religious organisations need to be studied in more detail, for example the impact on religious participation of the service opportunities afforded by other non-profits. Relations between religion and both business and government are also important, such as community development initiatives that bring public/ private together.

There has been a lot of interest lately in the service activities of faith-based organisations. INDEPENDENT SECTOR carried out a study on this in the early 1990s (Hodgkinson et al., 1992). The increased religious involvement sought by the current Bush administration in the Charitable Choice portion of its welfare reform initiative has brought this issue to the centre of the policy stage and galvanised vigorous debate and controversy. Charitable Choice, or Section 104 of the Personal Responsibility and Work Opportunity Reconciliation Act of 1996 (PRWORA),[3] encourages states to contract with faith-based organisations (FBOs) for delivery of social services to welfare recipients on the same basis as they contract with traditional, secular providers. The inclusion of Charitable Choice in welfare reform was premised on several assumptions: i) FBOs do a better job at a lower cost than traditional providers, ii) FBOs represent significant untapped resources that can be marshalled to help the needy, and iii) FBOs had previously encountered barriers to participation.

The first significant studies to examine religious organisations in light of this welfare reform initiative were by Cnaan and Chaves. Cnaan (1999) concludes that the current policy environment is rejoining religious and secular welfare provision, which had, historically, been separated in the United States. Chaves (1999, pp. 303-308) found that congregations and other religious organisations are no longer just member-serving, but are becoming new organisations in the service delivery system. He found that, overall, more than one-third of US congregations were potentially open to seeking government funding. In addition, liberal and moderate congregations (and especially African American congregations) were more likely to peruse government funding than conservative congregations.

The data to support the assumptions with respect to the comparative efficacy of faith-based service providers are sketchy at best, and while several case studies are supportive, there is no comprehensive research addressing these issues (Johnson et al., 2002). In the meantime, the involvement of faith-based organisations in charitable choice is growing (Sherman, 2002) and numerous projects to study the consequences are underway. This situation may afford researchers a good opportunity to assess the relative performance of non-profit, for-profit, and government organisations and assess the value of religion. Some results are starting to emerge.

Campbell (2002) found that a variety of faith-related organisations were involved and that coalitions and networks are important. Smith and Sosin (2001) found that faith-related organisations were differentially tied to faith and that the strength of the coupling had impacts on services and service delivery. Bielefeld and colleagues (2001) found evidence of holistic outlooks towards clients among faith-related providers as well as evidence of significant management difficulties.

Johnson (2002) has also compiled an extensive and interesting review of the literature on the relationship between religion and health and well-being outcomes. The research shows an impressive set of findings. Higher levels of religious involvement are positively associated with longer survival; less depression; and reduced drug and alcohol use, suicide, and delinquency and criminal activity. In addition, positive associations have been found, such as well-being, hope, purpose, meaning in life, and educational attainment.

## Sub-groups (women, religious and racial groups, age cohorts)

The United States is known for its diversity. It is the product of many cultures and traditions and is made up of a multitude of groups with a variety of outlooks and goals. This affects American philanthropy. This section will examine the philanthropic motivations of various subgroups in the United States and how they seek to use the non-profit sector to bring about conditions or changes. While this has not been done in a systematic or widespread fashion, these points could be used as a basis for evaluating how non-profit subsectors have performed. We will consider major religious and racial groups, women, and age cohorts (generations). It is important to note that the literature on each of these groups is extensive, and only a brief summary of salient points can be presented.

### Women

Ostrander and Fisher (1995) review the history of women's philanthropy in the United States. Besides support for numerous causes, a number of individual women (including African American women) have created and developed important institutions devoted to improving the lives of women and children. Women have been increasing in power and wealth in the United States. Data from 1994 show that 60 per cent of the wealth in the United States was owned by women. While there is little good work available on gender differences in philanthropy, a number of findings have been reported. These include the fact that women are more likely to give to charitable organisations, wealthy women are more likely than wealthy men to make charitable bequests, and younger women are more likely to give support to social action causes. In addition, it has been suggested that women are more likely to emphasise the cause and purpose of an organisation and their connection to and involvement in that cause. For example, they may seek to be involved with the organisation first and then give money to it if they are satisfied with their involvement (see also Sublett, 1993). A key factor is to want to make a difference and therefore needing to assess the impact and results of their giving and support. Sublett (1993) also points to the importance of family tradition and personal responsibility. The latter involves a feeling that everyone has a responsibility to others and a desire to teach philanthropy to the next generation.

McCarthy (2001) discusses the current state of research on women's philanthropy and suggestion for future directions. The current research focus is on political and economic aspects of women's philanthropy in "nation-building". Interest centres on the influence of women's philanthropy on participatory democracy, the empowerment of politically and economically disadvantaged groups, and civil society. Measurement could include quantitative measures such as the birth/death of initiatives, legislative gains made, and changes to underlying financial/social conditions. She cites several overarching needs, however, including research grounded in the social science disciplines (which have the necessary research tools), the examination of questions of broad nature that cut across disciplines, and practitioner-relevant research.

### Protestant

Given the large number and well-known nature of Protestant and Catholic groups, we will only briefly comment on relative motivations.

Hudnut-Beumler (1995) stresses the notion that the original Protestants were fundraising reformers, particularly Martin Luther whose disagreements with the money-raising practices of the Catholic Church at the time are well known. Concern about the wise or correct use of money for giving has continued to be a major characteristic of Protestant philanthropy. In addition, Tropman (1993) discusses the implications of the "Protestant ethic" which has been much written about since Max Weber's classic. This ethic includes an orientation to work as an important part of life and a view toward worldly success as a sign of being chosen or favoured. Other important notions include the distinction between worthy *versus* unworthy causes, a stress on personal responsibility in getting out of poverty, and the importance of freedom. For children, the values of initiative, integrity, industry, and thrift will be emphasised by parents.

These points can help us understand the goals of Protestant giving discussed by Hudnut-Beumler (1995). These include the desire for attachment, where preference is given to smaller causes or those where givers are needed and have a sense of ownership. This often translates into giving to local organisations, where these factors might be easiest to realise. In addition, internationality and accountability matter and the cause should be clearly identified as important. Many of the great American foundations were established by Protestant families and the programmes of these foundations exemplify the factors described above, including giving to institutions providing education, culture, health, or community building.

*Catholic*

Tropman (1993) outlines a Catholic ethic which, compared to the Protestant ethic, is characterised by more of a group-based (versus individual) self concept; more co-operative behaviour (versus competition), the seeking of contentment (versus seeking the optimal), and more interest in the consequences of poverty (versus its causes). It has also been asserted to be more charitable, particularly in regard to altruism, benevolence, compassion, and generosity.

Central tenets of the Catholic ethic include the notions that work and money are merely necessary to live (not a sign of personal quality), that mercy is important to deal with the cycle of sin and redemption, and that charity is important because you will get help in return for helping others. Other values include social relationships, equality, decentralisation, and government support for the needy. For children, loyalty, obedience, and patience are stressed.

Much giving is directly through the church and there are also numerous well-known Catholic non-profit organisations. McManus (1990) considers recent challenges the Catholic Church has faced, particularly the turbulence in the church and the drop in giving after the mid-1970s as a result of Vatican II and other social and economic changes. To deal with these, he advocates that renewed attention should be given to two important church traditions – stewardship and almsgiving. Catholics should be called upon to exercise stewardship by getting involved in voluntary activity in addition to giving money. The notion of almsgiving should, likewise, be expanded from a sense of obligation to help the poor and needy to also include helping due to compassion for them (charity). Each of these would result in more activity by Catholics in non-profits organised for Catholic purposes.

### Evangelical

Evangelicals are an important group to consider since they give twice as much as Protestants, three times more than Catholics, and four times more than the general population (Willmer, 1995). They give to ministries consistent with their faith, often headed by charismatic figures. These are often organisations that directly meet human needs and front line ministries.

Five factors are held to encourage evangelical giving. They include an earnest concern for the lost souls of the world, an adherence to the biblical notion of stewardship, and taking the Bible's instructions about possessions seriously by holding that giving is a part of worshipping. In addition, there is a desire to preserve the nation (as the place where religion can be practised) and a desire to build institutions that support evangelical values.

Giving is more often to individuals or projects than to larger institutions and the concern is more about an individual's salvation than it is about solving social problems. There are a number of large evangelical foundations and numerous smaller ones. Support goes to missionaries, Bible colleges, human welfare organisations, and para-church organisations (which supplement the work of churches).

### Jewish

The origin of the Jewish philanthropic tradition lies in religious texts. Proper philanthropy is held to be important acquired behaviour and much emphasis is placed upon teaching it to children. Much of it revolves around spending on holidays, and life-cycle events such as births and marriages, as well as everyday life. Tzedakah, or charity, is an important responsibility for everyone and its role in the correct way to live has been given much attention, for example in the eight degrees of charity laid out by Maimonides in the middle ages. In this oft-quoted scheme, the lowest form of charity is not to give enough while the highest form is giving that promotes the self-reliance of the recipient.

Jewish philanthropy has been heavily influenced by recent history, as outlined by Kosmin (1995). Historical changes have shaped changes in Jewish philanthropy. Earlier in the 20th century, Jewish philanthropic initiatives involved rescuing endangered or oppressed Jewish communities around the world and the security of Israel. However, history and successful efforts have reduced the need for these. Also important is a reduction of anti-Semitism in the United States as well as an increased acceptance of American society among the Jewish. In addition, the Jewish occupational profile is now professional and managerial as opposed to the earlier commercial and entrepreneurial profile. Women's roles and issues are now also more important.

The response to these changes has been a new emphasis on long-term and diversified financial resource development. This includes long-range strategies to finance ongoing Jewish fundraising from a variety of sources. It would also include building endowment programmes and securing, for perpetuity, some of the wealth of the older generation of loyal givers by means of bequests. The goal of these efforts should be to resist total assimilation as well as secure long-term viability. Jewish continuity is still very important, so activities should include identity-building efforts such as educational trips to Israel for young people. The concern for inner, rather than outer, direction should not be lost.

## African-American

Joseph (1995) considers the history and contributions of the major cultural traditions in the United States. For African Americans, one of the characteristics he stresses is the importance of a communal identity. Individuals are the stewards of the resources of the community and, as such, have moral duties and social obligations to it. As the bonds of the extended family were broken by slavery, the black churches, mutual aid societies, and other fraternal associations filled the void; they provided voluntary services and financial resources to free blacks, eased the transition from slavery to freedom, and worked to transform government and the laws which hindered social justice and civil rights. Throughout, the black church has been central. Service to God has been linked to service to humanity and the church has been the recipient of 75 per cent of all giving as well as most volunteering.

Fairfax (1995) points to the multitude of motives of black philanthropy, including caring for the community, solidarity with the oppressed, mutual assistance, self-help, social protest, the struggle for justice, and the enhancement of the education and economic status of blacks. This has led to disproportionate giving to black organisations, primarily the church. Being a trusted black-controlled institution that has not abandoned the inner city, the church is strategically positioned to continue to be a major vehicle for black charitable giving and volunteering. Important agendas for the future include the need to further engage the marginalised members of the community as well as focus on empowerment, capacity building, economic development, and the strengthening of community infrastructures. In addition, the role of the Muslim community and the role of charity in Islam (where it is one of the five pillars) should not be ignored.

Winters (1999) also discusses some of the challenges for the future as the black community moves from survival mode to self-sufficiency and economic empowerment. There is a need to build long-term philanthropic institutions through endowments, scholarships, family foundations, and support for black united funds and other major non-profit organisations (such as the new mega-churches with large budgets).

*Latinos*

Joseph (1995) describes several important dimensions of Latino culture. The primacy of the family is key among these. Another dimension is territory, for example the village or neighbourhood. In addition, there is the importance of "the race", or *la raza*. While there is racial diversity, the unifying elements of this concept include honour, dignity, the importance of spiritual over economic factors, and confidence in particular people. Other important factors are that social class plays a role in the solidarity and antagonisms among classes and that religion is a major source of bonding. More extensive discussions of these and a number of the other points considered below can be found in Wagner and Deck (1999).

While it is important to distinguish between major Latino groups because their origins and history in the United States resulted in somewhat different philanthropic activities and patterns, space prohibits this detailed discussion (see Joseph, 1995). We will consider common characteristics. Cortes (1995) outlines three major traditions that help clarify Latino philanthropy. These include the use of extended family networks to help individuals in need on a one-to-one basis, donations of time and money to the Catholic Church, and mutual assistance associations to promote and enable community survival. In addition, when philanthropy extends beyond the family and the church, it is mediated by personal relationships based on trust.

Ramos (1999) discusses several additional important factors. One is a historical tradition where government or the church met most social needs and individual philanthropy was informal and oriented to the family. Most philanthropic activity has been focused on Latino children, youth, and families. There has, understandably, been much concern over the issues associated with immigration and bilingualism. Recently, there has been growing support for self-help philanthropic activities oriented to a wider range of Latino interests. For example, support is growing for cultural arts activities that celebrate and promote Latino art forms and tradition. There is also a belief among important donors that efforts are needed to train and prepare Latinos at all levels to participate more extensively in giving.

### Asian-Americans

Shao (1995) points out that Asian Americans are one of the fastest growing segments of the American population. The 1990 census showed that their numbers doubled in each of the last three decades. Five states are home to the greatest part of the Asian American population. In addition, this is one of the most diverse and complex minority groups, composed of more than 20 different ethnic subgroups. Asian Americans come from countries with different histories, cultures, languages, customs, traditions, and religions. Moreover, there is great diversity within these countries. Immigrants basically came in three waves. The first arrivals were labourers in the 1800s, followed by a significant number of professionals following the relaxation of immigration policy in 1965, and finally the refugees after the Vietnam War. This has led to differences in patterns of assimilation into American culture.

Joseph (1995) discusses some of the philanthropic implications of the nation of origin for Chinese, Japanese, and Korean groups. Religion is an important factor in each case. Confucianism, for example stresses morality, humanism, commitment to public service, responsibility in social relations, equality, and benevolence. Buddhism promotes the notion that the individual alone cannot accomplish much and must work in groups.

Chao (1999) discusses the variety of philanthropic agendas of Asian Americans. Much giving is informal and for the care of the extended family and community. Important philanthropic institutions include churches and temples, alumni and professional associations, and schools (such as Saturday language and cultural schools). After the post 1965 influx of immigrants, activists established social service organisations oriented to providing health and human services for youth and the elderly, education, immigration services, cultural heritage preservation, and civil rights and social justice.

In giving, social and personal connections are important as is the obligation to "save face" among those in the social circle. This gives rise to giving to the causes of those who gave to yours. Stella Shao (1995) also points out the importance of the reciprocity of giving, the roles of ceremony and ritual, and the priority system starting with the family, then the ethnic community, and finally the larger society. Giving has been heavily focused on ethnic-specific, ritualistic, and institutionalised efforts to preserve Asian culture and assist Asian communities in foreign and hostile environments. More recently, however, as Asians have become more assimilated into

American culture, increases in the establishment of foundations contributing to non-Asians have been seen.

## Native-Americans

Native Americans form a very diverse group, composed of many tribes that have gone through many different transitions over the course of European colonisation and the periods thereafter. Joseph (1995) outlines some of the distinctive characteristics of a Native American *versus* a European worldview. The Native view is also described by Berry (1999).

One can contrast the European emphasis on science, objectivity, and technology to the Native American subjective and individualistic view. This is nowhere more evident than in regard to the Native American's direct experience with nature, which is spiritual. In addition, there is a stress on the oneness of the world and communal existence, including communal ownership. Also prominent are democracy, egalitarianism, and a tradition of generosity. Land and animals have an essence and spirit of their own and one must maintain a proper and respectful relation to them. This is opposed to considering them possessions to be used.

A reflection of these ideas is the notion that wealth is for distribution and not accumulation. This is shown through practices such as potlatch, or reciprocal generosity. In these practices, giving is not considered charity, but the honouring of the community and due to mutual responsibility. It is, thus, a unifying cultural trait, in which both the giver and the receiver are honoured and their equal status is validated. In this communally-centred giving, there is an obligation to pass gifts on as an extension of honour and the stewardship of all worldly resources.

In summary, a set of circular, concentric relationships involve the individual with the family, the clan, the tribe, and the native population respectively. This is reflected in philanthropy. Important forms of giving include informal and personal giving, giving to tribal foundations, tribal colleges, community foundations, Native American service organisations, tribal enterprise, tribal government, and intertribal consortia. Interests include education, cultural preservation, economic development, youth and the elderly, new forms of self-help, rehabilitation, and the environment. On the reservations, giving to family and community predominate, in urban areas support is also given to intertribal networks or larger Native American causes and activities.

## Generations

Eastman (1995) adapts a model that holds that four generational archetypes have repeated themselves throughout the history of the United

States. Briefly, an Idealist generation is a dominant type and sets the ideological framework for later generations. In contrast, a Reactive generation is more individualistic and pragmatic. When a Civic generation is dominant, it wins wars, overcomes social ills, builds institutions, and develops technology. Finally, an Adaptive generation is recessive and refines and improves upon the accomplishments of the Civic generation.

Applied to philanthropy, this model identifies the patterns of several generations coexisting in the United States today. The oldest givers today are from the GI generation born between 1901 and 1924. This is a Civic generation and has been the most collectivist in United States history. The extraordinary generosity and participation of this generation is well documented. Their numbers, however, are rapidly dwindling.

They have been followed by what has been termed the silent generation, those born between 1925 and 1942. This is an Adaptive generation that spanned a period, from a time of need to the age of rockets. They have wealth, but less meaning and direction than their parents do. They may have a sense of guilt, leading them to leave money to their children and grandchildren. Their focus may be more on calculation and results as opposed to idealism or emotion.

The baby boomers, born between 1942 and 1960, constitute an Idealist generation. Their idealism encompasses both liberal and conservative visions. Television, however, has fostered a habit of snap judgements and an expectation of quick resolutions. They are engaged in hands-on efforts that are part of grand moral movements, as is evident from the popularity of organisations like Habitat For Humanity and those providing HIV/AIDS services and environmental services.

Generation X – those born between 1961 and 1981 – is a Reactive generation. They question the ideological and civic orientations of previous generations. Many grew up in dysfunctional families during a time of jobs with relatively low wages and little promise of wealth. They are disenchanted with politics but will volunteer, seeing this as a more viable political expression. They will work hard for events and institutions that build relationships, perhaps seeking to replace what they missed in their families.

The newest generation, those born from the mid-1980s on, are labelled the Millennials. Numbers are not in for this generation yet, but indications are that they will be a Civic generation and perhaps as collectivist as their GI generation predecessors. If so, this holds promise for philanthropy and the non-profit sector.

## Conclusion

A survey of the current state of non-profit sector evaluation in the United States reveals a fragmented and partial field. It is a relatively recent focus in applied and academic areas and characterised by many disagreements about concepts, methods, and the interpretation of results. While there are frequent evaluations of individual organisations, they have often been the result of pressure from funders, opponents, or policy makers, whose concerns have generally been quite specific and narrow. Moreover, these and the larger or more encompassing evaluations that have been done have been carried out in a number of different substantive areas, with different focuses, and using different methodologies. The results have not added up to overall conclusions about any given area or sub-sector, much less conclusions across subsectors.

To the extent, however, that the sector or its subsectors is a focus of public or policy attention, evaluations of its impact will be called for. There is widespread disagreement about what can be accomplished, scientifically or substantively, with these evaluations. The literature we have reviewed contains discussions of numerous difficulties as well as suggestions for future directions. Several strike us as especially useful. There should be more discussion about what the concept of "value" might mean for the sector and how we can think about its social contributions. While economics and monetary valuation have made contributions and will continue to be applied, developing alternative conceptual and methodological models from other disciplines should be a key goal.

In addition, the research agenda should yield results that cumulatively shed light on key questions. This could be accomplished either through much more widespread research or through a more focused research programme. Given the narrow concerns of most of those in the policy or applied realms who currently initiate and support evaluation, it seems doubtful that a more systematic or widespread concern will develop. This may leave the future in the hands of the academic community. There are many intriguing intellectual and academic questions that could be pursued and we hope that the topic will increasingly become an area of vigorous research.

### Notes

1. United Way of America is a leading non-profit organisation whose mission is to improve people's lives by mobilising the caring power of communities. It operates through a network of 1 400 community-based independent organisations. See *www.unitedway.org*. INDEPENDENT SECTOR is a coalition of leading non-profits, foundations, and corporations seeking to strengthen not-for-profit initiative, philanthropy and citizen action. See *www.independentsector.org*

2. See *www.girlsscouts.org*; *www.bsa.scouting.org*; *www.bbbsa.org* and previous note for United Way.

3. This comprehensive bipartisan welfare reform bill dramatically changed the nation's welfare system into one that required work in exchange for time-limited assistance. The bill contained strict work requirements, a performance bonus to reward states for moving welfare recipients into jobs, comprehensive child support enforcement, and support for families moving from welfare to work.

ISBN 92-64-19953-5
The Non-profit Sector in a Changing Economy
© OECD 2003

PART III

# Chapter 11

# International and European Perspectives on the Non-profit Sector: Data, Theory and Statistics

by

Helmut Anheier,
Centre for Civil Society, London School of Economics, UK
and
Sybille Mertens,
Centre for Social Economy, University of Liège, Belgium

## Introduction

In the course of the last decade, the non-profit sector in OECD countries has generally seen an increase in its economic importance as a provider of health, social and educational services of all kinds (Anheier and Salamon, 1998; and Salamon *et al.*, 1999). This increase in economic importance is closely related to privatisation policies in most of the OECD countries that no longer see non-profit organisations as some outmoded form of service delivery and finance. Instead, they are seen as instruments of welfare state reform, be it under the heading of new public management, quasi markets, or public private partnerships (Ferlie, 1996; and Kendall, 2000).

Whatever the merits or demerits of this policy shift might be, the increased economic importance of non-profit organisations as providers of services, typically as contractors of services paid for, at least in part, by government, brings with it a greater need for systematic and up-to-date information on behalf of policy makers generally. Unfortunately, until recently, a huge gap existed in our knowledge about the size, scope and financing of non-profit activities in most OECD countries. It was only through efforts like the Johns Hopkins Comparative Non-profit Sector Project (see Salamon *et al.*, 1999) and complementary efforts (see Defourny and Mertens, 1999) that first international estimates on the economic weight of this set of institutions became available.

Ultimately, however, the ongoing collection and reporting on non-profit sector statistics has to be lodged with statistical agencies. The Handbook on Non-profit Institutions (United Nations, 2002) is a first step toward this goal of improving national and international coverage of the non-profit sector. The Handbook, linked to the System of National Accounts (SNA) (United Nations, 1993) builds on the Anheier-Salamon proposal (1998) for a satellite account of non-profit institutions, first formulated by Rudney and Anheier in 1996. Satellite accounts are integrated sets of statistical tables that focus on particular institutions (*e.g.,* government agencies), or fields (education, health, or environment) that are of special interest to policy makers and analysts.

The non-profit sector Handbook, officially accepted by the United Nations Statistical Commission in 2002, consolidates information on non-profit institutions (NPIs) in a user-friendly and systematic way. The guidelines established and presented in the Handbook, allow national statistical agencies to improve data coverage, incorporate paid and unpaid work into national economic statistics, and collect data on the contributions of these organisations as well as other policy-relevant aspects.

This, in turn, allows analysts to monitor the actual importance, structure and development of NPIs within national economies both cross-nationally as well as over time. The various satellite tables show aggregates and flows involving NPIs, presenting them as a sector next to government, corporations and households, as the Belgian example will demonstrate below. The satellite accounts make it possible to address many questions of great value to economists and policy analysts interested in macro-economic and institutional sector comparisons. For example, data on NPI employment would add useful information for policy analysts interested in employment issues. Moreover, capacity measures for NPIs in fields like health care or education would aid the policy planning process, particularly given the wealth of other information that is part of the SNA and could be incorporated in the satellite account. Therefore, once implemented, the satellite system can provide information on the following features of non-profit organisations, among others:

- Wage bill and other expenditures.
- Revenue through transactions (sales, fees) and transfers (grants, donations).
- Employees and structure of employment.
- Volunteering.
- Membership.
- Assets and liabilities.
- Contribution to value added.
- Role in the provision of health, education, welfare, culture, and related services.

Against this background, the present chapter will first offer an empirical profile of non-profit organisations in the context of a wider study on the size and scope of the non-profit sector in over 22 countries that are covered by the Johns Hopkins Comparative Non-profit Sector Project (Salamon et al., 1999). We will then explore the usefulness of an extended satellite system for the field of third sector research, an inter-disciplinary social science speciality at the intersection of economics, sociology and political science that looks at non-market/non-state organisations. Finally, we will present an application of the satellite accounts approach and methodology to the Belgian case within the context of the social economy. While Europe will serve as one focus of this chapter, we will also make reference to the wider, international relevance of the satellite account both for analytic and policy purposes.

## Background

One of the major barriers to the improved understanding of non-profit institutions (NPIs) at the international level at the present time is the persistent lack of basic and up-to-date statistical data about the scope, structure, financing, and activities of this set of organisations. This lack of information is, in turn, a product of the way these organisations are treated in the SNA, the data system for basic economic statistics throughout the world. The same applies to related systems like the European System of Accounts (ESA). Both systems, complimentary in nature, are a set of guidelines for the development of economic accounts and for reporting such statistics to international organisations in a manner comparable across countries.[1]

National accounting groups similar kinds of economic operators into institutional sectors[2]. The SNA-1993 states that "corporations, NPIs, government units and households are intrinsically different from each other" and that "their economic objectives, functions and behaviour are also different" (SNA-1993, 4.17). Similarly, the system acknowledges that NPIs are different from households, financial or non-financial corporations and governmental agencies, and groups them into a specific institutional sector called "Non-profit Institutions Serving Households" or NPISH.

Yet under SNA/ESA guidelines, which we will illustrate with the help of the Belgian case below, national statistical offices are to identify separately, and collect data on only a small subset of all non-profit organisations, i.e. those that receive most of their income and support from households in the form of charitable contributions. Other non-profit organisations, that is those that receive significant shares of their income from fees and service charges or government grants and contracts, are, under SNA guidelines, typically merged into either the business or government sector. SNA specialists have justified this treatment on the theory that these other non-profit institutions are rather limited in both number and size.

Specifically, a series of stipulations addresses the allocation of NPIs to different sectors (Table 11.1). First, NPIs considered of minor economic importance, deemed temporary and informal – because they do not have a legal status or do not employ paid staff – are excluded from the NPISH and allocated to the Households Sector (S14).[3] Secondly, NPIs that sell most or all output at prices that are economically significant are treated as market producers and allocated to the Non-financial (S11) or Financial Corporations (S12) Sectors.[4] This leaves a group of non-market NPIs, which provide most output to others freely or at prices that are not economically significant. The SNA/ESA divides them into two further groups: NPIs controlled and mainly financed by government, and other NPIs. The first group is allocated to the Government Sector (S13), while the second and residual group constitutes the NPISH Sector (S15).

Table 11.1. **The institutional sectoring of the non-profit sector**

| All NPIs | | |
|---|---|---|
| **Filter 1: Importance** | | |
| Formal NPIs | | Informal NPIs S14 |
| **Filter 2: Type of resources** | | |
| Market NPIs S11 – S12 | Non-market NPIs | |
| **Filter 3: Public funding and control** | | |
| Non-market NPIs controlled and mainly financed by government S13 | Other NPIs = NPISH S15 | |

*Source:* Mertens (2002).

Conventions about the classification of institutional units are thus causing the non-profit sector to break up, which consequently reduces its statistical visibility. The SNA acknowledges this problem when it states that, "with the exception of non-profit institutions, all institutional units of a particular type are grouped together within the same sector" (SNA-1993, 4.13). Moreover, the conventions imply a reduced vision of a non-profit sector, as represented in the residual NPISH sector. For Belgium, Mertens (2002), shows that the NPISH sector only covers some 15 per cent of existing NPIs and 12% of total NPI employment.[5] This study also challenges the SNA assumption that most NPIs are non-market producers;[6] in fact, only 18 per cent of NPIs can be considered as non-market producers according to SNA guidelines.

Some authors even suggest that SNA guidelines encourage a vicious cycle; whilst current conventions limit the statistical importance of the non-profit sector, they also reduce incentives to give appropriate acknowledgement to this sector of the national economy.[7] Even those that comply fully with current SNA requirements project an image of non-profit institutions that is grossly understated (see Anheier and Salamon, 1998). The few countries that show estimates of non-profit sector activities typically report that these account for one to two per cent of gross domestic product. This is well within the margin of error of estimates for larger economic aggregates in the corporate and government sectors. Within the SNA, moreover, virtually no information exists on the size and scope of the non-profit sector, including its relations with other parts of the economy. Several examples might illustrate how this treatment affects other parts of the SNA as well, leading to under-estimations and distortions:

- In most countries, non-profit value added is either not measured at all, or included in other sectors, usually government.
- The assets held by non-profit organisations such as foundations are either part of the personal savings or shifted to the financial corporate sector.
- The role of volunteers and unpaid work in non-profit organisations is ignored, or treated as part of the household sector.
- The international transfers and activities of non-governmental organisations are usually not captured or included in the governmental accounts.

The lack of basic information also makes specific applications of SNA/ESA information more complicated for policy and substantive application. NPIs are likely to differ from the other entities of the corporations and government sectors in a number of ways – in their objective function, in revenue sources, in governance structure, in legal and tax environment, etc. NPI managers may cross-subsidise the provision of goods and services that they consider particularly valuable, and non-profit producers typically have access to voluntary donations of labour inputs not available to corporations. Thus, as a by-product, identifying and separating "hidden" NPI components will improve data quality of other sectors.

An important case in the European context is the social economy, which groups together voluntary associations and foundations, but also mutual enterprises and co-operative societies (see below). According to the European Commission and several member states the social economy thus includes the non-profit organisations as a part of a broader component of national economies[8]. Put differently, European policy makers and economists are interested in statistical information on all the private organisations that serve a public benefit such as education, occupational training, employment, health, culture, protection of the environment. The problem, however, is that current statistical systems do not make such data readily available.

## A comparative profile of the third sector

Of particular interest are four critical dimensions of non-profit organisations: paid full-time equivalent (FTE) employment, volunteer employment converted to FTE, operating expenditures, and revenue sources (government payments, private fees and charges, and private philanthropy). Each of these dimensions, covered for over 20 countries by the Johns Hopkins Comparative Non-profit Sector Project (see Salamon et al., 1999), provides central input to the SNA generally and the satellite account particularly.

Specifically: In terms of employment, the third sector was found to be a major economic force. In the 22 countries covered by the Johns Hopkins Project, the sector constitutes a $1.1 trillion industry that employs close to 19 million full-time equivalent employees. Moreover, the sector attracts a considerable amount of volunteer effort. Indeed, within the countries studied, an average of 28 per cent of the population report contributing their time to non-profit organisations. This translates into another 10.6 million full-time equivalent employees, boosting the total number of full-time equivalent non-profit employees in the 22 project countries to 29.6 million.[9]

As shown in Figure 11.1, the third sector is larger in the more developed countries and much less in evidence in Latin America and Central Europe. Perhaps one of the most surprising outcomes is that the United States,

## Figure 11.1. **Economic size of the third sector, 1995**

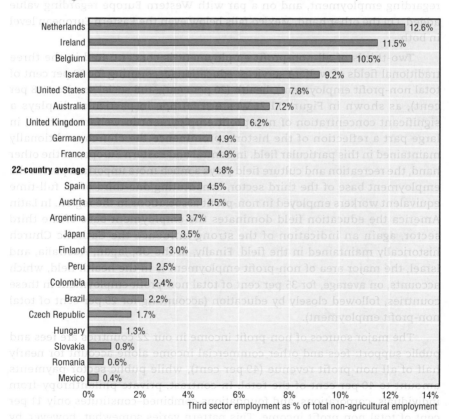

Netherlands 12.6%
Ireland 11.5%
Belgium 10.5%
Israel 9.2%
United States 7.8%
Australia 7.2%
United Kingdom 6.2%
Germany 4.9%
France 4.9%
**22-country average** 4.8%
Spain 4.5%
Austria 4.5%
Argentina 3.7%
Japan 3.5%
Finland 3.0%
Peru 2.5%
Colombia 2.4%
Brazil 2.2%
Czech Republic 1.7%
Hungary 1.3%
Slovakia 0.9%
Romania 0.6%
Mexico 0.4%

Third sector employment as % of total non-agricultural employment

*Source:* Johns Hopkins Comparative Non-profit Sector Project.

commonly thought to be the seedbed of non-profit activity, ranks only fifth in terms of paid employment as a percentage of non-agricultural employment, after the Netherlands, Ireland, Belgium, and Israel. The developed Western European countries turned out to have the largest third sectors among all project countries, surpassing their Eastern European neighbours by a ratio of about 7:1. In fact, the size of the third sectors in former socialist state countries turned out to be surprisingly low, accounting for a mere one per cent of non-agricultural labour.[10] The reason for the relatively small size of the non-profit sector in this region is found in a still somewhat weak institutional relationship with financially strained governments, which reduces the amount of funding available for non-profit service provision.

In comparison, the size of third sectors in Latin American countries is somewhere between those of Eastern and Western Europe, but there is also substantial variability among them. On the one hand, Argentina has a third sector that is only slightly smaller than many Western European countries regarding employment, and on a par with Western Europe regarding value added. On the other hand, Mexico falls below even the Eastern European level in both.

Two-thirds of all non-profit employment is concentrated in the three traditional fields of welfare services: education (accounting for 30 per cent of total non-profit employment), health (20 per cent), and social services (18 per cent), as shown in Figure 11.2. Western Europe in particular displays a significant concentration of non-profit employment in welfare services, in large part a reflection of the historic prominence the church traditionally maintained in this particular field. In Central and Eastern Europe, on the other hand, the recreation and culture field plays a much more important part in the employment base of the third sector, constituting one-third of all full-time equivalent workers employed in non-profit associations in the region. In Latin America the education field dominates the employment base of the third sector, again an indication of the strong influence the Catholic Church historically maintained in the field. Finally, in the US, Japan, Australia, and Israel, the major area of non-profit employment is in the health field, which accounts, on average, for 35 per cent of total non-profit employment in these countries, followed closely by education (accounting for 29 per cent of total non-profit employment).

The major sources of non-profit income in our 22 countries are fees and public support: fees and other commercial income alone account for nearly half of all non-profit revenue (49 per cent), while public sector payments amount to 40 per cent of the total. In contrast, private philanthropy–from individuals, corporations, and foundations combined–constitutes only 11 per cent of total non-profit income. This pattern varies somewhat, however, by country and region. Whereas fee income is predominant in Latin America and

Figure 11.2.   **Composition of the "third sector" by region, 1995**

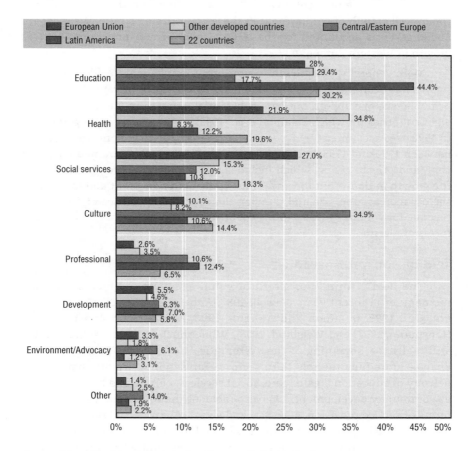

*Source:* Johns Hopkins Comparative Non-profit Sector Project.

Central and Eastern Europe, as well as in the US, Australia, and Japan, public grants and third party payments, primarily from public social insurance funds, are the most important sources of income for the third sector in the Western European region.

Not only is the non-profit sector a major economic force, it has also been an unusually dynamic one in recent years, surpassing the general economies in most of the Johns Hopkins Project countries in generating employment growth. Non-profit employment in Belgium, France, Germany and the United Kingdom grew by an average of 24 per cent, or by more than 4 per cent a year, between 1990 and 1995. In comparison, overall employment in these same

**277**

countries grew at a considerably slower rate during this same period – 6 per cent, or barely one per cent a year. The non-profit sector therefore outpaced the overall growth of employment in these countries by a ratio of almost 4:1. Social services accounted for the largest share of non-profit employment growth in Western Europe.

More generally, the growth in non-profit employment evident in these figures has been made possible not chiefly by a surge in private philanthropy or public-sector support, but by a substantial increase in fee income. In the eight countries for which Salamon *et al.* (1999) report revenue data going back to 1990, fees accounted for 58 per cent of the real growth in non-profit revenue between 1990 and 1995. In comparison, the public sector accounted for 34 per cent, and private giving, which includes foundation grants, eight per cent of the growth in non-profit income. Thus, while both non-profit and foundation sectors increased in size and number, the relative importance of foundation revenue for voluntary associations declined, compared to more "commercial" forms of revenue.

## The field of non-profit studies

The field of third, non-profit or voluntary sector studies has gained momentum in recent years (Powell, 1987; Anheier and Seibel, 1990; Ben-Ner and Gui, 1993; Salamon and Anheier, 1996; Anheier and Ben-Ner, 1997; Hansmann, 1997; and Weisbrod, 1998). While much has been achieved, it is still really the beginning of the systematic effort needed to describe and analyse more fully the role third sector organisations currently have in the delivery of education, health care, social services, culture and the arts as well as community development. This also includes the role of the third sector in terms of service provision, advocacy and social cohesion, and more generally, its relation to civil society. Moreover, we need to know how and why the role of non-profit institutions varies across countries, and what role this set of institutions is likely to play in the future.

But before research can begin in a systematic way, a better conceptual mapping of the areas between the state and the market sectors is needed for the great variety of forms located between household, market and state: membership associations, community groups, clubs, service providers, foundations, self-help groups, and other types of non-profit organisations. As a start, Salamon and Anheier (1997) suggest focusing on entities that are: i) organised, *i.e.* possessing some institutional reality; ii) private, *i.e.* institutionally separate from government; iii) non-profit-distributing, *i.e.* not returning any profits generated to their owners or directors; iv) self-governing, *i.e.* equipped to control their own activities; and v) voluntary, at least in part, *i.e.* involving some meaningful degree of voluntary participation, either in the agency's activities or management.

This mapping exercise, while usefully started, is by no means complete. Once NPIs have been identified and grouped according to the conceptual and operational definition laid out in the satellite account, however, we can begin to explore some of the fundamental research problems with new rigour. Three questions are central to the field of third sector research, and each can be addressed at the level of organisations, industries and economies (Table 11.2):

● In terms of **institutional choice**, we need to know why non-profit or third-sector institutions exist in the first place and what form they take in different countries. What are the rationales for the choice of form, and how do theoretical expectations relate to reality?

● How do non-profit institutions compare to alternative providers and forms in terms of efficiency, client base, and other aspects of **organisational behaviour**?

● What are the **implications and consequences** of non-profit forms in terms of equity and other distributional characteristics?

A number of theories have been proposed that explore at least some aspects of the "why" and "how" on non-profit provision in general and in specific fields such as education, health and social services. In the past, lack of data has prevented fuller tests of these theories; however, with the satellite account in place, greater data availability will over time offer more and more

Table 11.2.   **Basic third sector research questions**

| Basic question | Level of analysis and focus | | |
| | Organisation | Field/industry | Economy/country |
| --- | --- | --- | --- |
| Why? | Why is this organisation non-profit rather than for-profit or government? Organisational choice | Why do we find specific compositions of non-profit, for-profit, government firms in fields/industries? Field-specific division of labour | Why do we find variations in the size and structure of the non-profit sector cross-nationally? Sectoral division of labour |
| How? | How does this organisation operate? How does it compare to other equivalent organisations? Organisational efficiency etc.; management issues | How do non-profit organisations behave relative to other forms in the same field or industry? Comparative industry efficiency and related issues | How does the non-profit sector operate and what role does it play relative to other sectors? Comparative sector roles |
| So what? | What is the contribution of this organisation relative to other forms? Distinct characteristics and impact of focal organisation | What is the relative contribution of non-profit organisations in this field relative to other forms? Different contributions of forms in specific industries | What does the non-profit sector contribute relative to other sectors? Sector-specific contributions and impacts cross-nationally |

systematic opportunities for theory testing in this field (see Anheier and Ben-Ner, 1997):

- The "heterogeneity theory", associated with the work of Weisbrod (1977; 1988) suggests that unsatisfied demand for services in situations of demand heterogeneity is related to the presence of non-profit providers. Countries with heterogeneous demand would have a larger non-profit sector than countries with a more homogeneous demand.

  The heterogeneity theory suggests that the satellite account be extended to include information on the composition of the relevant population in terms of ethnic, religious, linguistic etc. heterogeneity. Moreover, data are needed to estimate median and non-median demand for different types of public goods, and how the provision of these goods is reflected in public budget allocations and layouts.

- A variation of the heterogeneity argument, the "supply-side theory", has been developed by James (1987), who suggests that ideologists and religious and social entrepreneurs use non-profit establishments to maximise non-monetary return. Accordingly, the greater ideological and religious competition in a country, the larger the third sector.

  In additional to the data needed for the heterogeneity theory, the supply-side theory would require better information on ideological and religious competition as well as data on "occupational groups" such as social workers, health care professionals, clergy, politicians, fund-raisers or activists.

- The "trust theory" (Hansmann, 1980; 1987; 1996), and related to it, the "stakeholder theory" developed by Ben-Ner and Van Hommissen (1993), suggests that trust goods, like services, involve serious information asymmetries to the potential detriment of the customer. Third sector organisations are one solution to this problem, as their non-distribution constraint and governance structure suggest "trustworthiness" (Hansmann, 1996).

  The trust theories have high data requirements. Not only are measures needed to gauge levels of trust relative to different institutional options, the theory also requires measures of information asymmetry across different types of services. Finally, the theory leads us to look for legal indications of the non-distribution constraint.

- The "interdependence theory" formulated by Salamon (1987) sees the third sector not as the antithesis to government action; rather it states a complementary relationship between both sectors. Synergetic effects develop over time in the sense that both sectors can complement each other's strengths and weaknesses.

The interdependence theory requires data on organisational founding and development over time, relative to changes in public budget allocations. Furthermore, the theory needs data on institutional synergies, *i.e.* welfare effects that arise from public-private partnerships.

● Finally, the "social origins theory" developed by Salamon and Anheier (1998) argues that the size, role and financing of the non-profit sector depends on the type of welfare regime in a country. The non-profit sector is seen as highly "path dependent" and part of a complex set of relationships among social classes, party politics, government regulations, and the influence of interest groups.

The social origins theory has the greatest data demand among the approaches introduced here. In addition to the data needed for the heterogeneity, supply-side and interdependence theories, it requires, at a minimum, information on social class compositions and strength, political mobilisation, and public spending and revenue figures over time.

It becomes clear that the satellite account would provide the core data needed for theory testing in terms of size and structure. Indeed, the satellite account would offer the measures for the "dependent variable" or *explanandum* of each theory; yet, at the same time, more information is needed for the independent variables or *explanans* of each theory. To a large extent, these data requirements refer to:

● Indicators of population characteristics (social composition, religion, ethnicity, voting, socio-economic status, etc.).

● Public budgets and expenditures.

● Information asymmetries in specific markets and industries.

● Social capital and trust.

● Indicators of social exclusion.

Of course, this list of theories is not exhaustive (see Anheier and Ben-Ner, 1997, for overview). Moreover, we need to keep in mind that very different conceptions of the third sector exist across countries, which portray these institutions in rather different policy scenarios. For example, the French notion of *économie sociale* brings the sector much closer to co-operatives and the communal economy (Archambault, 1996a); the German concept of "subsidiarity", in contrast, emphasises private social service provision and political decentralisation (Anheier and Seibel, 2000; Zimmer, 1997; Rauschenbach *et al.*, 1995), whereas the Italian concept of "associationalism" (Barbetta, 1997) and the Swedish concept of broad-based movements refer to local organising, community building and democratic inclusion (Lundstroem and Wijkstroem, 1997). Behind these concepts are specific state-society and third sector-economy relations and traditions (often in the sense of path dependencies) that need to be understood if we want to gain a deeper understanding of institutional choice processes. For example, why do some countries respond to old and new challenges such as AIDS, unemployment or the environment by establishing public agencies, others quasi-public institutions, while others opt for private sector solutions, and others do not seem to respond at all?

It is here that data gaps matter most for future developments, both theoretically and in terms of policy analysis. Why is this the case? There are several reasons for this:

● First, from a comparative, cross-national point of view, we find that third sector organisations are linked to strikingly different ideological orientations. For example, in the United States and Britain, the third sector is widely seen as an expression of individualism, whereas in Europe, particularly in the French tradition, this set of organisations is seen as a combined social force producing social solidarity and "sociability". How can it be that the same type of organisation, providing similar services, produces different effects and social outcomes in the end? Moreover, general ideological currents in some countries, such as the United States, traditionally, and Britain, in the 1980s particularly, posit a deep-seated opposition between the third sector and the state. In contrast, in countries like Germany, Sweden, Austria or the Netherlands, both government and the non-profit sector are seen to have a more symbiotic relationship with each other. How can we compare the contributions of the third sector, when it is alternatively positioned in opposition to, or in close vicinity of, the state? Obviously, there is a need to explore the cultural and political context of third sector organisations.

● Second, in trying to explain the existence and behaviour of non-profit organisations, theories frequently identify characteristics that are attributes of both the input side and the output side of this set of organisations. For example, trust in non-profit providers is treated as both an input and an output characteristic: people chose non-profit organisations because they are more trustworthy under conditions of information asymmetry than other providers (Hansmann, 1996), and non-profit organisations produce trust in the course of their operations (Fukuyama, 1994; and Putnam, 1993). Likewise, third sector organisations are both reflections and producers of heterogeneity (James, 1987), and diversity (Taylor, Langan and Hoggett, 1995), and are the consumers and producers of social capital (Edwards and Foley, 1997). The major point is that the rationales for the existence and comparative advantage of third sector organisations involve both input and output characteristics. Available data, however, are largely limited to the input side. This makes it difficult to test theories more fully, and points to a need to collect data on outputs and their

**282**

impacts more generally. Thus more and better data are needed on the "output side" generally.

● Third, beyond comparative advantages associated with the non-profit form, literature frequently speaks of "unique characteristics" of non-profit organisations – attributes and functions that neither government nor businesses can fulfil. Similarly, work on the role of non-governmental organisations (NGOs) in the development process and in humanitarian assistance, attributes several "distinct" characteristics to non-profit organisations (see Lewis, 1999). NGOs are assumed to be more in tune with indigenous cultures, and closer to the grass roots. They are seen as representatives of the powerless, engaged in community building, thereby enhancing the developmental capacities of third world societies (Fowler, 1997). In contrast, we also find attributions that see non-profit organisations as elitist, inefficient, dilettante, pre-modern and otherwise "sub-optimal" or "second-best" institutions when compared to the market and the state (see Seibel, 1993; 1996).

To what extent do these positive and negative characteristics attributed to third sector organisations apply generally, and to what extent do they vary across economies, societies and cultures that differ in their level of economic and social development? There is a need to test the assumption that non-profit organisations have "unique characteristics" and certain comparative advantages and disadvantages in a broad cross-section of settings. In this respect, the satellite account will make it possible to address the topic of third sector output, performance and impact with the help of three major questions:

● Characteristics: Do third sector organisations have distinct characteristics and make specific contributions to economy and society?

● Advantages: Do they have comparative advantages and disadvantages relative to government and business?

● Role: Do the cultural and political roles of non-profit organisations vary, to what outcome, and why?

For cross-national research, we suggest approaching these questions at the level of output, performance and impact:

● Output: Output and capacity of third sector provision relative to government and corporate provision.

● Performance: Efficiency and effectiveness of third sector provision relative to government and corporations.

● Impact: Distributional and equity aspects of third sector provision; contributions to solving social problems.

While the three basic questions indicate the theoretical reference of the research, the levels of analysis suggest that each question can be looked at from different aspects. When combined, they yield a conceptual *tableau* that circumscribes key aspects of a future research strategy on non-profit sector output, performance and impact (Table 11.3).

Each cell of the *tableau* indicates what the main thrust of the research problem would be:

● The Output column describes the phenomena under study ("what").

● The Performance column addresses the reasons underlying observed variations and commonalities ("why").

● The Impact column of Table 11.3 poses the "so what" question, *i.e.* the effects and consequences of both the phenomena themselves and those of possible alternatives.

The rows in Table 11.3 represent the particular theoretical interest that is brought to bear:

● Understanding third sector organisations as a distinct form in terms of their output ("Characteristics").

● Contrasting non-profit organisations with other organisational forms within a system of social division of labour that may vary cross-nationally ("Advantages").

● Exploring the broader social, cultural and political context in which third sector organisations operate.

Of course, the questions set out in Table 11.3 are fairly general, and have to be reformulated in concrete research settings. For example, in a project on the contributions of NPIs to employment growth relative to other sectors, we could ask in Field C2: What is the contribution of NPIs to employment stability? Do NPIs have cyclical swings in employment, and do they dampen, offset, or amplify for-profit labour market cycles? How great are the effects of the non-profit sector on income inequality? Of course, we are still some way off from being able to answer these questions, but a closer look at the Belgian example below reveals the critical importance of better information on non-profit institutions for both academic and policy purposes.

Table 11.3.   **Framework for the comparative analysis of NPI output, performance and impact**

| Theoretical reference | Level of analysis | | |
|---|---|---|---|
| | **A. Output**: Output and capacity of NPI provision relative to government and business | **B. Performance**: Efficiency of NPI provision relative to government and business | **C. Impact**: Distributional aspects and equity of NPI provision; contributions to solving social problems |
| **1. Characteristics**: Do NPIs have distinct characteristics and make distinct contributions to economy and society? | What are the contributions in terms of output? Do unique characteristics vary cross-nationally? | Why are non-profit contributions distinct? In what sense and why? | What is the impact of these distinct contributions on society in different countries? What other institutional forms and roles are possible? |
| **2. Advantages**: Do NPIs have comparative advantages and disadvantages relative to government and business? | What are the relative advantages and disadvantages in terms of non-profit output characteristics? What is the division of labour across form and country? | Why are there variations in non-profit performance relative to government and business, and across countries? How did particular profiles of division of labour come about? Are there crowding-out and crowding-in effects cross-nationally? | What are the economic and social effects of these variations in performance and division of labour? What is the institutional dynamic relative to equity? What other institutional arrangements are possible across different countries? |
| **3. Roles**: Does the cultural and political role of NPIs vary, to what outcome, and why? | What are non-profit outputs specific to the cultural and political role the sector plays cross-nationally? | Why are there variations in the roles of the sector cross-nationally? | What are the major implications that follow from sector roles for efficiency, equity, quality of life, and the problems-solving capacity of societies cross-nationally? |

## Towards a satellite account on non-profit institutions: the case of Belgium

As suggested above, SNA/ESA conventions about institutional classification have significant impact on measures of NPI output (see Table 11.4). Generally, the total NPI output – like that of any institutional unit – is equal to the sum of the output of its establishments (SEC-1995, 3.15). The SNA/ESA distinguishes among various types of outputs and, for each type of output, it uses a specific method to measure its current exchange value in monetary terms. Market output is valued at the basic prices at which goods

Table 11.4.  **The institutional distribution of the non-profit sector in Belgium, 1999**

| NPIs in | % of NPIs population | % of NPIs employment |
|---|---|---|
| Non-financial Corporations Sector (S11) Examples: Hospitals, nursing homes, sheltered workshops, institutions for the handicapped, crèches, business associations, fair trade organisations, etc. | 14.57 | 46.86 |
| Financial Corporations Sector (S12) Example: Pension funds | 0.03 | 0.04 |
| Government Sector (S13) Examples: Private schools, psycho-socio-medical centres, etc. | 3.40 | 40.90 |
| Households Sector (S14) Example: NPIs without paid employees | 67.02 | 0.00 |
| NPISH Sector (S15) Examples: Foundations, unions, religious organisations, political organisations, sport federations, etc. | 14.98 | 12.20 |

*Source:* Mertens (2001).

and services are sold and other non-market output is valued by the sum of the costs incurred in their production.[11]

## Sector allocations and output

According to national accounting conventions, the establishment of an institutional unit considered as a market producer (and classified in S11, S12 or S14) cannot be a producer of non-market output. Consequently, national accounting does not acknowledge the possibility for NPIs classified in the market institutional sectors to produce non-market goods and services as well. Their whole output is considered as market output and evaluated on the basis of their income from sales.[12] But, although these producers sell their output at economically significant prices, this does not mean that these prices necessarily cover their costs of production (Mertens, 2001). For example, as shown in Table 11.4, the analysis of the sales and the costs of production of Belgian NPIs seems to indicate that more than half the NPIs classified in the Corporations Sectors (S11 and S12) must resort to other forms of financing to ensure their viability. In reality, these "non-market" resources (subsidies or private donations) make it possible for these NPIs to sell their output at prices inferior to the price which would be defined by market mechanisms alone. Thus the total output of these NPIs is probably underestimated.

NPIs considered as non-market producers (classified in S13 or S15) may include establishments that produce market goods and services. In order to evaluate the total output of these NPIs, it would be necessary to know the production of their establishments. In principle, these outputs are estimated at basic prices if they occur in a market establishment and at the cost of production if they occur in a non-market establishment. This method makes it necessary to know how the costs of production and the sales are allocated among the different establishments. Without this information, it is impossible to identify different establishments and the NPI has to be considered as a sole non-market establishment. For operational reasons, total output is evaluated on the basis of the total production costs, even if part of their resources originate from the sale of output at a price different from zero (when users are asked to participate financially, be it to a very limited extent) or in a secondary market production (such as the sale of postcards in a museum or the sale of calendars or stickers).

According to SNA conventions, the estimation of NPI output depends on the category of producers to which the production unit belongs. Consequently, the estimation of NPI output is not homogeneous. We can illustrate this problem with the help of "the output curve" in Figure 11.3. The sales are represented on the X-axis, while the Y-axis shows the current estimation by the national account authorities. The costs of production are supposed to be constant (= 1 000). The output is estimated on the basis of the total cost of production (i.e. 1 000) up to the point where sales cover 50 per cent of these costs (i.e. 500). This point is a threshold beyond which the price is considered economically significant and the estimation starts following the linear progression of the percentage of sales. Only when the sales cover 100 per cent of the costs of production does the output value come back to the level it reached below the "threshold point". This output curve clearly shows the underestimation of NPI output when sales cover more than 50 per cent but less than 100 per cent of production costs.

Figure 11.3. **The output curve**

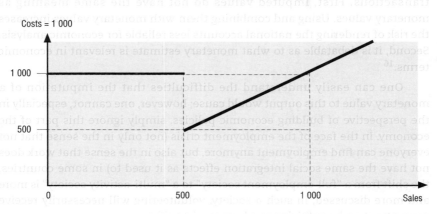

Source: Mertens (2002).

## Flows

NPIs and other institutional units generate economic flows that are not registered in the system of national accounts. Among these implicit flows, it is possible to distinguish between flows acknowledged by the SNA in principle, but which are difficult to measure in reality, and non-monetary flows outside the central scope of the SNA.

The first type of flow involves disposable NPI production factors, the cost of which is assumed by other organisations. For example, it frequently occurs that the wages of NPIs' workers are paid by public authorities, or that some buildings or equipment are made available to NPIs free of charge. The second type of flow includes savings realised – or, more precisely, costs avoided – by NPIs because some economic agents, in real transactions, waive their right to the payment to which they would normally be entitled.[13] The work carried out by volunteers is probably the best-known example of this phenomenon. Volunteering is a production factor freely offered by households to NPIs. It implies NPI output for sale at lower prices as well as lower production costs. While such output, from a conceptual point of view, meets the third party criterion,[14] it is, to a large extent, not measured statistically for SNA purposes.[15] This convention has particularly important consequences for the full range of NPI activities. Indeed, the presence of a volunteer workforce is often one of their specific features, yet volunteering is not registered as an implicit cost of production, corresponding to a resource put at NPIs' disposal by households. Furthermore, as the supply of services by volunteers is not considered as production, their use by NPIs is not recorded either.

The treatment of these implicit flows raises the question of the relevance of monetary imputations more generally. In reality, there are two main reasons why the SNA is reluctant to attribute imputed values to certain transactions. First, imputed values do not have the same meaning as monetary values. Using and combining them with monetary values increases the risk of rendering the national accounts less reliable for economic analysis. Second, it is debatable as to what monetary estimate is relevant in economic terms.[16]

One can easily understand the difficulties that the imputation of a monetary value to this output would cause; however, one cannot, especially in the perspective of building economic policies, simply ignore this part of the economy. In the face of the employment crisis (not only in the sense that not everyone can find employment anymore, but also in the sense that work does not have the same social integration effects as it used to) in some countries, the shift from a "full-employment society" to a "multi-activity society" is more and more discussed; in such a society, volunteering will necessarily receive more attention by politicians and economists alike.

## Classifications

If the institutional splitting of the non-profit sector is harmful in terms of visibility, it should not be considered that this sector forms a homogenous whole in all respects (see Salamon and Anheier, 1992 a, and b). In particular, the use of a classification system of NPIs according to their main activity allows a more accurate description of the field studied.

The International Standard Industrial Classification (ISIC) is the classification scheme that is applied in the SNA-1993. However, this system does not allow for the detailed classification of NPI activities. The activities of non-profit organisations are mainly concentrated in four industries: education, health and social services, miscellaneous non-profit activities, and recreational and cultural activities. These four industries, however, comprise few sub-divisions and contain very broad residual classes.[17]

Naturally, countries using the ISIC can create more detailed sub-divisions; EU countries, for example, use the NACE classification that is more detailed and allows for a better description of the economic activity in the member states. Moreover, the NACE system allows member states to create even more detailed classes and sub-classes. While this improves national coverage, it also stands in the way of international comparisons. It thus seems necessary to work out a harmonised classification system for the non-profit sector that could eventually contribute to the evolution of the ISIC, which the satellite accounts suggests and develops.

Another limit of the ISIC is linked to the fact that it does not distinguish clearly between the main activity of an organisation and its purpose. Generally speaking, NPIs are distinguished from other private sector organisations through the statement of an objective other than profit. Most of the time, the activity and the purpose are identical (education, health, culture, etc.). However, in certain situations, the objective of the organisation lies in the production method rather than in the product itself. What is emphasised is the process, the treatment of inputs, far more than the result. This is the case in sheltered workshops, fair trade organisations and organic agriculture, etc., for example.

National accounting provides for a functional approach. There is a functional classification for NPISH (COPNI) and the government (COFOG) sectors.[18] However, their use is limited to the analysis of the expenditure undertaken (means) and could be extended to the description of production (results) and use (impact).

## Concluding comments

Two approaches can overcome the current limitations of national accounting and respond to the quantitative information requirements of the sector. The first involves the construction of an "autonomous" information framework, capable of satisfying the requirements of the users of non-profit statistics (researchers, politicians, etc.). But this approach would result in the total separation from the SNA and the artificial isolation of non-profit organisations from the rest of the economy in statistical terms. The second possible option requires working in close co-operation with national accounts without interfering with the central logic and framework of the system.

It is the latter, of course, which we regard as the best way forward. A significant advantage of satellite accounts resides in their experimental nature: initially, they form rather a "progressive framework for the organisation of information" (Vanoli, 1986, p. 186). Indeed, satellite systems can be modified and expanded to suit special requirements and circumstances. This can be for analytic reasons, *e.g.*, to focus on the role of NPIs in the development process in Africa, or for policy-related purposes, *e.g.*, linking the satellite account with similar systems for health, education or the environment.

In Europe, one such special need for expanding the satellite account is around the notion of the social economy, which views NPIs as part of a broader sector.[19] As suggested above, this concept groups together associations and foundations, but also mutuals and co-operative societies. In Belgium and in Spain, the definition of the social economy, besides naming these four main components, also cites the four ethical principles which guide them: i) purpose of service to members or some specified larger community rather than profit to shareholders, ii) independent management, iii) democratic decision-making process, and iv) precedence of social aspects over capital in the distribution of income.

In the SNA/ESA, co-operatives and mutuals are integrated in the Corporations and Government Sectors, and reallocating them into a larger social economy account is, at least in principle, possible. However, for two reasons, it seems necessary to develop the NPI satellite account first. For one, statistical data are most fragmented for NPIs, and it is for this part of the social economy that the need for data is the greatest. Secondly, the analysis of the various conventions of national accounting reveals that the major weaknesses are in the treatment of NPIs and that, consequently, the development of a satellite account will require the most fundamental methodological changes.

## Notes

1. For a general overview see United Nations – SNA, 1993; and the European System of National Accounts issues by Eurostat, 1995. For discussion and background on the 1993 SNA see Keuning (1998, pp. 437-446). See also Carson (1996, pp. 25-72).

2. The SNA-1993 distinguishes six institutional sectors: the Non-financial Corporations Sector (S11), the Financial Corporations Sector (S12), the General Government Sector (S13), the Households Sector (S14), the Non-profit Institutions Serving Households Sector (S15) and the Rest of the World (S2).

3. The SNA-1993 does not explicitly consider allocating NPIs to the S14 (Households Sector). This is only provided for in the ESA-1995. Some NPIs, according to SNA-1993 proceedings, are allocated to the NPISH sector, while the ESA-1995 would more frequently consider them as assimilated to the S14.

4. According to the SNA-1993, *"prices are economically significant when they have a significant influence on the amounts the producers are willing to supply and on the amounts purchasers wish to buy"* (SNA-1993, 6.45). The ESA transposes this notion in operational terms: *"a price is economically significant as from the moment when the sales cover more than 50 per cent of the production costs"* (ESA-1995, 3.19). It is important to note that, in the system of national accounts, any intervention of public authorities which takes the form of "third-party payment" is also considered as being part of the sales.

5. Mertens (2002).

6. SNA-1993, 4.60: *"The majority of NPIs in most countries are non-market rather than market producers."*

7. See Mertens (2002).

8. It should not be thought, however, that Europe proposes a single model of the social economy or that this concept is equally widespread in all the member states. On this subject, see for example Archambault (1996b) and Jeantet (1999).

9. Data reported in this section draw on Salamon and Anheier, 1999.

10. Since these countries have relatively larger agrarian employment than their Western European counterparts, the gap between East and West would widen even further if total employment were used as the basis for a comparison.

11. The use of this method was suggested by Hicks (1940) and was taken up by national accounting systems SNA-1993, 6-91. By "costs of production", the SNA-1993 understands intermediate consumption, compensation of employees, consumption of fixed capital and other taxes, less subsidies on production. For a discussion on the inclusion of property incomes in NPIs' costs of production, see Mertens (2001).

12. This rule is also valid for NPIs classified in S14 since the Households Sector groups together unincorporated producers of market goods and services.

13. Various authors acknowledge the growing importance of these implicit transactions which reduce NPIs' production expenses: Archambault (1996a), Rudney and Anheier (1996), Slater and David (1994).

14. National accounting uses the "third party criterion" to determine the existence of production activity. An activity satisfies the third party criterion if a third party can – at least potentially – carry it out. This criterion was introduced for the first time by Hawrylshyn (1977).

15. Voluntary activities are only taken into consideration if they give rise to the production of goods. Voluntary work in services is left out even though it is infinitely more widespread than in the production of goods.

16. The SNA advances these arguments to explain its reluctance to impute values to flows generated by the production and the consumption of services within households (SNA, 6.21 and 6.22).

17. For example, in Belgium, the 91.99 ISIC class – "Activities of other membership organisations n.e.c." – comprises more than 14 per cent of NPIs.

18. The COPNI (Classification of the Purposes of the Non-profit Institutions Serving Households) and the COFOG (Classification of the Functions of the Government) are functional classifications which identify the functions – in the sense of purposes – for which certain groups of traders (here the NPISH or the government) engage in certain transactions. Examples of functions are: research and scientific services, education services, welfare services, etc.

19. On the conceptual differences and similarities between "social economy" and "non-profit sector", see among others Archambault (1996a and b), Defourny and Mertens (1999) or Mertens (2000) or Mertens (2002).

# Glossary*

**Accountability.** The concept of accountability has taken on a major importance over the last decade in the push by non-profit organisations to make business activity more transparent and to raise awareness of its impact on society in general. It is seen as a vital tool to connect business entities with the environment in which they operate. The provision of both financial and non-financial information, including wider social performance information, to discharge accountability is important for a number of reasons. Users of such information require it to make judgements and decisions that impact on economic and social wellbeing. It gives visibility to the resources, activities and achievements of an organisation; thus enabling informed discussions and decisions. Moreover, the need to discharge accountability encourages management to concentrate on the issues that are of importance to those stakeholders who are outside the immediate management of the organisation and who often provide the resources for the organisation to function.

**Charities.** A charity is an entity established for the altruistic purposes that common law regards as charitable. Charitable purposes are the relief of poverty, the relief of the needs of the aged, the relief of sickness and distress, the advancement of religion and education, and other purposes beneficial to the community. Thus, the main characteristics of a charity include the following: 1) it is either an institution or a trust fund, *i.e.* a separate legal entity that holds property or assets of some kind for the benefit of a specific person, group of people or organisation, 2) it exists for public benefit 3) it is non-profit making, and 4) its sole or dominant purpose is charitable.

**Civil society.** Civil society may be defined as a space or arena between households and the state, which affords possibilities of concerted action and social organisation. Thus, it encompasses all voluntary associations of citizens, whether politically motivated or active or not (although the term carries an implication of political consciousness and activity): business, labour, Non-Governmental Organisations, churches, special interest or purpose groups. These elements are the constituents of civil society, but none can individually be representative of it. Business is often excluded, given that

---

* This glossary contains only the most frequently-used terms of the publication which are explained with reference to the non- profit sector.

channels of communication between traditional organised business and labour and government are generally well established. Most frequently the term is used interchangeably with "NGO", though the latter does not have the attractive connotation of broad, democratic inclusiveness of the term "civil society".

**Community.** A key concept in the field of local economic development, the term community is commonly used in two very different senses. One meaning refers to any category of people who are related to each other by virtue of specific common interests and values (for example, the disabled, members of the Catholic Church, women, ethnic minority groups, low-income people, artists, etc). The other meaning specifies a category of people who are related to each other by virtue of living in the same geographical area (which implies that they also have some shared values and interests, arising from their common locality). The first meaning has a more limited and more specific target for the beneficiaries of development activities; the benefits or any ownership of assets are fairly readily assigned. In the second meaning, however, some benefits may be more broadly and indirectly assigned to all the residents of the entire locality. The definition and understanding of what constitutes a community is indeed crucial as this will make a difference when it comes to determining who are the beneficiaries and where the ownership resides for the assets created by the activities concerned. Moreover, definitions will also vary from one country to the next. Nonetheless, it is commonly agreed that the definition of a community includes the following criteria: 1) individual and collective interdependence, 2) voluntary activity, 3) a sense of belonging, 4) social and cultural interaction, 5) interaction with economic and political forces, 6) shared values and interests.

**Community-building.** A community can be defined in terms of *networks of linked relationships* (see also definition above). Community-building includes the social and political processes that result in creating alliances and strategic coalitions, and increasing social capital in networks of trust that facilitate co-ordination and co-operation among diverse organisations and agencies. Non-profit sector organisations play a key role in community-building.

**Community Development Entity (CDE).** CDE is a designation granted by the United States Department of the Treasury. A qualified CDE means any domestic corporation or partnership if 1) the primary mission of the entity is serving, or providing investment capital for, low-income communities or low-income persons; 2) the entity maintains accountability to residents of low-income communities through their representation on any governing board of the entity or on any advisory board to the entity; and 3) the entity is certified by the Fund as a CDE. A CDE may also be a limited liability company ("LLC") that meets the above criteria. (See also CFDIs.)

**Community Development Financial Institutions (CFDIs).** CDFIs are organisations that are certified by the United States Department of the Treasury as lending institutions whose primary mission is to promote community development. To be certified, an organisation must also serve a target market, offer development services, maintain accountability, and be a non-government controlled legal entity.

**Co-operative.** A co-operative is an association of persons united voluntarily to meet their common economic, social and cultural needs and aspirations through a jointly-owned and democratically-controlled enterprise. Examples of co-operatives in Europe can be traced back to the 19th century. Co-operatives are based on the values of self-help, self-responsibility, democracy, equality, equity, and solidarity. A co-operative includes one or more kinds of users or stakeholders: 1) consumers who use the enterprise to acquire products or services (such as a retail co-op, housing, healthcare or day-care co-op); 2) producers (such as independent entrepreneurs, artisans, or farmers) who use the enterprise to process and market the goods or services they produced, or to buy products or services necessary to their professional activities; and 3) workers who use the enterprise to secure their employment and control their working conditions. Co-operatives operate democratically (one person, one vote) through two bodies (general meeting of the members or delegates, and the board of directors, which is composed of members elected at a general meeting). The delegate structure may be required to reflect the size of the organisation or the distance covered by the co-operative. The co-operative's start-up capital usually comes *from co-op shares purchased* by members. Each member's liability is limited to the amount of his or her share in the capital. Since 1980, special co-operatives, known as social co-operatives, have become more widespread in OECD member countries.

**Credit unions.** Credit unions are member-owned, voluntary, self-help democratic institutions that provide financial services to their members. As member-owned, non-profit organisations they are value-driven and committed to serving the financial services needs of disadvantaged communities and individuals, many of whom have been abandoned by mainstream banking. Credit unions have a distinct economic and social philosophy. They are financial, co-operative institutions and their co-operative credentials encompass a number of attributes including open membership and democratic control. Equally, limited returns on share capital, with any surpluses belonging to members, are also indispensable defining features. The role of education, so that members can exercise real control of their co-operative, is similarly essential to co-operative identity. Credit unions are particularly well developed in the United Kingdom. In 2002, there were almost 1 000 credit unions in the UK, of which approximately half had been established in the ten previous years.

**295**

**Foundation(s).** Foundations are philanthropic organisations, organised and operated primarily as a permanent collection of endowed funds, the earnings of which are used for the long-term benefit of a defined geographical community or non-profit sector activity. Foundations operate as grant-making institutions, and also as providers of social, health and cultural services. It thus provides a significant link between the private and non-profit sectors, acting as a recipient of private capital and funder of non-profit organisations. Foundations are tax-exempt, incorporated, not-for-profit, organisationally autonomous, and cannot be controlled directly or indirectly by government at any level, corporations, associations and their members, or individuals. While recent trends point to a growth in the number of foundations, especially in the United States, largely due to the new wealth created by the stock market boom of the late 1990s, the shock of September 2001 that hit the country resulted in a reduction of foundations' grants (excluding contributions to September 11-related causes). Because they occupy a unique and central place in the non-profit sector, the development of foundations will strongly affect the future of the sector as a whole.

**Loan circles.** Loan circles were developed by the Bangladesh Grameen Bank in 1976. These consist of a group of four to seven people. The group decides who will apply for a loan first and repayment of that loan is the responsibility of the entire group. Loan circles are particularly well-established as a means of financing the non-profit sector in Canada, notably through the Montreal Community Loan Association. (See also Micro-credit)

**Loan pools.** Loan pools are micro-loan programmes where several banks contribute to and manage the loan fund, thus reducing the risk to any one bank. (See also Micro-credit.)

**Micro-credit.** Micro-credit is a financing option for small firms and individuals, which provides small volume loans for both working capital and investment purposes. It is widely used both in developed and developing economies. Micro-credit programmes seek to respond to the problem of inadequate credit supply in the enterprise creation market, both in the non-profit and commercial sectors of activity. As traditional banks are increasingly concentrating their credit activities on large business loans, credit unions, community development corporations, associations and other business start-up programmes have filled this segment of the market. Micro-credit schemes range from small one-off loans and guarantees to more sophisticated packages involving advisory services. Micro-credit programmes include, for example, loan circles, community loan funds, or loan pools. While the financial institutions and instruments found in the field of micro-credit are often independent, some co-operation with commercial banks has also been reported. Moreover, surveys show that non-profit organisations are more likely to resort to micro-credit than private SMEs.

**Mutual organisation.** A mutual organisation is an organisation owned and managed by its members and that serves the interests of its members. Mutuals can take the form of self-help groups, friendly societies and co-operatives. Mutual organisations exclude shareholding as they bring together members who seek to provide a shared service from which they all benefit. They are widely represented in the insurance sector.

**Non-profit sector.** The best known definition, while not commonly shared, most especially in European countries, is undoubtedly that supplied by the Johns Hopkins University in Baltimore (*www.jhu.edu/~cnp/*). According to this definition, the sector includes organisations which are voluntary, formal, private, self-governing and which do not distribute profits, such as hospitals, universities, social clubs, professional organisations, day-care centres, environmental groups, family counselling agencies, sports clubs, job training centres, human rights organisations and others. In fact, entities belonging to the non-profit sector can vary from country to country according to national history and tradition. The term non-profit, born in the USA, refers mainly to the absence of distribution of profits. This is substantially different to the European approach of "social economy", which includes co-operatives and their enterprises. However, this difference is less significant when investigated through empirical research. C. Borzaga and J. Defourny (*The Emergence of Social Enterprise*, 2001, Routledge, London) argue that the distribution of profits is in any case limited by internal and external regulations in co-operatives and mutual organisations in European countries.

**Plural economy.** This term was first used by the OECD/LEED Programme in 1996 (*Reconciling Economy and Society: Toward a Plural Economy*, OECD, 1996). It refers to an idea of economy in which various stakeholders, the private sector, the public sector, the civil society, contribute to the creation of a wealthier and more inclusive society. "*Mutual enrichment between a 'plural' economy and an 'active' conception of the society, both grounded in the concept of territory, can be seen as the essential components of a more comprehensive paradigm, one that can reconcile the economy with the society*" (p. 218).

**Satellite accounts.** Satellite accounts are integrated sets of statistical tables related to the central framework of national accounts. They focus on particular institutions (*e.g.*, government agencies), or fields (education, health, or environment) that are of special interest to policymakers and analysts. Recently, the use of satellite accounts has been advocated as a way to improve statistical knowledge on the non-profit sector. The Johns Hopkins Center for Civil Society Studies and the United Nations Statistics Division have jointly developed the Handbook on Non-profit Institutions in the System of National Accounts, which provides guidance to national statistical offices in improving the treatment of non-profit institutions in basic economic data gathering. Using this international methodology, national statistical agencies will be able to establish a satellite account that pulls together information on all non-profit institutions, classified by activity. The Handbook will be published by the UN in early 2003. The text is already available online at *www.jhu.edu/~gnisp*.

**Social capital.** Social capital refers to the institutions, relationships, and norms that shape the quality and quantity of a society's social interactions. Social capital is not just the sum of the institutions that underpin a society – it is the glue that holds them together (*www.worldbank.org/poverty/scapital/ whatsc.htm*). Social cohesion may be important for societies to prosper economically and it is clearly critical for sustainable development. The concept was popularised in sociology by James Coleman (1988) and then more generally by Robert Putnam. In *Bowling Alone: The Collapse and Revival of American Community* (2000, p. 19), Putnam gives the following definition: "*Social capital refers to connections among individuals – social networks and the norms of reciprocity and trustworthiness that arise from them.*" The central premise of social capital is that social networks have value. Social capital refers to the collective value of all social networks and the inclinations that arise from these networks to do things for each other ["norms of reciprocity"]. Putnam's major argument is that many of the ills in contemporary American societies can be explained through the decline of social capital and the rise of individualism. Social capital works through multiple channels including information flows (*e.g.*, learning about jobs, exchanging ideas with colleagues, etc), collective action (notably through the churches), mutual aid, solidarity and broader identities. It is thus not surprising that the concept of social capital features so prominently in non-profit sector studies. Besides its definition, the measurement of social capital has been a major issue of contention. Even among those using Putnam's definition, there is not an agreed-upon way to measure social capital. Most research has focused on looking for the positive benefits of social capital. These benefits have been held to accrue to individuals, organisations, and communities (*The Well Being of Nations: The Role of Human and Social Capital*, OECD, 2001).

**Social economy.** The term "social economy", also referred to in France as "économie solidaire" first appeared in this country at the beginning of the 19th century. It was nevertheless only at the beginning of the 20th century that it began to be employed to indicate various entities aiming at improving collective working conditions and individual lives. This concept is now also used by the Anglo-Saxon countries to refer to the production of goods and services provided not solely by the non-profit sector, but also, in some cases, by private enterprises with shareholder agreements that force the majority of shareholders to agree to social objectives undertaken by the firm. Among the organisations belonging to the social economy, one can find associations, co-operatives and mutual organisations and morerecently also foundations. This type of economy is essentially regulated by the stakeholder principle, which stands in stark contrast to the notion of shareholder capitalism. The "social economy" is a broader concept than the non-profit sector, as it is less strictly bound to the non-distributional constraint, according to which organisations cannot legally redistribute their surplus to their owners (see also "Third Sector").

**Social enterprise.**   This concept refers to any private activity conducted in the public interest, organised with an entrepreneurial strategy and whose main purpose is not the maximisation of profit, but the attainment of certain economic and social goals, and which, through the production of goods and services, brings innovative solutions to the problem of social exclusion and unemployment (see OECD, 1999). Social enterprises are part of the thriving and growing collection of organisations that exist between the private and public sectors. They stand out from the rest of the non-profit sector as organisations that use trading activities to achieve their goals and financial self-sufficiency. Social enterprises combine the entrepreneurial skills of the private sector with a strong social mission that is characteristic of the non-profit sector as a whole. They come in a variety of forms including employee owned businesses, credit unions, co-operatives, social co-operatives, development trusts, social firms, intermediate labour market (ILM) organisations, community businesses, or charities' trading arms. They mainly operate in two fields of activity: the training and integration into employment of persons excluded from the labour market, and the delivery of personal and welfare services ("services de proximité").

**Social innovation.**   Social innovation seeks new answers to social and economic problems by identifying and delivering new services that improve the quality of life of individuals and communities. This involves the design and implementation of new labour market integration processes, new competencies, new jobs, and new forms of participation. Social innovations thus contribute to the welfare of individuals and communities, both as consumers and producers. The elements of this welfare are linked to the attempt to restructure the work/life balance. Wherever social innovations appear, they always suggest new references or processes and imply new types of association and mobilisation of social actors. The difference with economic innovations is that these deal with new market products or new production functions, whereas social innovations deal with improving the welfare of individuals and communities through employment, consumption or participation. However, the two forms of innovation can be seen as complementary, as many social innovations will appear in private enterprises.

**Social venture capital.**   Social venture capital represents an innovative source of revenue generation for the non-profit sector. Also sometimes referred to as "socially responsible investment", this type of investment strategy developed in the United States and in Canada during the 1990s usually brings together a network of individual investors in an investment or equity fund. A given proportion of the assets is specifically earmarked for non-profit organisations or for stand-alone commercial companies that incorporate a social mission into their business. Social investors have large portfolios including commercial business, which reduce the risk of losing money if some of the investments do not make enough profit. In some cases, social venture capital may not be restricted to financial intermediation, but will also include support and counselling. The main defining characteristics of social venture capital is that investors are driven by their concern for a sustainable economy and that recipients are thus gauged in terms of a social return. However, it has been pointed out that this is difficult to measure or quantify. Moreover, it must be stressed that socially responsible venture capital remains a modest segment of the commercial capital investment and that its expansion is obviously linked to the overall climate of confidence in world markets.

**Third sector.** The concept of "third sector" is often used as a synonym to the non-profit sector and, more recently, also to "social economy", particularly in European literature. However, it is slightly more restrictive as it comprises charities, and mutual organisations, but excludes private enterprises and co-operatives. The term was chosen to reflect the idea that the sector assembles these otherwise disjointed entities, and that it sits between the public and private sectors and follows unique social goals and internal organisational rules. Its mode of financing is mixed, as it can seek both private and public funding. The idea of establishing a distinct "third sector" has given rise to many hefty debates, which have centred around the danger of using the third sector as a residual sphere or "dumping ground" for those individuals excluded from the private and public sectors. To avoid the danger of social polarisation, the third sector should not merely be seen as an alternative route or juxtaposition to the public and private sectors, but as an interactive and reflexive component of economy and society. Others have argued that the boundaries of the third sector cannot be established with certainty, and for this controversial reason the European Commission preferred the use of the term "Third System".

**Third system.** The term "Third System" was created by the European Commission in 1997 and refers to the economic and social fields represented by co-operatives, mutual companies, associations and foundations, as well as all local job creation initiatives intended to respond, through the provision of goods and services, to needs for which neither the market nor the public sector appear able to make adequate provision. On the initiative of the European Parliament, in 1997 the European Commission introduced a new pilot action entitled "Third System and Employment". The aim of the action was to explore and enhance the employment potential of the "Third System" with an emphasis on the areas of social and neighbourhood services, the environment and the arts (*http://europa.eu.int/comm/employment_social/ empl&esf/3syst/index_en.htm*).

**Venture philanthropy.** There is a relatively new approach to financing the non-profit sector, originally born from dissatisfaction with the perceived inefficiency of grant-making foundations. While there is currently no set definition for the term, venture philanthropy is generally considered as being the application of business-like approaches to making contributions to non-profit organisations. It brings together the notion of an undertaking that involves chance, risk or danger [venture] and the process of distributing excess income through contributions to charitable causes [philanthropy]. The investment approach is similar to that of using venture capital in the corporate sector since finance is raised from outsiders. However, venture philanthropy differs both from traditional private investment in business start-ups and discretionary philanthropic action via foundations. It is characterised by a much stronger engagement from donors in the ventures they fund. Donors tend to nurture their ventures more intensively than in traditional donor/recipient relationships. Venture philanthropy has developed across a wide spectrum with a variety of different models falling into three broad categories: venture-generated philanthropic funds, venture-influenced philanthropic funds and venture-parallel philanthropic funds (Morino Institute, *Venture Philanthropy: the changing landscape*, 2001, Washington, DC, USA). The main difference between these funds lies in the degree of donors' involvement in the non-profit organisations they finance. The development of venture philanthropy has been particularly strong in the United States.

**Voluntary organisation.** A voluntary organisation is a self-governing, independently constituted body of people who have joined together voluntarily to take action for the benefit of the community. They are not established for financial gain. The French translation of this term is "association".

**Welfare state.** The key elements of the Welfare State are social protection and the provision of social services on the basis of citizens' rights. In his classic essay, Asa Briggs ("The Welfare State in historical perspective", *European Journal of Sociology*, 1961, p. 228) defined the Welfare State as "*a state in which organised power is deliberately used through policies and administration in an effort to modify the play of pure market forces*".

Amongst the vast literature on Welfare States, mention could be made of the work done by Richard Titmuss who introduced the concept of an "integrated Welfare State" to refer to a welfare system which integrates economic and social objectives. Beyond this "ideal type", a frequent observation is that globalisation has spurred the reduction in welfare spending and thus led to a retrenchment of the welfare state. Moreover, there are many differences in the quality and scope of welfare state programs among OECD countries. In recent years a clear trend towards "Welfare pluralism" and local municipal welfare has been developing. These promote a "mixed economy of welfare", combining public sector, private-sector, non-profit sector and informal sources of financing and service delivery. It is especially associated with the idea of decreasing direct state involvement in the provision of social services and greatly increasing the role of the voluntary and informal sectors.

Esping Andersen's (*The Three Words of Welfare Capitalism*, 1990, Princeton University Press) influential contribution on the comparative study of advanced welfare states, which proposes a three-fold typology of welfare regimes – the social-democratic, liberal and conservative models – is now commonly used to analyse diverging and converging paths in welfare state reform. It has more recently been argued that rather than dismantling their welfare states, advanced industrialised countries are in fact proceeding to a process of "recalibration" (see for example Taylor-Gooby, *European Welfare States under Pressure*, Sage, 2001).

# Bibliography

AAFRC Trust for Philanthropy (2001),
   *Giving USA 2001*, in Center on Philanthropy, Indianapolis.

AGENZIA DEL LAVORO DELLA PROVINCIA AUTONOMA DI TRENTO (1997),
   *Monitoraggio e valutazione dell'attività del progetto per il supporto delle cooperative sociali di tipo b*, Trento.

AGUILAR VALENZUELA, Rubén (1997),
   "Apuntes para una historia de las organizaciones de la sociedad civil en México", *Revista Sociedad Civil*, No. 1, Mexico, pp. 9-32.

AGUILAR VILLANUEVA, Luis F. (2001),
   "Hacia una nueva relación Gobierno–Sociedad Civil", Mexico, *Foro Nacional del Consejo Nacional de la Sociedad Civil*.

AGUILAR VILLANUEVA, Luis F. (1997),
   "Las organizaciones civiles y el gobierno mexicano", *Revista Sociedad Civil*, No. 1, Mexico, pp. 83-101.

ALBERT, S., and WHETTEN, D.A. (1985),
   "Organisational Identity", in L.L. Cummings and Barry M. Staw (eds.): *Research in Organisational Behavior*, Vol. 7, JAI Press, Greenwich, Connecticut, pp. 263-295.

AMIT, R., BRANDER, J. and ZOTT, C. (1997),
   "Le financement de l'entreprenariat au Canada par le capital de risque", in Paul Alpern (ed.): *Le financement de la croissance au Canada*, University of Calgary Press, Calgary, pp. 261-307.

ANHEIER, H.K., and BEN-NER, A. (1997),
   "Shifting Boundaries: Long-Term Changes in the Size of the For-profit, Non-profit, Co-operative and Government Sectors", *Annals of Public and Co-operative Economics*, 68(3), pp. 335-354.

ANHEIER, H.K., KNAPP, M. and SALAMON, L.M. (1993),
   "Pas de chiffres, pas de politique. Est-ce qu'Eurostat peut mesurer le secteur non lucratif ?", RECMA, No. 46, pp. 87-96.

ANHEIER, H.K. and SALAMON, L.M. (1998),
   "Non-profit Institutions and the Household Sector", pp. 315-341, in United Nations Statistics Division (ed.): *The Household Sector*, United Nations, New York.

ANHEIER, H.K., and SEIBEL, W. (eds.) (1990),
   *The Third Sector: Comparative Studies of Non-profit Organizations*, DeGruyter, Berlin and New York.

ANHEIER, H.K., and SEIBEL, W. (2000),
   *The Non-profit Sector in Germany*, Manchester University Press, Manchester.

ANHEIER H.K. and TOEPLER, S. (1998),
   "Commerce and the Muse: Are Art Museums Becoming Commercial?", Chapter 12

in Weisbrod, Burton A. (1998): *To Profit or Not to Profit: The Commercial Transformation of the Non-profit Sector*, Cambridge University Press, Cambridge, United Kingdom, pp. 233-248.

ARCHAMBAULT, E. (1996a),
"Le secteur sans but lucratif", *Economica*, Paris, France.

ARCHAMBAULT, E. (1996b),
"Le secteur sans but lucratif : une perspective internationale", *RECMA, No. 59*, pp. 36-47.

ARREDONDO RAMÍREZ, Vicente (1997),
"Naturaleza, desarrollo y tipología de la sociedad civil organizada", *Revista Sociedad Civil*, No. 1, Mexico, pp. 165-184.

ASHMAN, D., BROWN, L.D. and ZWICK, E. (1998),
"The Strength of Strong and Weak Ties: Building Social Capital for the Formation and Governance of Civil Society Resource Organizations", *Non-profit Management and Leadership*, 9, pp. 153-177.

THE ASPEN INSTITUTE,
The Non-profit Sector and the Market: Opportunities and Challenges, Non-profit Sector Strategy Group, Internet: *www.aspeninst.org/nssg/pdfs/market.pdf*

ASSEMBLÉE NATIONALE (1998),
"Loi sur le ministère des Régions", *Gazette officielle du Québec*, 130th year, No. 3 (21 January), pp. 251-267.

AUSTIN, James R. (2000),
*The Collaboration Challenge*, Jossey-Bass Publishers, San Francisco.

AUSTRALIAN BUREAU OF STATISTICS (1998),
Australian National Accounts: National Income, Expenditure and Product Main Tables, 1996-97, ABS Cat No. 5204.0.40.002, ABS, Canberra.

AUSTRALIAN BUREAU OF STATISTICS (1998a),
Community Services 1995-96, ABS Cat. No. 8696.0, ABS, Canberra.

AUSTRALIAN BUREAU OF STATISTICS (2001),
Community Services 1999-2000, ABS Cat. No. 8696.0, ABS, Canberra.

AUSTRALIAN INSTITUTE OF HEALTH AND WELFARE (AIHW) (2001),
Australia's Welfare 2001, AIHW, Canberra.

AZIZ NASSIF, Alberto (1997),
"Miradas de fin de siglo", *Revista Sociedad Civil*, No. 1, Mexico, pp. 59-81

BACKMAN, Elaine V., and RATHGEB-SMITH, Stephen (2000),
"Healthy Organizations, Unhealthy Communities?", Non-profit Management and Leadership, 10:4, Summer, pp. 355-373.

BARBETTA, P. (1997),
*The Non-profit Sector in Italy*, Manchester University Press, Manchester.

BARON, S., FIELD, J. and SCHULLER, T. (2000),
*Social Capital: Critical Perspectives*, Oxford University Press, New York.

BEN-NER, A., and GUI, B. (eds.) (1993),
*The Non-profit Sector in the Mixed Economy*, The University of Michigan Press, Ann Arbor.

BEN-NER, A., and PUTTERMAN, L. (1998),
*Economics, Values, and Organization,* Cambridge University Press, New York.

BEN-NER, A., and VAN HOMMISSEN, T. (1993),
"Non-profit Organisations in the Mixed Economy: A Demand and Supply Analysis", in A. Ben-Ner and B. Gui (eds.): *The Non-profit Sector in the Mixed Economy,* The University of Michigan Press, Ann Arbor.

BERMAN, Gabrielle (2000),
"A Charitable Concern", *Agenda* 7(1), pp. 83-91.

BERRY, M.L. (1999),
"Native-American Philanthropy: Expanding Social Participation and Self-Determination", Ford Foundation, W.K. Kellogg Foundation, David and Lucy Packard Foundation, & Council on Foundations, *Cultures of Caring: Philanthropy in Diverse American Communities,* Council on Foundations, Washington, DC.

BIELEFELD, W., LITTLEPAGE, L. and THELIN, R. (2001),
"IMPACT in Indiana: Preliminary Comparisons of Faith-Based and Non-Faith-Based Providers", paper presented at the annual meeting of the Association for Research on Non-profit Organizations and Voluntary Action.

BIELEFELD, W., MAN, J., McLAUGHLIN, W. and PAYTON, S. (2002),
"Non-profit Organizations and Property Values: How the Presence of Non-profit Organizations Affects Residential Sales Prices", paper to be presented at the annual meeting of Association for Public Policy Analysis and Management (APPAM).

BLINDER, A.S. (1987),
*Hard Heads Soft Hearts,* Addison-Wesley, Reading, MA.

BODE, I. and EVERS, A. (1998),
"From institutional fixing to entrepreneurial mobility? The German Third Sector and its Contemporary Challenges", Mimeo.

BOGART, W.T., and B.A. CROMWELL (1997),
"How Much More is a Good School District Worth?", *National Tax Journal* 50, 2 (June), pp. 215-232.

BORIS, E.T (1999),
"The Non-profit Sector in the 1990s", in C.T. Clotfelter & T. Ehrlich (eds.): *Philanthropy and the Non-profit Sector in a Changing America,* Indiana University Press, Bloomington, Indiana.

BORZAGA, C. (1997),
"Introduzione, in AAVV", *Imprenditori sociali. Secondo rapporto sulla cooperazione sociale in Italia,* Edizioni fondazione G. Agnelli, Torino.

BORZAGA, C., CAMPBELL, M., GRANGER, B., GREFFE, X., LLOYD, P., OLABE, A. and SHERMAN, C. (2000),
*Rapport général sur la délimitation et le fonctionnement du troisième système,* European Commission DG V, Brussels.

BORZAGA, C., GUI, B. and POVINELLI, F. (1998),
*The Role of Non Profit Organizations in the Work Integration of Disadvantaged People,* European Commission DG V, Brussels.

BORZAGA, C., and MITTONE, L. (1997),
"The Multi-Stakeholders *versus* the Non-profit Organizations", Università degli Studi di Trento, Dipartimento di Economia, Discussion Paper No. 7.

BORZAGA, C., and SANTUARI, Alceste (eds.) (1998),
*Social Enterprises and the New Employment in Europe*, University of Trento, Trento, Italy.

BOUCHARD, M., BOUCHER, J. and SHRAGGE, E. (1997),
*Social Economy in Quebec – Theoretical Framework, History, Facts, Challenges*, Training Institute in Community Economic Development.

BOURQUE, G.L. (2000),
*Le modèle québécois de développement*, Québec, Presses de l'Université du Québec.

BOWLES, S., and GINTIS, H. (1997),
"The Evolution of Pro-social Norms in Communities", Working Paper, Amherst, University of Massachusetts.

BREMNER, Robert H. (1988),
*American Philanthropy*, University of Chicago Press, Chicago.

BRIGGS, Asa (1961),
"The Welfare State in Historical Perspective", *European Journal of Sociology*, 1961, p. 228.

BRITO VELÁZQUEZ, Enrique (1997),
"Sociedad civil en México: análisis y debates", *Revista Sociedad Civil*, No. 1, Mexico, pp. 185-204.

BROCKWAY, G.P. (1995),
*The End of Economic Man*, W.W. Norton & Company, New York.

BRODY, Evelyn (1997),
"Hocking the Halo: Implications of the Charities", Winning Briefs in Camps Newfound/Owatonna, Inc., *Stetson Law Review*, Vol. 27, No. 2, Autumn, pp. 433-456.

BRODY, Frances and WEISER, John (unpublished, 2001),
"Current Practices in Program-Related Investing", prepared for The San Francisco Foundation.

BRUNI, L. (2002),
"Per un economia capace di felicità", *Impresa sociale*, No. 62., March/April 2002, pp. 45-56.

BRUYN, S.T. (1987),
*The Field of Social Investment*, Cambridge University Press, Cambridge, MA.

BURLINGAME, Dwight F. and YOUNG, Dennis R. (eds.) (1996),
*Corporate Philanthropy at the Crossroads*, Indiana University Press, Bloomington, Indiana.

BUSSMANN, W., KLÖTI, U. and KNOEPFEL, P. (1997),
*Politiques Publiques: Evaluation*, Economica, Paris, France.

BYGRAVE, W.D., and TIMMONS, J.A. (1992),
*Venture Capital at the Crossroads*, Harvard Business School Press, Boston, MA.

CAISSE D'ÉCONOMIE DESJARDINS DE TRAVAILLEUSES ET TRAVAILLEURS (2000),
*Rapport Annuel 2000*, Québec.

CAMPBELL, M. *et al.* (1999),
"The Third System Employment and Local Development", European Commission DG V, pp. 10-11, in General Report on the Boundaries and Operation of the Third System, European Commission DG V, Brussels.

CAMPBELL, D. (2002),
"Beyond Charitable Choice: The Diverse Service Delivery Approaches of Local Faith-Related Organizations", *Non-profit and Voluntary Sector Quarterly*, 31, pp. 207-30.

CANADIAN VENTURE CAPITAL ASSOCATION (CVCA),
Association canadienne du capital de risque (ACCR), *Key Observations on 1998 Venture Capital Activity, (www.cvca.ca/statistical_review/lkey_observations.html).*

CARROLL, T.M., CLAURETIE, T.M. and JENSEN, J. (1996),
"Living Next to Godliness: Residential Property Values and Churches", *Journal of Real Estate Finance and Economics* 12, 3 (May) pp. 319-330.

CARSON, Carol S. (1996),
"Design of Economic Accounts and the 1993 System of National Accounts", Chapter 2, in John W. Kendrick, (ed.): *The New System of National Accounts*, Kluwer Academic Publishers, Boston, Dordrecht, London. pp. 25-72.

CASTANER, X. (2000),
"The Determinants of Artistic Innovation by Cultural Organizations: A Review and Extension", 11th Conference on Cultural Economics, University of Minnesota.

CAW (1999),
*Labour-Sponsored Funds: Examining the Evidence*, Prepared by the Canadian Automobile Workers' Research Department, February.

CECOP (1996),
Regione Trentino Alto-Adige, CGM, European Commission, "The contribution of social enterprises to the creation of new jobs: the field of services to people", proceedings of the Conference, Trento, Italy, 12-13 December.

CEDIOC,
Center for Information on Civil Organizations, *www.iztapalapa.uam.mx/ iztapala.www/cedioc/CEDIOC.htm*

CEMEFI,
Mexican Center for Philanthropy, *www.cemefi.org*

CEMEFI (2000),
*Introducción a las instituciones filantrópicas, asociaciones civiles e instituciones de asistencia privada*, Mexico, CEMEFI, Legal 1.

CENTRE CANADIEN DU MARCHÉ DU TRAVAIL ET DE LA PRODUCTIVITÉ (1995),
*Le rôle et le rendement des fonds d'investissement parrainés par le mouvement syndical dans l'économie canadienne : Un profil institutionnel*, Ottawa.

CGM-CECOP (1995),
*Social Enterprises: a chance for Europe*, Brussels.

CHANG, *c.f.* and TUCKMAN, H.P. (1990),
"Financial Vulnerability and Attrition as Measures of Non-profit Performance", in H.K. Anheier and W. Siebel (eds.): *The Third Sector: Comparative Studies of Non-profit Organizations*, de Gruyter, Berlin, pp. 157-164.

CHANTIER DE L'ÉCONOMIE SOCIALE (2000),
"De nouveau, nous osons...".

CHASKIN, R.J., BROWN, P., VENKATESH, S. and VIDAL, A. (2001),
*Building Community Capacity*, Aldine de Gruyter, New York.

CHAO, J. (1999),
"Asian American Philanthropy: Expanding Circles of Participation", Ford Foundation, W.K. Kellogg Foundation, David and Lucy Packard Foundation, & Council on Foundations: *Cultures of Caring: Philanthropy in Diverse American Communities*, Council on Foundations, Washington, DC.

CHAVES, M. (1999),
"Religious Congregations and Welfare Reform: Who Will Take Advantage of "Charitable Choice'?", *American Sociological Review*, 64, pp. 836-846.

CIRIEC et al. (1999),
The Enterprises and Organisations of the Third System, "Third System and Employment", Action Research Project conducted by the Employment and Social Affairs Directorate (DG V) of the European Commission.

CIRIEC (2000),
*The Enterprises and Organisations of the Third System. A Strategic Challenge for Employment*, University of Liège, Liège.

CLARK, C.M.A. (ed.) (1995),
*Institutional Economics and the Theory of Social Value: Essays in Honor of Marc R. Tool*, Kluwer Academic, Boston.

CLOTFELTER, C.T. (ed.) (1992),
*Who Benefits from the Non-profit Sector?*, Chicago and London.

CNAAN, R.A. (1999),
*The Newer Deal: Social Work and Religion in Partnership*, Columbia University Press, New York.

COBB, C.W. (2001),
"Measuring Failure to Find Success", in P. Flynn & V.A. Hodgkinson (eds.): *Measuring the Impact of the Non-profit Sector*, Kluwer Academic/Plenum Publishers, New York.

COLEMAN, J.S. (1988),
"Social Capital in the Creation of Human Capital", *American Journal of Sociology*, 94, S95-S120.

COMEAU, Y., FAVREAU, L., LEVESQUE, B. and MENDELL, M. (2001),
*Emploi, économie sociale et développement local*, Montréal: Presses de l'Université du Québec, 336 pages.

COMEAU, Y., and LÉVESQUE, B. (1993),
"Workers' Financial Participation in the Property of Enterprise in Quebec", *Economic and Industrial Democracy, An International Journal*, Vol. 14, No. 2, pp. 233-250.

COMEAU, Y. (1997),
"La structuration du mouvement de développement économique communautaire à Québec", *Économie et Solidarité*, Vol. 29, No. 1, pp. 101-112.

COMMISSION ON PRIVATE PHILANTHROPY AND PUBLIC NEEDS (1977),
*Research Papers*, Five Volumes, US Department of Treasury, Washington, DC.

CONNELL, P. et al. (1995),
*New Approaches to Evaluating Community Initiatives*, The Aspen Institute, Washington.

CORELLI, E. (1979),
*Il movimento cooperativo in Italia ieri e oggi*, Vallecchi, Firenze, Italia.

CORMAN, M., and GREFFE, X. (1999),
Rapport final sur l'action pilote: Partenariats locaux pour l'emploi, DG V A, Brussels.

CORTES, M. (1995),
"Three Strategic Questions About Latino Philanthropy", in H. Charles Hamilton and F. Warren Ilchman: *Cultures of Giving II: How Heritage, Gender, Wealth and Values Influence Philanthropy*, Jossey-Bass, San Francisco.

CRIMMINS, James C., and KEIL, Mary (1983),
*Enterprise in the Non-profit Sector*, The Rockefeller Brothers Fund, New York.

DEES, Gregory J. (1998),
"Enterprising Non-profits", *Harvard Business Review*, January/February, pp. 55-67.

DeFILIPPIS, J. (2001),
"The Myth of Social Capital in Community Development", *Housing Policy Debate*, 12, pp. 781–805.

DEFOURNY, J. (1999),
From Third Sector Concepts to a Social Enterprise Framework, Mimeo.

DEFOURNY, J., and MERTENS, S. (1999),
"Le troisième secteur en Europe: un aperçu des efforts conceptuels et statistiques", in B. Gazier, J-L. Outin, F. Audier (eds.) : *L'économie sociale*, L'Harmattan, Paris, pp. 5-20.

DEFOURNY, J., and MONZON CAMPOS, J.L. (eds.) (1992),
*Économie sociale. Entre économie capitaliste et économie publique: The Third Sector. Co-operative, Mutual and Nonprofit Organisations*, De Boeck Université, Brussels.

DEGL'INNOCENTI, M. (1981),
"Geografia e strutture della cooperazione in Italia", in G. Sapelli (a cura di): *Il movimento cooperativo in Italia. Storia e problemi*, Torino.

DEMOS Foundation,
*www.laneta.apc.org/demos/*

DEMOUSTIER, D. (2000),
"Les organisations d'économie sociale, acteurs de la régulation socio-économique", *Revue Internationale de l'économie sociale* (anciennement *Revue des études coopératives, mutualistes et associatives*- RECMA) Nos. 275-276, pp. 137-148.

DEPARTMENT OF EMPLOYMENT AND WORKPLACE RELATIONS (2002),
Submission to the Independent Review of Job Network, Internet: *www.pc.gov.au/inquiry/jobnetwork/subs/sub043.pdf*

DE TOCQUEVILLE, A. (1945[1835]),
*Democracy in America*, New York, Vintage Books.

DiMAGGIO, P. (2001),
"Measuring the Impact of the Non-profit Sector on Society is Probably Impossible but Possibly Useful: A Sociological Perspective", in P. Flynn & V.A. Hodgkinson (eds.): *Measuring the Impact of the Non-profit Sector*, Kluwer Academic/Plenum Publishers, New York.

DO, A.Q., WILBUR, R.W. and SHORT, J.L. (1994),
An Empirical Examination of the Externalities of Neighborhood Churches on Housing Values, *Journal of Real Estate Finance and Economics* 9, 2, pp. 127-136.

DOWLING, P.B. (1984),
*Environmental Economics and Policy*, Little Brown, Boston.

DWORKIN, G., BERMANT, G. and BROWN, P.G. (1977),
*Markets and Morals*, Hemisphere Publishing, Washington.

EARDLEY, Tony, ABELLO, David and MACDONALD, Helen (2001),
*Is the Job Network Benefiting Disadvantaged Job Seekers?*, Preliminary evidence from a study of non-profit employment services, University of New South Wales Social Policy Research Centre Discussion Paper No. 111, January.

EASTIS, C.M. (1998),
"Organizational Diversity and the Production of Social Capital", American Behavioral Scientist, 42, pp. 66–77.

EASTMAN, C.L. (1995),
"Philanthropic Cultures of Generational Archetypes", in Charles H. Hamilton & Warren F. Ilchman (eds.): *Cultures of Giving II: How Heritage, Gender, Wealth and Values Influence Philanthropy*, Jossey-Bass, San Francisco.

ECOTEC Research and Consulting Limited (2001),
"External Evaluation of the Third System and Employment Pilot Action", Final Report, August.

EDWARDS, B., and FOLEY, M. (1997),
"Social Capital, Civil Society and Contemporary Democracy", *American Behavioral Scientist*, Special Issue, 40, 5.

EMERSON, Jed (1999),
"The US Non-profit Capital Market", Chapter 10 in *Social Purpose Enterprise and venture Philanthropy in the Millenium*, Vol. 2, The Roberts Enterprise Development Fund, San Fransico, pp. 187-216.

EMERSON, Jed (unpublished 2000),
Social Enterprise Series No. 17, The Nature of Returns: A Social Capital Markets Inquiry into Elements of Investment and the Blended Value Proposition, Cambridge, available on *www.hbs.edu/socialenterprise*

EMERSON, Jed (unpublished, 2002),
A Capital Idea: Total Foundation Asset Management and The Unified Investment Strategy, available on *www.foundationnews.org*

EMERSON, Jed and TWERSKY, Faye (eds.) (1996),
*New Social Entrepreneurs*, The Roberts Foundation, San Francisco.

EMES, 2000 (1999),
*The Emergence of Social Enterprises in Europe. New Answers to Social Exclusion*, Brussels.

ENTERPRISE FOUNDATION (2000),
*www.enterprisefoundation.org/policy/crasummary.asp*

ESTES, C.L., BINNEY, E.A. and BERGTHOLD, L.A. (1989),
"How the Legitimacy of the Sector has Eroded", in Virginia A. Hodgkinson, R.W. Lyman and Associates (eds.): *The Future of the Non-profit Sector*, Jossey-Bass, San Francisco.

ETZIONI, A. (1988),
*The Moral Dimension: Towards a New Economics*, The Free Press, New York.

EUROPEAN COMMISSION (1995),
"Local Development and Employment Initiatives: An Investigation in the European Union", SEC 564/95, Brussels.

EUROPEAN COMMISSION (1996a),
*The First Report on Development and Employment Initiatives: Lessons for Territorial Employment Pacts*, DG V, Brussels.

EUROPEAN COMMISSION (1996b),
*European System of Account* – ESA-1995, Eurostat, Office for Official Publications of the European Communities, Luxembourg.

EUROPEAN COMMISSION (1998a),
"Exploiting the Opportunities for Job Creation at Local Level", paper for European Parliament/European Commission Seminar on the Third System and Employment, Brussels, 24-25 September.

EUROPEAN COMMISSION (1998b),
*The Era of Tailor-made Jobs: Second Report on Local Development and Employment Initiatives*, Forward Studies Unit, Brussels.

EUROPEAN COMMISSION (1999),
"Third System and Employment Pilot Action and Article Six ESF. Capitalisation Committee", Mimeo, Directorate General for Employment and Social Affairs, Brussels.

EUROPEAN COMMISSION (1999a),
*Employment Performance in the Member States: Employment Rates Report 1998*, DG V, Brussels.

EUROPEAN COMMISSION (1999b),
Employment in Europe 1998, DG V, Brussels.

EUROPEAN COMMISSION (2002),
The New Actors of Employment – Synthesis of the pilot action "Third System and Employment" – For a Better Understanding of Employment at Local Level.

EU TSEP (2000),
*Summary Booklet 1*, European Commission DG V, Brussels, April, p. 19.

ÉVALU ACTION (1999),
*Complément d'information SADC. Présentation des résultats généraux.*

EVERS, A. (1999),
"Social Capital: A key factor in the multiple goal and resource-structure which defines social enterprises", in Defourny, J. (ed.): *Social Enterprises in Europe*, London.

EVERS, A. (2000),
"Book Review", *Voluntas*, International Journal of Voluntary and Non-profit Organisations, Vol. 11, No. 1, pp. 371-379.

EVERS, J. and REIFNER, U. (eds.) (1998),
"The Social Responsibility of Credit Institutions in the EU", Nomos Verlagsgesellschaft, Baden Baden.

FAIRFAX, J.E. (1995),
"Black Philanthropy: Its Heritage and Future", in Charles H. Hamilton and

Warren F. Ilchman (eds.): *Cultures of Giving II: How Heritage, Gender, Wealth and Values Influence Philanthropy*, Jossey-Bass, San Francisco.

FAM,
Mutual Support Forum, *www.laneta.apc.org/fam/*

FAVREAU, L. and LÉVESQUE, B. (1996),
*Développement économique communautiare. Économie sociale et intervention*, Presse de l'Université du Québec, Québec.

FAVREAU, L. (1999),
"Économie solidaire et renouvellement de la coopération Nord-Sud : le défi actuel des ONG", *Nouvelles pratiques sociales*, Vol. 12, No. 1, PUQ, pp. 127-143.

FELKINS, P.K. (2002),
*Community at Work: Creating and Celebrating Community in Organizational Life*, Hampton Press, Cresskill, New Jersey.

FERLIE, E. (ed.) (1996),
*The New Public Management in Action*, Oxford University Press, Oxford.

FILGUEIRAS-RAUCH, Maria Joao (2000),
"Benchmarking of Insertion Enterprises", Ministry of Labour and Solidarity, Lisbon, Portugal.

FITZGERALD, Robert (2001),
"The Future of Non-Profit Organisations in Australia", Speech to The Power of the Association industry Unlocking the Potential, 25 May.

FLYNN, P. and HODGKINSON, Virginia, A. (eds.) (2001),
*Measuring the Impact of the Nonprofit Sector*, Kluwer Academic/Plenum Publishers, New York.

FONDS DE SOLIDARITÉ DES TRAVAILLEURS DU QUÉBEC (FTQ) (1983-1999),
*Rapports annuels.*

FOSTER, V., MOURATO, S., PEARCE, D. and OZDEMIROGLU, E. (2001),
*The Price of Virtue: The Economic Value of the Non-profit Sector*, Edward Elgar, Northampton, MA.

THE FOUNDATION CENTER (2002),
"Foundation Center Announces Estimates for 2001 Foundation Giving", April, available on *www.fndcenter.org*

THE FOUNDATION CENTER (2002a),
*Foundation Growth and Giving Estimates – 2001 Preview*, New York, available on *www.fndcenter.org*

THE FOUNDATION CENTER (2002b),
*Foundation Today Series – 2001 Edition*, New York, available on *www.fndcenter.org*

THE FOUNDATION CENTER (2002c),
*Foundation Yearbook – 2001*, New York, available on *www.fndcenter.org*

FOURNIER, P. (1987),
*La contribution des sociétés d'État au développement économique du Québec*, Montréal, Protocole UQAM/CSN/FTQ, UQAM.

FOURNIER, L. (1991),
*Solidarité Inc. Le Fonds de solidarité des travailleurs du Québec (FTQ). Un nouveau syndicalisme créateur d'emplois*, Québec-Amérique, Montréal, p. 288.

FOWLER, A. (1997),
Striking a balance: a guide to enhancing the effectiveness of non-governmental organisations in international development, Earthscan, London.

FRANCE-QUÉBEC,
www.unites.uqam.ca/econos/

FRANK, R.G. and SALKEVER, D.S. (1994),
"Non-profit Organisations in the Health Sector", Journal of Economic Perspectives,Vol. 8, No. 4, pp. 129-144.

FRONDIZI, R. (1963),
What is Value? An Introduction to Axiology, Open Court, Lasalle, IL.

FUKUYAMA, Francis (1994),
Trust: The social virtues and the creation of prosperity, Free Press, New York.

FUKUYAMA, Francis (1996),
La société de confiance: Vertus sociales et prospérité économique, Le Seuil, Paris.

FUNDAÇAO CALOUSTE GULBENKIAN (1998),
"Micro-credito contra la pobreza", Seminar Report, 2 October.

FUORI, Orario. (1999),
Bilancio sociale ed altri strumenti, 18/19, Milan.

GALANTE, P.S. (ed.) (1999),
An Overview of the Venture Capital Industry and Emerging Changes, The Private Equity Analyst, Newsletter, Wellesley, M.A. (See: www.vcinstitude.org/materials/galante).

GALASSO, G. (1987),
"Gli anni della grande espansione e la crisi del sistema", in V. Castronovo, G. Galasso and R. Zangheri (eds.): Storia del movimento cooperativo in Italia, la Lega Nazionale delle cooperative e delle mutue, Torino.

GAUSSIN, C. (1997),
"Analyse multidimensionnelle du coût des entreprises de formation par le travail en Wallonie", Le Cahiers du Cerisis, 97/3a.

GILLROY, J.M., and WADE, M. (eds.) (1992),
The Moral Dimension of Public Policy Choice: Beyond the Market Paradigm, University of Pittsburgh Press, Pittsburgh.

GOODMAN, A.C. (1989),
"Topics in Empirical Urban Housing Research", in Richard F. Muth and Allen C. Goodman (eds.): The Economics of Housing Markets, Harwood Academic Publishers, New York.

GOUVERNEMENT DU QUÉBEC (1999a),
Définition gouvernementale de l'économie sociale, www.cex.gouv.qc.ca/economiesociale/html/def_es.html

GOUVERNEMENT DU QUÉBEC (1999b),
Le Chantier de l'économie sociale, www.cex.gouv.qc.ca/economiesociale/html/ecosocif.htm

GOUVERNEMENT DU QUÉBEC (1999c),
Économie sociale. Portrait synthèse au 31 mars 1999, www.cex.gouv.qc.ca/economiesociale/html/portraitmars99.html

GOUVERNEMENT DU QUÉBEC (2000),
Fonds de lutte contre la pauvreté par la réinsertion au travail, http://mss.gouv.qc.ca/mes/org/fonlut/motprojet.htm

GRANGER, B. (1999),
Legal and Financial Tools to Support the Third System, Report for the European Commission (DG Employment and Social Affairs).

GRANGER, B., and INAISE (1998),
Banquiers du Futur – Les nouveaux instruments financiers de l'économie sociale en Europe, Editions Charles Léopold Mayer, Paris.

GRAY, B.H. (2001),
"Measuring the Impact of Non-profit Health Care Organizations", in P. Flynn and V.A. Hodgkinson (eds.): Measuring the Impact of the Non-profit Sector, Kluwer Academic/Plenum Publishers, New York.

GREENWAY, M.T. (2001),
"The Emerging Status of Outcome Measurement in the Nonprofit Human Service Sector, in P. Flynn and V.A. Hodgkinson (eds.): Measuring the Impact of the Nonprofit Sector, Kluwer Academic/Plenum Publishers, New York.

GREFFE, X. (1992),
Sociétés postindustrielles et rédéveloppement, Hachette, Paris.

GREFFE, X. (1998a),
Managing Local Partnerships for Employment, Programme LEDA, Pilot Action on Territorial Partnerships for Employment, Brussels, European Union, DG V A.

GREFFE, X. (1998b),
"The Role of the Third System in the Intertemporal Equilibrium", paper for the European Parliament/European Commission Seminar on the Third System, Brussels, September 4/25.

GREFFE, X. (1999a),
Third System and Cultural Activities, Brussels, European Union, DG V A.

GREFFE, X. (1999b),
Gestion publique, Dalloz, Paris.

GRIBBEN, Chris, PINNINGTON, Kate and WILSON, Andrew (2000),
Government as partners: The role of central government in developing new social partnerships, The Copenhagen Centre, Copenhagen.

GROUPE DE TRAVAIL SUR L'AVENIR DU SECTEUR FINANCIER CANADIEN (1998),
Rapport du groupe de travail. Ottawa, ministère des Finances, Document d'information, No. 4 (September), (see: http://finservtaskforce.fin.gc.ca/rpt/pdf/Main_F.pdf).

GROUPE FINANCIER BANQUE ROYALE (2000),
www.banqueroyale.com/communautaire/nouvelles_01.html

GUI, B. (2001),
"Economic Interactions as Encounters", Mimeo, Università di Padova, Italy.

GUÉRIN, I. (2000),
"Social Finance in France: Combining Social and Financial Intermediation", Revue internationale de l'économie sociale, No. 277, pp. 79-93.

GUY, G. (1999),
Economic Valuation of the Environment: Methods and Case Studies, Edward Elgar, Northampton, MA.

HALL, Peter D. (1992),
Inventing the Non-profit Sector, The Johns Hopkins University Press, Baltimore.

HALL, Peter D. (1998)
"Philanthropy, Public Welfare, and the Politics of Knowledge", in Deborah S. Gardner (ed.): *Vision and Values: Rethinking the Non-profit Sector in America*, PONPO Working Paper No. 251, Yale University, Program on Non-Profit Organizations, pp. 11-27.

HALPERN, Charles (1998)
"Foreword", in Deborah S. Gardner (ed.): *Vision and Values: Rethinking the Non-Profit Sector in America*, PONPO Working Paper No.251, Yale University, Program on Non-Profit Organizations, pp.5-9.

HANDY, R. (1970),
*The Measurement of Value: Behavioral Science and Philosophical Approaches*, Warren H. Green, St. Louis, MO.

HANSMANN, H. (1980),
"The Role of Non-profit Enterprise", *The Yale Law Journal*, Vol. 89, No. 5, pp. 835-901.

HANSMANN, H. (1987),
Economic Theories of Non-profit Organisations, in W.W. Powell (ed.): *The Non-profit Sector: A Research Handbook*, Yale University Press, New Haven, Connecticut.

HANSMANN, H. (1996),
*The Ownership of Enterprise*, Harvard University Press, Cambridge, MA.

HANSMANN, H.B (1986),
"The Role of the Non-profit Enterprise", in S. Rose-Ackerman (ed.): *The Economics of the Non-profit Institutions: Studies in Structure and Policy*, Oxford University press, New York.

HANSMANN, H.B. (1995),
Encouraging Entry and Exit of Non-profit Firms, paper prepared for the International Conference on Non-profit Organisations, Stresa, October.

HAUSMAN, D.M., and McPHERSON, M.S. (1996):
*Economic Analysis and Moral Philosophy*, Cambridge University Press, New York.

HAWRYLSHYN, O. (1977),
"Towards a Definition of Non-market Activities", *Review of Income and Wealth*, Series 23, pp. 79-96.

HEILBRUN, J. (1998),
"A Study of the Opera Repertory in the United States, 1982-83 to 1997-98", 10th Conference on Cultural Economics, Barcelona.

HENTON, D., MELVILLE, D. and WALSH, K. (1996),
*Grassroots Leaders: How Civic Entrepreneurs are Building Prosperous Communities*, Jossey Bass, San Francisco.

HERO, Peter (1998),
*Giving Back – The Silicon Valley Way*, self-published, San Jose.

HICKS, J.R. (1940),
"The Valuation of the Social Income", *Economica*, Vol. VII, No. 2, pp. 105-124.

HODGKINSON, Virginia A., WEITZMAN, M.S., KIRSCH, A.D., NOGA, S.M. and GORSKI, H.A. (1992),
*From Belief to Commitment: The Community Service Activities and Finances of Religious Congregations in the United States*, Washington, DC, Independent Sector.

HODGKINSON, Virginia A., WEITZMAN, Murray S., TOPPE, Christopher M. and NOGA Stephen M. (1992),
*Non-profit Almanac 1992-1993*, Jossey Bass Publishers, San Francisco.

HOME OFFICE (1998),
*Impact on Relations between Government and the Voluntary and Community Sector in Endland*, The Stationary Office, (CM 4100).

HUDNUT-BEUMLER, J. (1995),
"Protestant and Giving: The Tithes that Bind", Charles H. Hamilton & Warren F. Ilchmane: *Cultures of Giving: How Region and Religion Influence Philanthropy*, Jossey-Bass, San Francisco.

HUOT, G. (2000),
*Le regroupement des caisses populaires au sein de territoires en transformation: effets sur la proximité*, Montréal, UQAM, Sociology Department (mémoire de maîtrise).

ILO (1998),
*Enterprise Creation by the Unemployed: the Role of Micro-finance in Industrialised Countries*. An ILO Action Programme for 1998-1999.

INAISE (1997a),
*Financial Instruments of the Community-Based Economy in Europe*, European Commission, DG V, Brussels.

INAISE (1997b),
Financial Instruments of the Community Based Economy in Europe, July, for DG V.

INDEPENDENT SECTOR (1996),
*Measuring the Impact of the Independent, Not-For-Profit Sector on Society, Working Papers*, Independent Sector, Washington, DC.

INDUSTRY COMMISSION (1995),
"Charitable Organisations in Australia", Industry Commission, Report No. 45, AGPS, Melbourne.

INNER CITY PRESS (2000),
"Community Reinvestment", *www.innercitypress.org/cra.html*

INSINC (1997),
*The Net Result: Social Inclusion in the Information Society*, IBM, London.

INVESTISSEMENT QUÉBEC (2000),
*Rapport annuel 1999-2001*, Gouvernement du Québec, p. 93.

INVESTISSEMENT QUÉBEC (1999),
*Rapport annuel 1998-1999*, Gouvernement du Québec, p. 81.

JAMES, E. (1987),
"The Non-profit Sector in Comparative Perspective", in W.W. Powell (ed.): *The Non-profit Sector: A Research Handbook*, Yale University Press, New Haven.

JEANTET, T. (1999),
*L'économie sociale européenne*, CIEM, Paris.

JONES, G.H. (1967):
*History of Charity Law 1530-1827*, London.

JOHNSON, B.R., TOMPKINS, R.B. and WEBB, D. (2002),
*Objective Hope: Assessing the Effectiveness of Faith-Based Organizations: A Review of the Literature*, Center for Research on Religion and Urban Civil Society, University of Pennsylvania, Philadelphia, PA.

JOHNSTONE, H. (1998),
"Financing Ventures in a Depleted Community", in G. A. MacIntyre (ed.): *Perspectives on Communities. A Community Economic Development Roundtable,* University College of Cape Breton Press, Sydney (N.S.), pp. 91-104.

JOSEPH, J.A. (1995),
*Remaking America: How the Benevolent Traditions of Many Cultures are Transforming Life,* Jossey-Bass, San Francisco.

JOUET, P.A., and SOUBEYRAN, A.(1999),
"Contraintes de financement des firmes autogérées", *Revue internationale de l'économie sociale,* No. 265, pp. 73-84.

JOYAL, A. (1997),
"Le développement économique communautaire: l'exemple de Montréal", *Horizon Local.*

KENDALL, J. (2000),
"The Mainstreaming of the Third Sector into Public Policy in the late 1990's: whys and wherefores", *Policy and Politics* 28(4), pp. 541-562.

KEUNING, S. (1998),
"A Powerful Link between Economic Theory and Practice: National Accounting", *The Review of Income and Wealth,* Series 44, No. 3, September, pp. 437-46.

KIRSCH, A.D., HUME, K.M., JALANDONI, N.T., HAMMILL, K.C. and McCORMACK, M.T. (1999),
*Giving and Volunteering in the United States,* Independent Sector, Washington, DC.

KORTEN, David. (1990),
*Getting to the 21st Century. Voluntary Action and the Global Agenda,* Westford Kumarian Press, Connecticut.

KOSMIN, B.A. (1995),
"New Directions in Contemporary Jewish Philanthropy: The Challenges of the 1990s", in Charles H. Hamilton and Warren F. Ilchman (eds.): *Cultures of Giving II: How Heritage, Gender, Wealth and Values Influence Philanthropy,* Jossey-Bass, San Francisco.

KUTTNER, R. (1997),
"Lessons of the Community Reinvestment Act", *www.prospect.org/columns/kuttner/bk971111.html*

LABOUR SPONSORED INVESTMENT FUNDS ALLIANCE (1995),
*What Constitutes a Labour Sponsored Investment Fund? A Defining Statement,* November.

LAMOTHE, R. (interview with N. NEAMTAN) (1999),
"Des questions plein la tête !", *Autrement spécial,* Gouvernement du Québec, January, pp. 2-3.

LAMPKIN, Linda, and POLLAK, Thomas (2002),
*The New Non-profit Almanac & Desk Reference,* Urban Institute, Washington, DC.

LAND, Kenneth (2001),
"Social Indicators for Assessing the Impact of the Independent Not-For-Profit Sicial Sector of Society", in Flynn, P. and Hodgkinson, V.A. (eds.): *Measuring the Impact of the Non-profit Sector.* Kluwer Academic/ Plenum Publishers, New York.

LANG, R.E., and HORNBURG, S.P. (1998),
"What is Social Capital and Why is it Important to Public Policy?", *Housing Policy Debate*, 9, pp. 1-16.

LANGAN, J., and TAYLOR, M. (1995),
"The New Institutional Environment: Private and Voluntary Organisations in the Community Care Field", in B. Dallago and L. Mittone (eds.): *Economic Institutions, Markets and Competition: Centralisation and Decentralisation in the Transformation of Economic Systems*, Aldershot: Edward Elgar Publishers.

LAVILLE, J.L. (ed.) (1994),
*L'économie solidaire. Une perspective internationale*, Paris, DDB.

LAVILLE, J.L., and NYSSENS, M. (2000):
"Solidarity-Based Third Sector Organisations in the XProximity ServicesX Field. A European Francophone Perspective", *Voluntas*, International Journal of Voluntary and Non-profit Organisations, Vol. 11, No. 1, pp. 67-84.

LAVILLE, J.L., and SAINSAULIEU, R. (eds.) (1998):
*Sociologie de l'association. Des organisations à l'épreuve du changement social*, Paris, DDB, p. 404.

LEBOSSÉ, J. (1998),
"La Caisse d'économie des travailleuses et travailleurs, Québec (Canada)", in *Micro-finance et développement local*, p. 95-104, IFDÉC, Montréal.

LETTS, Christine, RYAN, William P. and GROSSMAN, Allen (1997),
"Virtuous Capital: What Foundations Can Learn from Venture Capitalists", *Harvard Business Review*, March/April, pp. 2-7.

LÉVESQUE, B. (1994),
"Une forme originale d'association capital-travail, les co-opératives de travailleurs au Québec", *Revue des études coopératives, mutualistes et associatives* (Paris), No 251 (1994), pp. 49-60.

LÉVESQUE, B. (1999),
*Originalité et impact de l'action des SOLIDE sur le développement local et sur l'emploi au Québec*, Montréal, Cahier du CRISES, p. 29.

LÉVESQUE, B. (2001),in Comeau, Y., L Favreau, B. Lévesque et M. Mendell (2001),
Emploi, économie sociale, développement local, Québec, Presses de l'Université de Québec, 336 p.

LÉVESQUE, B., and MENDELL, M. (1998),
"Les fonds régionaux et locaux de développement au Québec: des institutions financières relevant principalement de l'économie sociale", in Marc-Urbain Proulx (ed.) : *Territoire et développement économique*, Paris et Montréal, L'Harmattan, pp. 220-270.

LÉVESQUE, B., and MENDELL, M. (1999),
"L'économie sociale au Québec: éléments théoriques et empiriques pour le débat et la recherche", *Lien social et Politiques* (anciennement *Revue internationale d'action communautaire*), No. 41 (1999), pp. 105-118.

LÉVESQUE, B., and MENDELL,M. et al. (1997),
*Répertoire des fonds de développement local, régional et communautaire du Québec*, Montréal, Pro-Fonds-CRISES.

LÉVESQUE, B., and MENDELL, M. *et al.* (2000),
*La création d'entreprises par les chômeurs et les sans-emploi: le rôle de la microfinance*, Rapport de recherche soumis au Bureau international du Travail, Université Concordia, Montréal. p. 243.

LÉVESQUE, B., MENDELL, M and Van KEMENDADE, S. (1997),
*Socio-economic Profile of Quebec Local and Regional Development Funds*, Minister of Supply and Services Canada, Ottawa, Canada.

LÉVESQUE, B., VAN SCHENDEL, V., NEAMTAN, N. and VALLÉE, L. (2000),
"L'Alliance de recherche université-communauté en économie sociale: une infrastructure de partenariat pour la recherche, la formation, la diffusion et l'échange de connaissances", *Économie et solidarités*, Vol. 31, No. 135-150.

LEWIS, D. (ed.) (1999),
*International Perspectives on Voluntary Action*, Earthscan, London.

LEWIS, J. (1999),
"Relationships Between the Voluntary Sector and the State in Britain in the 1990s", *Voluntas*, Vol. 10, No. 3, September, p. 260.

LIGHT, Paul C. (2000),
*Making Non-profits Work*, Brookings Institution Press, Washington, DC.

LIN, N., COOK, K. and BURT, R.S. (2001),
*Social Capital: Theory and Research*, Aldine de Gruyter, New York.

LIPIETZ, A. (2000),
"Sur l'opportunité d'un nouveau type de société à vocation sociale", Final report, mimeo.

LIPMAN, Harvey, and SCHWINN, Elizabeth (2001),
"The Business of Charity", *The Chronicle of Philanthropy*, 18 October.

LUNDSTROM, T., and WIJKSTROM, F. (1997),
*The Non-profit Sector in Sweden*. Manchester University Press, Manchester.

LUTZ, M.A., and LUX, K. (1979),
*The Challenge of Humanistic Economics*, The Benjamin/Cummings Publishing Company, Menlo Park, California.

LYONS, Mark (1997),
"Australia", in L.M. Solamon (ed.): *The International Guide to Non-Profit Law*, John Wiley and Sons, New York.

LYONS, Mark (2001),
*Third Sector: The contribution of non-profit and co-operative enterprises in Australia*, Allen and Unwin, St. Leonards, Australia.

LYONS, Mark, and HOCKING, Susan (2000),
"Dimensions of Australia's Third Sector", A Report from the Australian Non-profit Data Project, Centre for Australian Community Organisations and Management (CACOM), University of Technology, Sydney.

MacDONALD and ASSOCIATES LIMITED (1995),
*Trends in Venture Capital Market in Quebec, Réseau Capital Annuel General Meeting*.

MacDONALD & ASSOCIATES LIMITED (1998),
*Trends in Venture Capital Market in Quebec, Réseau Capital Annuel General Meeting*.

MacDONALD & ASSOCIATES LIMITED (2000),
*www.canadavc.com/cfm/index.cfm*

MacINTYRE, G.A. (1998),
Perspectives on Communities. A Community Economic Development Roundtable, Sydney (NS), University College of Cape Breton Press.

MacLEOD, G. (1997),
From Mondragon to America. Experiments in Community Economic Development, Sydney (NS), University College of Cape Breton Press, p. 186.

MALO, Marie-Claire and IGNATIEFF, Nicholas (1997),
"Caisses Desjardins et cercles d'emprunt à Montréal: quelle configuration partenariale?", Économie et Solidarités, revue de CIRIEC Canada, Vol. 1, pp. 81-89.

MAN, J.F., and BELL, M.E. (1996),
"The Impact of Local Sales Tax on the Value of Owner-Occupied Housing", Journal of Urban Economics 39, pp. 114-130.

MANSBRIDGE, J.J. (ed.) (1990),
Beyond Self-Interest, Chicago, University of Chicago Press.

MARKANDYA, A., and RICHARDSON, J.(1993),
Environmental Economics: A Reader, St. Martin's Press, New York.

MASSARSKY, Cynthia, and BEINHACKER, Samantha (2002),
Enterprising Nonprofits: Revenue Generation in the Non-profit Sector, Yale University, New Haven, available on www.ventures.yale.edu

MATZNER, E., and STREECK, W. (eds.) (1991),
Beyond Keynesianism. The Socio-Economics of Production and Full Employment, Edward Elgar Publishing Limited, Aldershot, United Kingdom. p. 264.

McCARTHY, K.D. (2001),
"Women and Philanthropy: Charting a Research Agenda", in P. Flynn and V.A. Hodgkinson (eds.): Measuring the Impact of the Non-profit Sector, Kluwer Academic/Plenum Publishers, New York.

McGREGOR, A. et al. (1997),
"Bridging the Job Gaps. An Evaluation of the Wise Group and the Intermediate Labour Market", Training and Employment Research Unit, University of Glasgow, United Kingdom.

McGREGOR-LOWNDES (1999),
"Australia", in T. Silk (ed.): Philanthropy and Law in Asia, Jossey-Bass, San Fransisco.

McMANUS, W.E. (1990),
"Stewardship and Almsgiving in the Roman Catholic Tradition", Robert Wuthnow, Virginia A. Hodgkinson & Associates (eds.): Faith and Philanthropy in America, Jossey-Bass, San Francisco.

MENDELL, M. (2000),
"The social economy in Quebec. Discourse and Strategies", in Eleanor MacDonald and Abigail Bakan (eds.): Critical Political Studies; Debates and Dialogues for the Left, McGill-Queen's Press, forthcoming, Montreal.

MENDELL, M., and EVOY, L.(1997),
"Democratizing Capital: Alternative Investment Strategies", in Eric Shragge (ed.): Community Economic Development. In Search of Empowerment, Black Rose Books, Montreal, p. 232.

MÉNDEZ, José Luis (1997),
"El tercer sector y las organizaciones civiles en México. Evolución reciente y perspectivas", Mexico, Revista Sociedad Civil, No. 1, pp. 103-123.

MÉNDEZ, José Luis (ed.) (1998),
Las organizaciones civiles y las políticas públicas en México y Centroamérica, M.A. Porrúa, Mexico.

MERTENS, S. (1999),
"Non-profit Organisations and Social Economy: Two Ways of Understanding the Third Sector", Annals of Public and Co-operative Economics, Vol. 70:3, pp. 501-520.

MERTENS, S. (2000),
"A Satellite Account of Non-profit Organisations, Principles and Lessons from a Pilot Test in Belgium", paper presented at the 4th ISTR Conference, Dublin.

MERTENS, S. (2001),
"La production des associations dans les comptes nationaux", Working Paper, Centre d'Économie Sociale, Université de Liège.

MERTENS, S. (2002),
Vers un compte satellite des institutions sans but lucratif en Belgique, Thèse de doctorat en sciences économiques, Université de Liège.

MINISTÈRE DE L'INDUSTRIE ET DU COMMERCE (1999),
Taux de survie des entreprises co-opératives au Québec, Gouvernement du Québec, p. 52.

MINISTÈRE DE LA RECHERCHE, DE LA SCIENCE ET DE LA TECHNOLOGIE (2001),
Savoir changer le monde, politique québécoise de la science et de l'innovation, www.mrst.gouv.qc.ca/_fr/politique/P_politique.html

MINISTÈRE DES RÉGIONS (Québec) (1998),
www.sdr.gouv.qc.ca/poli331.htm

MONNIER, L., and THIRY, B. (1997),
"Introduction: the General Interest: Its Architecture and Dynamics", in Annals of Public and Co-operative Economics, Oxford, United Kingdom, Vol. 68, No. 3, pp. 313-334.

MORINO INSTITUTE (2001),
Venture Philanthropy: the Changing Landscape, Washington, DC, USA.

MUSSO, J.A., KITSUSE, A. and COOPER, T.L. (2002),
"Faith Organizations and Neighborhood Councils in Los Angeles", Public Administration and Development 22, pp. 83–94.

MUTH, Richard F., and GOODMAN, Allen C. (1989),
The Economics of Housing Markets, Harwood Academic Publishers, New York.

NATIONAL COMMUNITY CAPITAL DEVELOPMENT ASSOCIATION (2002),
Inside the Membership: 2000 Statistics and Analysis, Philadelphia, self-published, available on www.communitycapital.org

NELSON, Richard R., with WINTER, Sidney G. (1994),
An Evolutionary Theory of Economic Change, Harvard University Press.

NON-PROFIT PATHFINDER,
www.independentsector.org/pathfinder

NOWAK, M. (ed.) (1999),
Étude sur l'intégration des exclus par le travail indépendant et le micro-crédit en Europe – Identification du cadre législatif et réglementaire, report carried out by the Association pour le Droit à l'Initiative Économique on behalf of the European Commission, DG Science, Research and Development.

O'CONNELL, Brian (1997),
Powered by Coalition, Jossey-Bass Publishers, San Francisco.

O'CONNOR, J. (1999),
The Definition of Cultural Industries, Manchester Institute for Popular Culture.

OECD (1996),
Reconciling Economy and Society: Toward a Plural Economy, LEED Programme, OECD, Paris.

OECD (1996) and OECD (1998),
Local Management for More Effective Employment Policy, OECD, Paris.

OECD (1999a),
Note on the evaluation of social enterprises, LEED Programme, document [DT/LEED/DC(99)10], OECD, Paris.

OECD (1999b),
Decentralising Employment Policy, OECD, Paris.

OECD (1999c),
Social Enterprises, OECD, Paris.

OECD (2001a),
Innovations in Labour Market Policies: The Australian Way, OECD, Paris.

OECD (2001b),
Corporate Social Responsibility. Partners for progress, OECD, Paris.

OECD (2001c),
The Well-being of Nations: The Role of Human and Social Capital, OECD, Paris.

O'NEILL, Michael, and FLETCHER, Kathleen (eds.) (1998),
Non-profit Management Education, Praeger Publishers, New York.

O'NEILL, Michael, and YOUNG, Dennis R. (eds.) (1988),
Educating Managers of Non-profit Organizations, Praeger Publishers, New York.

ORTMANN, A., and SCHLESINGER, M. (1997),
"Trust, Repute and the Role of Non-profit Enterprise", Voluntas 8(2), 97-119.

OSTER, Sharon M. (1995),
Strategic Management for Non-profit Organizations, Oxford University Press, New York.

OSTRANDER, S.A., and FISHER, J.M. (1995),
"Women Giving Money, Women Raising Money: What Differences for Philanthropy?", in Charles H. Hamilton and Warren F. Ilchman (eds.): Cultures of Giving II: How Heritage, Gender, Wealth and Values Influence Philanthropy, Jossey-Bass, San Francisco.

OTTENSMANN, J.R. (2000),
Catholic Diocese of Cleveland: Economic Value of Selected Activities, in Center for Urban Policy and the Environment, Indianapolis.

PÉREZ YARAHUÁN, Gabriela., and GARCÍA-JUNCO, David (1998),
"¿Una ley para organizaciones no gubernamentales en México? Análisis de una propuesta", in José Luis Méndez (ed.): Las organizaciones civiles y las políticas públicas en México y Centroamérica, M.A. Porrúa, Mexico.

PESTOFF, V.A. (1994),
"Beyond Exit and Voice in Social Services. Citizens as Co-producers", in P. and I. Vidal (eds.): Delivering Welfare, Centre d'iniciatives de l'economia social, Barcelona.

**322**

PESTOFF, V.A. (1996),
"Renewing Public Services and Developing the Welfare Society through Multi-stakeholder Cooperatives", *Journal of Rural Cooperation*.

PESTOFF, V.A. (1998),
*Beyond the Market and the State*, Ashgate, Hampshire.

PHELPS, E.S. (1975),
*Altruism, Morality, and Economic Theory*, Sage, New York.

PIORE, M.J. (1994),
*Beyond Individualism*, Harvard University Press, Cambridge, USA.

POSEY, D.A (ed.) (1999),
*Cultural and Spiritual Values of Biodiversity*, Intermediate Technology, London.

POWELL, W.W. and FRIEDKIN, R. (1987),
"Organizational Change in Non-profit Organisations", in W.W. Powell (ed.): *The Non-profit Sector: A Research Handbook*, Yale University Press, New Haven, Connecticut.

PRESS, Eyal and WASHBURN, Jennifer (2000),
"The Kept University", *The Atlantic Monthly*, March, pp. 39-54.

PROCURA (2001),
*Caracterización del sector no lucrativo a nivel nacional y en el Distrito Federal*, Mexico, Procura (Investigaciones 2000-2001, 4).

PUTNAM, R.D. (1993),
*Making Democracy Work: Civic Traditions in Modern Italy*, Princeton University Press, Princeton, New Jersey.

PUTNAM, R.D. (2000),
*Bowling Alone: The Collapse and Revival of American Community*, Simon & Schuster, New York.

PUTNAM, R., LEONARDI, R. and NANETTI, R. (1993),
*Making Democracy Work: Civic Traditions in Modern Italy*, Princeton University Press, Princeton, New Jersey.

RAMOS, H.A.J. (1999),
"Latino Philanthropy: Expanding US Models of Giving and Civic Participation", in Ford Foundation, W.K. Kellogg Foundation, David & Lucy Packard Foundation, & Council on Foundations: *Cultures of Caring: Philanthropy in Diverse American Communities*, Council on Foundations, Washington, DC.

RAUSCHENBACH, T., SACHßE, C. and OLK, T. (eds.) (1995),
*Von der Wertegemeinschaft zum Dienstleistungsunternehmen. Jugend- und Wohlfahrtsverbände im Umbruch*, Suhrkamp, Frankfurt.

REED, P. (1994),
"What's it Worth When Nobody Pays for it: Considerations for a Social Theory of Values", paper presented at the annual meeting of the Association for Research on Non-profit Organizations and Voluntary Action.

REIS, Thomas K., and CLOHESY, Stephanie (2000),
"Unleashing New Resources and Entrepreneurship for the Common Good", International Society for Third Sector Research, Draft, June.

RESCHER, N. (1969),
*Introduction to Value Theory*, Prentice Hall, Englewood Cliffs, New Jersey.

RÉSEAU D'INVESTISSEMENT SOCIAL DU QUÉBEC (2000),
*Rapport annuel 1999*, RISQ, Montréal.

REYGADAS, Rafael (1998),
"Rastros históricos de prácticas identitarias de las organizaciones civiles", in *De lo cívico a lo público: una discusión de las organizaciones civiles*, CAM, Mexico, pp. 79-101.

REYGADAS, Rafael and ROBLES, Gil (1998),
*Abriendo veredas: iniciativas públicas y sociales de las redes de organizaciones civiles*, Convergencia de Organismos Civiles por la Democracia, Mexico.

RIDING, A.L. and ORSER, B. (1997),
*Beyond the Banks: Creative Financing for Canadian Entrepreneurs*, J. Wiley, Profit: the magazine for Canadian entrepreneurs, Toronto. pp. 289.

RILEY, Margaret (1995),
"Exempt Organization Business Income Tax Returns, 1991", *Statistics of Income Bulletin* 14(4), Spring, pp. 38-63.

THE ROBERTS FOUNDATION (1999),
"Social Purpose Enterprises and Venture Philanthropy in the New Millennium", San Francisco (three volumes).

ROGERS, E.M. (1995),
*Diffusion of innovations* (4th ed.), New York, NY: The Free Press

ROSE-ACKERMAN, S. (1990),
"Efficiency, Funding and Autonomy of the Third Sector", in H.K. Anheier and W. Siebel (eds.): *The Third Sector: Comparative Studies of Non-profit Organizations*, de Gruyter, Berlin, pp. 157-164.

ROSS, C.E., MIROWSKY, J. and PRIBESH, S. (2001),
"Powerlessness and the Amplification of Threat: Neighborhood Disadvantage, Disorder, and Mistrust", *American Sociological Review* 66, pp. 568–591.

ROTHENBERG, J., GALSTER, G.C., BUTLER, R.V. and PITKIN, J. (1991),
*The Maze of Urban Housing Markets: Theory, Evidence, and Policy*, The University of Chicago Press, Chicago.

RUDNEY, G. and ANHEIER, H. (1996),
"Satellite Accounts for Non-profit Institutions: a Proposal", paper presented at the 2nd ISTR Conference, Mexico.

RYAN, William P. (1999),
"The New Landscape for Nonprofits", *Harvard Business Review*, January-February, pp. 127-136.

SALAMON, Lester M. (1987),
"Of Market Failure, Voluntary Failure, and Third-Party Government: Toward a Theory of Government-Non-profit Relations in the Modern Welfare State", *Journal of Voluntary Action Research* 16, pp. 29-49.

SALAMON, Lester M. (1995),
*Partners in Public Service*, The Johns Hopkins University Press, Baltimore.

SALAMON, Lester M. (1997),
*Holding the Center, America's Non-profit Sector at a Crossroads*, The Nathan Cummings Foundation, New York.

SALAMON, Lester M. (1999a),
"America's Non-profit Sector at a Crossroads", in *Voluntas*, Vol. 10, No. 1, pp. 5-23.

SALAMON, Lester M. (1999b),
America's Non-profit Sector: A primer, The Foundation Center, New York.

SALAMON, Lester M. (2000),
The Non-profit Sector: For What and for Whom?, Working Paper, Johns Hopkins Comparative Non-profit Sector Project, Johns Hopkins Comparative Non-profit Sector Project, Baltimore, Maryland.

SALAMON, LesterM. (2002),
Philantrophy, Social Economy, Thirs Sector: Definitions and Concepts, Myths and Realities, paper presented at the seminar organised by the CDC Institute for Economic research of the Caisse des Depôts et Consignations, October, 22nd, Paris.

SALAMON, L.M. and ANHEIER, H.K. (1992a),
"In Search of the Non-profit Sector, I. The Question of Definitions", Voluntas, Vol. 3/2, pp. 125-151.

SALAMON, L.M. and ANHEIER, H.K. (1992b),
"In Search of the Non-profit Sector, II. The Problem of Classification", Voluntas, Vol. 3/3, pp. 267-310.

SALAMON L.M. and ANHEIER, H.K. (1994),
The Emerging Sector. An Overview, The Johns Hopkins University, Baltimore.

SALAMON L.M. and ANHEIER, H.K. (1996),
The Emerging Non-profit Sector: An Overview, Manchester University Press.

SALAMON, L.M., and ANHEIER, H.K. (eds.) (1997),
Defining the Non-profit Sector: A Cross-National Analysis, Manchester University Press, Manchester.

SALAMON, L., and ANHEIER, H.K. (1998),
The Emerging Sector Revisited, a Summary, the Johns Hopkins Institute.

SALAMON, L.M., and ANHEIER, H.K. (1998),
"Non-profit Institutions and the 1993 System of National Accounts", The Johns Hopkins Comparative Non-profit Sector Project, Working Paper, No. 25, Baltimore.

SALAMON, L.M., ANHEIER, H.K., LIST, R., TOEPLER, S. and SOKOLOWSKI, S.W. et al. (1999),
Global Civil Society: Dimensions of the Non-profit Sector, The Johns Hopkins Center for Civil Society Studies, Baltimore, MD.

SATTAR, D. (2000),
Upscaling Social Investment: 50 Case Studies, INAISE, Brussels.

SEGAL, Lewis M. and WEISBROD, Burton A. (1998),
"Interdependence of Commercial and Donative Revenues", Chapter 6 in Weisbrod: To Profit or Not to Profit: The Commercial Transformation of the Non-profit Sector, Cambridge University Press, Cambridge, United Kingdom. pp. 105-128.

SEIBEL, W. (1990),
"Organisational Behaviour and Organisational Function: Toward a micro-macro theory of the third sector", in H.K. Anheic and W. Seibel (eds): The Third Sector, Berlin, New York: Waller de Gruyten, pp. 107-121

SEIBEL, W. (1996),
"Successful failure", American Behavioral Scientist, 39(9), pp. 1011-1024.

SEIBEL, Wolfgang, BENZ, Arthur and MÄDING, Heinrich (Hrsg.) (1993),
Verwaltungsreform und Verwaltungspolitik im Prozeß der deutschen Einigung, 510 pages, Baden-Baden: Nomos Verlagsgesellschaft.

SENGE, P.M. (1997),
"Communities of Leaders and Learners", *Harvard Business Review*, Vol. 75, No. 5, p. 32.

SERVON, L.J. (1999),
*Bootstrap Capital. Micro-enterprises and the American Poor*, Brookings Institution Press, Washington.

SHAO, Stella (1995),
"Asian American Giving: Issues and Challenges", in Charles H. Hamilton and Warren F. Ilchman (eds.): *Cultures of Giving II: How Heritage, Gender, Wealth and Values Influence Philanthropy*, Jossey-Bass, San Francisco.

SHEARMAN (1999),
Local Connections: Making the Net Work for Neighbourhood Renewal, Communities Online UK.

SHEPPARD, I.F.(2001),
"Report of the Inquiry into the Definition of Charities and Related Organisations", Internet, *www.cdi.gov.au*

SHERMAN, A.L. (2002),
*Collaborations Catalogue: A Report on Charitable Choice Implementation in 15 States*, Hudson Institute, Indianapolis.

SIMON, W.H. (2001),
*The Community Economic Development Movement*, Duke University Press, Durham, NJ.

SIMONS, Rob (2000),
"Social Enterprise: An opportunity to harness capacities", *The Smith Family Briefing paper*, No. 7, December.

SIOS,
Information System for Civil Organizations, *148.245.85.197/sios/sitios*

SKLOOT, Edward (1987),
"Enterprise and Commerce in Non-profit Organizations", Chapter 21 in Walter W. Powell (ed.): *The Non-profit Sector: A Research Handbook*, Yale University Press, New Haven. pp. 380-393.

SKLOOT, Edward (ed.) (1988),
*The Non-profit Entrepreneur: Creating Ventures to Earn Income*, New York, The Foundation Center.

SLATER, C.M. and DAVID, M.H. (1994),
"The Not-for-profit Sector of the Economy: Measurement and Presentation in Federal Statistics", *Voluntas*, Vol. 4/4, pp. 419-444.

SMITH, D.H. (1983),
*The Impact of the Voluntary Sector on Society*, reprinted in Brian O'Connell (ed.): *America's voluntary spirit*, reprinted from Voluntary Action Research, 1973, Lexington Books, DC Heath & Co. Lexington, MA,

SMITH, S.R. and SOSIN, M.R. (2001),
"The Varieties of Faith-Related Agencies", *Public Administration Review*, 61, pp. 651-670.

SMITH, S.R., and LIPSKY, M. (1993),
*Non-profits for Hire: The Welfare State in the Age of Contracting*, Harvard University Press, Cambridge, USA.

SOLIDEQ (1992),
Pour une région SOLIDE un investissement régional. Guide d'implantation pour les MRC, SOLIDEQ, Québec.

SPEAR, R. (1995),
"Social Co-ops in the UK", in Social Enterprises: a Chance for Europe.

SPEAR, R. and THOMAS, A. (1997),
"Comparative Perspective on Worker Co-operative Development in Several European Countries", Annals of Public and Co-operative Economics, Vol. 68, No. 3, pp. 453-467.

SRDC Publishes a New Working Paper: "Understanding the Social Economy in Canada". www.srdc.org/english/announcements/SRDC_dual.gif

STOLLE, D. and ROCHON, T.R. (1998),
"Are All Associations Alike?", American Behavioral Scientist, 42, pp. 47–65.

STONE, M.M., and CUTCHER-GERSHENFELD, S.(2001),
"Challenges of Measuring Performance in Non-profit Organizations", in P. Flynn and V.A. Hodgkinson (eds.): Measuring the Impact of the Non-profit Sector, Kluwer Academic/Plenum Publishers, New York.

STORPER, Michael (1997),
The Regional World: Territorial Development in a Global Economy, The Guildford Press, New York.

STUART, Albert and WHETTEN, David A. (1985);
"Organizational Identity", in L.L. Cummings and Barry M. Staw (eds.): Research in Organizational Behavior, Vol. 7. JAI Press, Greenwich, Connecticut, pp. 263-295.

SUBLETT, D. (1993),
"Women's Approach to Philanthropy: A Learning Model", in Abbie J. Von Schlegell & Joan M. Fisher (eds.): Women as Donors, Women as Philanthropists, Jossey-Bass, San Francisco.

TASCH, Edward (unpublished, 2001),
"Mission-Related Investing: Strategies for Philanthropic Institutions", prepared for the Northwest Area Foundation.

TAYLOR, M., LANGAN, S. and HOGGETT, P. (1995),
Encouraging Diversity: Voluntary and Private Organisations in Community Care, Arena, Aldershot, United Kigdom.

TAYLOR-GOOBY (2001),
European Welfare States Under Pressure, Sage.

TEMKIN, K., and ROHE, W.M. (1998),
"Social Capital and Neighborhood Stability: An Empirical Investigation", in Housing Policy Debate 9,1, pp. 61-88.

THAKE, S. and ZADEK, S. (1996),
Practical People Noble Causes. How to Support Community-based Social Entrepreneurs, New Economics Foundation, London.

THOMAS, A. (1993),
"Worker Ownership in the UK 1992 and Financial Support Strategies for the Co-operative Movement", Economic and Industrial Democracy, An International Journal, Vol. 14, No. 4, pp. 557-571.

TICE, H.S., and SALAMON, L.M. (2000),
"The Handbook of Non-profit Institutions in the System of National Accounts: An Introduction and Overview", paper presented for the 26th General Conference of the International Association for Research in Income and Wealth, Krakow, Poland.

TOOL, M.R. (1986),
Essays in Social Value Theory: A Neoinstitutionalist Contribution, M.E. Sharpe, Armonk, NY.

TROPMAN, J.E. (1993),
"The Catholic Ethic and Charitable Orientation", in Transmitting the Tradition of a Caring Society to Future Generations, Working Papers from Independent Sector's Spring Research Forum, San Antonio, Texas, March, pp. 379-392.

TRUFFAUT, S. (1999),
"Martin ouvre les vannes", Le Devoir – édition Internet, 26 June.

TUCKMAN, Howard P. (1998),
"Competition, Commercialization, and the Evolution of Non-profit Organizational Structures", Chapter 2 in Weisbrod: To Profit or Not to Profit: The Commercial Transformation of the Non-profit Sector, Cambridge University Press, Cambridge, United Kingdom. pp. 25-46.

TURCOTTE, C. (1998),
"Le rapport McKay est bien reçu", Le Devoir – édition Internet, 16 September.

UNITED NATIONS (1993),
A System of National Accounts, New York.

UNITED NATIONS (1996),
Cooperative Enterprise in the Health and Social Care Sectors. A Global Review and Prospects for Policy Coordination, Geneva.

UNITED NATIONS (2002),
Handbook on Non-profit Institutions, United Nations, New York.

VAN KEMENADE, S. (1999),
"Sois ton propre patron. Le fonds d'une caisse populaire qui soutient les jeunes entrepreneurs", Cahiers du CRISES, Montréal, No. ES9906.

VAN KOOTEN, G.C., BULTE, E.H. and SINCLAIR, A.R.R. (eds.) (2000),
Conserving Nature's Diversity: Insights from Biology, Ethics, and Economics, Ashgate, Burlington, VT.

VAN LAAROVEN, P. et al. (1990),
"Achievement in Public and Private Secondary Education in the Netherlands", in H.K. Anheier, & W. Siebel (eds.): The Third Sector: Comparative Studies of Non-profit Organizations, de Gruyter, Berlin, pp. 165-182.

VANOLI, A. (1986),
"Sur la structure générale du SCN à partir de l'expérience du système élargi de comptabilité nationale français", Review of Income and Wealth, Series 32, No. 2, pp. 155-199.

VAN TIL, J. (1988),
Mapping the Third Sector: Voluntarism in a Changing Social Economy, The Foundation Center, New York.

VAN TIL, J. (2000),
Growing Civil Society: From Third Sector to Third Space, Indiana University Press, Bloomington.

VAN TONGEREN, Jan (1996),
"Discussion of Chapter 2", in John W. Kendrick (ed.): *The New System of National Accounts*, Kluwer Academic Publishers, Boston, Dordrecht, London. pp. 73-84.

VIENNEY, C. (1994),
*L'économie sociale*, La Découverte, Paris.

WAGNER, L., and DECK, A.F. (1999),
*Hispanic Philanthropy: Exploring the Factors That Influence Giving and Asking*, Jossey-Bass, San Francisco.

WATERMAN, R., and WOOD, D. (1993),
"Policy Monitoring and Policy Analysis", *Journal of Policy Analysis and Management*, 12, pp. 685-699.

WEISBROD, Burton A. (1977),
*The Voluntary Non-profit Sector*, DC Heat & Co. Lexington, Massachusetts.

WEISBROD, Burton A. (1988),
*The Non-profit Economy*, Harvard University Press, Cambridge, Massachusetts.

WEISBROD, Burton A. (1998a),
*To Profit or Not to Profit: The Commercial Transformation of the Non-profit Sector*, Cambridge University Press, Cambridge, United Kingdom.

WEISBROD, Burton A. (1998b),
"Institutional Form and Organizational Behavior", in Walter W. Powell and Elizabeth C. Clemens (eds.): *Private Action and the Public Good* Yale University Press, New Haven, CT., pp. 69-84.

WEISBROD, Burton A. (2001),
"An Agenda for Quantitative Evaluation of the Non-profit Sector: Needs, Obstacles, and Approaches", in P. Flynn and V.A. Hodgkinson (eds.): *Measuring the Impact of the Non-profit Sector*, Kluwer Academic/Plenum Publishers, New York.

WEITZMAN, M. S., JALANDONI, N.T., LAMPKIN, L.M. and POLLAK, T.H. (2002),
*The New Non-profit Almanac and Desk Reference*, Independent Sector, Washington, DC.

WESTLUND, H., and WESTERDAHL, S. (1997a),
*The Community Based Economy and Employment at the Local Level*, SCI/SISE, Stockholm.

WESTLUND, H., and WESTERDAHL, S. (1997b),
*The effects of the social economy on employment at the local level*, Stockholm, The Swedish Co-operative institute and the Institute for Social Economy (with the collaboration of the DG Employment and Social Affairs).

WILLIAMS, Caroline (1998),
*Financing Techniques for Non-Profit Organizations: Borrowing From the For-Profit Sector*, The President's Committee on the Arts and the Humanities, Washington, DC.

WILLIAMS, Caroline (unpublished, 2000),
"Financing Alternative – Sources of Capital", prepared for the board of the Coalition on Experiential Learning, available on *www.greyseal.org*

WILLIAMS, Caroline (unpublished, 2001),
"The Dividing Line Between Philanthropy and Investment", prepared for The Center on Arts and Culture, available on *www.greyseal.org*

WILLIAMS, Grant (2002),
"Health Conversion Organizations Saw Assets Top $15 billion in 2001", *The Chronicle of Philanthropy*, 2 May.

WILLMER, W.K. (1995),
"Evangelicals: Linking Fervency of Faith and Generosity of Giving", in Charles H. Hamilton and Warren F. Ilchman (eds.): *Cultures of Giving: How Region and Religion Influence Philanthropy*, Jossey-Bass, San Francisco.

WINTERS, M.F. (1999),
"Reflections on Endowment Building in the African-American Community", in Ford Foundation, W.K. Kellogg Foundation, David & Lucy Packard Foundation, & Council on Foundations: *Cultures of Caring: Philanthropy in Diverse American Communities*, Council on Foundations, Washington, DC.

WOLPERT, J. (2001),
"The Distributional Impacts of Nonprofits and Philanthropy", in P. Flynn and V.A. Hodgkinson (eds.): *Measuring the Impact of the Non-profit Sector*, Kluwer Academic/Plenum Publishers, New York.

WOLPERT, J., NAPHTALIK, Z. and SELEY, J. (2001),
"The Location of Non-profit Facilities in Urban Areas", *Lincoln Institute of Land Policy Working Paper*, Lincoln Institute of Land Policy, Cambridge, MA.

WRIGHT, D.J. (2001),
*It Takes a Neighborhood: Strategies to Prevent Urban Decline*, The Rockefeller Institute Press, Albany, NY.

WUTHNOW, R. (2001),
"The Religious Dimension of Giving and Volunteering", in P. Flynn and V.A. Hodgkinson (eds.): *Measuring the Impact of the Non-profit Sector*, Kluwer Academic/Plenum Publishers, New York.

WYSZOMIRSKI, M.J. (2001),
"Revealing the Implicit: Searching for Measures of the Impact of the Arts", in P. Flynn and V.A. Hodgkinson (eds.): *Measuring the Impact of the Non-profit Sector*, Kluwer Academic/Plenum Publishers, New York.

YOUNG, Dennis R. (1983):
*If Not for Profit, For What?*, Heath & Co. Lexington, Washington, DC.

YOUNG, Dennis R. (1989),
"Beyond Tax Exemption: A Focus on Organizational Performance Versus Legal Status", in Virginia A. Hodgkinson, Richard Lyman et al. (eds.), *The Future of the Non-profit Sector*, Jossey-Bass Publishers, San Francisco.

YOUNG, Dennis R. (1998a),
"Commercial Activity and Voluntary Health Agencies: When are Ventures Advisable?", *report*, National Health Council, Washington, DC.

YOUNG, Dennis R. (1998b),
"Commercialism in Non-profit Social Service Associations", Chapter 10 in Weisbrod: *To Profit or Not to Profit: The Commercial Transformation of the Non-profit Sector*, Cambridge University Press, Cambridge, United Kingdom. pp. 195-216.

YOUNG, Dennis R. (1999),
"Non-profit management studies in the United States: Current development and future prospects", *Journal of Public Affairs Education*, 5(1), pp. 13-24

YOUNG, Dennis R. (2001),
"Social Enterprise in the United States: Alternate Identities and Forms", prepared for: The EMES Conference, *The Social Enterprise: A Comparative Perspective*, Case Western Reserve University, Trento, Italy, December 13-15.

YOUNG, Dennis R. and STEINBERG, R. (1995),
*Economics for Non-profit Managers*, The Foundation Center, New York.

ZIMMER, A. (1997),
"Private-Public Partnerships: Staat und Dritter Sektor in Deutschland", in H.K. Anheier, E. Priller, W. Seibel and A. Zimmer (eds.): *Der Dritte Sektor in Deutschland*, Sigma, Berlin.

# Websites

| Country | Organisation | Website address |
|---|---|---|
| Australia | Area Consultative Committees | *www.acc.gov.au/rapguidelines.htm* |
| | Charities Definition Inquiry | *www.cdi.gov.au* |
| | Austrilian Jobsearch (government services for Australia) | *www.jobsearch.gov.au/* |
| | Australian Workplace | *www.workplace.gov.au* |
| Belgium | International Association of Investors in the Social Economy | *www.inaise.org* |
| | CWES | *www.terre.be/gi/economie_sociale.htm* |
| France | Association Française des Banques | *www.afb.fr* |
| | Comité National des Entreprises d'Insertion | *www.cnei.org* |
| | France Active | *www.franceactive.org* |
| | Institut de Socio-Economie des Entreprises et des Organisations | *www.iseor.com* |
| | France Initiative Réseau | *www.fir.asso.fr* |
| Netherlands | "Working together in a multicultural environment" | *www.seon.nl* |
| Portugal | Associação Portuguesa para o Desenvolvimento local | *www.animar-dl.pt* |
| Québec | Fond Action | *www.fondaction.com* |
| | ARUC | *www.aruc-es.uqam.ca* |
| | Chantier de l'économie sociale | *www.chantier.qc.ca* |
| United Kingdom | Area Consultative Committees | *www.acc.gov.uk* |
| United States | United Way | *www.unitedway.org* |
| | Public Radio Capital | *www.pubcap.org* |
| | Techno serve "Business solutions to rural problems" | *www.technoserve.org* |
| | INDEPENDENT SECTOR | *www.independentsector.org* |
| | Grey Seal Capital, LLC "Investment Banking for tax-exempt organisations" | *www.greyseal.org* |
| | Girl Scouts of America | *www.girlsscouts.org* |
| | Boy Scouts of America | *www.bsa.scouting.org* |
| | Community Reinvestment Act | *www.ffiec.gov/cra/default.htm* |
| | Community Foundation of Silicon Valley | *www.cfsv.org/communitysurvey/* |
| | Community Development Financial Institution Fund | *www.cdfifund.gov* |
| | National Community Capital Association | *www.communitycapital.org* |
| | Investors' Circle | *www.investorscircle.net* |
| | Guidestar | *www.guidestar.org* |
| | National Housing Trust | *www.nhtinc.org* |
| | The New Economics Foundation | *www.neweconomics.org* |
| | | *www.bbbsa.org* |
| | Big Brothers Big Sisters of America | *www.cfsb.org* |
| | Cartographics Services and Editorial Services | *www.muridae.com/nporegulation* |
| | The Chronicle of Philanthropy | *www.nonprofit.com* |
| | United Way | *www.national.unitedway.org* |
| | Share our Strength | *www.strength.org* |
| **International Organisations** | European Commission | *www.europa.eu.int/comm/employment_social/ empl&esf/3syst/index_en.htm* |
| | OECD/LEED | *www.oecd.org* |
| | World Bank | *www.worldbank.org/ngos* |
| | ILO | *www.ilo.org/public/english/comp/civil* |

# List of contributors

Mr. **Helmut K. Anheier** (Ph.D. Yale University, 1986) is the Director of the Center for Civil Society at UCLA's School of Public Policy and Social Research, where he is also a Professor of Social Welfare. He is also Centennial Professor at the London School of Economics, where from 1998 to 2002 he founded and directed the LSE Centre for Civil Society. Prior to this he was a Senior Research Associate and Project Co-director at the Johns Hopkins University Institute for Policy Studies, and Associate Professor of Sociology at Rutgers University.

Mr. **Wolfgang Bielefeld** is Associate Professor of Public and Environmental Affairs and Adjunct Professor at the Center on Philanthropy at Indiana University-Purdue University, Indianapolis. His interests include the relations between non-profit organisations and their environments, the dynamics of non-profit sectors, the development of human service delivery systems, and the social impacts of government human service policies and spending patterns.

Mr. **Carlo Borzaga** graduated in Social Science from the University of Trento, where he is now teacher (and professor) of Labour Economics and Economic Policy. He is director of Issan, a research institute on non-profit organisations and a member of the European Network EMES. He has participated in and co-ordinated several researches on non-profit organisations both in Italy and in Europe, paying particular attention to the so-called "social enterprises".

Mr. **Benoît Granger** is a consultant and expert and is the author of "Third system, financial and legal tools", a survey for the European Commission. Author of several books on micro finance, social banking and entrepreneurship, he is responsible for a large evaluation program on public aid to the micro enterprises in France.

Mr. **Xavier Greffe** is Professor at the Université de Paris 1 – Sorbonne and an Expert working for the European Commission and the OECD. He is the author of several papers including Public Management (*Gestion Publique*), Cultural Work in the Numerical Age and Local Development (*L'emploi culturel à l'âge du numérique le développement local*).

Mr. **Benoît Lévesque** is Professor of Sociology at the University of Quebec, Montreal, and Director of the Research Centre for Social Innovations in the

Social Economy, Enterprises and Trade Unions. He also manages the Communities-Universities Research Alliance. He is currently heading research in the following three fields: the social economy, local development and funding local development. He has published several articles and reports on these areas of research.

Mr. **Marco A. Mena** is the Director General for Institutional Development at the Mexico Ministry for Social Development (Sedesol). He has been Director General for Economic Analysis and Chief of Staff of the Under-secretary for Planning and Evaluation, also at Sedesol. In 1997 he obtained the International Fellowship at the Center for the Study of Philanthropy of the City University of New York. Mr Mena has an M.P.P. from the Harris School of Public Policy at the University of Chicago, where he was a Fulbright and Ford/MacArthur scholar. He is Delegate to the OECD/LEED Programme.

Mrs. **Marguerite Mendell**, economist, is Vice-Principal of the School of Community and Public Affairs, Concordia University, and Director of the Karl Polanyi Institute of Political Economy. She is co-director of the International Comparisons of the Social Economy network of ARUC (Alliance de Recherche Universités-Communautés. Her research interests are in community economic development, the social economy, alternative investment strategies, and the democratisation of capital. She has published widely in these areas as well as on the life and work of Karl Polanyi and the resonance of his work to contemporary society.

Mrs. **Sybille Mertens** is Lecturer in Social Economy at the University of Liège. She has completed her Doctorate (Ph.D.) in Economics with a dissertation on the non-profit satellite account in Belgium (2002). She is Scientific Co-director of the Centre for Social Economy (University of Liège) and Project Leader of the non-profit satellite account implementation at the National Bank of Belgium.

Mrs. **Nancy Neamtan** is President Executive Director of the Chantier de l'économie sociale, an independent corporation created in the context of the Quebec Summit on Economy and Employment of October 1996. She is also Vice-president – Strategic Development of the RESO (a group devoted to the economic and social development of Southwest Montreal) after having been Executive Director from 1989 to 1998. Since 1999 she has been Co-Director of ARUC-ÉS (Alliance de recherche Universités/Communautés en économie sociale).

Mrs. **Julie Novak** is an Assistant Director in the Strategic Policy and Analysis Branch, Australian Department of Family and Community Services (FaCS). She has worked previously in the Department of Industry, Tourism and Resources, the Australian Treasury, and in the State public sector.

**336**

Mr. **Ralph Rouzier** is a graduate from the Université du Quebec à Montreal, having completed his Doctorate (Ph.D.) in sociology. His thesis is on public sector investment in Quebec.

Mr. **Alceste Santuari** (Ph.D. Law – Cantab) is lecturer of Non Profit Law and Tourism Law at the University of Trento. His main areas of interest and expertise are non-profit and mutual organisations, co-operatives, social and health care systems, non-profit comparative law, foundations and trusts. He is a member of several Scientific Committees of Journals and Reviews (both Italian and international), as well as various boards of directors of non-profit organisations

Ms. **Caroline Williams** joined The Nathan Cummings Foundation in May 2001 as Chief Financial and Investment Officer. She has worked as an investment banker in both the non-profit and for-profit sectors. She began a 20-year career in investment banking in 1971 and most recently served as a Managing Director of Donaldson, Lufkin and Jenrette. In 1992 she left the field to pursue interests in the non-profit sector and set up Grey Seal Capital, LLC to provide financial consulting services to tax-exempt organisations and socially responsible venture stage companies.

Mr. **Dennis R. Young** is Professor of Non-profit Management and Economics at Case Western Reserve University and CEO of the National Center on Non-profit Enterprise in Arlington, Virginia. From 1988 to 1996 he was Director of the Mandel Center for Non-profit Organisations. He is the founding editor of the journal Non-profit Management and Leadership and past President of the Association for Research on Non-profit Organisations and Voluntary Action (ARNOVA). He is the author of many scholarly articles, as well as either author or editor of several books on non-profit organisations.

OECD PUBLICATIONS, 2, rue André-Pascal, 75775 PARIS CEDEX 16
PRINTED IN FRANCE
(84 2003 02 1 P) ISBN 92-64-19953-5 – No. 52735 2003

OECD PUBLICATIONS, 2, rue André-Pascal, 75775 PARIS CEDEX 16
PRINTED IN FRANCE
(84 2003 02 1 P) ISBN 92-64-19953-5 – No. 52735 2003